最新汉英特色词汇词典
（第7版）

中国日报网　编

清华大学出版社
北　京

本书封面贴有清华大学出版社防伪标签，无标签者不得销售。

版权所有，侵权必究。举报：010-62782989，beiqinquan@tup.tsinghua.edu.cn。

图书在版编目(CIP)数据

最新汉英特色词汇词典 / 中国日报网编. —7版. — 北京：清华大学出版社，2019（2022.11重印）
ISBN 978-7-302-51731-3

Ⅰ.①最… Ⅱ.①中… Ⅲ.①英语—词典②词典—汉、英 Ⅳ.① H316

中国版本图书馆 CIP 数据核字(2018)第 267491 号

责任编辑：张立红
封面设计：梁　洁
版式设计：方加青
责任校对：王　玲
责任印制：杨　艳

出版发行：清华大学出版社
网　　址：http://www.tup.com.cn，http://www.wqbook.com
地　　址：北京清华大学学研大厦 A 座　邮　　编：100084
社 总 机：010-83470000　邮　　购：010-62786544
投稿与读者服务：010-62776969，c-service@tup.tsinghua.edu.cn
质 量 反 馈：010-62772015，zhiliang@tup.tsinghua.edu.cn
印 装 者：天津鑫丰华印务有限公司
经　　销：全国新华书店
开　　本：135mm×210mm　印　　张：13.75　字　　数：539 千字
版　　次：2019 年 7 月第 7 版　印　　次：2022 年 11 月第 4 次印刷
定　　价：75.00 元

产品编号：080157-01

《最新汉英特色词汇词典》(第7版)

编委会

编者：中国日报网（http://www.chinadaily.com.cn）

主编：马文英

编委：王　浩　韩　蕾　吴艳鹏

编辑：陈丹妮　董　静　许雅宁

To Our Readers
致读者

时隔三年多，《最新汉英特色词汇词典》（第7版）终于和大家见面了。

自2002年首次出版以来，该系列词典一直努力为广大读者提供紧跟时代的词条和权威地道的例句，内容涉及时政、经济、金融、文化、军事、外交、体育、环保、生活等诸多领域，例句均摘自《中国日报》、新华社、英国广播公司、美联社等国内外权威媒体。

新版词典在以往版本的基础上，删减了数百个内容陈旧、过时的词条，同时新增了近几年引发热议、广为传播的新词和热词，比如：人类命运共同体（a community of shared future for mankind）、"四个全面"战略布局（the four-pronged comprehensive strategy）、厕所革命（toilet revolution）、鄙视链（chain of contempt）、高质量发展（high-quality development）、分享经济（sharing economy）、网络借贷（P2P lending）、粤港澳大湾区（Guangdong-Hong Kong-Macao Greater Bay Area），等等。

同时，我们还对附录进行了微调，删除了一些过时的类别，增加了社交媒体常用语、常用军事词汇、报纸行业相关词汇以及冬季奥运会词汇等内容，便于读者更新和查找相关词汇。

本词典能够顺利出版有赖众多尽责用心的编、译、校以及排版人员的辛勤付出，在此向他们致以衷心的谢意。

我们在编辑本词典的过程中，虽然尽力做到准确无误，但是错误或不足之处在所难免，希望各方读者不吝指正。

中国日报网英语点津
2018年8月

Contents 目录

A	1
B	5
C	21
D	45
E	72
F	75
G	95
H	124
J	148
K	194
L	208
M	228
N	241
O	247
P	248
Q	256
R	270
S	276
T	304
W	315
X	332
Y	358
Z	383

附录 Appendices	409
社交媒体常用语	409
常用军事词汇	409
报纸行业相关词汇	410
房屋词汇	413

- 交通词汇 415
- 美容词汇 417
- 手机词汇 418
- 旅游词汇 419
- 工作及薪酬词汇 423
- 环保词汇 424
- 选举词汇 426
- 夏季奥运会词汇 428
- 冬季奥运会词汇 431
- 体育比赛结果词汇 432

A

APEC蓝 APEC blue
APEC期间,污染严重的北京出现了久违的蓝天,中国网友称其为"APEC蓝"。蓝天重现是严厉减排措施的结果,中国人民希望"APEC蓝"能够成为一种"新常态"。

"APEC blue" is a popular phrase coined by China's netizens to describe the blue sky in the heavily-polluted Beijing during the APEC week, which was a result of tough emission-reduction measures. The Chinese people hope to make APEC blue a "new normal".

AR录取通知书 AR-enabled admission notice
西北工业大学向学生发出了使用增强现实(AR)技术的录取通知书。这是国内首份使用AR技术的大学录取通知书。

The Northwestern Polytechnical University issued the letter of acceptance using Augmented Reality (AR) technology to students. This is the first AR-enabled university admission notice in China.

A4腰 A4 waist
A4腰挑战在中国,尤其是女性当中十分流行,社交媒体已经被A4腰刷屏。

In China, the A4 waist challenge is going viral, especially with women, and social media is flooded with the results.

爱国、创新、包容、厚德(北京精神)patriotism, innovation, inclusion and social morals (Beijing Spirit)

爱国统一战线 patriotic united front
党号召加强爱国统一战线。

The Communist Party of China has called for further efforts to solidify the patriotic united front.

安家费 settling-in allowance
拿到安家费,你可以如愿给新家买台电脑了。

Now that you have the settling-in allowance in hand, you can buy the computer you've always wanted to have for your new home.

安检 security check
由于客流巨大，携带腰包等小包的乘客事实上可以逃过安检。
Because of the huge passenger flow, passengers with small bags, such as waist packs, can actually escape security checks.

安检级别 security level
周日上午，北京首都国际机场国内航班的安检级别从三级升至二级，导致部分情绪激动的旅客发生了冲突。
Fights broke out among angry passengers at Beijing Capital International Airport on Sunday morning, after the security level for domestic flights was raised from Level three to Level two.

安居工程 government-subsidized housing
今年保障性安居工程新安排740万套。
We will build an additional 7.4 million units of government-subsidized housing this year.

安全大检查 safety overhaul
中国交通部负责人周日要求各地方部门开展全面彻底的安全大检查，彻底杜绝严重交通事故的发生。
China's transportation authority on Sunday ordered local departments to launch a thorough safety overhaul to resolutely curb severe traffic accidents.

安全岛 safety island; traffic island
有了安全岛，行人说他们现在感觉更安全了。
Pedestrians say they now feel more comfortable with the safety islands laid out.

安全警戒线 security cordon
在事件发生后不久，巴基斯坦边境的军队和警察在该地区周围设下了安全警戒线。
Soon after the incident, Pakistani Frontier Corps and police put a security cordon around the area.

安全隐患 hidden danger
现代设计和玻璃围裹的摩天大楼随之而来，这些富有美学意味的美景也带来了安全隐患。
With modern designs and skyscrapers wrapped in glass, aesthetic beauty has brought hidden danger with it.

安慰奖 consolation prize
即使参赛选手没有答对任何提问，也将会得到一份安慰奖，以感谢其参与。
Even if the contestant fails to give a correct answer to any question, he or she will get a consolation prize in appreciation of participation.

按劳分配 distribution according to performance
按劳分配制度是劳动价值的市场体现。
The system of distribution according to performance is a reflection of labor value in the market.

案例分析 case analysis ; case study
我们通常用案例分析为客户提供咨询服务。
We provide consulting services to clients, usually through case analysis.

暗池交易 dark pools
与其他市场玩家一样，这些系统交易的也是公开发行的股票。但是它们不会向公众披露它们的交易，这也是人们叫它们"暗池交易"的原因。
These systems trade the same public stocks as other market players do. But they do not publicly report their trades. This secrecy explains why they also have another name "dark pools".

暗恋 unrequited love
为歌颂情人节，她写了首诗记述自己的暗恋经历。
As a tribute to Valentine's Day, she wrote a poem about her unrequited love.

暗网 dark web
美国司法部称，世界最大暗网市场AlphaBay已被关闭。与此同时，荷兰执法者关闭了全球第三大暗网犯罪市场Hansa。
The US Justice Department said that the world's largest dark web marketplace, AlphaBay, has been shut down. The crackdown coincided with efforts by Dutch law enforcement to take down Hansa, the world's third largest criminal marketplace on the dark web.

暗物质 dark matter
我国已将国内首枚暗物质粒子探测卫星送入太空。科学家相信，肉眼无法看见的暗物质构成了宇宙质量的绝大部分。
China has sent into space the country's first dark matter particle explorer satellite. Scientists believe dark matter, an invisible material, makes up most of the universe's mass.

A

暗箱操作 covert deal

为杜绝暗箱操作,参建单位日前与供水工程总部签订了质量安全终身责任书。

To prevent covert deals, the construction unit and the water supply project headquarters signed a lifelong responsibility contract on quality and safety.

奥斯卡荣誉奖 Academy Honorary Award

因其在电影业取得的杰出成就,中国演员成龙被授予奥斯卡荣誉奖。

The Chinese actor Jackie Chan received an Academy Honorary Award for his noted achievements in motion pictures.

奥运特许商品 Olympic merchandise; franchised goods for the Olympics

只有在授权专卖店里才能买到奥运特许商品。

You can only buy the Olympic merchandise in those authorized shops.

巴黎气候协定 Paris climate agreement
美国总统特朗普宣布，美国将退出2015年达成的巴黎气候协定。他表示，接下来会展开谈判，以达成一个全新的、不会让美国企业和工人陷入不利境地的"公平的"协议。

US President Donald Trump announced that the US is withdrawing from the 2015 Paris climate agreement. He said moves to negotiate a new "fair" deal that would not disadvantage US businesses and workers would begin.

把握大局 see the whole picture
把握大局并正确行动，往往就能避免造成不可挽回的错误。

When one sees the whole picture and acts accordingly, one can usually avoid making irrevocable mistakes.

白领犯罪 white-collar crime
白领犯罪呈上升趋势。

The white-collar crime is on the rise.

白领工人 white-collar worker
有工会组织的蓝领工人报酬明显高于那些没有加入工会的同行，而白领工人是否加入工会对他们的收入影响倒不大。

Unionized blue-collar workers are paid considerably more than those without a union. White-collar workers receive almost the same salary whether they are in a union or not.

白马王子 Prince Charming
灰姑娘和她的白马王子的幸福结局打动了几代读者的心。现实生活中，你的白马王子是谁呢？

Cinderella's happy ending with her Prince Charming has captured the hearts of readers for generations. Who's your Prince Charming in real life?

白皮书 white paper; white book
白皮书指出，到目前为止，包括医疗基础设施建设、服务提供以及医保覆盖等在内的医疗卫生服务体系已经成型，覆盖13亿多城乡居民。

So far, a medical and healthcare system including medical infrastructure construction, service supply and health insurance coverage has taken shape, covering more than 1.3 billion people in urban and rural areas, according to the white paper.

B

白色污染 white pollution (using and littering of non-degradable plastics)
城市白色污染已趋严重，而且有向农村蔓延的危险。
White pollution has gotten worse in cities and is threatening to spread to the countryside.

白手起家 start from scratch
许多农民白手起家，创立了自己的公司。
Starting from scratch, many farmers set up their own companies.

百年老店 century-old shop
这家百年老店里陈列着许多黄铜器皿、装饰灯、织篮、陶罐等物品。
A lot of brassware, chandeliers, woven baskets, and clay pots are on display at this century-old shop.

摆渡服务 shuttle service
有网友建议提供高速舒适的摆渡服务，吸引政府部门工作人员乘坐，使他们放弃使用公车。
Netizens have suggested a shuttle service with comfort and speed to attract people working at government agencies and get them to abandon their official vehicles.

摆花架子 talk the talk
在拳坛，人们会问："你摆花架子行，动真格的行吗？"意思是，你说你拳下无健将，但若真让你上阵恐怕就不行了。
In boxing circles, they ask, "You can talk the talk, but can you walk the walk?" meaning you say you can fight, but probably you cannot actually do it.

摆架子 put on airs; act arrogant and superior
某些领导和你在公开场合说话时老摆架子。
Some officials always put on airs when they talk to you in public.

摆平 take care of
别担心，我会为你摆平这事儿。
Don't worry. I will take care of it for you.

摆谱儿 show off
最初，我买汽车就为摆谱儿，让大家知道我买得起。

At first, my purpose of buying a car was to show off, to let everyone know that I could afford it.

摆脱贫困 shake off poverty
浙江省今年计划使6万残疾人摆脱贫困。
Zhejiang province plans to help 60,000 disabled people shake off poverty this year.

拜把兄弟；哥们儿 sworn brothers; buddies; very close friends
这两个人现在几乎连话都不说，在大学时他们可是拜把兄弟，是最好的哥们儿。
The two men are hardly on speaking terms, but back in the university, they were sworn brothers, the best friends.

拜金 worship money
对年轻人，有些老年人总有的指责，什么浪费了、轻率了、不负责任了、拜金了。
Some old people always find something to criticize about the young. Youngsters are scolded for being wasteful, flippant, irresponsible, and for worshipping money.

拜年 pay a New Year's visit
拜年是中国的传统习俗，人们借此拜访亲戚朋友，互致祝福。
Paying a New Year's visit is a traditional custom in China. People visit friends and relatives, giving them best wishes.

班车 shuttle bus
免费提供观光、购物班车。
A free shuttle bus is provided for sightseeing and shopping.

斑马线；人行横道 crosswalk; pedestrian crossing; crossing zone; zebra crossing
某些国家交通法规规定，一旦行人走上斑马线，机动车必须让路。
According to traffic regulations in some countries, motor vehicles must yield to pedestrians in crosswalks.

搬迁 relocate
自今年初以来，这个区已经有615家搬迁户被妥善安排。
Since the beginning of this year, 615 units in this neighborhood have been well relocated.

版权法 copyright law
版权法在中国远远没有得到充分执行，盗版和其他非法印刷猖獗。
Given the prevalence of piracy and other illegal printings, the copyright law is far

from being fully enforced in China.

版权贸易 copyright business
涉外版权代理机构是指有权经营涉外版权贸易的中国企业。
The "foreign-related" copyright agencies are Chinese enterprises authorized to handle foreign-related copyright businesses.

版税率 royalty rate
一般来说，当红的作者版税率在10%以上。
Generally speaking, the royalty rate for popular writers is above 10 percent.

办年货 Lunar New Year's shopping; do Lunar New Year's shopping
正如西方的圣诞节采购一样，春节办年货在中国也是件大事。
Lunar New Year's shopping is a big event in China, as Christmas shopping is in the West.

办丧事 conduct a funeral service
办丧事的文化习俗比办婚礼要普遍。
The cultural practices to conduct a funeral service are more popular than those for conducting a wedding ceremony.

半成品 semi-finished product
这次行动抓获罪犯32人，还缴获了各类假证件和大批半成品。
Thirty-two criminals were arrested with various forged certificates and a lot of semi-finished products.

半自由行 semi-guided tour
多家旅行社针对即将到来的3天元旦假期推出"半自由行"旅游套餐吸引游客。
Many travel agencies have introduced semi-guided tour packages to attract travelers for the upcoming 3-day New Year's Day holiday.

包车 chartered vehicle; charter a bus, train, taxi
该公司提供长期包车业务。
The company offers long-term chartered vehicles.

包揽；收入囊中 clean sweep; wrap up; bag
中国羽毛球队首次包揽了奥运会羽毛球比赛的全部金牌。
Chinese badminton team achieved an unprecedented clean sweep of all Olympic golds in the event.

包容性增长 inclusive growth
这次会议的主题是"开发人力资源、大力促进就业、实现包容性增长"。

The theme of the meeting is "Developing Human Resources, Vigorously Promoting Employment and Realizing Inclusive Growth".

包修、包换、包赔的三包承诺制度 "three guarantees" policy which covers repair, replacement or compensation for faulty products
这只坏了的鞋按照商家的三包承诺制度可以调换。三包说的就是包修、包换和包赔。
The broken shoe can be taken back to the store for exchange in accordance with the company's "three guarantees" policy which covers repair, replacement or compensation for faulty products.

包月服务 monthly subscription service
亚马逊正式推出了一个新的包月服务,用户每月支付12元即可阅读所有的电子书。
Amazon officially unveiled a new monthly subscription service that offers all-you-can-read digital books for 12 yuan per month.

保护价格 support price
夏粮收购的保护价格旨在保护农民利益。
Support prices for summer grains are aimed at protecting farmers' interests.

保护生态环境 preserve the environment
随着经济和社会的发展,人们越来越意识到保护生态环境的重要性。
Along with the economic and social development, people have become increasingly aware of the importance of preserving the environment.

保护性关税 protective duty; protective tariff
泰国政府对进口钢铁征收保护性关税以保护本国企业。
To protect Thai enterprises, the government of Thailand imposes a protective duty on steel imports.

保护主义 protectionism
从长远来看,地方贸易保护主义弊大于利。
In the long run, local trade protectionism hurts rather than helps.

保健食品 health food
据说,在墨西哥仙人掌作为保健食品受到珍视。
The cactus is said to be highly valued in Mexico as a health food.

保姆黑名单 nanny blacklist
为了更好地规范市场,防止业主雇用到不合格保姆,上海30家家政公司组成的联盟创建了"保姆黑名单",首批名单已出炉。
The first names have been added to a nanny blacklist created by an alliance of 30 housekeeping service agencies in Shanghai to better regulate the market and deter unsuitable caregivers.

保释 on bail
她付了1000美元后被保释。
She was released on bail of $1,000.

保税仓库 tariff-free warehouse; bonded warehouse
除了保税仓库之外,康柏还在中国投资建立研发中心。
Apart from tariff-free warehouses, Compaq has invested in China to set up a research and development center.

保税区 tariff-free zone; bonded area
香港商人大多在保税区投资开店。
By and large, Hong Kong's businessmen have set up shops in tariff-free zones.

保修期 warranty period
保修期为两年,自购买日期开始。
The warranty period lasts two years from the date of purchase.

保障性住房 indemnificatory apartment
中国已拨出600多亿元建造580万套保障性住房,以遏制飞涨的房价。
China has allocated more than 60 billion yuan to build 5.8 million indemnificatory apartments to curb the skyrocketing housing prices.

保证金;押金 collateral; cash deposit
回到机场后他们才恍然大悟——总共2万元的保证金恐怕是要不回来了。
Having returned to the airport, they came to realize that they could lose their collateral of 20,000 yuan altogether.

保值储蓄 inflation-proof bank savings
政府已采取措施稳定经济,如严格控制纸币发行、推出保值储蓄等。
The government has taken measures to stabilize the economy, such as controlling the issuance of paper money and introducing inflation-proof bank savings.

保质期 shelf life
这种全麦面包在常温下保质期为4天。
The whole-grain bread has a shelf life of four days under normal temperatures.

报复性反弹 retaliatory rebound
社科院经济蓝皮书预测，如果楼市调控力度放松，房价会出现"报复性反弹"。
According to the Blue Paper of the Chinese Academy of Social Sciences on the Chinese economy, housing prices will see a "retaliatory rebound" if the government were to relax measures aimed at cooling the market.

报复性关税 retaliatory duty
鉴于美国威胁说要对中国钢铁征收抑制性关税，中国也考虑对一系列美国产品加收报复性关税。
To counter America's threat to impose prohibitive duties on Chinese steel, China is contemplating retaliatory duties on a string of US products.

报价单 quote sheet
本产品报价单所报价格可能变更。
Prices on this quote sheet are subject to change.

暴发户 nouveau riche
许多暴发户靠房地产发家，他就是其中之一。
He's one of the nouveau riches who have made a fortune in the real estate business.

暴力冲突 mayhem
2016年欧洲杯俄罗斯对战英格兰的比赛结束后，双方球迷发生暴力冲突。数十名俄罗斯球迷冲入坐满英格兰球迷的看台，扔东西、撕扯国旗，与尚未撤离的英格兰球迷互殴。
The Euro 2016 game between Russia and England ended with scenes of mayhem as scores of Russian fans charged into a section full of rival supporters, throwing missiles, tearing down flags and fighting with anyone who remained in their way.

暴力分拣 rough handling of parcels
国家邮政局已对这家快递公司做出罚款1万元的行政处罚。这是国家管理部门针对快递公司的"暴力分拣"问题开出的首例罚单。
The State Post Bureau has fined this express delivery firm 10,000 yuan for rough handling of parcels. It is the first time the bureau has imposed such a punishment against a courier for rough handling.

爆发期 outbreak period
在爆发期内，大约有90万只鸡在被传染和隔离的农场里被扑杀。
Approximately 900,000 chickens were destroyed on infected and quarantined farms during the outbreak period.

B

背包游 backpack tour
越来越多的游客选择"背包游",这让旅游业、酒店业和零售市场更加多样化。
An increasing number of tourists are taking backpack tours, bringing more diversity to the tourism, hospitality and retailing markets.

背黑锅 be the scapegoat; bear the blame
一有差错,总是我来"背黑锅"。
If anything goes wrong, I'm always the scapegoat.

备件 spare parts
伊朗一些服役期长的波音和空中巴士客机由于技术问题和缺少备件已经停飞。
Several of Iran's aging Boeing and Airbus planes have been grounded because of technical problems and a lack of spare parts.

被动房 passive house
中国首座被认可的"被动房"外观类似于一组朝四个方向开的抽屉,"被动房"的意思是该房屋能在零能耗的情况下在任何季节都保持舒适的室内温度。
The building, which resembles a set of drawers opening in four directions, is China's first certified "passive house", meaning it consumes zero energy while maintaining comfortable room temperatures in all seasons.

被动吸烟 second-hand smoking
被动吸烟可导致儿童哮喘和呼吸系统疾病。
Second-hand smoking causes asthma and respiratory illness in children.

被告席 defendants' pen; defendants' seat
独自站在被告席上的他有时表现出与法庭合作的态度。
Standing alone in the defendants' pen, he cooperated with the court at times.

被隔离 under quarantine
目前大约一共有650个家禽农场被隔离。
A total of about 650 poultry farms are now under quarantine.

被解除隔离 be released from quarantine
动物直到5个月大才能被解除隔离。
Animals will not be released from quarantine unless they are five months old.

被判无罪 be cleared of all charges; acquittal; find someone not guilty
在经历了一年半隐士般的生活后,乔治•齐默尔曼走出佛罗里达州的一家法院,重获自由，他在17岁少年特雷翁·马丁枪杀案中的所有指控均被判不成立。
After a year and a half of living as a hermit, George Zimmerman emerged from a Florida courthouse a free man, cleared of all charges in the shooting of 17-year-old Trayvon Martin.

本本主义 dogma and bookishness; bookishness; dogma
中国共产党中央委员会号召全党发扬理论联系实际的作风，反对本本主义。
The Central Committee of the Communist Party of China calls on all Party members to uphold the spirit of linking theory with actual practice and opposing dogma and bookishness.

本命年 the year of one's animal sign
他计划在自己的本命年骑摩托车飞跃黄河。
He plans to cross the Yellow River on a motorcycle during the year of his animal sign.

本土电影 homegrown production; homegrown film
票房收入前十名的影片中有七部是本土电影。
Among the top 10 films in terms of box office revenue, seven were homegrown productions.

本土疫苗 homegrown vaccine
为了应对可能出现的冬季甲型流感大爆发，中国批准了第一批本土H1N1流感疫苗，该疫苗的生产者北京科兴称这种疫苗只需注射一次就能起到防护作用。
China granted approval to its first homegrown H1N1 flu vaccine, which producer Sinovac says is effective after only one dose, as the country braces for a feared winter outbreak.

笨鸟先飞 A slow sparrow should make an early start.
如果你认为技不如人，可以通过早起步、多投入、更努力来弥补。俗话说，笨鸟先飞嘛。
If you think others are more skilled than you, you can offset that by starting sooner, putting in more hours and working harder. A slow sparrow should make an early start, as the saying goes.

蹦极 bungee jumping
对于那些喜爱冒险的人来说，攀岩、蹦极值得一试。
For those who enjoy adventures, rock climbing and bungee jumping are worth trying.

逼近 bear down on
敌舰企图逼近我们的小汽艇。
The enemy warship tried to bear down on our small airboat.

鼻烟壶 snuff bottle
鼻烟壶是中国传统民间工艺品,最早出现在17世纪中期。鼻烟壶的价值不在于其实际用途,而在于其内画艺术。
A snuff bottle is a traditional Chinese folk craftwork, which first appeared in China in the mid-17th century. A snuff bottle is special not because of its practical use but the fact that it's painted on the inside.

比赛脸 game face
比赛脸即准备好应对某件棘手的事情或迎接挑战时做出的表情。
Game face refers to the face you put on when you are about to get ready to tackle something difficult, or when you are about to take on a challenge.

鄙视链 disdain chain; chain of contempt
传说中的"鄙视链"是这样的,英剧迷瞧不起美剧迷,美剧迷瞧不起韩剧迷,而鄙视链中地位最低的则是国产剧迷。
The so-called "disdain chain" works like this: British drama fans look down on folks who prefer US shows, and they in turn look down on South Korean soap opera fans. The lowest of the low in the disdain chain are fans of domestic dramas.

必胜 be bound to win
我们的球队必胜。
Our team is bound to win the match.

闭关政策 closed-door policy
明朝对外国交流和投资实行开放政策,促进了经济发展,清朝的闭关政策阻碍了经济发展。
The Ming dynasty opened up China to foreign interaction and investment, stimulating the country's economy; the Qing dynasty adopted a closed-door policy, which had the opposite effect.

闭门羹 be given the cold shoulder
展销会上,家用电器受到欢迎,而服装和纺织品却吃了闭门羹,让人难以相信。
Electrical appliances are popular at the trade fair. Incredibly, clothes and textile products were given the cold shoulder.

避税；逃税 tax evasion
逃税犯法。
Tax evasion is punishable by law.

边际报酬 marginal return
上半年这家银行实现了超过3700万美元的投资利润和4%的边际报酬。
In the first half of the year the bank realized investment profits of over $37 million with a marginal return of 4 percent.

边际成本 incremental cost
为改善碳的使用率，相关的能源产业不得不增加边际成本，但最终，这些边际成本还是会转移到消费者身上。
Energy-related industries will have to face incremental costs to improve their carbon efficiency, but ultimately, such incremental costs will have to be shouldered by the consumers.

边境检查 border inspection
在世博会的最后准备阶段，上海将为陆续抵达的外国参展团提供专用通道来实行快速边境检查。
International delegations arriving in Shanghai for the upcoming World Expo would be entitled to a special passage for the swift border inspection as the metropolis gears up for the final run-up to the international event.

边境控制 border control
边境控制政策收紧始于两年前保守党和自由民主党联合政府上台之时。
The program to tighten border controls began two years ago when the Conservative-Liberal Democrat coalition took office.

边缘科学 borderline science
信息促进边缘科学的发展。
Information facilitates the development of borderline science.

边远贫困地区 remote, poverty-stricken area
我们必须普及九年义务教育，包括边远贫困地区。
We must ensure nine-year compulsory education for children, including those in remote, poverty-stricken areas.

贬值 depreciate; devaluate
由于受到亚洲金融危机的影响，日元也贬值了。

Affected by the financial crisis in Asia, the yen has also depreciated.

变相涨价 disguised inflation
专家们认为这次价格调整实际上是变相涨价。
Experts perceive the current price adjustments as a form of disguised inflation.

变性手术 sex change surgery
泰国针对变性手术颁布的法规使得在该国进行变性手术更加困难。法规要求申请者穿异性服装一年，以防止一些手术者仓促决定变性。
Thailand has issued rules making sex change surgery more difficult—including a requirement that potential candidates cross-dress for a year—over fears that some patients are rushing into the operation.

便民拖鞋 replacement slipper; backup slipper
除了便民拖鞋，该地铁站还准备了几百件雨衣以及医药箱以备不时之需。
In addition to the replacement slippers, the station has also prepared hundreds of raincoats and medical kits for emergencies.

便衣警察 plain-clothes policeman; plain-clothes police officer
目击者说，便衣警察在他散发传单之前将其抓获。
Plain-clothes policemen got their hands on him before he was able to give out any leaflet, witnesses said.

标书 bid document
项目经理已经把明天投标要用的标书文件都准备好了。
The project manager has got all the bid documents ready for tomorrow's bidding.

表面文章 lip service
在总统竞选中他承诺要搞好环保，但那不过是在做表面文章。
During his campaign for the presidency he paid lip service to the idea of environmental protection.

濒危野生动物 endangered wildlife
大熊猫是濒临灭绝的珍稀动物，现在已被列入世界最濒危野生物种的名单。
Pandas are rare animals close to distinction. They have now been listed among the world's most endangered wildlife species.

冰雕 ice sculpture
会议中心外面树起一座巨大的代表地球的冰雕，上面用红色颜料绘出世界五大洲的图案。

A large ice sculpture representing the earth stands outside the conference center with a red pattern depicting the five continents of the world.

冰雪运动项目 ice and snow sports
北京计划把冰雪运动项目作为中小学生体育课的必修内容。
Beijing is planning to list ice and snow sports as a compulsory course for primary and middle school students.

病毒变异 mutation of the virus
世界卫生组织表示，乌克兰甲型H1N1流感病毒样本的检测结果显示，该病毒并未出现显著变异。
The World Health Organization (WHO) said tests on A/H1N1 flu samples from Ukraine show no significant mutation of the virus.

病毒性感染 viral infection
血液检查显示，在所有坚持按进度治疗的病人中，病毒性感染都继续得到了抑制。
Blood tests showed the viral infection continued to be suppressed in all the patients who had maintained the treatment schedule.

玻璃雨 glass rain
专家认为，在那些案件中高温固然是致使安全玻璃自爆的原因，但引发"玻璃雨"的根本原因是政府对玻璃幕墙安全的忽视。
High temperature is blamed for the cracking of safety glass in those cases, but experts said the fundamental cause of "glass rain" is the government's inattention to the safety of glass curtain walls.

玻璃栈道 glass/see-through walkway
北京市旅游发展委员会的一名官员称，北京将叫停玻璃栈道的建设，因为其安全标准主体责任不明确。
An official from Beijing Municipal Commission of Tourism Development said the city will suspend the construction of glass walkways as it is not clear who is responsible for ensuring they are of a safe standard.

剥夺 strip of
由于赛后药检呈阳性，这位保加利亚举重选手后来被剥夺了金牌。
The Bulgarian weightlifter was later stripped of his gold medal after he tested positive in a drug test following the competition.

薄利多销 small profit margins, big sales; small profits but quick returns
由于市场竞争日益激烈，许多家用电器厂家执行薄利多销的策略。
Due to the increasingly fierce competition, many household appliance companies have adopted the strategy of "small profit margins, big sales".

补缺选举 by-election
补缺选举必须遵照法律，由同一个选举单位选出新代表以填补代表空缺。
By law, a by-election should be held by the same electoral unit in order to pick a new deputy for the vacancy.

补习班 tutoring center
澳门教育暨青年局下令暂时关闭两家当地的私立补习班，因为该局收到有关这两家补习班对男生进行性虐待的举报。
Macao's Education and Youth Affairs Bureau has ordered two local private tutoring centers to be temporarily shut down as it received reports of a sexual abuse case involving the two centers to boy students.

补助奖励机制 reward-compensation mechanism
他号召当地政府在新的补助奖励机制的基础上认真研究制定推进牧区又好又快发展的政策措施。
He called on authorities to devise policies for the sound and fast development of pastoral regions, on the basis of the new reward-compensation mechanism.

不安全性行为；无保护性行为 unprotected sex
艾滋病病毒主要通过无保护性行为传播。
The HIV virus is mainly spread through unprotected sex.

不败纪录 remain unbeaten or undefeated; perfect record
上海队以2比1战胜客队青岛队，继续保持主场不败的纪录。
The Shanghai team remained unbeaten at home by beating the visiting Qingdao team 2∶1.

不动产统一登记制度 unified real estate registration system
作为全国调控房地产市场行动的一部分，北京已开始实施不动产统一登记制度。
Beijing has begun to implement unified real estate registration system as part of a national campaign for regulating the real estate market.

不分上下；难分伯仲 neck-and-neck
不分上下的总统选情表明，近期两党都难有好日子过。
The neck-and-neck presidential election points to tough days ahead for both parties.

不记名投票 secret ballot
在代表雇员的四名委员中，两名由工会以不记名投票的方式选出，其余两名则由政府委任。
Of the four members representing employees, two were elected by trade unions via secret ballot, while the other two were appointed by the government.

不可推卸的责任 unshakeable responsibility
中国外交部发言人表示，在解决化学武器问题上，日本政府负有不可推卸的责任。
The Chinese Foreign Ministry spokesman said that the Japanese government had an unshakeable responsibility to resolve the chemical weapons issue.

不可再生资源 non-renewable resources
据信，不可再生资源，如煤、石油和天然气等的储备都在急剧下降。
Reserves of non-renewable resources such as coal, oil and natural gas are believed to be declining drastically.

不良贷款 non-performing loan
自今年初开始，国务院决定整顿金融领域，打击违法行为，如高额的不良贷款率、违规贷款和金融欺诈。
Since the beginning of this year, the State Council has vowed to reorganize the financial industry by clamping down on irregularities such as high non-performing loan ratios, irregular lending and financial fraud.

不良反应 adverse reaction
北京市卫生局称，参加十一国庆游行和表演的超过1万名学生和表演人员接种了疫苗，未发现不良反应。
More than 10,000 students and performers in Beijing who are to take part in the National Day parade and performances on October 1 received vaccinations, with no adverse reactions, the Beijing Municipal Bureau of Health said.

不明飞行物 unidentified flying object (UFO)
电影《宇宙与人》科学地讲述了一系列神秘现象，如宇宙和生命的起源、不明飞行物以及恐龙的灭绝。
The film *Man and the Universe* presents a scientific view on a series of mysteries such as the origin of the universe and life, UFOs, and the extinction of dinosaurs.

不忘初心 stay true to the mission
中共中央总书记习近平号召同志们"不忘初心"，不要忘记中国共产党95年前成立之时的最初使命。

Xi Jinping, general secretary of the Communist Party of China (CPC) Central Committee, called on his comrades to "stay true to the mission" taken up by the CPC 95 years ago.

不文明行为 inappropriate behavior
我国发布了一项新规,屡现不文明行为的游客和旅游从业人员将被纳入黑名单。
China issued a new regulation to blacklist tourists and tourism service providers who indulge in inappropriate behaviors.

不惜一切代价 spare no effort; go all out
我们会不惜一切代价保卫祖国的主权不受侵犯。
We will spare no effort to safeguard the sovereignty of our motherland.

不夜城 a city that never sleeps; sleepless city
纽约24个小时运转不停,因此,有时被称作"不夜城"。
New York is sometimes referred to as a city that never sleeps because life in the city continues 24 hours a day.

不在服务区 out of reach
您所呼叫的用户不在服务区。
The number you dialed is now out of reach.

不作为;失职 dereliction of duty
昆明市一所小学发生校园踩踏事故,导致6名小学生死亡,26名小学生受伤,作为相关责任人,7名官员因严重失职被解职或停职。
Kunming sacked and suspended seven officials over serious dereliction of duty after a stampede left six pupils dead and 26 injured at a primary school.

步行街 pedestrians-only street
王府井商业街现在是步行街。
Wang Fu Jing Shopping Street has now become a pedestrians-only street.

部长通道 ministers' passage
"部长通道"指的是人民大会堂北门外一条百米长的通道,也被称为"部长红毯",是部长们进入会议厅的必经之路。
Ministers' passage, also known as ministers' red carpet, is the 100-meter passage near the northern gate of the Great Hall of the People where ministers have to go before entering the meeting hall.

擦网球 net ball
幸运的是,他靠擦网球赢得赛点。
It turned out the match point was a lucky net ball in his favor.

才疏学浅 be wanting in skills and knowledge
人们需要独立工作时才发现自己才疏学浅。
It is when one is asked to work on their own that they find themselves wanting in skills and knowledge.

财产申报 asset declaration
为打击腐败,广东已开展官员财产申报试点工作。
Guangdong has launched a pilot official asset declaration program in a bid to fight corruption.

财产税 property tax
收入所得税是最广义上的财产税。然而,财产税通常指的仅是对不动产征收的税。
Income tax meets the broadest definition of a property tax. The term, however, is often limited to taxes based on real property.

财产所有权 property ownership
尽管有人抱怨说在结婚前就得讨论离婚的事,但最高人民法院表示,新的司法解释旨在防止离婚案件中的财产所有权的纠纷。
While some people complain about having to discuss divorce even before tying the knot, the Supreme People's Court said the new rulings are aimed at heading off disputes over the property ownership in divorce cases.

财务报表 financial statement
银行、保险、证券公司必须在招股说明书和财务报表中披露资产质量信息,包括不良资产状况。
Firms in sectors like banking, insurance and securities are required to disclose information on asset quality, including non-performing assets, if there are any in their prospectuses or financial statements.

财务造假 financial fraud
中国证监会表示,将严打不断增加的财务造假等违法违规交易行为。
The China Securities Regulatory Commission said it will crack down on increasing illegal trading activities like financial fraud.

财政包干体制 fiscal responsibility system
财政包干体制是指各单位自负盈亏的财政合同体制。
The fiscal responsibility system is a financial contract system by which each unit is responsible for its own surplus or deficit.

财政赤字 fiscal deficit
阿根廷政府的紧缩计划要求年底前减少财政赤字15亿美元,可谓雄心勃勃。
Argentina has an ambitious, belt-tightening program aimed at shaving $1.5 billion off its fiscal deficit by year's end.

财政年度 fiscal year
日本内阁通过了将于明年4月开始的财政年度的预算准则。
The Japanese cabinet approved budget guidelines for the fiscal year starting next April.

财政收入 fiscal revenue
同一时期,政府财政收入下降了7.5%。
In the same period, the government's fiscal revenue dropped by 7.5 percent.

财政性科技投入 financial input in science and technology

财政悬崖 fiscal cliff
贸易纠纷以及美国的财政悬崖有望成为此次会议的首要议题。
Trade disputes and the US fiscal cliff are expected to top the agenda of the meeting.

裁减冗员 lay off surplus staff
当地政府今年将裁减冗员500人。
The local government will lay off 500 surplus staff this year.

采购经理人指数 Purchasing Managers' Index(PMI)
中国制造业1月份有所增长,采购经理人指数(PMI)为50.5,比去年12月份的50.3略有回升。
China's manufacturing sector expanded in January, as indicated by a slight rise in the Purchasing Managers' Index(PMI)to 50.5 from 50.3 in December.

彩礼 betrothal gifts
河南省某县出台了一项针对红白事的指导意见,其中有一条指出,男方给女方家的彩礼礼金不得超过6万元。
A county in Henan province issued a guideline on arranging weddings and funerals, in which it stated that the total amount of money a man gives his fiancee's family as betrothal gifts should not exceed 60,000 yuan.

参与式扶贫 participatory poverty reduction
"参与式扶贫"让贫困家庭在扶贫资金的使用上有更多话语权。
Participatory poverty reduction allows poverty-stricken families to have a bigger say in how the money intended to benefit them is used.

餐桌污染 dining table pollution
我国将继续加强对食品安全的监管力度,以解决"餐桌污染"问题。
China will continue to strengthen food safety supervision to solve "dining table pollution".

仓储式超市;大型廉价商店 warehouse store
山姆坚持即使在少于5000人的小镇也要照开仓储式超市。
Sam insisted that warehouse stores should be opened even in small towns with fewer than 5,000 people.

藏身之处 hideout
警方突袭歹徒的藏身之处。
Police raided the gangster's hideout.

藏书票 book label
17世纪以来,收藏和交换藏书票成为一种时尚。
Collecting and exchanging book labels has been fashionable since the 17th century.

操办 make arrangements
把婚事的要求告诉他,让他马上操办。
Tell him what you want for the wedding. Let him begin making the arrangements right away.

操纵比赛 game-rigging
有关(足球)幕后交易和非法操纵的流言四起,为此公安部设立了一支特别工作组,负责调查传言的操纵比赛一事。
The Ministry of Public Security set up a special task force to investigate alleged game-rigging, when rumors of under-table deals and fixing ran rife.

操纵股票市场 manipulate the stock market
纽约官方周三透露,有5人被指控操纵股票市场,其中一人是联邦调查局特工。
Five people, including one FBI agent, have been indicted on manipulating the stock market, New York officials announced Wednesday.

操纵市场 market manipulation
中国最高人民法院有望今年出台有关操纵市场、证券市场内幕交易等违法犯罪行为的司法解释。
China's top court is expected to release new judicial interpretations this year to help define criminal conduct involving market manipulation and illegal trading using insider information in the securities market.

厕所革命 toilet revolution
我国要继续推进"厕所革命",发展国内旅游业,提升群众生活品质。
China should continue to upgrade the country's toilets as part of its "toilet revolution" aimed at developing domestic tourism and improving people's quality of life.

测评体系 testing and rating system
教育部正在草拟国家英语能力测评体系。
The Ministry of Education is drafting a national English proficiency testing and rating system.

测图卫星 mapping satellite
北京时间周二下午3点10分,我国在西北的酒泉卫星发射中心成功地发射了一颗测图卫星"天绘一号"。
China successfully launched a mapping satellite, "Mapping Satellite-I", from the northwestern Jiuquan Satellite Launch Center at 3:10 p.m. (Beijing time) Tuesday.

插件 plug-in
这些浏览器所附带的定制插件可以帮助人们在铁道部官方购票网站12306.cn购得车票,在春运期间很受欢迎。
The browsers have plug-ins designed to help people buy tickets at 12306.cn, the Railways Ministry's official ticketing website, and have been popular during the Spring Festival travel rush.

茶道;茶艺 tea ceremony; sado
茶道发源于中国,在日本得到高度发展。

Cha Dao, or the tea ceremony, originated in China, and is highly developed in Japan.

茶话会 tea party
正式会晤结束后，市长陪同5位外国来宾参加了茶话会。
After the formal meeting, the mayor accompanied the five foreign guests to a tea party.

差额选举 competitive election
十九届中央委员会委员和候补委员将由参加十九大的当选代表和特邀代表通过无记名投票选举产生，中央委员会委员和候补委员都实行差额选举。
Delegates and specially invited delegates to the Party congress will select members and alternate members of the 19th CPC Central Committee through secret ballot in competitive election.

差旅费 traveling allowance (for business trips)
所有人员出公差时都有资格得到差旅费。
All members shall be entitled to traveling allowance in respect to a journey performed in connection with the business of the company.

拆东墙补西墙 rob Peter to pay Paul
要是今天他要我还钱的话，我就又得跟别人借。我可不想老是拆东墙补西墙。
If I had to pay him back today, I'd have to borrow from someone else again. I don't want to keep robbing Peter to pay Paul.

拆迁费 relocation compensation
店主称，基于现行的北京市拆迁费标准，最终的拆迁补偿应该可以达到（每平方米）3万至5万元人民币。
The shopkeeper said the final compensation should be 30,000 to 50,000 yuan per square meter, based on the current relocation compensation in Beijing.

拆迁户 household or unit to be relocated
拆迁户中有三家拒不搬走，除非给他们加倍的搬迁费。
Three households to be relocated refused to go unless they get double compensation.

掺水股票 watered-down stocks; ordinary stocks that can be bought by insiders at a cost lower than their face value
掺水股票听起来就像有什么猫腻。

Watered-down stocks smack of foul play.

产假 maternity leave
自2016年1月1日全面二孩政策落地以来，我国30个省级地区延长了产假。
Thirty provincial regions in China have extended maternity leave since the introduction of the universal two-child policy on Jan 1, 2016.

产科床位 maternity bed
我国将提供更多产科床位、培养更多专业人员，以满足不断增长的产科资源需求。
China will offer more maternity beds and train more professionals to meet the growing demand for maternity resources.

产能过剩 excess manufacturing capacity; overcapacity
我国将与世界接轨，创造新动能，目标就是要利用我国产能过剩提升外部需求。
China will reach out internationally to create new drivers for growth. The goal is to boost external demand by taking advantage of China's excess manufacturing capacity.

产品积压 product surplus; excess inventory
我们现在的问题不再是没有生产，而是我们的产品没人要。现在让我头疼的是产品积压。
The problem is no longer that we are not producing, but that our products are unwanted. Product surpluses are giving me headaches.

产品结构 product mix
产品结构的调整将成为下阶段结构调整的重点。
An adjustment in the product mix will be the focus of the next round of restructuring.

产权保护 property rights protection
国务院常务会议后发布的公告指出，依法平等保护公有制和非公有制经济产权，加强企业自主经营权和合法财产所有权保护。对居民产权的保护也将加强。
Businesses will enjoy better protection of their operational and property rights, and private businesses will enjoy equal protection for their property rights as companies in the public sector, according to the statement following the State Council executive meeting. Protection of residents' property rights will also be enhanced.

产业生态系统 industry eco-system
他表示，由于当时中国缺少成熟的产业生态系统，TD-SCDMA技术的使用大多局限在了国内市场。
He said because China lacked an industry eco-system at that time, the use of TD-SCDMA technology was largely restrained to the domestic market.

产业政策 industrial policy
钢铁和汽车等行业将得到各省政府产业政策及资金方面的支持。
Industries such as steel and automobiles will be backed by provincial governments with favorable industrial policies and funding.

长臂管辖 long-arm jurisdiction
发言人表示"中国反对针对外国企业的'长臂管辖'",并指出中国已经对美国明确表明立场。
"China opposes 'long-arm jurisdiction' on foreign enterprises," the spokesperson said, adding that China has made this stance very clear to the United States.

长江后浪推前浪,一代更比一代强 The river surges forward wave upon wave. The new generation performs better than the old.

长江三角洲 Yangtze River Delta
江苏位于长江三角洲,紧靠上海。
Jiangsu is located in the Yangtze River Delta, close to Shanghai.

长江中下游 the middle and lower reaches of the Yangtze River
长江中下游城市污水处理不是没有问题。
Sewage water disposal in the middle and lower reaches of the Yangtze River has not been problem-free.

长期共存、互相监督、肝胆相照、荣辱与共 long-term coexistence, supervision of one another, sincere treatment and sharing of well-being or woe

长途航班 long-haul flight
法国航空预计将恢复所有长途航班和几乎全部欧洲航班。
Air France is expected to resume 100% of its long-haul flights and nearly all of its European flights.

长途漫游费 long-distance and roaming charges
我国三大电信运营商取消了国内长途漫游费。
China's three major telecom carriers scrapped domestic long-distance and roaming charges.

长治久安 lasting political stability
长治久安是全国人民的共同愿望。

The entire Chinese people cherish the hope for lasting political stability.

常规裁军 conventional disarmament
核裁军与常规裁军是两项优先任务。
Nuclear disarmament and conventional disarmament are two priorities.

常规武器 conventional weapon
除了《欧洲常规武器协议》的签署，没有别的消息可以减轻人们对日益加剧的军备竞赛的忧虑。
Except for the signing of the *European Conventional Weapons Agreement*, there was no news to relieve people's worries about an escalating arms race.

常设国际法庭 permanent international tribunal
许多国家支持建立常设国际法庭，审判战争罪犯。
Many nations support the idea of establishing a permanent international tribunal to try war criminals.

常务董事 managing director; executive director
该常务董事将于周日抵京，开始他的亚洲四国之行。
The executive director will arrive in Beijing on Sunday to begin his visit to four Asian countries.

常驻代表 permanent representative
他被任命为肯尼亚共和国驻联合国人类住区（生活环境）中心的常驻代表。
He was appointed Permanent Representative of the Republic of Kenya to the United Nations Center for Human Settlements (Habitat).

常驻记者 resident correspondent
该作者是《聊望》杂志常驻日本东京的记者。
The author is a resident correspondent of *Outlook* magazine in Tokyo, Japan.

常驻联合国代表 permanent representative to the United Nations
中国常驻联合国代表致函联合国秘书长重申一个中国原则。
China's permanent representative to the United Nations has sent a letter to the Secretary-General of the UN reiterating the One-China Principle.

偿付能力 solvency
一种办法是向保险公司开放股票市场，以便他们筹集必要的资金来增强偿付能力。
One solution is to open the stock market to insurance companies, which will allow them to raise the money needed to improve their solvency.

场内交易人 floor trader; floor broker
作为场内交易人,他的年收入为10万美元。
As a floor trader, he makes $100,000 a year.

场外证券市场上的股票 over-the-counter (OTC) stock
场外证券市场上的股票通常是高风险的,因为这些股票数额小、不稳定,没有资格在正规股票交易所交易。
OTC stocks are usually very risky since they are the stocks that are not considered large or stable enough to trade on a major exchange.

唱对台戏 put on a rival show
老板讲话时你们不要交头接耳,不然他会认为你们和他唱对台戏。
Don't chatter while the boss speaks, or he'll think you're putting on a rival show.

唱高调 all talk and no action
他总说要动手做实事却不见行动,真是只唱高调不干事。
He's all talk and no action; he always says he's going to do things but he never does.

超大机构、城市 megacity behemoth
到那时,北京、上海、成都、重庆、广州、深圳、天津、武汉这八个城市将成为人口超过一千万的超大城市,而其中有些城市已经成为超大城市。
By then eight cities, Beijing, Shanghai, Chengdu, Chongqing, Guangzhou, Shenzhen, Tianjin and Wuhan, will have populations of more than 10 million with some already megacity behemoths.

超短波 ultra-short wave
他是最早使用超短波激光显微镜诊断疾病的人。
He was the first to use the ultra-short wave laser microscope in diagnosing diseases.

超国民待遇 super-national treatment
为迎接即将到来的中国国庆假期,境外商家计划向中国游客推出"超国民待遇"来拉动消费。
Overseas sellers plan to give "super-national treatment" to Chinese tourists to promote their spending during the upcoming China's National Day holiday.

超级计算机 supercomputer
我国新型超级计算机"神威太湖之光"取代"天河二号"问鼎全球超级计算机500强榜单。

A new Chinese supercomputer, Sunway Taihu-Light, dethroned the country's Tianhe-2 from the top of a list of the 500 most powerful supercomputers in the world.

超级水稻 super grain
中国顶尖农业科学家袁隆平近日实现了他80岁生日的愿望之一——他的超级水稻每公顷的产量达到了13.9吨,创造了水稻产量新的世界纪录。
Yuan Longping, China's leading agricultural scientist, realized one of his 80th birthday wishes recently when his super grain brought yields of 13.9 tons of rice a hectare, setting a new world record for the rice output.

超级网银 super online banking system
中国人民银行正式推出网上支付跨行清算系统,或称"超级网银"。该系统支持跨行转账实时到账以及跨行余额查询。
The People's Bank of China (PBOC), China's central bank, put its online payment interbank clearing system, or "super online banking system" into service. The system supports real-time interbank transfers and interbank balance inquiries.

超前消费 excessive consumption
毫无疑问,媒体对超前消费模式的形成也负有责任。
The media undoubtedly played their part in the creation of excessive consumption patterns.

超售 overbooking
美联航一趟航班上出现常见的超售问题,却以一名男子被强行赶下飞机收场,给这家本已问题缠身的航空公司带来了更多负面报道。
A common overbooking problem on a United Airlines flight ended with a man being violently removed from the flight and an already troubled airline earning more bad press.

超水平发挥 outdo oneself
我那次真是超水平发挥,之前、之后都没有过那么好的表现。
I really outdid myself that time. I had never given a better performance before and haven't since.

超现实主义 surrealism
超现实主义的特点是痴迷于异乎寻常的事物。许多人认为它不合时宜,也不够理性。
Surrealism, which is characterized by a fascination with the bizarre, is considered by many to be incongruous and irrational.

超优惠税收政策 super-preferential tax policy
在对外资企业改革开放的早期，我国就在税收方面对外企实行超优惠税收政策，努力促进经济发展。外资企业得以免除部分税费。
Early on in its reform and opening to foreign enterprises, China launched super-preferential tax policies for international companies in a bid to propel its economic growth, and the internationals were exempt from some taxes.

朝阳群众 Chaoyang residents
为了密切警民关系，北京市公安局朝阳分局发布了一款以"朝阳群众"命名的app。
The Chaoyang Branch of Beijing Municipal Public Security Bureau launched an app named after Chaoyang residents in a bid to better connect the police and ordinary citizens.

潮汐车道 reversible lane; tidal flow
北京将推出潮汐车道以缓解道路拥堵状况。
Reversible lanes will be introduced in Beijing to relieve road congestion.

潮汐电站 tidal power station
浙江温岭的江厦潮汐电站是中国最大的潮汐电站。
The Jiangxia Tidal Power Station at Wenling, Zhejiang province is the largest of its kind in China.

炒汇 speculate in foreign currency
中行广东分行是中国首家为个人提供网上炒汇业务的银行。
The Bank of China's Guangdong Branch was the first bank in China to provide a program that allowed individuals to speculate in foreign currency online.

炒作 hype; commercial speculation
看这部新片的媒体报道可别当真。有些纯粹是炒作。
Don't take media reports on the new movie seriously. Some reports are just hype.

车补 traffic subsidy
根据中央政府控制交通费用的最新指导意见，取消一般公务用车，司局级每人每月领取车补1300元，处级每人每月800元，科级及以下每人每月500元。
Instead of having cars provided by the government, officials at bureau level will receive monthly traffic subsidies of 1,300 yuan, while those at director level and section level will get 800 yuan and 500 yuan a month, according to the new guideline to rein in vehicle expenses for the central government.

车船使用税 vehicle and vessel tax
这名司机请税务局退还今年他所缴纳的部分车船使用税,因为他和所有其他北京驾车者一样,每周都有一天因为首都的"无车日"车辆限行政策而不能开车。
The driver asked the tax office to refund part of the vehicle and vessel tax he has paid this year because he, like all other Beijing drivers, is not able to drive one day each week as a result of the car limitation policy in the capital—the so-called "no car day".

车牌摇号 license-plate lottery
从周五开始,车辆登记将采用车牌摇号的方式进行。
Starting on Friday, car registration will be allocated by a license-plate lottery system.

车展 auto show
福特公司计划在本月即将到来的北京车展上展出Edge越野车(SUV),试图在中国消费者中挖掘对SUV车型快速增长的需求。
Ford plans to introduce its Edge sports utility vehicle (SUV) at the upcoming Beijing Auto Show this month in a bid to tap fast-growing demand for SUVs among Chinese customers.

扯后腿 hold someone back
英国作家、演员史蒂芬·弗莱写道:"农民意识在扯英国的后腿。"
A peasant attitude holds Britain back, wrote the British writer and actor Stephen Fry.

扯皮 pass the buck; shirk
火灾事故发生后,厂里所有与事故有干系的工人都一直在推诿扯皮,说错在别人,不关自己的事儿。
After the accidental fire in the factory, all the workers involved kept passing the buck, saying it was someone else's fault and not theirs.

撤军 withdraw troops
国防部要求印度立即从我国领土撤军,提醒印度领导人不要心存侥幸,不要抱着不切实际的幻想。
The Ministry of Defense has demanded India immediately withdraw its troops from Chinese territory, warning its leaders not to leave things to luck or have unrealistic expectations.

撤离区 evacuation zone
工程师对遭特大海啸袭击的6座核反应堆的修复工作进展缓慢,严重受损的核电站周围辐射水平居于高位,日本计划将"撤离区"扩大。
Japan plans to extend the evacuation zone around its crippled nuclear plant because of high radiation levels, with engineers no closer to regaining control of six reactors hit by a giant tsunami.

撤侨 evacuation of one's nationals
中国于周六决定加快从利比亚撤侨。在未来两周,中国航空当局每天会派出15架飞机接运滞留在这个非洲北部国家的中国同胞回国。
China on Saturday decided to hasten evacuation of its nationals from Libya, as Chinese aviation authorities prepare 15 planes per day during the next two weeks to carry home citizens stranded in the northern African country.

撤销职务 dismiss someone from one's post
他因为经济犯罪被撤销了职务。
He was dismissed from his post for economic crimes.

尘肺病 pneumoconiosis; black lung disease; coal worker's pneumoconiosis
今年,宫颈癌、乳腺癌、肺癌以及尘肺病等20种重大疾病将被纳入医疗救助项目。
This year, 20 major diseases including cervical, breast and lung cancer as well as pneumoconiosis will be included in medical aid programs.

成活率 survival rate
他的努力没有白费,他种的树成活率在全地区最高。
His hard work wasn't in vain, as the survival rate of the trees he planted tops the region.

成就感 sense of achievement
人只有在努力工作并克服重重困难之后才会有成就感。
One won't feel a sense of achievement unless he has worked hard and overcome many obstacles.

成品油定价机制 oil product pricing system; fuel pricing scheme; fuel pricing mechanism
中国推出了一个更加以市场为导向的成品油定价机制,以便能更好地反映产品成本并适应全球油价波动。
China launched a more market-oriented oil product pricing system to better reflect costs and adapt to fluctuations in global oil prices.

城际高铁 intercity high-speed rail
连接中国东部江西省南昌市和九江市的城际高铁周一开始运行,这是我国铁路运输的长期规划项目之一。新城际高铁将把135公里路程的运行时间缩短至45分钟。
The intercity high-speed rail line connecting Nanchang and Jiujiang in East China's Jiangxi province began operation on Monday, as part of the long-term plan of the railway network in China. The new train service will cover the 135-km journey in 45 minutes.

城市病 urban disease
一项最新报道警告称,中国大城市正濒临严重的资源短缺、基础设施承载能力不足等一系列城市问题,这些问题被统称为"城市病"。
Big cities in China are on the brink of a major shortfall in resources and infrastructure capacity, under a problem termed "urban diseases", a new report has warned.

城市低保对象 urban residents entitled to basic living allowances
我们增加了城市低保对象的保障水平。
We increased subsidies for urban residents entitled to basic living allowances.

城市规划 urban planning
作为中国改革开放政策的试验区,深圳是中国首批将城市规划向海外设计人士开放的城市之一。
An experimental area for China's Reform and Opening-up, Shenzhen was among the first Chinese cities to open urban planning to overseas designers.

城市竞争力 urban competitiveness
全球城市竞争力格局正在发生剧烈变化,中国城市的排名正迅速提高。
The pattern of urban competitiveness in the world is changing dramatically, and Chinese cities are rapidly upgrading their rankings.

城市热岛效应 urban heat island effect
根据中国气象局的最新统计,在气候变暖导致的气温上升中,大约有1/4是由城市热岛效应导致的。城市化导致的其他现象包括城市干岛效应、湿岛效应、混浊岛效应和雨岛效应。
According to the latest statistics from the China Meteorological Administration, about one-fourth of the temperature rise caused by climate warming can be blamed on the "urban heat island effect". Other phenomena resulting from urbanization include dry islands, wet islands, dark islands and rain islands in cities.

城市通风廊道 urban air corridor
北京将于年底出台一项城市新规划,规划中首次计划留出生态绿色的"城市通风廊道"。

Beijing will issue a new urban planning strategy by the end of this year that will for the first time contain a plan to preserve green "urban air corridors".

城市增长边界 urban growth boundary

为了控制无计划的城市扩张，保护环境，北京拟设4类"城市增长边界"，将其70%的行政区域变为生态保护区。

Beijing will set 4 urban growth boundaries while 70% of its administrative districts will become ecological protection areas in order to control unplanned city expansion and aid the environment.

城乡一体化 rural-urban integration

中国承诺进一步协调城市与农村的发展，更好地推动城乡一体化进程。

China pledges to push coordinated development of cities and villages for better rural-urban integration.

城镇社会保障体系 urban social security system

我们将改善城镇社会保障体系。

We will improve the urban social security system.

城镇住房公积金 urban housing fund

我们要建立城镇住房公积金制度，加快改革住房制度。

We shall establish an urban housing fund to speed up housing reform.

惩罚性关税 punitive duty

商务部发言人姚坚周四表示，中国坚决反对欧盟针对中国太阳能企业征收惩罚性关税，政府将维护中国企业的权利。

China is firmly opposed to any punitive duty set by the European Union targeting Chinese solar companies, and the government will defend the rights of domestic companies, Yao Jian, a spokesman for the Ministry of Commerce, said on Thursday.

橙色预警 orange alert

中央气象台昨天上午发布了强冷空气和暴雪预警，将预警级别提高到了二级橙色预警。

The Central Meteorological Station (CMS) yesterday morning extended the warning of a strong cold spell and snowstorms by issuing an orange alert, the second-highest level.

吃饱穿暖 have enough food to eat and enough clothing to wear; have adequate food and clothing
农村贫困人口最渴望的是吃饱穿暖。
What the impoverished people in rural areas desire is to have enough food to eat and enough clothing to wear.

吃醋 be jealous; be green with envy
她要他来接她,让室友看看她有了新男友。她们吃醋才好呢。
She wants him to pick her up so that her roommates see she has a new boyfriend. If they are jealous, that's just fine with her.

吃回扣 receive kickbacks
医务人员吃回扣、乱收费将被严肃查处。
Medical staff found to be receiving kickbacks or arbitrarily charging fees will be severely punished.

吃老本 rest on one's laurels; live off one's past gains or achievements
吃老本的人很快会落后。
Those who rest on their laurels soon find themselves falling behind.

吃香 sought-after
招聘中最吃香的是20多岁的年轻女子。
Young women in their twenties were the most sought-after candidates for the job.

迟到卡 late card
上海、广州地铁会给受到地铁晚点和其他交通故障原因影响的乘客发放"迟到卡",使其免受像扣工资这样的惩罚。
Subway lines in the Shanghai municipality and Guangzhou will hand out "late cards" to commuters affected by train delays and other traffic reasons so they can get exemption from punishment by employers such us wage deduction.

持平 hold the line
经济状况不稳定,公司的雇用计划和支出计划刚好持平。
Businesses are holding the line on hiring and spending plans because of uncertainty about the economy.

赤潮 red tide
根据星期五发布的水样检测结果,当地海滩赤潮本周继续消退。
The red tide continued to diminish this week at local beaches, according to water sample test results released Friday.

赤贫人口 destitute population; people living in abject poverty
中国的赤贫人口大多集中在内陆地区。
Most of China's destitute population lives in inland areas.

冲动购买 impulse shopping; impulse buying
她有一次冲动大采购，花了5000美元买衣服和鞋子，买来的物件又大都待在衣柜里，一次也没派上用场。
In one of her impulse shopping sprees, she spent $5,000 on shoes and clothing, most of which are hanging in the closet untouched.

冲销账目 write off accounts; write-off
信达资产管理公司已经着手帮助中国建设银行冲销坏账。
The Cinda Assets Management Corporation has set out to help the China Construction Bank write off bad accounts.

充电（进一步学习或培训） brush up on something
去美国旅行以后，我意识到得把英语捡起来给自己充充电了。
After traveling to America, I realized I needed to brush up on my English.

充分调动人的积极性和创造性 give full play to people's initiative and creativity
只要你能充分调动各位员工的积极性和创造性，就不愁公司在这一行业没有好的业绩。
Giving full play to the employees' initiative and creativity, the company is sure to do well in the field.

充值卡 rechargeable card
这是一个充值卡。只要你每月记着往卡里充值，这个手机你就可以一直用下去。
It is a rechargeable card. Remember to put money on the card every 30 days and then you can use the mobile phone as long as you want.

重考；补考 make-up test
受影响的考生有两种选择：他们可以选择参加免费重考，也可以获得GRE考试费用205美元的全额退款。
The affected examinees have been offered two options: they can choose to take a free make-up test, or receive a full refund of their GRE test fee of $205.

崇洋媚外 worship everything foreign
"外国的月亮比中国的圆"，这句话常用来贬斥那些崇洋媚外的中国人。
That "the foreign moon is fuller in their eyes" is a common disparaging remark directed at those Chinese people who worship everything foreign.

宠物医院 pet clinic
近来,宠物医院也"顾客"盈门。
Pet clinics have been crowded with "patients" lately.

抽检 spot check
国家质量监督检验检疫总局对手机电池的质量进行了抽检。
The General Administration of Quality Supervision, Inspection and Quarantine did a spot check on the quality of mobile phone batteries.

仇外情绪 xenophobia
词典网提供了对"仇外情绪"一词的两种定义:对外国人、不同文化背景的人或陌生人的恐惧或仇恨,对不同文化背景的人的习俗、着装等的恐惧或厌恶。
Dictionary.com offers two definitions for xenophobia: fear or hatred of foreigners, people from different cultures, or strangers; fear or dislike of the customs, dress, etc., of people who are culturally different from oneself.

筹资 raise capital
如果你想筹资,就必须讲清楚资本将作何用。
If you want to raise capital, you've got to explain how it is going to be used.

臭氧污染 ozone pollution
环保部称,北京、天津及河北省部分地区可能遭遇臭氧污染。
Beijing, Tianjin, and parts of Hebei may suffer from ozone pollution, the Ministry of Environmental Protection said.

出厂价格 factory-gate price
在这一新机制下,如果喷气燃料综合购买成本达到一定水平,航空公司将可以自己决定是否收取或收取多少燃油附加费。喷气燃料综合购买成本为喷气燃料国内出厂价和进口燃料价格的加权平均值。
Under the new mechanism, airline companies could decide themselves whether to charge fuel surcharge and how much to charge if the jet fuel comprehensive purchasing cost, which is the weighted average of domestic factory-gate prices for jet fuel and prices of imported fuel, reaches a certain level.

出场费 appearance fee
伦敦奥运会金牌得主回到家乡,又迎来新一轮收获,包括一大笔奖金和参加商业活动的高额出场费。
Gold medalists of the London Olympics welcome a new round of harvest back to homeland, including a large sum of bonus money as well as high appearance fees

in commercial opportunities.

出境签证 exit visa
申请出境签证需要10个工作日。
Applications for exit visas take 10 working days to process.

出境游 outbound trip
国家旅游局称，七天春节假期，中国大陆游客出境游人次达到创纪录的615万。
A record 6.15 million outbound trips were made by Chinese mainland tourists during the seven-day Spring Festival holiday, according to the China National Tourism Administration.

出口关税 export duty
自2015年5月1日起，我国取消稀土的出口关税。分析师指出此举将刺激中国这一稀缺资源的出口。
Export duties on rare earths were eliminated on May 1, 2015. Analysts said the move will stimulate China's exports of the limited resource.

出口管制 export control
奥巴马访华期间，中美商务官员的会晤议题包括（对华）高技术出口管制、反贸易保护主义以及保护知识产权等。
Hi-tech export control is among the topics, including anti-protectionism and intellectual property rights, to be discussed between Chinese and US trade officials during Obama's visit.

出口退还税款 export tax rebate
出口退还税款帮助许多企业渡过了金融危机。
Export tax rebates have helped many enterprises survive the financial crisis.

出气筒 punching bag
他靠充当那些醉鬼商人的出气筒来谋生。
He makes a living as a punching bag for drunken businessmen.

出勤率 attendance rate
用奖励的方法能够提高出勤率，但并非屡试不爽。
Incentives can raise the attendance rate, but not all the time.

出租车价格机制 taxi fare system
北京市交通委主任表示，北京将推出一系列措施缓解首都打车难的问题，其中包括调整出租车价格机制。

Beijing will adjust the taxi fare system as part of a series of measures to ease the difficulty of hailing a taxi in the capital, the city's top transport official has announced.

初审 preliminary censor
根据国家广播电影电视总局发布的新规定，省级广电审查部门负责当地电影公司拍摄完成的所有影片的立项和初审工作。
Provincial censorship branches will be able to process script submissions and preliminarily censor all completed films in local studios, under new regulations by the State Administration of Radio, Film and Television（SARFT）.

处理价格 bargain price; reduced price
周日，在每月例行的甩卖中，几百台计算机和其他家用电器将以处理价格出售。
Hundreds of computers and other household appliances will be sold at bargain prices Sunday at the monthly sale.

处理品 items for disposal
打折商品不是处理品，自然要区别对待。
Commodities for discount are not items for disposal, and are therefore treated differently.

处女作 maiden work
艺术设计的工作不再让他感到满足，于是他开始写剧本，并且在1994年为他的处女作拿到了一笔银行贷款。
The job as an art designer could no longer satisfy him. He started writing scripts and in 1994, he got a bank loan for his maiden work.

穿梭外交 shuttle diplomacy—a figure of speech referring to frequent diplomatic activities
欧盟特使的穿梭外交旨在降低斗争演变为战争的危险。
Shuttle diplomacy by European Union envoys was supposed to reduce the threat of fighting spilling over into war.

传销 pyramid scheme; pyramid selling
传销活动已经在全国明令禁止。
Pyramid schemes are banned by government decree throughout the country.

闯黄灯 ignore yellow traffic lights; ignore amber lights
公安部宣布对闯黄灯的驾驶员将主要进行警示教育，暂时不予处罚。

Drivers who ignore yellow traffic lights will mostly receive warnings and education, and for the time being, they will not be penalized, the Ministry of Public Security announced.

创刊号 inaugural issue
峰会官方英文会刊周一发行了创刊号。
The official English-language journal of the summit launched its inaugural issue on Monday.

创利 generate profit
钱应该投在最需要的地方，投在能创利的地方。
Money should be invested where it is needed the most, and where it can generate profit.

创新全面伙伴关系 innovative comprehensive partnership
国家主席习近平与到访的以色列总理内塔尼亚胡在北京宣布，双方建立创新全面伙伴关系。
Chinese President Xi Jinping and visiting Israeli Prime Minister Benjamin Netanyahu announced in Beijing an innovative comprehensive partnership between both countries.

创新型国家 innovation-driven country
我们将深入贯彻新发展理念，全面深化改革，加快建设创新型国家，推动形成全面开放新格局，建设现代化经济体系。
We will act on the new vision of development, comprehensively deepen reform, turn China into an innovation-driven country at a faster pace, break new ground in pursuing opening-up on all fronts and build a modern economic system.

创新战略伙伴关系 innovative strategic partnership
中国和瑞士将建立创新战略伙伴关系，以促进两国共同发展和繁荣。
China and Switzerland will establish an innovative strategic partnership to promote common development and prosperity.

创业精神 entrepreneurial spirit
完成这些任务需要有创业精神。
Fulfillment of the tasks calls for an entrepreneurial spirit.

创业企业；创始企业 start-up company
此外，我们还帮助有发展前景的创业公司联系风险投资人。

In addition, we help to connect venture capitalists with promising start-up companies.

创业友好城市 start-up friendly city
凭借蓬勃的创业文化、巨大的人才库、地方政府有效的政策支持和有前景的市场定位，北京、上海等国内创业友好城市正在吸引越来越多的企业家。
With a vigorous entrepreneurial culture, huge talent pool, efficient local government policy support and promising market niches, China's start-up friendly cities such as Beijing and Shanghai are attracting an increasing number of entrepreneurs.

创意毕业照 creative graduation photo
临近毕业季，我国大学生正绞尽脑汁地试图想出完美的创意毕业照。
Graduation season is drawing near and Chinese college students are racking their brains trying to come up with the perfect creative graduation photos.

创造性思维 think outside the box; out-of-box thinking
美国学校鼓励学生进行创造性思维、提出质疑、并挑战老师的权威，中国学生到美国后常对此感到惊叹不已。
Arriving in the US, the Chinese students often marvel at how American schools encourage students to think outside the box, to ask questions and challenge the teachers.

吹风会 briefing
在周一举行的关于新规定的吹风会上，政府公布了第一批准备进行国际招标的5块地皮。
In a Monday briefing on the new regulations, the government identified the first five pieces of land to be up for international bidding.

春茶 spring tea
在中国，春茶的采摘时间通常是每年的3月至5月初。碧螺春、瓜片茶等其他知名春茶的价格每斤也将高达2万元。
The picking time for spring tea in China is usually from March to early May. The price for other famous spring tea, like Spring Snail or Melon Seed, will be as high as 20,000 yuan per 500 grams.

春运 the annual Spring Festival travel rush
我国一年一度的春运被誉为世界最大规模人口迁徙。
The annual Spring Festival travel rush marks the world's largest human migration.

辞旧迎新 ring in the new year; bid farewell to the old year and usher in the new
年轻人挤满了酒吧,等着倒计时一起辞旧迎新。
Young people crowded in the bar, waiting for the countdown to ring in the New Year.

辞职;下台 step down
布什内阁的许多高级官员辞职了。
Many high-ranking officials of the Bush Administration stepped down.

次级债务 subordinate debt
中国银行现在已经获准发行高达320亿元的次级债务,以改善资本结构。
The Bank of China has now received regulatory approval to issue up to 32 billion yuan worth of subordinate debt to improve its capital structure.

次生地质灾害 secondary geological hazard
有关部门还应防范次生地质灾害,将受灾群众送往安全地区,为他们提供充足的住处、食物、饮用水和医疗物资。
Authorities should also guard against secondary geological hazards, transport people affected to safe areas and provide them with sufficient shelter, food, drinking water and medical services.

次生灾害 secondary disaster
雨季将至,我国高度关注四川地震灾区对山体滑坡等次生灾害的防范。
China is on high alert for secondary disasters like landslides in the quake-hit region in Sichuan as the rainy season approaches.

从众行为 inclinations to conform
投资者的从众行为也会影响金融市场的稳定。
Investors' inclinations to conform can also destabilize the financial market.

凑份子 whip-round
你们可以凑份子合伙给她买个礼物。
You might have a whip-round to buy a joint present for her.

粗加工产品 rough-wrought product
他身穿一套粗加工制服,做工粗糙。
He wore a rough-wrought uniform. It had been manufactured in a rough way.

促销 promote sales
政府的住房促销措施似乎已见成效。

Government measures to promote housing sales seem to have taken effect.

篡改历史 tamper with the history

金砖国家应该同世界上所有热爱和平的国家和人民一道,坚决反对否认、歪曲甚至篡改第二次世界大战历史的图谋和行径,共同维护第二次世界大战的胜利成果和国际公平正义。

The BRICS countries should join all the peace-loving countries and peoples in the world in firmly opposing any attempt or action to deny, distort or even tamper with the history of that war, and in upholding its victorious outcome and international equity and justice.

篡改食品标签 doctor food label

国内媒体曝出北京一家赛百味快餐连锁店的员工篡改食品标签并使用过期食材,赛百味美国总部正对此进行调查。

US fast food chain Subway is investigating media reports in China that workers at a Beijing outlet doctored food labels and used produce beyond its expiration date.

催泪弹 tear gas

警方使用催泪弹驱散人群。

Tear gas was used by the police to disperse the crowds.

错峰上下班方案 staggered rush hour plan

错峰上下班方案需更多公交和地铁列车配合——周一开始实行新的错峰上下班政策后,北京多达80万名上班族的上下班高峰时间将会调整。

More buses and trains needed for staggered rush hour plan—As many as 800,000 commuters in Beijing will change their rush hour schedules as the new adjusted work-hour policy kicks off on Monday.

D

搭售 tie-in sale
顾客都讨厌搭售。
Customers hate tie-in sales.

搭送；额外奉送 throw in
我买这套家具时，经理搭送了几块地毯和窗帘。
When I bought the furniture set, the manager threw in a few carpets and curtains as well.

打车软件 taxi-hailing app; cab-hailing app
北京叫车中心将8个手机打车软件整合到其服务平台，而上海在考虑复制这一模式。
Beijing's taxi booking center has integrated eight smartphone taxi-hailing apps into its service, while Shanghai is considering copying the model.

打出王牌 play one's trump card
在谈判中，王牌打得太早可能是致命错误。
In negotiations, playing your trump card too soon can be fatal.

打翻身战 turn the things around; turn the situation around
困境中，这家网络公司开始提供免费邮件和网上购物服务，力求打个翻身战。
The struggling internet company began providing free e-mail and online shopping in a bid to turn the things around.

打黑 campaign against mafia-style gangs; crack down on mafia-style gangs
在打黑运动中，本市公安局特别培训了70多位干警。
The city trained more than 70 police officers specifically to participate in its campaign against mafia-style gangs.

打击报复 conduct reprisals; retaliate
美国国务院的谴责中并未提及以色列人的其他报复行为。
The US State Department's condemnation made no mention of other reprisals conducted by the Israelis.

打击非法投机活动 crack down on speculation
1929年纽约证券市场大震荡后，政府采取了措施打击非法投机活动。

After the stock market crashed in 1929, the US government took measures to crack down on speculation.

打破沉默者 The Silence Breakers
"打破沉默者"当选《时代》杂志2017年"年度人物",他们在全美范围内引发了对性骚扰的愤慨。

"The Silence Breakers" who sparked a national outcry over sexual harassment across the US have been named as *Time* magazine's 2017 Person of the Year.

打破僵局 break the deadlock
人们都在观望,看对峙双方能否做出让步以打破谈判僵局。

People are waiting to see whether the rival parties will make compromises to break the deadlock.

打破垄断 break up a monopoly
电信体系改革包括将中国电信拆分为两个公司,目的是打破电信产业的垄断。

The telecom system reform, including the split of China Telecom into two companies, is aimed at breaking up the monopoly in the telecom industry.

打破世界纪录 shatter/break/smash/rewrite the world record
自周六在400米个人混合泳最后一段的自由泳部分以惊人的速度打破世界纪录以来,叶诗文一直受到密切关注。

Since shattering the world record for the 400m individual medley with an eyecatching last-leg freestyle sprint on Saturday, Ye Shiwen has been put under the microscope.

打小报告 squeal on someone
办公室里最可恨的就是那些打小报告讨老板喜欢的人。

Those who squeal on colleagues in return for favors are the most hated in the office.

大包大揽 take on all things
他爱大包大揽,好像他什么都行。其实,他什么也不行。

He takes on all things as though he's good at all of them. In fact, he's good at none.

大病保险全覆盖 full coverage of the serious illness insurance nationwide
政府工作报告指出,年内要实现大病保险全覆盖。

The Government Work Report stated that full coverage of the serious illness insurance nationwide will be completed by the end of this year.

大丰收 bumper harvest
农业部一位高级官员表示,虽然今年国家粮食会大丰收,但消费者还是要面临粮价适度上涨的局面。
Consumers will still face moderate grain price hikes this year, despite the country seeing a bumper harvest, a senior agricultural official said.

大功率电器 high-power electrical appliance
严令禁止在学生宿舍使用大功率电器。
The use of high-power electrical appliances in student dormitories is strictly prohibited.

大规模枪击事件 mass shooting
一名携带突击步枪的男子在佛罗里达州奥兰多市一家拥挤的同性恋夜总会枪杀了49人。这是美国历史上最严重的大规模枪击事件。
A man armed with an assault rifle killed 49 people at a packed gay nightclub in Orlando, Florida, in the worst mass shooting in US history.

大排档 snack stand; food stand
闹市区里大排档和小食铺里的中式小吃和葡式美食让人大快朵颐。
People can fully enjoy Chinese-style snacks and Portuguese-style dishes at snack stands downtown.

大选焦虑 election anxiety
大选焦虑确实存在。很多美国人因长时间争来辩去的竞选活动而感到"压力山大"。
Election anxiety is a real thing. Lots of Americans have become uncomfortably stressed-out by the long, contentious campaign.

大闸蟹 hairy crab
在每年的这个时节,大闸蟹是大家争相购买最多的食材之一,而从江苏省阳澄湖中捕捞的大闸蟹则被认为是最美味的。
Hairy crabs are one of the most sought-after ingredients at this time of year and those caught in Yangcheng Lake in Jiangsu province are considered to be the tastiest.

大众传媒 mass media
大众传媒包括定期出版的印刷媒体、广播、电视、影像制品、纪录片及任何其他的大众信息传播形式。
The mass media include print media, radio, TV and video programs, documentaries, and any other form of the periodical distribution of mass information.

大众富裕阶层 mass affluent class
《福布斯》杂志联合宜信财富发布的报告指出,到2015年底,中国的大众富裕阶层已增长至1530万人。
The number of China's mass affluent class has jumped to 15.3 million by the end of 2015, according to the report released by *Forbes* magazine and CreditEase Corp.

大众旅游 mass tourism
落实带薪休假制度,加强旅游交通、景区景点、自驾车营地等设施建设,规范旅游市场秩序,迎接正在兴起的大众旅游时代。
We will ensure people are able to take their paid vacations, strengthen the development of tourist and transport facilities, scenic spots and tourist sites, and recreational vehicle parks, and see that the tourist market operates in line with regulations. With these efforts, we will usher in a new era of mass tourism.

大专毕业生 junior college graduate
尽管他的分数足够,他父母却没有允许他上本地的专科学校,因为他们担心大专毕业生难找工作。这种担忧后来证明是没有根据的。
His parents refused to allow him to enroll in the local polytechnic college even though he scored sufficient marks because they thought it would be difficult for him to find a job as a junior college graduate, a fear that proved to be unfounded.

大做文章 make a fuss
同其他领导不同,史蒂夫从不会因为谁迟到3分钟而大做文章。
Unlike other bosses, Steve will never make a fuss if you are late to work by three minutes.

呆账 bad account
呆账多、工作效率低一直困扰着这些银行。
These banks are plagued by bad accounts and low efficiency.

代工厂商;贴牌生产商 OEM (original equipment manufacturer)
泰祥公司只是个代工厂商。我们计划创建我们自己的品牌,打入海外市场,但这真的需要时间。
Taixiang has been an OEM. We are planning to create our own brand for overseas markets, but it really takes time.

代沟 generation gap
"代沟"一词据信早在20世纪40年代就出现了。
The term "generation gap" is believed to have been coined as early as the 1940s.

代金卡 gift card
有调查显示，越来越多的美国大公司为员工发放代金卡或者提供其他奖励，以鼓励他们减肥和戒烟。
An increasing number of America's largest employers are offering gift cards and other incentives to encourage workers to slim down and quit smoking, a survey found.

代课教师 substitute teacher
广东省委书记表示，该省的代课教师今后的道路喜忧参半。
Substitute teachers will have a mixed future in Guangdong, the provincial Party secretary said.

代理市长 acting mayor
他被任命为上海市代理市长。
He was appointed as acting mayor of Shanghai.

代孕母亲 surrogate mother
广东省卫生厅成立专项小组对通过代孕母亲用人工受精方式生下"八胞胎"的富商夫妇进行调查。
The Guangdong provincial department of health has set up a task force to investigate a wealthy couple who used in vitro fertilization to have "octuplets" with the help of surrogate mothers.

代孕行为 practice of surrogacy
为给国内夫妇提供安全、规范、有效的辅助生殖技术服务，我国将继续打击代孕行为。
China will continue to crack down on the practice of surrogacy in a bid to provide safe, standard and efficient assisted reproductive technology to Chinese couples.

带薪产假 paid maternity leave
目前，欧盟各国的雇主普遍允许丈夫享有带薪产假。
At present, the paid maternity leave for husbands is being granted universally by employers in EU countries.

贷款额度 lending quota
据四位知情人士透露，中国几家最大银行的年度贷款额度已接近用完，计划停止发放新贷款以避免超出限额。
China's biggest banks are close to reaching annual lending quotas and plan to stop expanding their loan books to avoid exceeding the limits, according to four people with knowledge of the matter.

单边主义 unilateralism
单边主义只会使该国更加孤立于国际社会。
Unilateralism will only further isolate the country from the international community.

单独重赛 re-race alone; solo re-run
美国队通过申诉成功获得单独重赛的机会后，中国队无缘里约奥运会女子4×100米决赛。
China lost the chance to enter the women's 4×100m final at Rio Olympics after the US successfully appealed its chance to re-race alone.

单日票房纪录 single-day box office record
大年初一，全国票房收入达7.95亿元，创单日票房新纪录。
China's box office raked in 795 million yuan on Lunar New Year's Day, setting a new single-day box office record.

单双号限行 traffic restrictions based on even- and odd-numbered license plates
北京将在污染天实施单双号限行。
Beijing is to impose traffic restrictions based on even- and odd-numbered license plates on polluted days.

单/双人舞 solo-duo dance
来自11个国家的专业舞蹈演员将于11月1日到8日期间在尼日利亚的拉各斯参加名为TRUFESTA 09的国际单/双人舞表演赛。
Professional dancers from 11 countries are expected at the international solo-duo dance festival tagged "TRUFESTA 09" on Nov. 1-8 in Lagos, Nigeria.

单挑；单干 do something by oneself; work on one's own
要是他能说了算，他就自己单干。
If he had it his way, he'd have done it by himself.

单循环制比赛 single round-robin tournament
此次比赛采用单循环制，中国队将在1月17日首先迎战伊朗队。
In this single round-robin tournament, the Chinese team's first match is against Iran on January 17.

单一窗口 single-window system
国务院常务会议指出，"单一窗口"要覆盖所有口岸。

The State Council's executive meeting announced that a "single-window system" will be adopted at all ports nationwide.

单一货币 single currency; unified currency
马来西亚财政部副部长林祥才表示，中国经济规模庞大，应当在建立亚洲单一货币方面起到带头作用。
China should take the lead in formulating a single currency for Asia, given the large size of its economy, suggested Lim Siang Chai, Malaysia's deputy minister of finance.

单一经济 single-product economy
改革使得中国农村摆脱了单一的农业经济模式。
The reform has enabled rural China to break away from single-product economies that focused on farming only.

当前用户 active user
促销活动期间，当前用户可享受9折优惠。
During the promotion, active users will get a 10 percent discount.

（把……）当作耳旁风；（对……）置之不理 turn a deaf ear to something/somebody
他把所有人的反对建议都当作耳旁风。
He turned a deaf ear to all the people who had advised him against it.

挡箭牌 excuse; pretext
拿客户来电话做挡箭牌，他的中途退场把在场的每个人都气坏了。
Using a phone call from a client as an excuse, he left in the middle of the meeting, infuriating everyone in attendance.

党的全面领导 overall Party leadership
深化党和国家机构改革的首要任务是，完善坚持党的全面领导的制度，加强党对各领域各方面工作领导，确保党的领导全覆盖，确保党的领导更加坚强有力。
A primary task of deepening reform of the Party and state institutions is to improve the system for upholding overall Party leadership in a bid to strengthen the CPC's leadership in every sector, ensure its all-encompassing coverage and make it more forceful.

党内法规 Party rule; Party regulation
中央政府为确保政治稳定，从群众和专家学者中广泛收集意见和建议，着手制定两部长期的新党内法规。
The central government is collecting ideas and suggestions from the grassroots

and think tanks, and is planning two new long-term Party rules to ensure political stability.

党内票决 caucus ballot
时任总理吉拉德在党内票决中以12票之差负于陆克文。
The then Prime Minister Gillard lost to Rudd in the caucus ballot by a 12 vote margin.

党外人士 non-Party personage; public figure outside the Communist Party of China
作为一名党外人士，他在政界广受尊敬。
As a non-Party personage, he is well respected in political circles.

导航栏 navigation bar
导航栏以一种简易而有趣的方式引导访客在网站的各个主要频道间畅游。
Navigation bars provide an easy and visually interesting way for visitors to navigate among the site's main sections.

导航卫星 navigation satellite
我国发射了两颗导航卫星。
China has launched two navigation satellites.

导游自由执业 freelance tour guide
导游自由执业试点工作是我国导游体制全面改革的一部分，将为导游群体创造更多的就业机会，并建立一个公平有序的旅游市场。
The freelance tour guide pilot program is part of a comprehensive reform of China's tour guide system that will tap more job opportunities for tour guides and create a fair and orderly tourism market.

倒春寒 unusually cold spells in early spring
农民最头疼的气候问题就是倒春寒。
Unusually cold spells in early spring are the biggest climatic problems facing farmers.

到位 be adopted; be in place
有管理的浮动汇率制度已经到位。
A managed floating exchange rate has already been adopted.

盗版书 pirated book
湖南省查处了一个印刷盗版书的团伙，没收了约62.7万本总价值2030万元的盗版书。

Hunan province smashed a gang producing pirated books. About 627,000 pirated books worth 20.3 million yuan were seized.

悼念仪式 memorial service
在悼念活动上,挪威国王哈拉尔五世向围聚在奥斯陆斯佩克特姆音乐堂的6000多名民众发表讲话,对500万名国民表示,挪威会战胜这次痛苦。
Addressing over 6,000 people who gathered in Oslo's Spektrum arena for the memorial service, Norwegian King Harald V told the nation of 5 million people that Norway would surmount its pain.

道德银行 morality bank
针对被惯坏和自私的一代学生,中国一所大学开办了"道德银行"来鼓励善行。
Targeting a generation of students considered spoiled and selfish, a Chinese college runs a "morality bank" to encourage good deeds.

德才兼备的人 person of integrity and professional competence
像他这样德才兼备的人不多。
He's a person of integrity and professional competence. You don't see the likes of him every day.

德高望重 be of high prestige; command respect
请一位德高望重的作家写序会为书增色不少,至少青年作家是这样认为的。
A preface written by a writer of high prestige lends credibility to a book, or so young writers think.

登记失业率 registered unemployment rate
登记失业率连续第三个月下降。
The registered unemployment rate has fallen for the third consecutive month.

登陆 make landfall
根据中央气象台网站消息,热带风暴"梅花"登陆朝鲜民主主义人民共和国后,大约于凌晨2点在中国东北辽宁省减弱为热带低压。
According to the website of the Central Meteorological Station, the tropical storm Muifa weakened to a depression at about 2:00 a.m. in Northeast China's Liaoning province, after making landfall in the Democratic People's Republic of Korea (DPRK).

低调 low profile
抢劫银行后,他有一段时间行事一直低调。他不做任何可能会引人注意的事情。
After robbing the bank, he kept a low profile for a while and refrained from doing anything that would draw attention to himself.

低谷 at a low point
美国经济的衰退正在导致全球经济走入低谷,美国经济占世界经济总量近1/3。
The global economy is at a low point as a result of the downturn of the American economy, which constitutes nearly one-third of the world's total.

低空飞行 fly at a low altitude
超低空飞行的战机有时可以避开敌方的雷达。
Flying at an extra low altitude, planes can sometimes evade enemy radar.

低空空域 low-altitude airspace
专家表示,政府批准向民用航空工业开放部分低空空域的方案将有可能使一直受抑制的私人飞行服务得到释放,从而创造出一个价值超过万亿的市场。
Government approval of plans to open part of its low-altitude airspace to the general aviation industry may unleash pent-up demand for private air services and create a market worth more than one trillion yuan, experts said.

低生育率陷阱 low fertility trap
中国目前的总和生育率只有1.4,已经非常接近国际上公认的1.3的"低生育率陷阱"的警戒线。
The fertility rate in China is now 1.4 children per woman, almost touching the warning line of 1.3 that is recognized globally as the "low fertility trap".

低俗弹幕 vulgar bullet-screen comments
一些视频网站上的低俗弹幕十分不利于青少年成长,需设立审查机制。
Vulgar bullet-screen comments on some video websites are harmful to the development of teenagers and a review mechanism should be set up.

低俗作品 vulgar productions
文化部长对纸媒和电子媒体中的"低俗作品"和"媚俗"风气提出批评,并严厉抨击了那些用八卦奇闻做噱头,宣传拜金主义和消费主义的文化出版物。
The culture minister criticized the trend of "vulgar productions" and "kitsch" in print and on electronic Chinese media, and lashed out at publications with gossip and sensational stories that advocate money worship and consumerism.

低碳城市 low-carbon city
一份报告称,未来5年,我国将投资6.6万亿元用于建设低碳城市。
China is set to invest 6.6 trillion yuan on developing low-carbon cities in the next five years, according to a report.

低碳经济 low-carbon economy
国家发展与改革委员会已证实政府将采取切实行动来发展低碳经济。
The National Development and Reform Commission has confirmed the government will take concrete actions to develop a low-carbon economy.

低头族 phubber
低头族的表现是手机依赖症。
Phubbers show symptoms of addiction to their mobile phones.

地地常规导弹 surface-to-surface conventional missile
国庆阅兵展示的导弹包括两种地地常规导弹、一种陆基巡航导弹、一种核常兼备的地地中远程导弹和一种洲际战略核导弹。
Missiles displayed at the National Day Parade included two types of surface-to-surface conventional missiles, a land-based cruise missile, surface-to-surface intermediate and long-range missiles that could be equipped with either nuclear or conventional warheads, and nuclear-capable intercontinental missiles.

地方保护主义 regional protectionism
由于地方保护主义、垄断、暗箱操作，当前的建筑市场确实有些混乱。
The current building market is somewhat chaotic because of regional protectionism, monopolies and covert deals.

地方政府融资平台 local government-backed investment unit
中国政府表示，与地方政府融资平台贷款有关的风险"整体可控"，不会给经济带来系统性的风险。
The Chinese government said risks related to borrowing by local government-backed investment units are "controllable" and would not cause systemic damage to the economy.

地沟油 gutter oil
政府最近的这次严厉打击行为旨在阻止所谓的"地沟油"流入居民厨房。
The latest crackdown in the government's battle is aimed at eliminating the so-called "gutter oil" from the country's kitchens.

地理国情普查 national geoinformation survey
国务院新闻办公室在新闻发布会上公布，我国植被覆盖总面积达到756.6万平方千米，房屋建筑（区）占地15.3万平方千米。这些数据是我国首次地理国情普查的部分结果。
China boasts a total of 7.566m sq km of vegetation cover, while buildings

cover 153,000 sq km of land, the State Council Information Office unveiled at a press briefing. The numbers are part of the results of China's first national geoinformation survey.

地面塌陷 earth sinking
自武广高速铁路开工建设以来，金沙洲住宅区已上报10余起地面塌陷事故。
More than 10 cases of the earth sinking have been reported in the Jinshazhou housing estate since the construction of the Wuhan-Guangzhou express railway began.

地面训练 ground training
周二，日本和美国在日本南部的宫崎县的雾岛演习场开始举行大规模的地面训练。
Japan and the United States launched a major ground training in Kirishima Training Area in southern Japan's Miyazaki Prefecture Tuesday.

地区霸权主义 regional hegemonism
中国一贯反对地区霸权主义。
China consistently opposes regional hegemonism.

地区差异 regional difference
由于地区差异，沿海城市上海的成功经验不一定适用于山西这个内陆省份。
Because of regional differences, what makes coastal Shanghai successful may not work in Shanxi, an inland province.

地热资源 geothermal resources
尽管这个地区有丰富的土地、日照和地热资源，但是水资源的缺乏制约着该地区经济的发展。
Despite being rich in land, sunlight, and geothermal resources, this area is short on water, which restrains its economic development.

地铁消防队 subway fire brigade
北京将于5月成立中国首支地铁消防队，以更好地保障地铁安全。在北京，每天有数百万人乘坐地铁出行。
Beijing will establish China's first subway fire brigade in May to better ensure the safety of subway lines that millions use each day.

地下核试验 underground nuclear test
朝鲜官方的朝中社报道，朝鲜民主主义人民共和国已于周二成功进行了第三次地下核试验。
The Democratic People's Republic of Korea（DPRK）said on Tuesday it has

successfully conducted the third underground nuclear test, according to the official KCNA news agency.

地下排污 pumping emissions underground
山东省某市政府近日提供高额悬赏金来征集当地企业地下排污的线索或证据。
A municipal government in China's Shandong province has offered a huge reward for clues or evidence of local enterprises' pumping emissions underground.

地下钱庄 illegal bank
中国警方和财政部门上月在广东一举查获26个地下钱庄。
Chinese police and finance authorities broke up 26 illegal banks in Guangdong last month.

地震活跃期 active seismic period
有地震学家表明,地球已经进入了地震活跃期。
Seismologists are now suggesting the Earth has entered an active seismic period.

地质信息系统 geology information system
三维城市地质信息综合系统将为城市规划和发展提供地质技术支持。
A comprehensive three-dimensional (3D) urban geology information system will provide geological assistance for urban planning and development.

第二课堂 the second classroom; experiential learning
博物馆在寒假期间成为同学们的第二课堂。
Museums become the students' second classroom during the winter vacation.

第三产业 the service sector; the tertiary industry
今年政府指望第三产业创造几万个就业机会。
The government is counting on the service sector to create tens of thousands of jobs this year.

第三卫生间 gender-neutral bathroom
国家旅游局敦促国内5A级旅游景区配备"第三卫生间"。
China National Tourism Administration has urged the country's 5A-class scenic spots to install gender-neutral bathrooms.

第一手材料 first-hand information
同他以前的一些作品不同,他写这篇文章用的都是第一手材料,大多取材于对当事人以及参与调查这桩案件的警方的采访。
Unlike some of his previous works, he wrote this article based on the first-hand

information, mostly from interviews with people and police involved in the case.

点钞费 counting fee
储户曹某上周去中国农业银行北京某支行存了300个一元硬币到个人账户上，令她吃惊的是，银行竟然向她收取了6元的"点钞费"。
A depositor surnamed Cao went to a Beijing branch of the Agricultural Bank of China last week to deposit 300 yuan in 1-yuan coins. To her astonishment, the bank charged her 6 yuan as "counting fee".

点击诱饵 clickbait
"点击诱饵"指的是网站上用来吸引你的注意，引你去点击的链接。"点击诱饵"的主要目的是让某网站获得点击量，而不是真的为你提供什么信息。
Clickbait is a link on a website designed to draw your attention and make you click! The main aim of the clickbait is to get hits to a site rather than genuinely inform you.

点名 roll call
他点名未到，所以被关了禁闭。
He was put into solitary confinement for missing roll call.

点球 penalty kick
保罗·加斯科因早些时候赢得一个点球机会，但是他的队友没能罚中。
Paul Gascoigne had earlier won a penalty kick, which his teammate failed to convert.

点心债券 dim sum bond
钢铁制造商宝钢集团于11月成功发行了2年、3年和5年期总额达36亿元的"点心债券"，成为首家发行人民币债券的非金融类公司。
The first-ever issue by a non-financial firm was conducted by steelmaker Baosteel Group Corp in November, when it raised 3.6 billion yuan of dim sum bonds in two-, three- and five-year notes.

点赞 give a thumbs-up; give a like
别给微信运动垫底的人点赞，人家不会觉得那是赞美，会以为是嘲讽。
Don't give a thumbs-up to someone ranked at the bottom of WeChat Exercise. They won't take it as a compliment or encouragement. They'll consider it a sneer.

电动飞机 electricity-powered aircraft
我国首款自主研发的电动飞机已获得民航主管部门批准投入生产。

China's first domestically developed electricity-powered aircraft has been approved for production by civil aviation authorities.

电动轮滑车 electric self-balancing scooter
继上海和其他几个大城市禁止电动轮滑车上路后,北京也开始规范电动轮滑车的使用。
Beijing has started to regulate electric self-balancing scooters after Shanghai and several other major cities recently prohibited their use on roads.

电动汽车 electric car
在英国很多城市,电动汽车将免收交通拥堵费。
Electric cars will be exempt from congestion tolls in various cities around the UK.

电话储值卡 pre-paid phone card
由于电话储值卡很方便,很多人都使用它。
Many people use a pre-paid phone card because of the card's convenience.

电话访谈节目 call-in program
中国男足连续第三次负于韩国,愤怒的球迷纷纷打电话到广播电话访谈节目发泄不满。
Angry calls from fans flooded radio call-in programs after the Chinese men's soccer team lost to Republic of Korea for the third straight time.

电话窃听 phone hacking
《世界新闻报》涉及犯罪受害者的电话窃听事件是在本周早些时候曝光的,有报道揭露,米莉·道勒的手机留言在她失踪后数天内被拦截。
The disclosure that the *News of the World* phone hacking involved victims of crime began earlier this week with the revelation that Milly Dowler's mobile phone voicemails had been intercepted in the days following her disappearance.

电脑病毒 computer virus
中国是否受到了破坏力极大的"红色代码"电脑病毒的重创,各家媒体众说纷纭。
There have been conflicting reports about whether China has been hard hit by the deadly Code Red computer virus.

电脑盲 do not know how to use a computer; computer illiterate
因为是电脑盲,他没能竞争上这份工作。
He lost out on the job because he didn't know how to use a computer.

电脑派位招生 enroll students on a random computer-generated waiting list
征求意见稿指出,通过电脑随机派位方式招收的学生比例将逐年增加,到2016年将达到90%。
Under the draft regulation, the percentage of enrolled students on a random computer-generated waiting list will continue to increase over the years, to reach 90 percent in 2016.

电脑综合征 computeritis
工作压力问题专家们说"电脑综合征"问题如果不解决，会引起长期健康问题。
Workplace stress experts are saying that "computeritis" can cause long-lasting health problems if not addressed.

电视派生剧 TV spin-off
罗伯特·帕丁森正在与顶峰娱乐公司的老总们就拍摄《暮光之城》电视派生剧进行协商。
Robert Pattinson is in negotiations with bosses at Summit Entertainment regarding the TV spin-off of the *Twilight* blockbuster.

电信运营商 telecom operator
中国联通是中国第二大电信运营商，仅次于中国移动。
China Unicom is the second largest Chinese telecom operator after China Mobile.

电信诈骗 telecom fraud
多部门、多所高校正加大努力，增强大学新生防范电信诈骗的意识。
Authorities and universities are strengthening their efforts to improve new college students' awareness of telecom fraud.

电影版权费 movie royalties
该协会收取的电影版权费中，90%将归该协会的成员所有，剩下的10%该协会将作为管理费使用。
The association's members will share 90 percent of the movie royalties collected and the association will keep the remaining 10 percent as management fees.

电影分级制度 film rating system
中国消费者协会呼吁，尽快建立电影分级制度，避免儿童看到不适宜的镜头。
The China Consumers Association called for a film rating system as soon as possible to protect minors from inappropriate scenes.

电影网络院线 internet-based cinema
联盟方表示，电影网络院线将确保网友观看到正版电影，提供高清播放，而且价格合理。

The alliance said that the internet-based cinema would ensure netizens authorized copies of films and provide high definition viewing at a reasonable price.

电影预告片 movie trailer
在魏楠看来，电影预告片是促使观众去看电影的最主要的一个手段。
In Wei Nan's opinion, movie trailers play a dominant role in all the means of encouraging people to see a movie.

电影展映 film panorama
法国电影展映将于4月再度在中国举行，此次影展还会有其他形式的表演项目，到访的艺术家代表团也是有史以来规模最大的。
The French Film Panorama is coming back to China in April with an extended program and the largest ever artist delegation.

电影制片厂 movie studio
随着国内的娱乐公司纷纷转向资本市场筹措资金，中国第三大电影制片公司也预备上市，而且是在纽约证券交易所上市。
A third leading Chinese movie studio is aiming for a listing—this time on the New York Stock Exchange—as the country's entertainment companies turn to the capital markets to raise funds.

电子出版 electronic publishing
方正集团是中国电子出版的软件开发商和十大科技企业之一。
Founder Group is a developer of software for electronic publishing and one of China's 10 largest technology firms.

电子护照 electronic passport; e-passport; digital passport
电子护照是按照国际标准设计的，采用防伪技术，并内置智能芯片，将为持照人带来更多便利。
The electronic passport is designed according to international standards, featuring anti-counterfeiting technology and intelligent chips that will bring greater convenience to passport holders.

电子竞技 electronic competitive sports; e-sports
"电子竞技运动与管理"专业成为我国职业学校新增的13个专业之一。
The major "Electronic Competitive Sports and Management" is listed among 13 new majors for vocational schools in China.

电子垃圾 e-waste
根据该条例，无证经营电子垃圾回收的人可能会被处以罚款，罚金从5万到50万元不等。
Recyclers who engage in e-waste recycling business without certificates could face fines ranging from 50,000 yuan to 500,000 yuan, according to the regulation.

电子商务 e-commerce; electronic commerce; e-business
人们已不像几年前那样热衷于电子商务。
People are not as keen on e-commerce as they were a few years ago.

电子设备禁令 ban on electronic devices
中国民航局表示，将解除飞机上使用便携式电子设备的禁令，交由航空公司自行决定。
China's civil aviation authority said that it will lift its ban on the use of portable electronic devices on aircraft, and airlines will make the decision themselves.

电子身份证 electronic identification card
我国首张电子身份证在广东省广州市签发。
China's first electronic identification card was issued in Guangzhou, Guangdong.

电子阅读器 e-book reader
中国高科技公司汉王科技公司表示，由于国内外对便于携带的电子阅读器的需求量都在增加，他们预计今年该公司电子阅读器的发行量将增长400%。
The Chinese hi-tech firm Hanwang Technology said it expected shipments of its e-book readers to increase 400 percent this year, as the demand for the portable reading devices grows both domestically and overseas.

电子证据 electronic evidence
电子证据是以数位形态储存或传输，并可作呈堂证据用的数位电子资讯，由控方或辩方其中一方呈上作为法庭案件裁判时的理据。
Electronic evidence is any probative information stored or transmitted in digital form that either party to a court case may use at trial.

吊胃口 pique someone's interest
老师播放电影来吊学生的胃口，以启发他们学习英语口语的兴趣。
Movies were shown to pique students' interest in learning spoken English.

吊销执照 revoke a license
在被美国吊销执照的一年中，他仍能到国外进行比赛。
During the year in which his license was revoked in the US, he was still able to go for a match abroad.

钓鱼WiFi phishing WiFi
"钓鱼WiFi"在北京、上海、广州等大城市十分猖獗,有8.5%的公共WiFi信号为钓鱼WiFi。
Phishing WiFi has been rampant among public WiFi accesses in China's major cities like Beijing, Shanghai and Guangzhou, featuring 8.5% of public WiFi connections.

钓鱼执法 sting/entrapment operation
在一次钓鱼执法行动中,美国移民部门建立了一所假冒大学,最终破获一起学生签证造假案并进行大规模逮捕,21名嫌疑人被捕。
A fake university established as part of a sting operation to expose student visa scams has netted 21 suspects in mass arrests carried out by American immigration authorities.

调查失业率 surveyed unemployment rate
31个大城市的调查失业率保持在5%左右。
Surveyed unemployment rate has stayed at around 5% in 31 big cities.

掉价 degrade oneself
无论他说什么脏话你也不要还嘴,否则你就太掉价了。
Don't respond in kind to any foul language he uses. You'd be degrading yourself if you do.

跌眼镜 be caught out; be exposed; be proven wrong
专家们让人大跌眼镜——他们的预测成绩完全落空。
The experts were caught out as all their predictions proved to be way off the mark.

丁克一族(双收入、无子女)DINK(Double Income, No Kids)
许多丁克族表示,一想到孩子可能会带来的压力就不寒而栗。
Many from so-called DINK families say they shudder at the thought of the pressures kids might bring.

盯防 man-mark
马拉多纳摆出了4-3-3阵形,使梅西在场上拥有了更多的自由,并且使尼日利亚队手忙脚乱,因为他们没办法跟上他的脚步,或者对他进行盯防。
Maradona played 4-3-3, which allowed Messi greater freedom and caused confusion for Nigeria because they were unable to track him or man-mark him.

钉子户 nail household
许多与这种(拆迁)事件有关的建筑都被标为"违规建筑",而那些拒绝搬迁的住户则被称为"钉子户"。
Many of the buildings involved in such cases are labeled "illegal", and those who refuse to relocate are called "nail households".

顶包者；替罪羊 fall guy; scapegoat; whipping boy
为了应对公众及受害者家属的质疑，深圳警方周二公开了相关的监控视频和照片，以证明在致命的车祸发生后几小时来自首的这个人不是自愿替人承担过错的"顶包者"。
Shenzhen police showed videos and pictures on Tuesday in an attempt to convince a cynical public and victims' families that the person who turned himself in hours after a deadly accident was not a fall guy willing to take the blame.

顶尖人才 top talents
虽然中国已发展成为人力资源第一大国，但其顶尖人才流失非常严重。
China is hemorrhaging top talents despite the nation now boasting the world's largest team of human resources.

定点医院 designated hospital
这些病人应该住进定点医院，安置到隔离病房，防止再传染给其他病人。
These patients should be admitted to a designated hospital and placed in an isolated room to avoid infecting other patients.

定调子 set the tone
父母的态度往往会给孩子的体育价值取向定调子。如果孩子参加体育比赛后父母只是问谁赢了，那他就是在教孩子重视结果而不是过程，重视输赢而不是提高技艺。
Parents' attitudes often set the tone for children's attitudes toward youth sports. If after a game, all a parent asks is, "Who won?" he is teaching his child to focus on the outcome rather than the process (skill improvement).

定价机制 pricing mechanism
天然气定价机制改革在很久以前就已经被提上了中央政府的日程。
Reform of the natural gas pricing mechanism has been on the central government's agenda for a long time.

定锚婴儿 anchor baby（出生在美国、自动获得美国国籍的婴儿，他们在年满21岁后就可以为父母和兄弟申请美国绿卡）
一位共和党议员表示，（中期选举后）新成立的国会将举行有关"定锚婴儿"的一系列听证会，以结束有关非法移民子女自动获得公民权这一饱受争议的做法。
A Republican congressman says the new Congress will hold a series of hearings

on the issue of "anchor babies" as it works to end the controversial practice of awarding automatic citizenship to the children of illegal immigrants.

（给……）定心丸 set one's mind at rest
数月之久的等待后,《南京市房屋安全管理办法》的颁布终于给了居民一颗定心丸。
After months of waiting to see what the outcome would be, the passage of the *Nanjing Municipality Housing Security and Management Rules* has finally set the citizens' minds at rest.

定制日历 customized calendar
我国最高反腐机构禁止政府公款购买日历、贺卡、明信片等新年礼物后,传统日历遇冷,定制日历开始走俏。
Customized calendars are gaining popularity while traditional calendars are languishing after China's top anti-graft body banned government spending on New Year gifts, such as calendars, greeting cards and postcards.

丢车保帅 give up a pawn to save the king; sacrifice something minor to save something major
下棋时棋手有时不得不丢车保帅。
In Chinese chess, one sometimes has to give up a pawn to save the king.

东道国；东道主 host country
俄罗斯是2018年世界杯的东道主。
Russia is the host country for the 2018 World Cup.

东亚经济共同体 East Asian Economic Community
国务院总理李克强在菲律宾出席第二十次东盟与中日韩（10+3）领导人会议时提出构建东亚经济共同体,促进地区融合发展和共同发展。
Premier Li Keqiang advanced building an East Asian Economic Community in order to promote regional integration and common development at the 20th Association of Southeast Asian Nations, China, Japan and Republic of Korea (10+3) leaders' meeting in the Philippines.

动土仪式 ground-breaking ceremony
该工程于当天早上举行了动土仪式。
A ground-breaking ceremony for the project was held in the morning.

动员讲话 pep talk
他应邀给即将参加世界杯预选赛的英国足球队做动员讲话。

He was asked to give a pep talk to England's soccer team for its World Cup qualifying match.

冻雨 freezing rain
冰冷天气和冻雨将继续侵袭中国南方5个地区。
Icy weather and freezing rain continue to batter five regions across South China.

豆腐渣工程 jerry-built project
所有工程项目都必须根据相关的法律和规定进行公开招投标，以避免出现豆腐渣工程。
All project bids must be made in public and in compliance with relevant laws and regulations to prevent jerry-built projects.

（某人受到）毒舌抨击 knock somebody down a few pegs
每个伟大的作家，都会受到另一个伟大作家的毒舌抨击。尽管这里的作家是文化圈公认的大文学家，然而他们之间似乎彼此并不怎么欣赏。
For every great author, there's another great author eager to knock him or her down a few pegs. Although the writers here are typically deemed canonical by literary tastemakers, there wasn't much mutual admiration amongst them.

毒跑道 toxic running tracks
全国多所学校卷入"毒跑道"丑闻。
Many schools across the country have been embroiled in the "toxic running tracks" scandal.

毒校服 toxic school uniform
上海警方已对当地一家生产毒校服的服装公司立案调查。
Police in Shanghai have started investigating a local garment firm about the toxic school uniforms it has manufactured.

独栋房子 detached house
许多人都想在郊区拥有一套独栋房子。
Many people want to have detached houses in suburbs.

独家新闻 scoop
《汽车》杂志抢先独家报道了有关此款豪华新车的情况。
Automobile was the first magazine to get the scoop on the background of this new luxurious car.

独角兽企业 unicorn company
北京最具价值科技创业公司数量居全球第二位。北京"独角兽企业"（估值达到10亿美元以上的初创企业）的数量已经达到40家，仅次于美国硅谷。
Beijing boasts the world's second-largest number of most valuable tech startups. The number of so-called unicorn companies—startups valued at more than $1 billion each—has reached 40, second to Silicon Valley in the US.

"独狼式"恐怖袭击 "lone wolf" terror attack
美国可能面临"独狼式"恐怖袭击的威胁。
The United States was warned against the threat of "lone wolf" terror attack.

独立候选人 independent candidate
中国立法机关表示，没有所谓的"独立候选人"，"独立候选人"没有法律依据。
China's legislative body said that there is no such a thing as an "independent candidate", as it's not recognized by law.

独立展馆 stand-alone pavilion
准备搭建独立展馆的42个国家中，有38个国家的展馆已经举行了奠基仪式或是已经开工。
Among the 42 countries to build stand-alone pavilions, 38 have already celebrated ground-breaking or begun construction.

独立罪名 independent charge
酒后驾车将被列入《中华人民共和国刑法》第八次修正案，成为一项独立罪名。
Driving under the influence of alcohol (DUI) will be listed as an independent charge in the eighth amendment of the *Criminal Law of the People's Republic of China*.

赌球 football gambling
11月，公安部在全国范围内展开了一场打击赌球和非法操纵比赛的行动。
The Ministry of Public Security launched a nationwide crackdown on football gambling and match-fixing in November.

度蜜月 honeymoon trip
周日他们出发去度蜜月了。
They embarked on a honeymoon trip Sunday.

短途近郊游 excursions to suburban areas
一项调查显示，在端午节假日期间，短途近郊游将成为国内游客出行首选。

Excursions to suburban areas would be the most popular choice for Chinese travelers during the Dragon Boat Festival holiday, according to a survey.

断电 power outage
异常寒冷的天气和随之而来的能源消耗剧增导致华中和华东部分地区断电和天然气的短缺。
Unusually cold weather and the resulting soaring energy consumption for heating have caused power outages and shortages of natural gas in parts of central and eastern China.

断交信 a Dear John letter (from a woman to a man, ending a relationship between them)
他本来打算去见她的,可是她送了他一封断交信,于是他就留在阿肯色州了,心碎不已。
He had been planning to visit her, but she sent him a Dear John letter so he stayed in Arkansas. He was crushed.

断章取义 take one's words out of context
针对那篇说他仇恨非洲裔美国人的文章,参议员说他的话被断章取义了,还说他爱所有种族的人民。
In response to the article that said he hated African-Americans, the senator said his words had been taken out of context and that he loved people of all races.

对口味 to one's taste
他带给她一束康乃馨,很合她口味。
Quite to her taste, he brought her a bunch of carnations.

对口支援 partner assistance
即将实施的对新疆的对口支援模式借鉴了汶川地震灾后重建的模式。
The new partner assistance model in Xinjiang has been copied from the Wenchuan earthquake recovery model.

对内搞活,对外开放 revitalize the domestic economy and open up to the outside world
我们的经济改革概括起来就是对内搞活,对外开放。
Our economic reform can be summarized in two phrases: revitalize the domestic economy and open up to the outside world.

对台军售 arms sale to Taiwan
外交部就美国对台军售一事表示强烈反对,警告美国此举将损害中美关系。

The Foreign Ministry has expressed its strong opposition to the US over its arms sale to Taiwan and warns that this move will harm China-US ties.

对外直接投资 outbound direct investment (ODI)
商务部称，我国2016年1月非金融类对外直接投资达到120.2亿美元，同比增长18.2%。
China's non-financial outbound direct investment (ODI) reached $12.02 billion in January, 2016, which is 18.2% higher than January 2015, said the Ministry of Commerce.

兑奖 claim the prize
这是迄今为止全国范围内金额最高的彩票大奖。尽管这位幸运儿还没有现身兑奖，但对于这个大奖能买来多少幸福，人们都议论纷纷。
The prize is the country's biggest jackpot to date. Despite the fact that the lucky winner has not yet stepped forward to claim the prize, many have an opinion on how much happiness it might buy.

敦煌石窟 Dunhuang Grottoes
外国游客游览西安之后继续西行，去参观著名的敦煌石窟。
Foreign visitors, after visiting Xi'an, went further west to see the famous Dunhuang Grottoes.

多边税收协议 multilateral agreement on tax matters
我国签署了一项多边税收协议，作为共享跨国企业涉税信息并打击国际避税行为举措的一部分。
China signed a multilateral agreement on tax matters as a part of efforts to share tax information of multinational companies to fight international tax avoidance.

多部门制 multi-department structure
我国已经将总参谋部、总政治部、总后勤部、总装备部四总部改为由中央军委领导的15个职能部门。多部门制将有助于军委实现其职能，巩固党对军队的绝对领导。
China has reorganized its four military headquarters—staff, politics, logistics and armaments—into 15 new agencies under the Central Military Commission (CMC). The multi-department structure will help the CMC function better and is conducive to consolidating the absolute leadership of the Party over the armed forces.

多重国籍 multiple citizenship
申请新国籍之前需要弄清楚申请国是否允许多重国籍，以免无意中丢掉自己的原国籍。
In order not to lose your citizenship in another country by accident, when applying

for citizenship in a new country you should find out in advance if the country concerned permits multiple citizenship.

多次往返签证 multiple-entry visa
法国将向更多中国游客提供5年有效期多次往返签证。
France will offer more multiple-entry visas to Chinese visitors that are valid for five years.

多（跨）国公司 multinational company
一半以上的大跨国公司选择在北京建立中国研究和开发中心。
Over half of the leading multinational companies have chosen to locate their Chinese research and development centers in Beijing.

多极化 multi-polarization
中俄应该联合推动多极化进程，为建立一个民主、公正的国际政治经济秩序而共同努力。
China and Russia should make a joint effort to push forward the multi-polarization process and to help establish a just, democratic international political and economic order.

多劳多得 more pay for more work
以前大家混日子，因为干多干少一个样。现在是多劳多得，干得好还有奖赏。
In the past, people lazed away because they received the same wages regardless of how much work they did. Now, people are getting more pay for more work, and are rewarded for working extra hard.

多数股权 majority stake
中国零售业巨头苏宁云商集团买下了国际米兰的多数股权，这是资金雄厚的中资企业进军欧洲足球市场的一大动向。
China's retail giant Suning Commerce Group bought a majority stake in Inter Milan, marking a big entry into the European soccer market by cash-rich Chinese firms.

多元文化 multi-culture
越来越多的西方人来中国学习汉语以及其多元文化。
More and more people from the West are coming to China to study the Chinese language and learn about its multi-culture.

多证合一 integrating multiple certifications and licenses into one consolidated business license

我国将继续推行工商登记制度改革，推进"多证合一"，持续降低市场主体的制度性成本，激发市场活力。

China will keep integrating multiple certifications and licenses into one consolidated business license, which is to further reduce institutional costs for market entities and stimulate market vitality as part of the country's business registration reform.

夺冠 win a championship; win a title

中国男篮如愿在亚洲锦标赛中夺冠。

As expected, China won the Asian men's basketball championship.

恶搞 spoof
中国导演陈凯歌对自己的电影被恶搞感到非常气愤。
Chinese director Chen Kaige is furious at a spoof of his film.

恶名市场 notorious market
阿里巴巴集团就美国政府将其重新列入"恶名市场"黑名单的决定提出质疑。
Alibaba Group questioned a US government decision to return it to a blacklist of "notorious markets".

恶评 malicious comments
"恶评严重破坏了电影行业的生态环境"的指控在网上引发轩然大波。
The allegation that malicious comments seriously damaged the ecosystem of the film industry causes a stir online.

恶性循环 vicious circle; vicious cycle
郁闷了我就吃，吃了又让我感到郁闷，这真是一种恶性循环。
I eat because I'm unhappy, and I'm unhappy because I eat. It's a vicious circle.

恶意透支 malicious overdraft
今后，信用卡使用者"恶意透支"将被指控，"恶意透支"者被界定为故意透支并在银行两次催款3个月后仍未还款者。
Card users could be charged for "malicious overdraft", which means someone intentionally overdrafts and delays payment three months after the second notice from the bank arrives.

恶意营销 smear campaign
之前被广泛报道的奶粉致女婴乳房过早发育事件也许是来自竞争对手的恶意营销手段。
A highly publicized incident about milk products that caused baby girls to develop breasts may have been a smear campaign by a competitor.

恩格尔系数 Engle coefficient
地方政府在制定低保标准时，应将基本生活费用支出和当地恩格尔系数水平考虑在内，恩格尔系数就是消费支出比例。

Local governments should take the basic subsistence costs, local Engle coefficient level or the expenditure-income ratio, into account when setting their own allowance standards.

儿童肥胖 childhood obesity
《中国儿童肥胖报告》预言,如果不加以干预,到2030年,我国7~18岁学生超重及肥胖率预计将达到28%。
The *Report on Childhood Obesity in China* predicts that the prevalence rate of overweight and obese students aged 7 to 18 will reach 28% in 2030 without intervention.

儿童福利 child welfare
这位歌手一直都在积极地倡导儿童福利。
The singer has been active in promoting child welfare.

儿童锁 child safety lock; child-proof lock
开车的何某告诉交警,他2岁的女儿不知怎么从后排爬到了没有儿童锁的前排。
The driver surnamed He told police his two-year-old daughter somehow managed to crawl from the back into the front seat which has no child safety locks.

儿童早期教育 early childhood education
教育部发布了有关儿童早期教育的指南,以遏制日益盛行的超前教育行为。
The Ministry of Education released guidelines on early childhood education, in an effort to curb the growing practice of young children being educated in a way that pushes them beyond what children at their age should learn.

二次探底 double dip
中国最高产业监管机构周二表示,今年下半年,我国不太可能出现经济"二次探底"的情况。
China's top industrial regulator said on Tuesday that the country is unlikely to see a "double dip" in its economy in the second half of this year.

二次污染 secondary pollution
日益增长的工业固体废弃物占用大片土地,对空气、地表水和地下水造成二次污染。
The growing pile of industrial solid waste occupies a large amount of land causing secondary pollution to the air, surface water and ground water.

二房东 "middlemen" landlords
中介充当"二房东"蓄意抬高房租或鼓动房东提价是此次房租上涨的主要原因。
Agents purposefully driving up rents while acting as "middlemen" landlords or encouraging landlords to increase the prices are the main reasons for the increases.

二孩经济 second-child economy
随着全面二孩政策的实施,"二孩经济"在我国兴起,带动相关行业迅速升温。
With the adoption of the overall two-child policy, China has seen a boom of its "second-child economy", heating up related industries.

2030愿景 Vision 2030
32岁的沙特王储去年公布了"2030愿景",目的是在2030年之前,使沙特居民在文化娱乐活动中的消费由2.9%增加到6%。沙特的经济增长主要依赖石油。
"Vision 2030", unveiled by the 32-year-old crown prince last year, aims to increase household spending on cultural and entertainment activities in the oil-dependent kingdom from 2.9% to 6% by 2030.

二流货 cut-rate goods
这些二流货的质量都不好。
These cut-rate goods are of low quality.

二十四节气 The Twenty-Four Solar Terms
联合国教科文组织已将中国的"二十四节气"列入人类非物质文化遗产代表作名录。
The United Nations Educational, Scientific, and Cultural Organization (UNESCO) has inscribed China's "The Twenty-Four Solar Terms" on the Representative List of the Intangible Cultural Heritage of Humanity.

二手房 second-hand house
专家预测,今后几年北京的二手房价格将会保持稳定。
Experts have predicted that prices of second-hand houses in Beijing will remain stable in the coming years.

二维码支付 QR code payment
全国性银行卡联合组织中国银联推出了自己的二维码支付应用和安全规范。
China UnionPay, the national bankcard association, launched its own application and security standard for QR code payment.

二氧化碳监测卫星 carbon dioxide monitoring satellite
2016年12月22日凌晨,我国在酒泉卫星发射中心用长征二号丁运载火箭将我国首颗二氧化碳监测卫星发射升空。
China launched its first carbon dioxide monitoring satellite via a Long March-2D carrier rocket from Jiuquan Satellite Launch Center early December 22, 2016.

发表政见 express one's political views
你必须分清发表政见和进行人身攻击的根本区别。
You must distinguish the fundamental difference between expressing one's political views and launching a personal attack.

发动机排量 engine capacity
对占中国现有乘用车总量58%、发动机排量在1.6升及以下的车辆，征税幅度将小幅降低或保持不变。
Taxes on vehicles with an engine capacity equal to or smaller than 1.6 liters—which account for 58 percent of Chinese cars—will be either reduced slightly or unchanged.

发射升空 blast off
宇宙飞船发射升空了。
The spaceship blasted off.

发射时限 launch window
最佳发射时限计划在7月13日到31日之间。
The planned launch window is from July 13 to 31.

发射台 launch pad
六名入选的宇航员已抵达位于内蒙古的发射台。
The six short-listed astronauts have arrived at the launch pad in Inner Mongolia.

发行价 issue price
本公司股票目前形势很好，每股40美元左右，是发行价的两倍。
Our company's shares are doing well at the moment, trading at around $40 per share, twice the issue price.

发展不平衡 be disparate in development; disparate development
中国是一个人多地广、地区发展不平衡的国家。
China is populous and vast but disparate in regional development.

发展是硬道理 Development is of utmost importance.

罚薪 salary deduction as penalty
如果我迟到,就会被罚薪。
If I am late, I will get a salary deduction as penalty.

法定货币 legal tender
欧元是大部分欧盟国家唯一的法定货币。
The euro was the sole legal tender in most of EU countries.

法定赔偿金上限 legal cap on liability
英国石油业巨头英国石油公司已向法院承诺放弃该公司对海湾漏油事件的法定赔偿金上限,此前该公司的赔偿金限额在7500万美元以内。
British oil giant BP has told a court it was committed to waiving the legal cap on its liability from the Gulf oil spill that could have limited the company's liability cost to 75 million US dollars.

法律漏洞 legal loophole
由于市场低迷和许多法律漏洞的存在,中国的股票经纪行业在过去的4年里陷入极大的困境。
China's stock brokerage sector has had great difficulties over the past four years because of the sluggish market and many legal loopholes.

法律援助 legal aid
司法部一名高级官员表示,中国将扩大法律援助的范围,以保护弱势群体的权利。
China will expand the scope of legal aid in a bid to protect the rights of vulnerable groups, a senior official at the Ministry of Justice said.

法治知识 legal knowledge
根据教育部、司法部、全国普法办联合发布的有关校园法治教育的大纲,今后法治知识将被纳入中考和高考。
Legal knowledge will be included in high school and college entrance exams in the future, according to a guideline for legal education in schools jointly issued by the Ministry of Education, the Ministry of Justice and the legal knowledge popularization office.

翻老账 open old wounds
过去的就让它过去吧,他破坏你们两家关系已是陈年老账,不要再去翻了。
Let bygones be bygones. Don't open old wounds by mentioning his part in the feud between your families.

翻两番 quadruple
中国信息产业部部长周五在北京说，中国计划2010年实现信息产业产值翻两番。
China plans to quadruple the output of its information industry by 2010, the Minister of the Information Industry said in Beijing Friday.

翻拍 reshoot; remake; reproduce
在中国，"四大文学名著"深深植根于人们的心中。20世纪末，这些作品已被拍成电视剧，受到观众喜爱。而如今，电视制作者开始对名著电视剧进行翻拍。
In China, "the four masterpieces of literature" are deeply rooted in the hearts of Chinese people. At the end of the 20th century, these works were filmed as TV series and welcomed by audiences. Now TV producers are set to reshoot the plays.

翻新 face lift
著名的中国八达岭长城可能不久将迎来一次翻新。现代人对这段长城的破坏比古代侵略者的破坏严重。
The popular Badaling section of China's Great Wall, which has suffered more at the hands of modern visitors than ancient invaders, may soon get a face lift.

反补贴税 countervailing duties
美国参议员表示，他们会敦促奥巴马政府对中国和中国出口商征收反补贴税作为惩罚，因为中国一直在"用低估币值的不正当手段补贴其出口商"。
The US Senators said they will urge the Obama Administration to punish China and its exporters by imposing countervailing duties, because China has been "subsidizing its exporters unfairly by undervaluing its currency".

反串表演 cross-gender performance
TNT剧院创立于1980年，以其简洁的舞台设计、纯正的英伦风和反串表演等特点而独树一帜。它曾经在中国上演过查尔斯·狄更斯的《雾都孤儿》和莎士比亚的《哈姆雷特》等戏剧，颇受中国观众的好评。
The TNT Theater, founded in 1980, has been distinguished for its simple stage decoration, strong British style and cross-gender performances. It has previously won acclaims of Chinese audience with dramas such as Charles Dickens' *Oliver Twist* and Shakespeare's *Hamlet*.

反对党 opposition party
反对党通过如下活动来反对现行政府：对政府政策提出批评，提出替代现行政策之建议，向公众传播有关政府管理的信息。
The role of an opposition party is to oppose the government by criticizing

government policies, suggesting alternatives and keeping the public informed about issues related to government administration.

反分裂国家法 Anti-Secession Law
反分裂国家法旨在遏制"台独"势力,有利于台湾和大陆之间关系的稳定和发展。
The Anti-Secession Law is aimed at curbing "Taiwan independence" forces, and the law is conducive to stability and the development of relations between Taiwan and the mainland.

反腐倡廉 fight corruption and build a clean government
反腐倡廉将是一项长期的任务。
Fighting corruption and building a clean government will be a long-term task.

反腐巡视 anti-graft inspections
中纪委宣布,我国将向中管高校派出反腐巡视组。本轮反腐巡视将对29所高校党委进行详查。
China will send anti-graft inspectors to centrally-administrated universities, discipline authority of the Communist Party of China (CPC) announced. The anti-graft inspections will scrutinize Party committees of 29 universities.

反恐部队 counter-terrorism unit
美国高官表示,中情局追踪到了本·拉登藏身之地,之后顶级军事反恐部队"海军海豹突击队"的精英部队第六分队搭乘四架直升机飞往该地。
US officials said the CIA tracked bin Laden to his location, then elite troops from Navy SEAL Team Six, a top military counter-terrorism unit, flew to the hideout in four helicopters.

反垄断调查 anti-monopoly probe
中国电信和中国联通表示将配合国家发改委就宽带接入问题展开反垄断调查。
China Telecom and China Unicom said they will cooperate with an anti-monopoly probe of their broadband internet services by National Development and Reform Commission.

反倾销措施 anti-dumping measures
欧盟对于从中国和越南进口的皮鞋实行了新的反倾销措施。
The European Commission drew up new anti-dumping measures for shoes from China and Vietnam.

反倾销税 anti-dumping duty
商务部发言人称,中方坚决反对欧盟对华光伏产品征收临时反倾销税。

China firmly opposes the European Commission's decision to slap provisional anti-dumping duties on Chinese solar panels, a spokesman for the Ministry of Commerce said.

返工忧郁症 back-to-work blues
当首都人民从节日庆祝的宿醉中清醒过来返回到工作当中的时候,该市的一些专家也开始为人们应对返工忧郁症支招儿了。
As the capital's residents shake off their hangovers following the holiday celebrations, some of the city's experts are chiming in with advice on how to beat the back-to-work blues.

返聘 rehire after retirement
他是公司返聘的四位元老之一。
He's one of the four veterans who were rehired by the company after retirement.

返校购物季 back-to-school shopping season
进入9月份以来,中国的返校购物季高峰已经到来。
The September back-to-school shopping season in China is in great shape.

饭友 meal pal
那家泰国餐馆很棒,是我的那些饭友们最喜欢的餐馆。
That Thailand restaurant is great. It's my meal pals' favorite.

方便食品 instant food; snacks
他第一次到中国时由于担心找不到可口的东西,便随身携带了大量方便食品。
When he first visited China, he carried with him a large amount of instant food for fear of finding nothing that would suit his taste.

防尘口罩 anti-dust mask
天猫商城的一位店主说,他们通常每天能收到100～200个防尘口罩的订单。
An online vendor at Tmall.com said they usually receive 100 to 200 orders for anti-dust masks a day.

防红包协议 anti-bribery agreement; hongbao stipulation
医患双方须在就诊前签署防红包协议,医生保证不向患者索要红包,患者保证不向医生送红包。
Doctors and patients will be required to sign an anti-bribery agreement before treatment in which the doctor vows he or she will not ask for money, and the patient vows he or she will not attempt to hand over bribe money.

防洪 flood control

中国计划投资1500亿元用于黄河防洪工程建设。

China plans to spend 150 billion yuan on flood control along the Yellow River.

防护林；防护林带 shelter forest belt

这项工程将重点建设一个65万公顷的防护林带，以防止风沙向我国东北部的半干旱地区蔓延。

The project will focus on planting a 650,000-hectare shelter forest belt to halt the progression of deserts in Northeast China's semi-arid areas.

防火 fire prevention

因近日全国多地发生火灾，导致人员死亡和经济损失，消防部门提醒人们注意冬季防火。

Firefighting authorities are urging people to pay attention to fire prevention in winter, as several fires broke out around the country recently, claiming lives and causing economic losses.

防火隔离带 firebreak

为抵御外火烧过边界，中国已分别在北部的中俄和中朝边境线设了大面积的森林防火隔离带。

Extensive firebreaks have been made along North China's woody borderlines with Russia and the Democratic People's Republic of Korea （DPRK） to prevent wildfires from spreading across borders.

防窃听电话 eavesdropping-proof telephone

一家德国公司推出了一款防窃听电话机。

A German company has released an eavesdropping-proof telephone.

防沙治沙 desertification control

防沙治沙工程、水土流失治理工程、生态安全屏障监测工程得到全面实施。

Desertification control, water and soil conservation, and ecological safety barrier monitoring are in full swing.

防身术 personal defense skill

他的跆拳道班上多数学生是女性。对她们来说，学几招儿防身术也许真用得着。

More than half of the students who attend his taekwondo classes are women, for whom a few personal defense skills may come in handy.

防暑降温补贴 high temperature subsidy

北京市政府将防暑降温补贴的数额增加了1倍。根据人力资源和社会保障局新出台的法规，在气温高于33度的户外工作的工人每个月将能领到120元补助，而室内工作的工人能领到的最低补助金额从原先的45元提高到90元。
Beijing government doubled the high temperature subsidy. Workers will receive 120 yuan each month for working outside in temperatures higher than 33 degrees Celsius and indoor workers will receive a minimum subsidy of 90 yuan, up from 45 yuan, according to the new Municipal Human Resources and Social Security Bureau regulation.

防卫白皮书 defense white paper
中国国防部对日本发布的防卫白皮书表示强烈不满，称其肆意渲染"中国威胁论"是别有用心的。
China's Defense Ministry expressed "strong opposition" to Japan's defense white paper, saying the document plays up the "China threat theory" and has ulterior motives.

防汛抗旱 flood control and drought relief
密苏里河上的六个大水坝是用来防洪抗旱的，河水在降水量大的时候被挡进水库，干旱的时候又被放出来。
The six large Missouri River dams were designed for flood control and drought relief—water would collect in the reservoirs during heavy rainfalls and be released during dry spells.

防作弊措施 anti-cheating measures
今年高考期间，多地将首次采取人脸识别、指纹验证系统等高科技防作弊措施。
High-tech anti-cheating measures such as facial recognition and fingerprint verification systems, will be used for the first time in many places for this year's gaokao, or the national college entrance exam.

房产估价师 real estate evaluator
据这位房产估价师说，将于周三拍卖的那幢别墅至少会卖到30万美元。
According to the real estate evaluator, the villa to be auctioned Wednesday will fetch $300,000 at the very least.

房产库存 housing inventory
专家认为，随着房地产市场成交量下降，房产库存开始不断累积，中国高昂的房价有望逐渐松动。
Experts expect China's skyrocketing home prices to gradually ease, as housing inventories have begun to pile up as a result of slumping transactions in the property market.

房产税 property tax
在政府发出扩大房产税试点范围的信号后,我国多个城市已完成房产税试点技术准备工作。

Several Chinese cities are "technically ready" to join the property tax pilots after the government signaled it will expand the program to more areas.

房产证 (property) ownership certificate
从法律上讲,在拿到房产证之前,即使拿到了钥匙你也还不是业主。

Even though you've got the keys, legally, you won't be regarded as the owner of the house until you have your ownership certificate in hand.

房地产去库存 reduce real estate inventory
2016年我国房地产去库存取得了积极的进展。

China made good progress in reducing real estate inventory in 2016.

房屋拆迁 housing demolition and relocation
在致全国人大常委会的一封信中,学者们表示目前的《房屋拆迁管理条例》与国家的宪法和物权法相抵触。

In a letter to the National People's Congress (NPC) Standing Committee, scholars said the current *Housing Demolition and Relocation Management Regulation* is a breach of the country's constitution and property law.

房屋征收 expropriation of houses; house expropriation
经过近一年的讨论和修改,国务院开始就广泛热议的国有土地上房屋征收与补偿条例(第二次征求意见稿)公开征求社会意见。

After almost one year of discussion and revision, the State Council, or China's cabinet, started soliciting public submissions on the second version of the much-discussed draft regulation on expropriation of houses on State-owned land and compensation.

仿人机器人 humanoid robot
来自约20个国家的100多所大学的仿人机器人将参加5个类别包括田径、球类、格斗、舞蹈以及清洁和医疗护理之类的家政服务等16个项目的比赛。

More than 100 universities from about 20 countries are expected to send humanoid robots to compete in 16 events in 5 categories, including track and field, balls, combat, dancing as well as domestic service such as cleaning and medical care.

仿真枪 imitation gun
北京警方缴获了316支仿真枪,其中大部分是通过网络售出的。

Beijing police seized 316 imitation guns, most of which had been sold via the internet.

放贷款 extend a loan
学校给低收入家庭的学生发放贷款。
Loans were extended to students from low-income families.

放疗 radiotherapy; radiation treatment
他拒绝接受放疗,担心会因此引起基因变异并导致后代残疾。相反,医生们认为他的担心纯属无稽之谈。
He refuses to have radiotherapy for fear it will cause genetic mutations leading to handicaps in his offspring. Doctors, on the other hand, say such fears are groundless.

放射性污染 radioactive contamination
安全检查员检查了每个集装箱,没有发现放射性污染的迹象。
Safety inspectors checked every container and found no trace of radioactive contamination.

放生 release of captive animals
没有严格的管理,即使是善意的放生活动也可能造成严重后果。
Without strict regulation, albeit well-intended, release of captive animals could have serious consequences.

放眼全球 have a global view; with a global view
放眼全球,我们能更清楚地认识我国近年来取得的进步。虽然在许多方面我们仍然远远落后于西方,但我们的经济发展确实是最快的。
With a global view, we can put China's recent progress into better perspective. We're lagging far behind the West in many areas, but we do enjoy the fastest economic development.

飞絮 fluffy catkins
开花的柳树和杨树产生的杨柳飞絮每年会导致许多人产生过敏症状,并引发呼吸系统疾病。杨柳絮还会降低城市道路的能见度。
Fluffy catkins, from blooming willows and poplars, are an annual annoyance for many people who suffer from allergies and respiratory diseases. They also reduce visibility.

非常设机构 ad hoc organization
安全生产委员会是隶属国务院的非常设机构。

The Safety Production Committee under the State Council is an ad hoc organization.

非传统安全威胁 nontraditional security threat
实际上，两国在全球稳定、经济增长和打击非传统安全威胁方面有着共同的基本战略目标。非传统安全威胁包括气候变化、恐怖主义，以及流行病等。
In reality both countries share fundamental strategic goals in global stability and economic growth and in reduction of nontraditional security threats such as climate change, terrorism and pandemics.

非典；非典型肺炎 severe acute respiratory syndrome（SARS）
当时还没有治疗非典的相应措施，所以，非典疫情刚出现时曾引起民众一片恐慌。
The outbreak of SARS（severe acute respiratory syndrome）, with no known cure for victims afflicted at that time, had brought a widespread panic to people.

非法采金 illegal gold mining
近些年来不时传出加纳警方抓捕涉嫌非法采金的中国矿工的新闻。
There have been reports in recent years of Chinese workers being arrested by the Ghanaian authorities on suspicion of illegal gold mining.

非法取证 illegal collection of evidence
全国人大常委会周二继续审议刑事诉讼法修正案草案，建议增加更多阻止非法取证行为的细节规定。
Standing Committee of NPC on Tuesday read a draft amendment to the Criminal Procedural Law again, suggesting more detailed stipulations to stem illegal collection of evidence.

非法行医 illegal medical practice
卫生部周三表示，已责成北京市卫生局调查这家医院涉嫌非法行医导致一名教授死亡的事件。
China's Health Ministry said Wednesday it has ordered its Beijing bureau to investigate this hospital for alleged illegal medical practice that caused the death of a professor.

非法移民 illegal immigrant
欧洲正遭遇着二战以来规模最大的移民危机，而周五联合国难民署公布的一份报告将危机进一步放大。报告估计，今年迄今为止，乘船逃往欧洲的非法移民比2014年全年增加了40%。
The migrant crisis, the biggest wave to hit Europe since World War II, was further

amplified on Friday by a report from the United Nations refugee agency estimating a 40 percent jump this year in the number of illegal immigrants fleeing to the Continent by boat compared with all of 2014.

非婚生子女 baby/child born out of wedlock; illegitimate child
非婚生子女的夭折率是婚生子女的两倍。
Babies born out of wedlock run twice the risk of early deaths than children born to married couples.

非居民用电 non-residential electricity
我国的非居民用电价格根据地域和行业的差别而有所不同,但比居民用电价格要高。
China's non-residential electricity prices differ according to the areas and sectors, but are higher than the price of power for residential use.

非劳动收入 non-labor income
非劳动收入包括股息、资产租贷、利息等收入。
Non-labor income includes earning from dividends, rental of an asset, interest and so on.

非流通股 non-tradable share
只要2/3的非流通股股东同意,就可进行股改。
Approval of only two-thirds of holders of non-tradable shares is needed to launch the reform.

非全日制研究生 part-time postgraduate student
考研人数暴涨的原因之一是新政策要求报考非全日制研究生的人也参加统考。
The surge of the students taking the postgraduate exam was partly due to a newly implemented policy requiring people who apply for part-time postgraduate programs to take the exam.

非物质文化遗产 intangible cultural heritage
非物质文化遗产代表作,如手工艺术、节日仪式和语言等,都将在国家博物馆首次展出。
Examples of the intangible cultural heritage, including craftsmanship, festival rituals and languages, are to be showcased together for the first time at the National Museum.

非再生资源 non-renewable resource
石油是一种非再生资源。

Petroleum is a non-renewable resource.

非战争军事行动 noncombatant actions
人民解放军还承担抢险救灾、国际维和、国际救援等非战争军事行动任务。
The PLA undertakes noncombatant actions and missions such as disaster relief, international peacekeeping, and search and rescue work.

非制造业采购经理人指数 Purchasing Managers Index of non-manufacturing sector
周一发布的一份官方调查显示，11月份中国非制造业采购经理人指数为55.6%，比上月上升0.1个百分点。
The Purchasing Managers Index of China's non-manufacturing sector was 55.6 percent in November, up 0.1 percentage point from October, an official survey showed on Monday.

非自然死亡 unnatural death
专家敦促政府公布更多有关官员非自然死亡的信息，包括患有抑郁症而自杀的官员。

Experts are encouraging authorities to publish more information about unnatural deaths of government officials, including those who killed themselves after suffering from depression.

非自住业主 non-owner-occupier
目前政府在收紧信贷和对非自住业主房贷的政策方面还不是太严格。据报道，今年在北京国贸举办的春季房展成交的房产价值达29亿元。
The government's efforts to tighten credit and mortgage requirements for non-owner-occupiers have not bitten deeply so far. This year's spring real estate fair at the Beijing World Trade Center sold property worth 2.9 billion yuan, according to reports.

废热发电厂 co-generation power plant
新加坡上市的中国热轧钢圈生产商德龙控股有限公司宣布它已经建成了该公司的首个废热发电厂，以减少碳足迹。
Singapore-listed Chinese hot-rolled steel coil manufacturer Delong Holdings said it has completed the construction of its first co-generation power plant in a bid to reduce its carbon footprint.

废物的循环使用 recycling of waste
中国需投资100亿美元用于废物的循环使用。
China needs $10 billion for the recycling of waste.

分包商 subcontractor
作为分包商,我们只负责广告这一部分。
As the subcontractor, we are paid to handle advertising alone.

分分合合的恋情 on-again-off-again relationship
如果她现身,那么就意味着他们俩七年分分合合的恋情还没有告吹。
If she turns up, it'll be a sign that their on-again-off-again relationship of seven years hasn't yet run out of steam.

分红 distribute dividends
这是该公司第一次给股东分红。
Now, for the first time, the company is distributing dividends to investors.

分级诊疗制度 hierarchical medical system
我国将建立分级诊疗制度,以提高县镇级卫生中心的服务水平。
China will set up a hierarchical medical system to improve services at county- and township-level health centers.

分级制度 rating system
在青少年游戏玩家数量剧增的情况下,有关方面会在今年启用网络游戏分级制度,打击游戏中粗俗的内容。
Authorities will introduce a rating system for online games this year to crack down on vulgar content amid a soaring number of young gamers.

分流 reposition of superfluous employees
日本松下公司宣布将裁减或分流5000名员工。
Panasonic of Japan has announced that it will dismiss or conduct a reposition of 5,000 superfluous employees.

分期付款 installment payment
你可以申请从你的存款账户自动扣除分期付款。
You can request for installment payments to be automatically deducted from your savings account.

分时度假房 timeshare(度假目的地的酒店、度假村或者公寓、别墅等旅游住宿场所的客房使用权,按时段进行分解,用锁定并且优惠的价格按份销售给固定的消费者;消费者在约定的年限内,每年拥有一周或几天到该场所住宿、度假的权利,同时还享有对timeshare进行转让、出租等权利)
玛格丽塔岛是委内瑞拉的主要旅游胜地之一,岛上的酒店拥有300多个房间和约

150个分时度假房,此外还有数家饭馆、一家赌场、若干家纪念品商店和一个小艇停靠区。

Margarita Island is one of Venezuela's main tourist destinations, and the hotel has more than 300 rooms and about 150 timeshares, plus restaurants, a casino, souvenir shops and a marina.

分时计价系统 time-of-use pricing system
一种是阶梯用电计价系统,另一种是分时计价系统。两种系统完全不同。

The first is the tiered electric pricing system, and the other is time-of-use pricing system. The two systems are completely different.

分享冰箱 sharing fridge
设立分享冰箱是为了把富余的食物分给贫困家庭,让这些家庭把钱省下来用于教育或医疗。

The sharing fridge was founded with the intention of giving away excess food to poorer families, so that the family can save the money for education or medical care.

分享经济 sharing economy
国家发改委近日在一份意见稿中表示,为规范分享经济领域,我国计划对其适当征税。

China plans to impose appropriate taxes to regulate the sharing economy sector, the National Development and Reform Commission said in a draft proposal.

风险投资 venture capital; risk investment
中国的实际风险投资额预计仅为3亿美元。

The actual venture capital investment in China is estimated at only $300 million.

风险图 risk map
为了改善城市规划,避免可能发生的灾害,政府机构正在绘制一张全国性的自然灾害"风险图"。

Authorities are drawing up a national "risk map" for natural disasters in an attempt to improve urban planning and avoid potential catastrophes.

封闭式管理 closed-off management
近日在北京一些流动人口数量超过常住人口数量的村落实施的封闭式管理得到了公安部领导和市委书记的认可,此举将会在首都进一步推广实施。

Closed-off management, which has been implemented in some Beijing villages where migrant residents outnumber permanent residents, will be further promoted across the capital after the move received approval from both the official of

Ministry of Public Security and secretary of Beijing Municipal Committee of the CPC.

封闭式基金 close-ended fund
33个封闭式基金机构都已公布了它们的年度报告，收益总额达160亿元。
All 33 close-ended funds have published their annual reports, with a combined profit reaching 16 billion yuan.

封锁禁运 embargo
联合国大会绝大多数的成员国都谴责美国对古巴进行封锁禁运的行为。
The US embargo against Cuba is condemned by an overwhelming majority of member-states of the United Nations General Assembly.

封锁消息 news blackout
随着互联网和移动电话的普及，封锁消息已不再可能。
With the widespread use of internet and mobile phones, a news blackout is no longer possible.

疯牛病 mad cow disease; bovine spongiform encephalopathy（BSE）
仅上周就有几千头疑似疯牛病奶牛被宰杀。
Thousands of cattle believed to have mad cow disease were slaughtered in the past week alone.

奉子成婚 shotgun wedding
看上去这两个人好像是奉子成婚。
It looks like that it's a shotgun wedding for those two.

否决 vote down
他们投票否决了修正案。
They have voted down the amendment.

伏旱 summer drought
高温和少雨天气使宁夏回族自治区、内蒙古自治区，以及甘肃、贵州和湖南等省的伏旱进一步加剧。
Soaring temperatures and little rainfall have worsened the summer drought in the Ningxia Hui and Inner Mongolia autonomous regions, as well as the provinces of Gansu, Guizhou and Hunan.

扶贫 poverty alleviation; poverty relief
扶贫工作是中国政府一项长期而又艰巨的任务，也是联合国开发计划署最重要的工作之一。
Poverty alleviation is a long-term and arduous task facing the Chinese government. It is also a top priority for the United Nations Development Program.

扶贫线 poverty threshold
我国决定将扶贫线标准提升至农民人均年纯收入2300元。
China has decided to raise the poverty threshold to 2,300 yuan in terms of the annual net income of farmers.

服务特色；卖点 selling point
他们发现电影制作者们并不试着去理解音乐家，而只是把他们的音乐作为一个卖点。
They discovered the filmmakers were not trying to understand the musicians, but merely using their music as a selling point.

服务外包 service outsourcing
正在蓬勃发展的南京服务外包行业今年将为大学毕业生提供约1万个工作岗位。
Nanjing's booming service outsourcing industry will provide about 10,000 jobs to college graduates this year.

服务业；餐饮业 catering industry
去年杭州市的餐饮业发展迅速，市民人均饮食消费达到1700元。
Residents contributed an average of 1,700 yuan to Hangzhou's booming catering industry last year.

辐射防护 radiation protection
目前正在研制的辐射防护屏幕高75厘米、宽105厘米。
Radiation protection screens being built are 105cm wide and 75cm high.

福利彩票 welfare lottery
在未来5年里，中国的福利彩票预计将在慈善事业集资方面起到更大的作用。
In the next five years, China's welfare lottery is expected to play a bigger role in pooling money for charitable causes.

福利分房 welfare-oriented distribution of public housing
福利分房已成过去。
Welfare-oriented distribution of public housing is a thing of the past.

福利院 charity house; welfare house
他是个私生子，从小在福利院长大。

As an illegitimate child, he grew up in a charity house.

抚恤金 comfort fund
当地一些商人提议为地震受灾者筹集抚恤金。
Some local businessmen proposed to raise a comfort fund for the earthquake victims.

辅警 auxiliary police
《关于规范公安机关警务辅助人员管理工作的意见》明确规定，辅警由县级及以上地方人民政府或者公安机关采取正式合同方式招聘。
Opinions on Regulating the Management of Auxiliary Police specified that auxiliary police are employed with formal contracts by public security organs and governments at or above the county level.

辅助生殖 assisted reproduction
该市最大的辅助生殖中心已经停止接收新患者，以防止让那些想做父母的人无望地等待。
The city's biggest assisted reproduction center has closed its doors to new patients to prevent hopeless waiting by prospective parents.

辅助自杀 assisted suicide
辅助自杀在瑞士是合法的，前提是辅助者不从病人的死亡中获取私利。
Assisted suicide is legal in Switzerland provided the helper doesn't personally benefit from a patient's death.

父亲假/陪产假 paternity leave
韩国劳动部称，韩国将从明年开始允许男性享受5天的父亲假，此举是为了提高韩国的低生育率。
South Korea is set to allow 5 days of paternity leave starting next year, in an attempt to raise the country's low birth rate, the labor ministry said.

付费订阅 pay-to-read
腾讯旗下通信应用程序微信计划推出付费订阅的新功能，允许微信公众号向读者收取费用。
Tencent's messaging app WeChat is mulling a new pay-to-read feature that allows its official accounts to request payment from readers.

付费下载音乐 charge users for music downloads; pay for music downloads
据报道，华纳音乐集团、环球音乐以及索尼音乐娱乐正与国内主要在线音乐提供商商讨建立用户下载音乐收费制度。
The Warner Music Group, Universal Music and Sony Music Entertainment are reportedly talking with major online music providers in China to set up a scheme that will charge individual users for music downloads.

负增长 negative growth
在第三个季度国内生产总值减少了0.6%之后,专家预测下季度的国内生产总值仍将保持负增长。
After the country's GDP fell 0.6 percent in the third quarter, experts predicted more negative growth in the next.

负债经营 manage with a loan
许多提供宽带服务的公司,不是负债经营,就是面临倒闭。
Many of the broadband service companies are either facing bankruptcy or managing with a loan.

妇科检查 gynecological examination
公益组织北京益仁平中心建议取消公务员录用考试体检中的妇科检查项目。
Beijing Yirenping Center (BYC), a public welfare organization, proposed that gynecological examinations be removed from the physical exams for civil service recruitment.

附加税 tax surcharge
年收入超过30万美元的家庭会被征收收入附加税。
A tax surcharge is levied on households with incomes exceeding $300,000 a year.

附加意外险 supplemental accident insurance
为了刺激目前不景气的寿险市场,又有3家寿险公司获得了开办诸如附加意外险等新险种的许可证。
Another three life insurance companies have received licenses to offer new services, such as supplemental accident insurance, in a move to inspire the currently sluggish life insurance market.

复读生 return and repeat student—students reattending classes after failing the college entrance examination
通常复读生很难考上清华和北大,但每年总是会有人成功。
Normally, it is difficult for the "return and repeat student" to be enrolled by Tsinghua University or Peking University, but a few of them do succeed every year.

复式住宅 duplex apartment
北京市政府已拨出特别款项和土地用于在城西建造12幢复式住宅。
The Beijing municipal government has allocated special funds and land for 12 duplex apartment buildings to be built in the western part of the city.

复映 return to screens
大约一个月前被戏剧化停映的电影导演昆丁·塔伦蒂诺的反奴隶制巨制《被解救的姜戈》于周日起在中国各影院复映。
Film director Quentin Tarantino's anti-slavery saga *Django Unchained* returned to China's screens on Sunday after being dramatically pulled from the country's theaters about a month ago.

复员 be discharged from active military service
同等学历下，复员军人比本地青年更有可能找到工作。
Army men discharged from active military service are more likely to find jobs than local youths with identical education.

复制文化 copy culture
杨先生的故事仅仅是"复制文化"在微博领域日益盛行的一个例子。
Mr. Yang's story is just one example of the "copy culture" that is becoming more prevalent among micro bloggers.

副中心 subcenter
北京城市副中心通州的建设进展迅速。
Construction of Tongzhou, Beijing's subcenter, is moving at a fast pace.

富二代 rich second generation
近几年，"富二代"一词时常见诸报端，通常都是与飙车及醉酒驾车等负面新闻相关。
In recent years, the phrase "rich second generation" has hit the headlines, associated with negative news such as car races and drunk driving.

富豪榜 rich list
这份富豪榜反映出了中国经济以及人们对财富的态度和认识的变化。
The rich list reflects the changes in China's economy and also people's attitude and knowledge about wealth.

富豪消费价格指数 Luxury Consumer Price Index (LCPI)
胡润发布的一份报告显示，过去10年，我国富豪消费价格指数累计上涨了

81.7%，是全国居民消费价格指数（CPI）涨幅的两倍多。
Luxury Consumer Price Index (LCPI) in China saw an accumulated rise of 81.7% over the past 10 years, more than doubling the growth rate of nationwide Consumer Price Index (CPI), according to a Hurun report.

富豪之都 home to the world's most billionaires
根据2016胡润全球富豪榜，北京首次超越占据榜首多年的纽约，成为全球"富豪之都"。
Beijing is home to the world's most billionaires, pushing New York out of the top slot it had held for years, according to the Hurun Global Rich List 2016.

G

GDP核算 gross domestic product (GDP) calculation
我国采用了一种新的国内生产总值(GDP)核算方法,分析人士称此举是迈向与国际标准接轨、提高数据准确性的一步。
China has adopted a new gross domestic product (GDP) calculation method, a move that analysts have called a step toward meeting international standards and improving data accuracy.

GDP万亿俱乐部 one-trillion-yuan GDP club
全国31省级区域公布了当地的GDP数据,25省加入了"GDP万亿俱乐部"。
Thirty-one provincial-level regions had released their local gross domestic product (GDP) data, 25 of them joined the "one-trillion-yuan GDP club".

改版 makeover; revamp
每晚7点在央视一套和各省卫视播出的《新闻联播》将在此次改版中启用新人,加入新的关注点。
Xinwen Lianbo, which runs every night at 7:00 pm on CCTV1 and all provincial satellite channels, is expected to get new faces and a new focus in the makeover.

改革促进派 reform promoters
领导干部应争当"改革促进派",正确解决改革道路上遇到的问题。
Top cadres should strive to become reform promoters and correctly deal with problems on the path of reform.

改革开放 reform and opening-up
改革开放政策是社会主义中国富强之路。
The policy of reform and opening-up is the way to lead socialist China to prosperity.

改革试点 trial reform; pilot reform; reform experimentation
许多企业正在通过引进国外教学方式开展职业教育改革试点。
Many enterprises are carrying out trial reforms in vocational education by introducing foreign teaching methods.

改善投资环境 improve the environment for investment
改善投资环境对于吸引外资很重要。

To improve the environment for investment is vital for attracting foreign investment.

改组 reshuffle
总统改组了顾问委员会。
The president reshuffled the advisory committee.

盖帽了 superb; great; excellent; wonderful
姚明篮球打得那么好,真是盖了帽了。
Yao Ming plays basketball so well that he is indeed a superb player.

概念车 concept car
宝马公司将在这次展示会上推出他们的最新款概念车车型。
BMW will unveil their newest concept car models at the exposition.

干旱期 dry spell
11月开始的干旱期已导致至少953万公顷农田受旱,波及至43%的冬小麦产区。
The dry spell since November has affected at least 9.53 million hectares of farmlands, or 43 percent of the country's winter wheat supplies.

甘居下游 be resigned to lagging behind; lack ambition; be resigned to losing
如果你甘居下游,别人即使乐意也很难帮得了你。
If you were resigned to lagging behind, there would be little other people could do for you even if they wanted to.

赶时髦 be trendy; follow trends; be hip; be fashionable
她穿的毛衣正是目前电视广告上的那种。她真能赶时髦,总在时尚前沿。
She wears a sweater that's being advertised on TV right now. She's very trendy, and always on the cutting edge of the latest fashion.

感情投资 investment in human relationships
我认为感情投资是一个人最好的投资。
I believe investment in human relationships is the best investment one can make.

感染病毒 contract the virus
和死禽进行接触并非人们感染上病毒的唯一途径。
People don't just contract the virus through contact with dead poultry.

干细胞疗法 stem cell treatment
干细胞疗法每年会吸引数千名外国患者,中国卫生部将严格管理干细胞疗法这一尖端疗法,以确保患者安全并使该技术有序发展。

China's top health authority will strictly regulate the cutting-edge stem cell treatment, which attracts thousands of patients from abroad each year, to ensure patient safety and the orderly development of the technology.

岗位津贴 post allowance
补助工资是指按国家有关规定支付给工作人员的津贴、补贴,包括各项岗位津贴、加班费等。
Subsidiary salary refers to the allowance and subsidies paid to staff according to the relevant state policies, including post allowance and overtime pay.

港人治港 Hong Kong governed by the people of Hong Kong
中国政府将落实基本法,坚决全面贯彻"一国两制""港人治港"的方针。
The Chinese government is determined to fully implement the policy of "One country, Two systems", allowing Hong Kong to be governed by the people of Hong Kong in accordance with the Basic Law.

高才生 top student
我小学算是高才生,但是从那以后就一直走下坡路了。
I was one of the top students at my primary school. But I've been going downhill since then.

高档餐饮业 high-end dining sector
中国政府推行节俭政策以来,国内餐饮业,尤其是高档餐饮业,深感压力。
The Chinese government's frugality campaign has turned up the heat on China's catering industry, especially the high-end dining sector.

高档食品 upmarket food
近日,卜蜂莲花和正大广场宣布在上海新天地创立首个高档食品零售品牌——莲花集市。
Recently, the owner of CP Lotus and Super Brand Mall announced the launch of its first upmarket food retail brand, Bazaar by Lotus, in Shanghai's Xintiandi.

高度好评 rave review
那位青年导演执导的影片获得了热烈的好评。
The young director won rave reviews for his film.

高端产品 high-end product
一项调查发现,电器和汽车等主要消费品的价格出现适度下跌的趋势,这将刺激消费者去购买一些更为高端的产品。
A survey noted a trend of moderate price drops in major consumer goods, including

electrical appliances and automobiles, saying this would push consumers to look for higher-end products.

高发季节 high-occurrence season
他指出，秋冬季是流感的高发季节，并敦促权威部门提升疾病防御和治疗能力，阻止疾病在全国迅速传播。

He noted that autumns and winters were high-occurrence seasons for the flu, and urged the authorities to improve disease prevention and treatment in order to stop the disease from fast spreading across the country.

高分低能 high scores but low ability
长期以来，这种教育制度因培养出的学生高分低能而受到批判。

This educational system has long been criticized for producing students with high scores but low ability.

高峰期 peak season
流感的高峰期即将到来。

The peak season for influenza is approaching.

高耗能老厂 obsolete energy-consuming production facilities
工信部最近要求2000多家企业在2个月内关闭其下属的高耗能老厂，违者将面临减少贷款额及吊销生产许可等处罚。

China's industry chiefs have warned more than 2,000 companies to close obsolete energy-consuming production facilities within two months or they will face cuts in credit and a suspension of government approvals.

高精尖技术 cutting-edge technology; advanced technology
据悉，这批高精尖技术的所有者都是来自北京经济技术开发区的企业。

It is reported that the owners of these cutting-edge technologies are all from enterprises in the Beijing Economic and Technological Development Zone.

高净值家庭 high-net-worth families
报告显示，北京每万户家庭中高净值家庭数量超过200户。

The report said there are more than 200 high-net-worth families out of every 10,000 families in Beijing.

高考保姆 gaokao nanny
一家叫嘉乐会的北京家政服务公司说，在北京，高考保姆是按日计酬的，平均一天300元。

In Beijing, gaokao nannies are paid by the day, 300 yuan on average, according to a Beijing domestic service company named Coleclub.

高科技板块 high-tech sector
高科技板块渐渐显示出它的盈利潜力。
The high-tech sector is showing signs of profitability.

高科技作弊 hi-tech cheating
中国在高考前严打高科技作弊。
China targets hi-tech cheating before national college entrance exam.

高龄津贴 old age allowance
全中国80岁以上的居民将享受统一的高龄津贴。
Residents older than 80 will get a unified old age allowance across China.

高清晰度 high definition
中国第一个高清晰度宽带有线电视网络系统于周一在深圳问世。
China's first wide-band, high-definition cable television network was introduced in Shenzhen Monday.

高手 master; expert
经过几年的努力,他已成了象棋高手。
After years of effort, he has become a master chess player.

高速飞行列车 HyperFlight
中国航天科工集团公司宣布,我国将研发设计时速高达4000公里的超音速"高速飞行列车"交通网。
China will develop a supersonic speed HyperFlight transport network with a designed speed of up to 4,000 km/h, China Aerospace Science and Industry Corporation announced.

高速费 highway toll fees
交通部将逐步建立一个稳定的、低标准的收费系统,让全国范围内的高速公路收费更合理。
Highway toll fees will be made more affordable nationwide, as the Ministry of Transport will gradually introduce a stable and cheap charging system.

高速铁路 high-speed rail
国际铁路联盟高速铁路部(UIC)总监伊格纳西奥·巴伦称,经过几年的快速发展,中国有望在世界高速铁路建设方面处于领先者地位。
China will become a high-speed rail leader in the world after several years of rapid

development, Ignacio Barron, the director of High Speed of International Union of Railways (UIC) said.

高危人群 high-risk group
某些群体属于易感染艾滋病病毒的高危人群，吸毒者就属于此类。
Certain groups of people are at a higher risk of contracting HIV than others, drug addicts represent one such high-risk group.

高温补贴 high-temperature subsidies
北京、山西等北方地区的员工在6月到9月期间可获得高温补贴，而海南的员工可在4月到10月期间获得该补贴。
Employees in northern regions such as Beijing and Shanxi are entitled to high-temperature subsidies from June to September while those in Hainan get the subsidy from April to October.

高消费 high consumption
虚荣心是造成大学生高消费的一大原因。
Vanity contributes to high consumption on campus.

高效节能 energy-efficient
国家质量技术监督局对北京、上海、天津等10个省市72家企业生产的高效节能灯进行了抽查，结果却不尽如人意。
The State Bureau of Quality and Technical Supervision carried out a spot check on energy-efficient lamps produced by 72 enterprises in 10 provinces and municipalities, including Beijing, Shanghai, and Tianjin. The findings, however, were disappointing.

高原反应 altitude sickness
四川省和北京国际救助办公室最近救助了一名22岁的法国大学生。这名学生在西藏旅行途中差点因高原反应而丧生。
Sichuan province and the Beijing International S-O-S Office rescued a 22-year-old French university student who was dying from altitude sickness in Tibet.

高职教育机构 school of higher vocational education
中国目前有约1184所高职教育机构。
China currently has about 1,184 schools of higher vocational education.

高质量发展 high-quality development
国有企业要通过改革创新，走在高质量发展前列。

Our SOEs (State-owned Enterprises) should, through reform and innovation, become front-runners in pursuing high-quality development.

告别赛 final game; farewell match; swan song
篮球明星科比·布莱恩特在告别赛中砍下60分，结束20年NBA职业生涯后，我国网络被"向科比致敬"刷屏。
Tributes to Kobe Bryant went viral on the internet in China after the basketball star scored 60 points in his final game, ending 20 years in the NBA.

告别演讲 farewell address
美国总统奥巴马在自己的第二故乡芝加哥发表告别演讲。
US President Barack Obama delivered his farewell address in his adopted hometown of Chicago.

告急 report an emergency; be in an emergency; ask for emergency help
西线情况也告急，请求增援。
Emergencies were also reported from the western front. They were asking for reinforcements.

告密者 whistleblower
美国告密者爱德华·斯诺登表示，美国政府已入侵中国香港和内地的电脑系统多年。
US whistleblower Edward Snowden said the US government had been hacking into computers in Hong Kong and on the Chinese mainland for years.

搁浅 run aground
周日，在南沙群岛附近海域搁浅的一艘海军护卫舰在救援兵力协助下脱浅。
A navy frigate that ran aground in the waters off China's Nansha Islands was refloated with the help of the navy's rescue force on Sunday.

隔离带（公路）median
警方说当时这名男子正和他的妻子驾车在路上行驶，突然他的车冲向公路隔离带，并撞上了电线杆。
Police said the man was driving with his wife when his car hit the median and smashed into a telegraph pole.

个案 individual case
这是个个案，不能说全城的警官都是腐败的。
This is an individual case. It doesn't mean all police officers in the city are corrupt.

个人财产申报 personal asset declaration
立法要求公职人员申报个人财产,是防止腐败、增加政府透明度的一项举措。
Legislation requiring public officials to submit their personal asset declarations is seen as a move to prevent corruption and improve government transparency.

个人对个人模式 P2P model
我们的个人对个人模式为有闲钱的城里人和想贷款的农村人提供了一个平台。
Our P2P model has established a platform for people in the city to loan their money to those in need in rural areas.

个人对个人移动支付服务 person-to-person (P2P) mobile payment service
苹果公司正与多家美国银行洽谈开发个人对个人移动支付服务。
Apple Inc. is in talks with US banks to develop a person-to-person (P2P) mobile payment service.

个人所得税 personal income tax
提高个人所得税起征点,增加子女教育、大病医疗等专项费用扣除,合理减负,鼓励人民群众通过劳动增加收入、迈向富裕。
We will raise the personal income tax threshold and create expense deductions for items like children's education and treatment for serious diseases, appropriately lightening burdens, and encouraging our people to increase their incomes and achieve prosperity through hard work.

个人信息权 rights to personal information
近年来,获取和买卖他人个人信息的事件越来越多,严重损害了人们的个人信息权。
In recent years, there have been increasing incidents of people acquiring others' personal information and selling it, which has seriously harmed people's rights to personal information.

个人信用记录 personal credit records
旅游管理部门将要求旅行社监督旅行团,并将探索使用个人信用记录,以提前了解可能会有不良行为的人员身份。
Tourism authorities will urge travel agencies to monitor tour groups and will explore the use of personal credit records to identify possible offenders in advance.

个人信用体系 individual credit rating system
中国建设银行今年将要建立该行第一个全国个人信用体系。

The China Construction Bank will establish its first national individual credit rating system this year.

个人演唱会 solo concert
去年9月她在北京举行的个人演唱会竟是她的告别演出。
Her solo concert in Beijing last September turned out to be her swan song.

个人隐私 privacy
有些家长几乎没有个人隐私概念，经常查看子女的私人信件，使家长同孩子的关系更加紧张。
Some parents have little sense of privacy. They often read letters sent to their children, further straining parent-child relations.

个人域名注册 individual domain name registration
我们正在研究如何确保个人注册者的信息真实、完整、准确。在此基础上我们才能加快起草有关个人域名注册的规定。
We are now working to check whether individual registrars' information is true, complete and accurate, and based on this we can quicken our speed in drawing up the regulation on individual domain name registration.

个税改革方案 reform plan for individual income tax
个税改革方案预计将于今年4月提请全国人大常委会审议。
The reform plan for individual income tax is expected to be submitted to the Standing Committee of the National People's Congress for review in April this year.

个税税级 income tax bracket
草案将九级税级调整至七级。
The draft cut the number of income tax brackets from nine to seven.

根除腐败 root out corruption; eliminate corruption; eradication of corruption
我们需要用新法约束官员，为根除腐败现象提供法律依据。
New laws are needed to regulate officials and provide a legal basis for the eradication of corruption.

跟踪服务 follow-up service
如今，几乎所有家电厂商都提供长至一年的免费售后跟踪服务。
Nowadays, almost all household appliance makers provide free follow-up services up to a year after purchase.

耕地流失 arable land loss
分析人士认为导致耕地流失有几个主要因素，一个是建筑占用耕地现象越来越多，一个是森林或草地返耕项目影响，还有自然灾害带来的损毁。
Analysts believed several major factors contributed to the arable land loss, such as increasing use of arable land for construction purposes, forest or grassland replanting programs as well as damage caused by natural disasters.

更快、更高、更强的奥林匹克精神 the Olympic Spirit of Faster, Higher, Stronger, or Citius, Altius, Fortius
践行更快、更高、更强的奥林匹克精神，助力实现中华民族伟大复兴的中国梦。
We should practice the Olympic Spirit of Faster, Higher, Stronger in helping to realize the "Chinese Dream" of national rejuvenation.

工笔画 traditional Chinese realistic painting
年轻人中，耐得住寂寞研习工笔绘画的人很少。
Few young people can bear the solitude involved in practicing traditional Chinese realistic painting.

工夫茶 congou—a kind of Chinese tea prepared with care
在工夫茶风行的闽南、粤东和台湾，几乎家家户户都置有一套雅致的工夫茶具。
In south Fujian, east Guangdong, and Taiwan, where congou is popular, nearly every household has a delicate congou tea set.

工间操 daily workout
北京市总工会日前发布通知，要求数百万名机关、企事业单位员工每天做20分钟的工间操以保证身体健康。
Millions of municipal workers in the capital are being asked to take part in 20 minutes of daily workout in a bid to keep them fit, according to a news release of the Beijing Federation of Trade Union (BFTU).

工龄工资 seniority pay
为本公司工作10年以上的员工还可得到一份按月发放的工龄工资。
Those who have been working for our company for more than ten years are also entitled to monthly seniority pay.

工伤 work-related injuries
对工伤死者家属的赔偿金调整为年度全国城镇居民人均可支配年收入的20倍。
The compensation to families of those who die from work-related injuries has been raised to 20 times the per capita disposable annual income in urban areas.

工伤保险 employment injury insurance
劳动和社会保障部正忙于研究以灵活的形式解决就业人员的工伤保险问题。
The Ministry of Labor and Social Security is busily engaged in the study of the issues related to employment injury insurance for people in flexible forms of employment.

工薪阶层 wage earners
工薪阶层是纳税的主力军。
Wage earners are major taxpayers.

工休 day off; holiday
下月我有几天工休,我们那时聚会好吗?
Can we get together next month, when I have a few days off?

工业大迁移 great industry transfer
工资上涨和出口需求缩减迫使制造业厂商迁移到邻近的东南亚国家,那些尚未迁移的也在认真考虑这个问题。这一迁移行为被称为"工业大迁移"。
Rising wages and shrinking export demand are forcing manufacturers to relocate to neighboring Southeast Asian nations and many that remain are seriously considering moving in a trend that is called the great industry transfer.

工业固体废物 industrial solid waste
堆积的工业固体废物不仅占用大量土地,而且会对空气造成二次污染。
The piling-up of industrial solid waste occupies a large amount of land and will cause secondary pollution to the air.

工业控制一体化 integrated industrial control
随着竞争加剧,生产工业控制一体化装置的厂商开始想办法降低成本。
Due to the increasing competition, manufacturers of integrated industrial control equipment are looking for ways to cut costs.

工业明胶 industrial gelatin
周一早上在网上发布的消息警告消费者称,酸奶和果冻中可能含有用废弃皮鞋熬制的工业明胶。
The messages, which were posted online on Monday morning, warned consumers that yogurt and jelly might contain industrial gelatin made from discarded leather shoes.

工资封顶 have one's pay capped
根据该草案规定,国有垄断企业的员工,尤其是高管的工资将"封顶"。
Employees, especially those at the senior management level in State-owned

monopolies, will have their pay capped, according to the draft.

工资税 payroll tax
工资税对企业来说历来是一个棘手的问题。
Payroll tax has long been a sticky issue for businesses.

工资协商制度 negotiation system on wages
根据官方数据显示，中国的1300家中小型企业中约有1000家目前没有建立工资集体协商制度。
According to official statistics, about 1,000 out of 1,300 small and mid-sized enterprises in China currently lack a collective negotiation system on wages.

工资形成机制 wage formation mechanism
该报告预计由低端劳动力市场开始的工资形成机制改革将会延伸到高端市场并启动收入分配变革。
The report predicted the wage formation mechanism reform that originated from the low-end labor market will spread to the high-end market and trigger shifts in income distribution.

工作狂 workaholic
她是个工作狂。工作就是她的全部生活！
She is a workaholic. Her job is her life!

工作午餐 working lunch
为弥补时间上的损失，明天我们共进工作午餐吧。
To make up for lost time, let's have a working lunch tomorrow.

工作作风 work style
多省党委均已按照中央领导集体要求，制定出改进工作作风的详细政策。
Many provincial Party committees have created detailed policies to improve their work style, as required by the country's core leadership.

公厕新标准 new standards on public toilets (restrooms)
卫生部最新发布的草案规定了公厕新标准，对公共厕所的臭味强度和蝇蛆数量等评价指标规定了限值。
Health authorities have issued a draft regulation that sets new standards for public toilets, including limits for odor intensity and the number of flies and maggots.

公车私用 use government cars for private purposes
今年晚些时候起，广州市想要公车私用的官员将需要支付一定的费用。

Officials in Guangzhou will have to pay when they want to use their government cars for private purposes later this year.

公费生 government-supported student
如果你是公费生，就不用付学费了。
If you are a government-supported student, you don't have to pay the tuition.

公费医疗 free medical service; free medicare; public health service
他们使用电脑检查公费医疗处方。
They used computers to check for free medical service prescriptions.

公共服务型政府 public service-oriented government
中国改革发展研究院院长迟福林表示，建立更多公共服务设施以及建设公共服务型政府将为扩大内需奠定基础。
Chi Fulin, head of the China Institute for Reform and Development, said the establishment of more public services and a public service-oriented government will lay the foundation for boosting domestic demand.

公共外交 public diplomacy
中国需要大力开展公共外交活动，把中国更好地介绍给世界。
China needs a bigger public diplomacy campaign to better present the country to the world.

公关 public relations
这里的公关业务营业额现在以10亿美元计数。
Public relations is now a multi-billion dollar business here.

公检法机关 public security organs, procuratorial organs and people's courts
中国公检法机关在处理未成年人案件上已形成比较成熟的做法。
China's public security organs, procuratorial organs and people's courts have become experienced in dealing with cases involving minors.

公交专用车道 bus lane
交管部门已在北京市交通堵塞最严重的路段新开设了9条指定的公交专用车道。
Traffic police have opened nine bus lanes on some of Beijing's most notoriously congested roads.

公开选拔 public selection
周三是北京公开选拔领导干部网上报名的第一天，截至当晚6时，公选报名网站点击量已高达67万。

Beijing's public selection for leading officials attracted as many as 670,000 clicks on its application website as of 6 pm Wednesday, the first day of its application.

公开预算 publicize the budget; make the budget public

公开征求意见 solicit the public opinion
北京市教委近期正就周三发布的《北京市中长期教育改革和发展规划纲要》草案公开征求意见。
The Beijing Municipal Education commission is soliciting the public opinion on the draft *Guidelines on Beijing's Long-and-Mid-Term Education Reform and Development*, which was issued on Wednesday.

公款吃喝 wining and dining on public funds; entertainment on taxpayers' money
中共中央发出通知，禁止一切形式的公款吃喝。
The Central Committee of the Communist Party of China has issued a notification banning all wining and dining on public funds.

公立学校 public school
如果你没有多少钱，你可以把孩子送到免费的公立学校读书。
If you don't have much money, you can send your kid to a free public school.

公立医院改革 public hospital reform
中国已决定在各省、自治区、直辖市中选取部分城市或辖区率先进行公立医院改革试点。
China has decided to start public hospital reform with pilot programs in selected cities or districts in each province, autonomous region and municipality.

公路隧道 highway tunnel
中国开始建设世界最高公路隧道。
China begins construction of world's highest highway tunnel.

公民投票 referendum; plebiscite
全国公民投票已经决定停止核电计划。
A national referendum on nuclear power was decided in favor of discontinuing the program.

公民新闻 citizen journalism
7月23日D301动车上的一名乘客发布的微博无疑是呼救，但由此也引发了微博上前所未有的"公民新闻"热潮。
The words tweeted by a passenger on high-speed train D301 on July 23 were

clearly a cry for help. But they also initiated a wave of unprecedented "citizen journalism" on China's Twitter-like micro blogs.

公平补偿 fair compensation
该草案着重关注现行法第四十七条，建议对征地农民进行"公平补偿"以"确保农民生活水平有所提高，他们的长期生活有保障"。
The draft amendment, which focuses on Article 47, proposes to give "fair compensation" to farmers to "ensure their living standards improved and their long-term livelihood is guaranteed" after land expropriation.

公务用车 government car
国家计划进一步推进公务用车的改革，以减少不必要的花费，建设绿色政府。
China plans to further reform the use of government cars in an effort to cut unnecessary expenditure and build a green government.

公务员 civil servant
400多名学生和公务员于周六聚集北京大学，进一步了解新开设的公共行政管理硕士课程。
More than 400 students and civil servants gathered at Peking University on Saturday to learn more about the school's new Master of Public Administration (MPA) program.

公益唱片 benefit album
周三，公益唱片《给海地希望》将以美国流行音乐排行榜冠军的位置首度亮相。这张唱片是Billboard 200专辑榜近54年的历史上第一张创下如此佳绩的数字专辑。
The *Hope For Haiti Now* benefit album will debut at No. 1 on the US pop chart on Wednesday, becoming the first digital-only release to achieve this feat in the nearly 54-year history of the Billboard 200.

公正、公平、公开 just, fair and open
新规定旨在确保评选能够做到公正、公平、公开。
The new regulations are designed to ensure a just, fair and open contest.

公证 notarize (one's documents)
在每座城市，你都能找到提供免费公证服务的公证部门。
In every city, you'll find a notary office where you can get your documents notarized free of charge.

公租房 public rental housing
我国将继续发展公租房等保障性住房。

China will continue to develop public rental housing and other forms of government-subsidized housing.

功夫片 kung fu film
影片《卧虎藏龙》大获成功，一举赢得3项奥斯卡奖，引起了许多人对中国功夫片的极大兴趣。
The great success of *Crouching Tiger, Hidden Dragon*, which won three Oscars, has kindled many people's interests in Chinese kung fu films.

功利足球 Result Football
荷兰队主帅贝尔特·范马尔维克一改荷兰队20世纪70年代"全攻全守"足球的天赋和自发性，为求胜利转而使用功利足球战术。
Netherlands coach Bert van Marwijk changed the "Total Football" of flair and spontaneity of the 1970s into "Result Football", using cynical plotting for victory.

恭喜发财 may you be prosperous; wish you all the best
中国人爱听吉利话，"恭喜发财"是春节熟人见面时常说的客套话。
Chinese people love to hear auspicious words. "May you be prosperous" is a polite greeting frequently heard when acquaintances meet during the Spring Festival.

共建共治共享 collaboration, participation and common interests
打造共建共治共享的社会治理格局。
We will establish a social governance model based on collaboration, participation and common interests.

共同财产 mutual property; common wealth
婚姻法之前的条款规定，传统上由男方在婚前购买的房产在离婚时被认定为夫妻的共同财产，并接受估价。
The previous clause in the Marriage Law dictated that a house, which is traditionally bought by the bridegroom before the marriage, is regarded as the couple's mutual property and appraised for its value on divorce.

共同抚养权 joint custody
声明表示，两人将对他们的两个儿子享有共同抚养权，但没有透露任何关于两人财产分割的细节。
The statement indicated that the two would have joint custody of their two sons, but did not disclose any detail on how the couple's assets would be divided.

共同富裕 common prosperity
他呼吁成员国共同努力促进该地区的共同富裕。
He called for member countries to make joint efforts toward common prosperity in the region.

共同申报准则 Common Reporting Standard(CRS)
我国的共同申报准则办法开始实施以后，国税总局将掌握我国公民在101个国家和地区的境外账户信息。
The State Administration of Taxation will monitor Chinese citizens' foreign accounts information in 101 countries and regions following the implementation of the localized Common Reporting Standard (CRS).

共享充电宝 sharable chargers
在西安，包括餐厅和商场等37处区域都出现了共享充电宝。
Sharable chargers are available at 37 sites in Xi'an, including restaurants and shopping malls.

共享单车实名制 real name registration for shared bikes
交通运输部发布关于鼓励和规范共享单车发展的指导意见（征求意见稿），进行为期两周的公开征求意见。意见稿要求共享单车实行实名制。
The Ministry of Transport released a draft guideline to encourage and regulate the development of shared bikes, soliciting public opinions for two weeks. The draft requires real name registration for shared bikes.

共享睡眠舱 shared sleep cabin
由于存在火灾隐患等原因，上海有关部门关停了在写字楼里新开张的共享睡眠舱。
Authorities in Shanghai have shut down newly opened shared sleep cabins in office buildings for fire hazards and other reasons.

共有产权住房 home with joint property rights
北京市政府宣布，将向市场推出更多政府与居住者共有产权住房，以降低房价，满足北京无房人士的需要。
More homes with joint property rights between the government and occupiers will come on the market in Beijing to bring down prices and meet the needs of local people without a home, the municipal government said.

供给侧结构性改革 supply-side structural reform
我国应着力加强供给侧结构性改革，着力提高供给体系质量和效率，为可持续经济发展提供增长动力。

China should strengthen supply-side structural reform to increase the quality and efficiency of supply system and provide a growth impetus for sustainable economic development.

狗仔队 paparazzi—journalists who haunt celebrities
加州颁布了保护名人隐私的新法令，狗仔队可能很快将无法像以前那样肆无忌惮地追踪名人。
The paparazzi's feeding frenzy in California may soon be over due to the new privacy legislation designed to protect the celebrities.

购房移民计划 property-for-residency scheme
香港特区行政长官本周三宣布了冷却地产市场的新举措以平息民众对于房价不断攀升的怒气，举措包括中止面向有钱人的购房移民计划。香港房地产市场目前在全世界最热。
Hong Kong's Chief Executive on Wednesday outlined new steps to cool the world's hottest property market, including halting the property-for-residency scheme for rich buyers, in the face of simmering the public anger over the rising prices.

购汇 purchase foreign currency
打算购汇的个人须在申请书中提交更详细的信息。
Chinese individuals intending to purchase foreign currency now have to file more detailed information in their applications.

购买力平价 purchasing power parity（PPP）
明年中国将通过购买力平价这一国际通用的方法来换算国内生产总值。
China next year will measure its gross domestic product（GDP）using purchasing power parity（PPP）, an internationally accepted methodology.

购物狂 shopaholic
一份美国杂志近来声称这位女演员是个购物狂。
An American magazine recently alleged the actress is a shopaholic.

购物欺诈 shopping scam
很多中国游客成为日本购物欺诈的受害者，导游与当地免税店都参与了这种欺诈行为。
Many Chinese tourists have fallen victim to shopping scams perpetrated by tour guides and local duty-free stores in Japan.

购物优惠券 discount coupon
凭购物优惠券采购，主妇们每个星期最多能在食品方面节省100美元。

With discount coupons, housewives can save up to $100 a week on food.

估值偏低货币 undervalued currency
美国一直在指责中国的"估值偏低货币",并声称这是中国保持在海外市场廉价出口的手段。
The US has been criticizing China's "undervalued currency", claiming it is a way China keeps its exports cheap in overseas markets.

股份有限公司 limited liability company
据统计,在城市股份合作企业、股份有限公司和控股公司的从业人员为79.3万人。
According to statistics, 793,000 people work in urban joint-stock cooperative enterprises, limited liability companies, and shareholding companies.

股票期权 stock option
财政部将首次允许某些高科技企业试用股票期权。
The Ministry of Finance is going to allow some high-tech enterprises to try out stock options for the first time.

股指 stock index
上海证券交易所股指下跌47.68点,以1645.16点收盘。
The stock index at the Shanghai bourse dropped 47.68 points to close at 1645.16.

股指期货 stock index futures
中国证券业监管部门于周二批准位于上海的中国金融期货交易所推出股指期货交易。
China's securities regulator on Tuesday approved Shanghai-based China Financial Futures Exchange (CFFEX) to undertake stock index futures trade.

故意抬杠 argue for the sake of arguing
他似乎故意与作者抬杠。
It seemed that he was arguing with the author just for the sake of it.

雇佣协议 employment agreement
雇主必须根据雇佣协议支付每个员工的工资。
The employer must pay each employee according to the employment agreement.

挂靠 be attached to; be affiliated with; be a subordinate of
中国康复医学会心血管病专业委员会挂靠在福建医科大学附属协和医院。
The Cardiovascular Committee of the Chinese Association of Rehabilitation Medicine is attached to the Affiliated Union Hospital of Fujian Medical University.

挂职 serve temporary positions
北京市东城区政府宣布,该区计划派干部到美国和日本等国的政府部门去挂职,学习他们的管理经验。

The national capital's Dongcheng district is planning to have officials serve temporary positions in government departments in countries such as the United States and Japan to learn from their governance experience, district authorities said.

官话;官方语言 political jargon; official language
官方文件往往重形式、官话连篇、旋绕费解。

Official documents tend to be formal, confusing, and full of technical language known as political jargon.

关键词过滤 keyword filtration
该省官员还强调称,短信过滤系统采取的是关键词过滤的办法,而不是对公民的每条短信都查看。

The provincial official also stressed that the operation of its text message screen system is based on keyword filtration and not all text messages are actually checked.

关键少数 critical minority
全面依法治国必须抓住领导干部这个"关键少数"。

We will seize the critical minority of top cadres to promote rule of law across the nation.

关系网 relationship network; connections
这些人际关系网使得硅谷的公司创业者们快速获取所需基金、赢得合作伙伴并建立一个可靠的领导班子。

These interpersonal relationship networks enable Silicon Valley business starters to quickly gain needed funds, find cooperative partners, and establish credible leadership.

观察员国 observer state
联合国大会周四以大多数赞成票通过决议,决定将巴勒斯坦在联合国的地位由"观察员实体"升格为"观察员国"地位。

The UN General Assembly on Thursday voted overwhelmingly to grant an upgrade of the Palestine's status at the United Nations from "entity" to "observer state".

观潮派;观望态度 fence-sitter; those who take a wait-and-see attitude
楼盘销售的火爆推动着准备购房的观潮派纷纷加入到买房的浪潮中。

The active estate market induces more and more fence-sitters to purchase residential houses now.

光棍危机 bachelor crisis
国家统计局数据称将有3000多万男性人口打光棍。这一数据凸显了我国的光棍危机。
According to data released by the National Bureau of Statistics, more than 30 million males will have to stay single. The statistic highlights the country's bachelor crisis.

光缆 optical cable
中国首条商业海底光纤电缆日前通过中国信息产业部验收,为规模生产铺平了道路。
China's first commercial seabed fiber optical cable has passed an evaluation commissioned by China's Ministry of Information Technology, paving the way for mass production.

光量子计算机 photon quantum computer
我国科学家已构建出世界首台超越早期经典计算机的光量子计算机,为最终实现量子计算铺平了道路。
Chinese scientists have built the world's first photon quantum computer that goes beyond the early classical computers, paving the way to the ultimate realization of quantum computing.

光盘行动 "clear your plate" campaign
北京已有近750家饭店加入"光盘行动",通过提供小份菜减少食物浪费。
Nearly 750 restaurants in Beijing have joined the "clear your plate" campaign against wasting food by offering smaller dishes.

光污染 light pollution
据悉,中国南部的广东省省会广州市将率先在全国开征光污染排污费。
The provincial capital of South China's Guangdong province, GuangZhou is expected to take the lead in collecting light pollution fees in the country.

广而告之 spread the word; advertise; get the word out
广而告之一下吧!也算是给您的亲戚朋友和同事帮忙,告诉他们我们网站英语学习资源丰富、内容广泛。
Do a favor to all your friends, relatives, and associates; tell them about the vast array of English-learning resources on our website. Spread the word!

广告明星 poster star
刘翔在雅典奥运会勇夺110米栏金牌，还平了世界纪录，一夜之间成为广告明星。
Liu Xiang's world record tying performance at the Athens Olympics won him a 110m hurdles gold medal, making him a poster star overnight.

广告时段 advertising slot
中央电视台广告时段招标拍卖总额达158.8亿元，比上年增长11.4%。
The auction for advertising slots held by China's top TV broadcaster earned a total of 15.88 billion yuan, up 11.4 percent year-on-year.

广交会 China Import and Export Fair (Canton Fair)
广交会的成交额最大，是中国最大的商品交易会。
China Import and Export Fair (Canton Fair) is China's largest trade fair with the largest turnover.

广义货币供应量 broad measure of money supply (M2)
今年的广义货币供应量（M2）增长目标将会更灵活，意在给予实体经济更多支持。
This year's broad measure of money supply growth target will be more flexible, aiming to better support the real economy.

归国华侨 returned overseas Chinese; Chinese who lived overseas but have returned to China
我国海外华侨人数已超过3400万，遍布世界170多个国家和地区。归国华侨人数约为3000万。
China has more than 34 million people living overseas, scattered in more than 170 countries and regions worldwide. The returned overseas Chinese number some 30 million.

归国留学生 students who return to China after studying overseas; returned overseas students
海外归国的中国留学生在创业初期可以获得一笔政府特别津贴，用于创业。
Students who return to China after studying overseas will receive subsidies from the government to start their own businesses.

归属感 sense of belonging
招聘网站智联招聘发布的一份报告称，居住在北京、上海等一线城市的白领的归属感较低。
A report issued by recruitment website zhaopin.com said white-collar workers who live in first-tier cities such as Beijing and Shanghai have a lower sense of

belonging.

规模经济 economies of scale; scale economy
显而易见，个性化并不适合规模经济。
Customization is not beneficial for economies of scale, for obvious reasons.

柜族 cupboard tribe （迫于生活压力，蜗居在集装箱里的人们）
这位老人被网友称为"柜族"。老人希望在长沙租一个房间，但是长沙的房租太贵，一个房间每月约400元，他根本负担不起。
Dubbed online as the "cupboard tribe", the old man wishes to rent a room for himself but the cost in Changsha, where the rent for a single room is around 400 yuan a month, is far beyond what he can afford.

贵宾 distinguished guest; honored guest
这家餐馆吸引了来自世界各地的贵宾，其中不乏国王、总统。
The restaurant attracts distinguished guests from all over the world, including quite a few kings and presidents.

滚雪球 snowball
刚开始是1家银行倒闭，现在竟又有3家关门，雪球越滚越难控制。
It began with the collapse of one bank, but now three more have shut their doors. It's starting to snowball out of control.

棍棒教育 stick parenting
继"虎妈"热潮之后，"狼爸"再一次激起了关于"棍棒教育"的争论。
Following the roars of a "tiger mom", a "wolf dad" stirred controversy again on "stick parenting".

国产航母 home-built aircraft carrier
我国首艘国产航空母舰001A在中国船舶重工集团公司大连造船厂下水。
China's first home-built aircraft carrier 001A hit the water in Dalian shipyard of the China Shipbuilding Industry Corp.

国产化率 localized production
预计随着零部件国产化率的提高，该轿车的售价将降至6万元以下。
It is estimated that with the increase in localized production of parts and components, prices for this car will drop to below 60,000 yuan.

国产客机 homemade passenger jet
虽然备受期待的首架国产客机C919完成首飞，但初来乍到的C919也许需花更多时间才能在航空市场中立足。
While the much-awaited first homemade passenger jet C919 made its maiden flight, it may take much longer for the newcomer to take off in the aviation market.

国防和军队改革 defense and military reforms
深化国防和军队改革是实现中国梦、强军梦的时代要求。
Deepening defense and military reforms is a call of the time to realize the Chinese dream as well as a strong military dream.

国防预算 defense budget
我国的国防预算和军队改革举措将是重要议题。
Defense budget and new reform measures concerning army building will be top on the agenda.

国货 homemade products
澳门空调市场出现了国货热。
Homemade products are sought after in the air conditioner market in Macao.

国际板 international board
汇丰银行首席执行官周三表示,欧洲市值最大的银行汇丰控股已做好准备在上海国际板上市。
HSBC Holdings plc, Europe's biggest bank by market value, is ready to list its shares on the proposed international board in Shanghai, Chief Executive Officer said on Wednesday.

国际标准化组织 International Organization for Standardization (ISO)
另外,ISO 标准还有助于保护消费者的权益。
ISO standards also serve as a safeguard for consumers' rights.

国际多边金融机构 international multilateral financial institution
国际货币基金组织、世界银行等国际多边金融机构应在加强自身改革的同时加强和完善金融监管。
While pursuing internal reform, international multilateral financial institution such as the IMF and World Bank should strengthen and improve supervision of global finance.

国际惯例 common international practice
在加入世界贸易组织之后,中国必须遵守国际惯例。
After its accession to the WTO, China is required to comply with common

international practices.

国际化城市 a city of global clout
深圳将发展成为"全国经济中心",同时成为汇聚文化、经济和技术交流的"国际化城市"。
Shenzhen is to become "a national economic center" and "a city of global clout" in exchanges of culture, economy and technology.

国家安全 national security
全面贯彻落实总体国家安全观,开创新时代国家安全工作新局面。
China will fully implement a holistic approach to national security and break new ground in national security in the new era.

国家大数据战略 national big data strategy
要推动实施国家大数据战略,更好服务我国经济社会发展和人民生活改善。
Implementing the national big data strategy to better serve social and economic development and improve people's lives should be accelerated.

国家大数据中心 national big data center
我国将建设全国一体化的国家大数据中心,推进公共数据开放和基础数据资源跨部门、跨区域共享,提高数据应用效率和使用价值。
China will establish a national big data center to promote the opening up of public data and the trans-departmental, trans-regional sharing of basic data, in order to improve the practical value of data and its efficient use.

国家公务员考试(国考) national civil service exam; national examination for admissions to the civil service
2016年国考报名人数已超过上一年,星期二的通过审核人数超过13.2万人,创单日新高。
The number of candidates for the 2016 national civil service exam has surpassed last year's numbers, with more than 132,000 applicants deemed qualified for the exam on Tuesday, the most in a single day.

国家公园 national park
我国发布国家公园发展及管理总体方案,要求对自然生态进行最严格的保护,并世代传承下去。
China released an overall plan on the development and management of national parks, which calls for the strictest measures to protect the country's natural beauty and pass it on to generations to come.

国家公园体制 national park system
全面深化改革领导小组决定,建立国家公园体制,加强对大熊猫和东北虎、远东豹的保护。
China is set to establish a national park system to beef up the protection of giant pandas, Siberian tigers and Amur leopards, according to a decision made by the country's leading group for overall reform.

国家基因库 national gene bank/pool
国家基因库耗时5年建设,由国家发改委等四部委批复、深圳华大基因运营。
The national gene bank, which took five years to create, was approved by four government departments including the National Development and Reform Commission, and is operated by BGI-Shenzhen.

国家赔偿 state compensation
我国最高人民法院发布了关于审理国家赔偿决定上诉案件的若干新规。
China's top court issued a set of new rules on handling appeals to state compensation decisions.

国家形象宣传片 national publicity film
中国首部国家形象宣传片将在首都北京开拍,该宣传片是中国最近向全世界宣传国家形象的举措之一。
China will start shooting its first national publicity film in the capital Beijing as part of latest efforts to boost its image worldwide.

国家一级保护 first-grade state protection
黑颈鹤和西藏雉鸡被列为国家一级保护动物。
Black-necked cranes and Tibetan pheasants are under first-grade state protection.

国家账本 State balance sheet
全国和地方资产负债表编制工作方案获得国务院批复。有媒体报道,中央政府编制的首部国家账本或于今年底完成。
The State Council approved the compiling of balance sheets for both the central and local governments. The central government reportedly may finish its first State balance sheet by the end of this year.

国家重点科技攻关项目 national key scientific and technological project
国家重点科技攻关项目中国实验性数码图书馆周三通过了专家鉴定。
China's Trial Digital Library, a national key scientific and technological project, passed an expert appraisal on Wednesday.

国家专营 state monopoly
我国打破食盐生产与销售的国家专营局面,废除已实行了2000多年的食盐专营制度。
China shakes up the state monopoly on production and sale of table salt, dismantling a system that has been in place for more than 2,000 years.

国家最高科技奖 State Preeminent Science and Technology Award
火炸药专家王泽山和病毒学家侯云德获2017年度国家最高科学技术奖,这是我国最高科学奖项。
Explosive expert Wang Zeshan and virologist Hou Yunde received the 2017 State Preeminent Science and Technology Award—the nation's highest scientific award.

国民生产总值 gross national product (GNP)
农业对非洲发展至关重要,目前,农业产出对非洲国民生产总值的贡献为40%。
Agriculture is crucial to African development as it currently generates 40% of African GNP.

国民营养计划 national nutrition plan
国务院印发国民营养计划。计划提出以下目标:到2030年,在减少学生肥胖、贫血、5岁以下儿童生长迟缓以及提高居民营养意识方面取得明显改善。
A national nutrition plan was released by the State Council, setting a target to make substantial improvements by 2030 in reducing student obesity, anemia, and stunted development afflicting children younger than 5, as well as raising residents' nutritional awareness.

国内生产总值 gross domestic product (GDP)
工业行业生产总值占中国国内生产总值的1/3。
The industrial sector accounts for about one-third of China's GDP.

国事访问 state visit
盛夏时节,我很高兴再次对德国进行国事访问,并出席二十国集团领导人汉堡峰会。
It gives me great pleasure to pay a state visit to Germany again and attend the G20 Hamburg Summit in the height of summer.

国土空间开发规划 territory development plan
一位政府官员表示,中国将出台全国性的国土空间开发规划,这是中华人民共和国建国以来第一个国土开发规划。
China will issue a national territory development plan, the first of its kind since the founding of the People's Republic of China, said a government official.

国有股减持 reduce the state's stake in listed companies
中国宣布有关国有股减持的两步走计划。

China has announced a two-step program to reduce the state's stake in listed companies.

国葬 state funeral
官方宣布，撒切尔夫人将不会享受国葬，她的葬礼将以最高军事荣誉礼仪在伦敦圣保罗大教堂举行。
Baroness Thatcher will receive a ceremonial funeral with full military honors at St Paul's Cathedral in London but not a state funeral, it has been announced.

国债投资 treasury bond investment
中国用于支持西部地区基础设施建设的国债投资已达430亿元。
China's treasury bond investment in infrastructure construction in western areas has amounted to 43 billion yuan.

国资监管 State-owned capital supervision
我国将继续深化国有企业改革，进一步加强国有资本监管，以保证其安全和升值。
China will continue to deepen the reform of State-owned enterprises (SOEs) and further strengthen State-owned capital supervision to ensure their safety and appreciation.

过度包装 excessive packaging
专家表示，为满足网购用户需求，快递公司在派送商品时过度包装，产生的垃圾量越来越大，现有的回收利用系统无法应对。
Experts say excessive packaging for products dispatched through courier agencies to meet online shoppers' demand is generating increasing amounts of trash and the existing recycling system cannot cope with them.

过度放牧 overgraze
过度放牧是造成土地沙漠化和水土流失的一个原因。
Overgrazing is one cause of desertification and soil erosion.

过度开垦土地 excess land reclamation
这些地区正在开展一场"绿色"战役，要将大面积贫瘠土地变为森林，旨在遏制因战争年代过度开垦土地而造成的生态系统的恶化。
These areas are now undergoing a green campaign to turn huge tracts of barren farmland into forests, in order to curb the deterioration of the ecological system caused by excess land reclamation during the war.

过渡人物 seat warmer
分析人士早就猜测梅德韦杰夫只是普京受宪法限制不得不屈就总理期间的"过渡

人物"。
Analysts long speculated that Medvedev was merely a "seat warmer" while Putin served as Prime Minister due to constitutional restrictions.

过火 go too far
不高兴被换下场可以理解,可是他为发泄不满朝教练扔毛巾就有点过火了。
To be unhappy after being benched is understandable. But to show his frustration by throwing a towel at the coach is going a bit too far.

过境旅客 transit passenger
上海及杭州、无锡等周边城市从免签政策中获益良多,目前上海对过境旅客实行免签政策,即外国游客可免签停留48小时。
Shanghai and neighboring cities, such as Hangzhou and Wuxi, have benefited greatly since Shanghai introduced a visa waiver for transit passengers, as it means foreign tourists can travel during a 48-hour stay.

过境签证 transit visa
非澳大利亚公民经澳大利亚去其他国家须在海外办理过境签证方可入境。
Non-Australian citizens crossing through Australia on their way to another country must obtain a transit visa overseas before traveling to Australia.

过劳的 over-fatigued
中国大陆白领的健康状况堪忧,有60%的白领处于过劳状态,另有76%的白领处于亚健康状态。
The condition of Chinese white-collar workers on the mainland has received a bad prognosis with 60 percent over-fatigued and 76 percent in sub-health.

过路费 road toll
北京取消五环路过路费,司机们现在高兴了。
Drivers in Beijing are happy that road tolls for the Fifth Ring Road have been lifted.

(商品)过剩 glut; surplus
目前市场上西瓜过剩,瓜价可能还会下跌。
There's a glut of watermelons right now. Prices may drop even further.

过硬 competent
他的职业技术很过硬。
In terms of skills and techniques, he is competent.

H

孩奴 child's slave
一个新词汇——"孩奴"最近在国内媒体很流行,这是从有关"房奴"的报道演变而来的。"房奴"指的是背负房、车、信用卡等大量开支负担的人。
A new phrase—"child's slave"—has become popular in the Chinese media, playing on reports of "mortgage slaves" saddled with large payments for apartments, cars and credit cards.

海关检查站 customs checkpoint
按照该法规,如果欠账不还的"老赖"(汉语中对欠账不还的顽固分子的称呼)试图离境,警方有权在海关检查站予以阻止。
It gives police officers the power to stop people at customs checkpoints if the deadbeat, or Laolai—a derogatory term in Chinese used for diehard debtors—tries to leave the country.

海归 overseas returnees
科技园区已成功吸引了许多高级海归人员,他们平均拥有10年的美国硅谷工作经验。
The science park has been successfully alluring many senior overseas returnees with an average of 10 years of working experience in the Silicon Valley in the US.

海绵城市 sponge city
作为世界上缺水问题最严重的城市之一,北京打算转型成为有效收集和利用雨水的"海绵城市"。
Beijing, one of the world's cities facing the greatest water scarcity, aims to transform into a "sponge city" to effectively collect and use rainfall.

海上核电站 maritime nuclear power plant
我国有关部门已就海上核电站标准和相关关键技术开展研究。
Chinese authorities have already researched on relevant core technologies as well as the standardization of maritime nuclear power plants.

海上丝绸之路 Maritime Silk Road
国家主席习近平对南亚三国的访问凸显了中国对区域合作和"21世纪海上丝绸之

路"的重视。
Visits by President Xi Jinping to three South Asian countries show China's commitment to regional cooperation and the "21st Century Maritime Silk Road".

海市蜃楼 mirage
在海市蜃楼中，沙漠有时会现出湖泊的形象。
In a mirage, the desert could mimic a lake sometimes.

海淘 cross-border online shopping
我国对海淘实行了一套新的税收政策，海淘是为迎合中国消费者对海外产品的青睐而生且日益壮大的商业领域。
A new tax system is imposed on cross-border online shopping that forms a growing business catering to Chinese consumers with an appetite for foreign goods in China.

海外保障基地 overseas logistical base
2017年8月1日，中国人民解放军迎来90华诞之际，我国首个海外保障基地开始投入使用。
China's first overseas logistical base began operations on August 1, 2017, the same day as the 90th birthday of the Chinese People's Liberation Army.

海外代购 overseas shopping representative
新规定或将迫使个人海外代购和小公司要么洗手不干，要么转变经营模式。
The new regulation is expected to force private overseas shopping representatives and small companies to quit the business or transform their business model.

海外抢房 snap up properties overseas
越来越多的中国富人奔向海外抢房。
An increasing number of China's rich are snapping up properties overseas.

海峡交流基金会（海基会）Straits Exchange Foundation (SEF)
海峡两岸关系协会与海峡交流基金会之间的对话仍在继续。
Talks have been ongoing between the Association for Relations Across the Taiwan Straits and the Straits Exchange Foundation.

海峡两岸经济合作框架协议 Economic Cooperation Framework Agreement (ECFA)
6月末签署的《海峡两岸经济合作框架协议》（ECFA）被看作是海峡两岸签署的对深化经济组织合作、减少关税和商业壁垒影响最深远的协议。
The *Economic Cooperation Framework Agreement* (ECFA), signed in late June, is seen as the most sweeping agreement between the mainland and the island to

deepen cooperation between financial organizations and to reduce tariffs and commercial barriers.

海洋经济发展指数 ocean economic development index
中国海洋经济发展指数体系包括发展水平、发展成效和发展潜力3个分项指数，共29个指标。
The China Ocean Economic Development Index includes three sub-indices (development level, efficiency and potential) and covers 29 indicators.

函授课程 correspondence program
2004年离职后，我决定集中精力提高我的中文水平，随后加入了厦门大学开办的海外函授班。
When I left that job in 2004, I decided to focus on improving my Chinese skills so I enrolled in the Overseas Correspondence Program at Xiamen University.

韩流 Korean wave; South Korean fad
韩国尼尔森公司（调查机构）称，当调查机构询问来自中国、日本和泰国这3个国家的600名游客到首尔旅游的主要原因时，出现得最多的一致回答是"因为韩剧和首尔的广告"，这反映了该国文化的强大影响力和在过去几年里席卷亚洲的"韩流"的影响。
When the research agency asked 600 travelers from China, Japan and Thailand visiting Seoul for their main reason of visit, the consensus top response was "because of South Korean TV shows and Seoul advertisements", reflecting the country's strong influence over cultural contents and the impact of the so-called "Korean wave" that swept Asian fans over the past few years, Nielsen Korea said.

韩流签证 hallyu visa
"韩流签证"允许持有者在有效期内随时访问韩国，每次最长可停留30天。购买价格17350元以上四天韩国游专享套餐的中国游客可申请该签证。
Hallyu visa, which allows holders to return for stays of up to 30 days during the period of validation, is open to Chinese tourists who buy specialized four-day travel packages costing 17,350 yuan or more.

寒潮 cold snap
英国正在遭受1981年以来历时最长的寒潮。
Britain is suffering through its longest cold snap since 1981.

汉语文化圈 Chinese-speaking community
在韩国，一个新的汉语文化圈正在形成。

In South Korea, a new Chinese-speaking community began taking form.

汉字处理软件 Chinese character processing software
中文之星是流行的汉字处理软件。
Chinese Star is a popular Chinese character processing software.

汗血马 blood-sweating horse
阿克哈—塔克马，中国俗称"汗血马"，是世界上最古老最独特的马种之一。
Akhal-Teke, nicknamed "blood-sweating horse" in China, is one of the world's oldest and most unique horse breeds.

旱地滑雪场 mock ski park
香山滑雪场是北京第一家旱地滑雪场。
The mock ski park at the Fragrant Hills is the first of its kind in Beijing.

航班延误 flight delay
一位空域管制专家表示，作为全国飞行管制实施者，中国空军将出台多项措施，缓解民航航班延误。
China's Air Force, the country's airspace regulator, will introduce measures to ease flight delays of civil planes, an airspace regulation expert has said.

航班延误险 flight delay insurance
为了应对不断增加的"航班延误"投诉，廉价航空公司上海春秋航空联合上海大众保险公司推出了中国首个"航班延误险"。
With complaints about flight delays on the increase, Shanghai Spring Airlines—a budget airline—and the Shanghai-based Dazhong Insurance Company Limited are offering flight delay insurance for the first time in China.

航空母舰 aircraft carrier
据国防部官网报道，中国首艘航空母舰于周二正式交接进入中国人民解放军海军服役。
China's first aircraft carrier was delivered and commissioned to the People's Liberation Army (PLA) Navy Tuesday, according to report by National Defense Ministry's official website.

航母 style Carrier Style
网友们上传了模仿"航母style"姿势的各种照片，并称"航母 style""炫酷，强势，自信又带有娱乐和喜剧效果"。
Nicknamed "Carrier Style", it was deemed "cool, powerful and confident as well

as amusing and comical" by netizens who uploaded pictures showing various takes on the gesture.

航天员候选人 reserve astronaut
航天员评选委员会的一名高级医学专家称，首批两名女性航天员候选人的评选标准和男性一样。

The first two female reserve astronauts have to meet the same criteria as their male counterparts, said a senior medical expert from the astronaut selection panel.

航线 flight route
国航于周三发布消息称，连接华中地区工业中心武汉及日本东京的直飞航线将于8月27日开通。

Air China will launch a non-stop flight route linking central China's industrial hub of Wuhan with Tokyo on August 27, the airline said on Wednesday.

好莱坞大片 Hollywood blockbuster
没多少演员能宣称自己主演过好莱坞大片。

Not many people can claim to have played a starring role in a Hollywood blockbuster film.

好心人；见义勇为者 good Samaritan
面对遭遇不幸而需要帮助的人，很多中国人会犹豫不决，因为担心自己会被牵连。很多引人注目的此类案件最终结果都是，伸出援手的好心人却不得不向受助者支付一大笔赔偿金。

Many people in China are hesitant to help people who appear to be in distress for fear that they will be blamed. High-profile law suits have ended with good Samaritans ordered to pay hefty fines to individuals they sought to help.

号贩子 hospital appointment scalper
一名愤怒的女子在医院斥责号贩子害她挂不上号的视频走红后，北京警方已在市中心3家医院抓获12名号贩子。

Beijing police have arrested 12 people scalping outpatient appointments in three downtown hospitals following a viral video that showed a furious woman at a hospital blaming hospital appointment scalpers for her failure to get a ticket.

耗水产业 water-intensive industry
火电、纺织、造纸及钢铁等耗水产业在节水方面可努力的空间最大。

Water-intensive industries, such as thermal power, textiles, paper, iron and steel, have the most potential for water conservation.

合并重组 merger and consolidation
今年,为了增强央企的市场活力而进行的国有资产合并重组中,将至少有27家央企会被重组,届时央企总量将减至大约80到100家。
At least 27 central enterprises will be regrouped this year amid the ongoing merger and consolidation among State-owned assets, trimming the heavyweight bloc to about 80 to 100 firms, in a bid to beef up their market vitality.

合乎国情,顺乎民意 conform with the national conditions and the will of the people
这项政策合乎国情,顺乎民意。
This policy conforms with the national conditions and the will of the people.

合拍片 co-production
第12届上海国际电影节最高奖项由丹麦、瑞典合拍片《原创人生》获得,该片也是(两位)年轻导演首度拍摄的电影长片。
Top award at the 12th Shanghai International Film Festival went to *Original*, a Danish-Swedish co-production and a feature debut for its two young directors.

合群 be one of the guys; get on well with others; mix well with others
他并不特别喜欢跳舞,但还是和大家一道去了。作为新人,他最怕别人说他不合群。
He's not keen on dancing, but he went along with others. As a newcomer, the last thing he wanted was for others not to consider him one of the guys.

合议庭 collegiate bench
根据这项五年改革方案,中国还将努力建立新的合议庭庭长选举制度。
According to the five-year reform plan, China is also pushing for a new system to select the chief judge of the collegiate bench.

和平发展 peaceful development
中国将始终不渝走和平发展道路,坚定奉行独立自主的和平外交政策。
China will unswervingly follow the path of peaceful development and firmly pursue an independent foreign policy of peace.

和平共处五项原则:互相尊重领土主权、互不侵犯、互不干涉内政、平等互利、和平共处 Five Principles of Peaceful Coexistence: mutual respect for territorial integrity and sovereignty, mutual non-aggression, non-interference in each other's internal affairs, equality and mutual benefit, and peaceful coexistence

和平尊 Zun of Peace
"和平尊"以中国古代青铜礼器"尊"为原型。"尊"取"敬重"之义,在中国传统文化中是十分隆重的青铜礼器。
Zun of Peace is modeled after Zun, a bronze ritual object used in ancient China. Zun means reverence in Chinese, and this bronze ritual object is highly important in traditional Chinese culture.

和气生财 Harmony brings business
他说:"和气生财嘛,无论如何也不能和主顾吵架。"
"Harmony brings business," he said. "On no account should you quarrel with a client."

河道整治 waterway dredging project
中国最大的河道整治工程的第一阶段已通过官方验收。
First-phase construction of China's largest waterway dredging project has passed official approval.

河长制 river chief system
我国将全面建立省、市、县、乡四级河长体系,并任命地方各级政府领导为河长。
China will establish provincial, municipal, and county- and township-level river chief systems, and appoint heads of local government at various levels as river chiefs.

核安全 nuclear security
中美两国重申对全球核安全的共同承诺,承诺在核安全峰会之外继续在该领域加强合作。
China and the US reaffirmed their joint commitment to global nuclear security and pledged to continue cooperation in this area beyond the Nuclear Security Summit process.

核安全合作 nuclear security cooperation
核安全合作已成为中美之间建立新型大国关系的一个亮点。
Nuclear security cooperation has become a bright spot in the building of a new type of major-country relations between China and the US.

核裁军 nuclear disarmament
作为世界核大国,中国已为全球核裁军做出不懈努力。
As a world nuclear power, China has made unremitting efforts toward the global nuclear disarmament.

核讹诈 nuclear blackmail
伊朗正式向联合国"上书"指责美国新的核政策是"核讹诈",应被视为违反国际法。
Iran has formally complained to the United Nations that the new American nuclear policy is "nuclear blackmail" and should be considered a violation of international law.

核辐射 nuclear radiation
日本强震受灾地区不仅面临更多余震,而且还面临着另一个震后危机——核辐射。
While the affected areas in Japan brace for more aftershocks, the country is also being afflicted by another earthquake-engendered crisis—nuclear radiation.

核恐怖主义 nuclear terrorism
国际社会应该借助多边框架,削减对危险核材料的依赖,消除核恐怖主义。
The international community should cut its dependence on hazardous nuclear materials and eradicate nuclear terrorism with the aid of multilateral frameworks.

核武器数量 size of nuclear arsenal
上月得知美国的核武器数量后,他感到很震惊。
He was stunned last month when he learned about the size of the US nuclear arsenal.

核心舱 core module
中国空间站首个核心舱将搭载新一代长征五号重型运载火箭于2018年发射升空。
The first core module of China's space station will be launched in 2018 on board a new-generation Long March-5 heavyweight carrier rocket.

核心家庭 nuclear family
尽管大城市的核心家庭不断增加,几世同堂的传统在中国广大的农村地区依然存在。
Despite the growing number of nuclear families in big cities, the tradition of several generations living under one roof persists in China's vast rural areas.

核心竞争力 core competitiveness
该集团主动采取措施来扩大收入来源,并积极加强其核心竞争力。
The group took the initiative to expand its source of revenue and to strengthen its core competitiveness.

黑车 illegal taxi
北京打击黑车行动本周一正式启动,旨在治理公共交通混乱状况,改善首都交通体系。"黑车"指的是非法搭载乘客以牟利的私人交通工具。
A crackdown on Beijing's illegal taxis—private vehicles illegally carrying

passengers for money—kicked off on Monday in a bid to stop the disarray in public transportation and improve the capital's traffic system.

黑寡妇 black widow （大多是被俄联邦军队打死的车臣武装分子的遗孀，平常总是蒙着黑色头巾、身着黑色长袍，心怀黑色的仇恨，动辄带来黑色的死亡，所以被称为"黑寡妇"）
与俄当局较难控制的北高加索地区有关的"黑寡妇"组织有可能是莫斯科国际机场致命的自杀式袭击的幕后黑手。警方正在搜捕4名携带炸药混进机场的嫌疑犯。
A "black widow" linked to Russia's restive Northern Caucasus region could be behind the deadly suicide attack at Moscow's international airport and police were on the look out for four men who sneaked in with explosives.

黑马 dark horse
黑马候选人是指那种意外获得提名，而事先并没有人谈及或关注的人。
A dark horse candidate is one who is nominated unexpectedly, without previously having been discussed or noticed.

黑色星期五 Black Friday
据称，"黑色星期五"这种说法在20世纪60年代起源于美国费城，用来描述感恩节过后的周五，购物者涌入城市的商业中心，导致交通异常拥堵，给交警和出行司机都带来不小的麻烦。
The term "Black Friday" is said to have originated in Philadelphia during the 1960s to describe the difficulty of police and drivers to deal with exceptionally heavy traffic on that day as shoppers flooded into the city's commercial center.

黑哨 black whistle; referee who accepts bribes
中国足球协会宣布整顿中国足球，消灭"黑哨"。
The Chinese Football Association announced a campaign to clean up the sport in China, with the aim of eliminating "black whistles", or referees who accept bribes.

黑社会 Mafia-style organization
斯里兰卡警方逮捕了5名黑社会分子。该组织在佛教卫塞节当天杀害多人。
Five members of a Mafia-style organization responsible for killings on Vesak Day were arrested by Sri Lankan police.

黑市 black market
人体器官黑市的经营很有组织性，运作起来就像一条生产流水线。

The black organ market is so organized that it runs like an assembly line.

黑匣子 black box
中国打捞人员周二找到了一个黑匣子。
Chinese rescue workers found one black box Tuesday.

红包（婚礼用）red envelope (containing money) as a gift
在北京和中国其他许多地方，赴婚宴的宾客都要给新郎新娘送红包。
In Beijing and many other places in China, wedding guests each give the newlywed couple a red envelope as a gift.

红包照片 red envelope photo
微信用户可以分享被系统模糊处理的照片，想要查看照片的人需要先向其发红包。这一新功能被称为"红包照片"。
WeChat users can share a photo that is blurred by the system. People who want to view the photo will have to give the user a red envelope first. The new function is called the "red envelope photo".

红筹股 red chips
在香港上市的内地公司发行的股票被称为红筹股。
Stocks of mainland-funded corporations listed in Hong Kong are referred to as red chips.

红船精神 Red Boat Spirit
要认真贯彻习近平总书记关于弘扬"红船精神"等革命精神的重要指示，为实现党的十九大提出的任务不懈努力。
General Secretary Xi Jinping's instructions on carrying forward revolutionary spirit such as that embodied in "Red Boat Spirit" should be implemented earnestly amid the Party's efforts to strive toward fulfilling the goals set at the 19th CPC National Congress.

红股 bonus share
持有股票1年以上的散户按其所持有股票数额获赠忠诚红股，每20股获赠1股，持股2年以上者每15股获赠1股。
Each private investor receives one loyalty bonus share for every 20 shares for having held the stock for one year, and one for every 15 shares for having held the stock for two years.

（用了）洪荒之力 give one's full play
我国游泳选手傅园慧在2016年里约奥运会女子100米仰泳半决赛中游出个人最好

成绩后的夸张反应在网上爆红。她向央视记者表示："我已经用了洪荒之力。"
A new internet meme has emerged after Chinese swimmer Fu Yuanhui reacted exaggeratedly to her personal best performance in Rio 2016 women's 100 meters backstroke semi-final. "I have given my full play," she told a CCTV reporter.

红领 red-collar worker
根据一项新调查，成为公务员，也就是中国所谓的"红领"，是许多城市白领的梦想。
Becoming a civil servant—known as a red-collar worker in China—is the ambition of many white-collar workers in the city, according to a new survey.

红色通缉令 red notice
国际刑警组织中国国家中心局发布了一份100名全球通缉人员的名单，名单上77名男性、23名女性均涉嫌腐败，且都在国际刑警组织红色通缉令名单中。
Interpol's National Central Bureau of China has released a list of 100 persons wanted worldwide. On the list are 77 men and 23 women allegedly involved in corruption and all on Interpol's red notice list.

红色遗迹 red relics
今年西藏将向中央政府申请超过2300万元人民币用来保护"红色遗迹"（革命遗址），第一批保护工程已经启动。
Tibet will apply to the central government for more than 23 million yuan to protect the "red relics" (revolutionary sites) this year, with the first batch of construction for protection projects already started.

红色炸弹 red bomb （意指婚礼请柬）
过去的7天假期让这个25岁的女人感到精疲力竭。她不是去旅行，也没有加班，而是在各地之间奔忙，准备好一叠叠钞票来应对"红色炸弹"。
The 25-year-old woman has had an exhausting holiday during the past seven days. Rather than traveling or working overtime, she was busy hopping from one place to another bracing against "red bombs" with piles of cash.

红色资源 red resources
近日中国在全国范围内开展了一项针对烈士纪念设施的调查，力求为加强保护这些宝贵的"红色资源"提供信息。
China has launched a survey on its martyr memorial facilities nationwide, aiming to offer information for enhanced protection on these precious "red resources".

宏观经济基本状况 macroeconomic fundamentals
良好的宏观经济基本状况使得中国能够从亚洲开发银行获得更多的贷款。
Sound macroeconomic fundamentals have enabled China to secure more loans from the Asian Development Bank.

宏观审慎的政策框架 macro-prudential policy framework
中国央行行长表示,中国目前应采用宏观审慎的政策框架,以推动后全球金融危机时代的金融改革。
The time is right for China to adopt a macro-prudential policy framework in order to facilitate financial reforms in the post-global financial crisis era, the country's central bank governor said.

虹膜识别技术 iris recognition technology
不远的将来,虹膜识别技术或将在我国打击拐卖儿童的行动中发挥作用。
Iris recognition technology might play a role in the battle against child trafficking in China in the near future.

洪峰 flood crest
长江洪峰正涌向大海,南京等沿江城市将脱离危险。
The Yangtze River's flood crest is rolling closer to the sea, leaving Nanjing and other cities safe.

喉舌;代言人 mouthpiece
行业协会既不是国家机构的延伸,也不是某一个企业的喉舌,它代表的是行业中所有企业的共同利益。
An industrial association is neither an extension of the State nor the mouthpiece of any single enterprise, but a representative of the interests of all enterprises in the industry.

后高考经济 after-gaokao economy
随着逾900万名学生参加完高考,他们如今已成为商家和所谓"后高考经济"的目标。
As more than 9 million students finish taking the national college entrance exam, or gaokao, they now become the target of businessmen and the so-called after-gaokao economy.

后悔期 cooling-off period
周二提交人大常委会审议的《消费者权益保护法》修正案草案提出,网购消费者应享有7天的"后悔期",在此期间,消费者有权退货。

Online shoppers should be granted a seven-day cooling-off period, within which they would be able to get a refund, a draft amendment presented to the legislature on Tuesday has proposed.

后危机时代发展模式 post-crisis development model
区域各国正在寻求一个后危机时代的发展模式。
Regional countries are seeking a post-crisis development model.

候补委员 alternate committee member
候补委员们必须参加区委会议。
Alternate committee members must attend district meetings.

候选城市 candidate city
所有候选城市必须遵守国际奥委会的有关规定。
All candidate cities shall abide by the rules set by the International Olympic Committee.

呼叫转移 call forwarding
这款手机具备多种功能，包括会议呼叫、呼叫转移、来电显示、呼叫等待，等等。
The model features many functions including conference calling, call forwarding, caller ID, and call waiting.

呼吸衰竭 respiratory failure
广东省卫生厅一位官员说已有5位病人死于呼吸衰竭。
An official with the Guangdong Provincial Health Bureau said five patients had died of respiratory failure.

户主 head of a household
在中国，人们通常认为丈夫是户主。
In China, the husband is generally acknowledged as the head of the household.

互动演示 interactive demonstration
你需要一个支持Java语言的网络浏览器来实现互动演示。
To be able to use this interactive demonstration, you must have a web browser that is Java compatible.

互联网保险 online insurance
我国的互联网保险用户基数扩张迅猛，其市场前景一片光明。
China's online insurance market has a bright future as the user base expands fast.

互联网从业者 internet professionals
报告显示，我国互联网从业者大多在北上广深等一线大都市就业。
Most of China's internet professionals work in first-tier metropolitan cities such as Beijing, Shanghai, Guangzhou and Shenzhen, according to reports.

互联网法院 Court of the Internet
杭州互联网法院在浙江省杭州市正式挂牌成立，集中管辖日益激增的网络争端案件。
Hangzhou Court of the Internet, set up to handle the soaring number of online disputes, has gone online in Hangzhou, Zhejiang province.

互联网服务提供商 Internet Service Provider（ISP）
互联网服务提供商又称互联网通道提供商。
ISPs are also called IAPs（Internet Access Providers）.

互联网金融 online finance
国务院承诺将加强对包括P2P（个人对个人）平台在内的互联网金融市场的监督，以减少风险，支持行业健康发展。
The State Council pledged to improve supervision over the online finance market, including peer-to-peer (P2P) platforms, to reduce risks and support the healthy development of the sector.

互联网投资基金 Internet Investment Fund
分析人士指出，新设立的中国互联网投资基金有望通过市场手段在互联网行业促进创新和创业发展。
The newly established China Internet Investment Fund is expected to foster innovation and entrepreneurship within the internet sector via a market approach, analysts said.

互联网+政务服务 Internet Plus government services
大力推行"互联网+政务服务"模式，实现政府部门间数据共享，让居民和企业少跑腿、好办事、不添堵。
We will carry out the "Internet Plus government services" model and promote better data sharing between government departments, so that the public and businesses need to make fewer visits to government departments to get things done, find procedures simpler, and find the service satisfactory.

户外外交 outdoor diplomacy
李克强总理与澳大利亚总理特恩布尔在海湾漫步，又一起观看了一场激烈的澳式足球比赛，展现户外外交，增强两国人民之间的联系。
Chinese Premier Li Keqiang took a casual harbor walk and watched an exciting

Australian football game with his Australian counterpart Malcolm Turnbull, extending his outdoor diplomacy to strengthen the ties between the two peoples.

沪港通 Shanghai-Hong kong Stock Connect
中国银行成为"沪港通"独家结算银行。
Bank of China was named the exclusive settlement bank for the Shanghai-Hong kong Stock Connect.

花葬 flower burial
华中地区的湖北省武汉市号召市民采用花葬,将骨灰倒进花坛下方的地窖。
Residents of Wuhan, in Central China's Hubei province, are asked to consider flower burials by pouring ashes into the cellar beneath flower beds.

滑草场 grass-skating field
白云滑草场平均坡度为18度,总占地面积为6500平方米。
The Baiyun grass-skating field with an average slope of 18 degrees is 6,500 square meters in area.

滑出跑道 overshoot the runway
上月,一架满载乘客的加勒比航空客机滑出跑道,在峡谷边缘断成两截。
A packed Caribbean Airlines passenger jet broke in two at the edge of a ravine after overshooting the runway last month.

化学阉割 chemical castration
韩国将对一名恋童癖罪犯实施化学阉割,这是韩国首次动用此刑。
A convicted pedophile will be offered chemical castration for the first time in Republic of Korea.

画饼充饥 feed on illusions
他总是给你许诺说会和你结婚,快醒醒吧,他只是在给你画饼充饥!
He always gives you an empty promise that he will marry you. Please wake up. He just feeds you on illusions!

环保彩票 environmental lottery
去年,世界上第一款环保彩票亮相英国,旨在削减温室气体排放,缓解气候变化。
Last year, the world's first environmental lottery was unveiled in UK, aimed at reducing greenhouse gas emissions and limiting climate change.

环保产品 environment-friendly product
这款机器用水少、耗电低,是真正的环保产品。

With low consumption of water and electricity, the machine is a real environment-friendly product.

环保警察 environmental police force
北京市组建环保警察队伍，以此加强环境保护。
Beijing organized an environmental police force to strengthen environmental-protection.

环境保护税 environmental protection tax
环境保护税法以环境保护税取代现行排污费系统，成为管理中国企业环境污染的主要经济工具。
The Environmental Protection Tax Law is poised to replace the existing pollutant discharge fee system with a pollution tax as the main economic tool regulating environmental pollution by businesses in China.

环境事故 environmental accident
据环保部统计，去年全国共处理542起环境事故。
Last year, 542 environmental accidents were handled across the country, statistics from the Ministry of Environmental Protection showed.

环境污染强制责任险 compulsory environmental pollution liability insurance (pollution insurance)
专家表示，中国正在抓紧制订环境污染强制责任保险实施计划，联合监管和产品设计将是重点考虑的问题。
China is quickening the pace of putting together its compulsory environmental pollution liability insurance implementation plan, and joint regulation and product designs could be key issues, experts said.

环幕电影 circular-screen movie
环幕电影是完全不同的感受，比普通电影感觉生动得多、真实得多。
Circular-screen movies are an entirely different experience. They look far more vivid and real.

缓冲室"buffer zone" rooms
中国东部的江苏省正计划在婚姻登记处设立离婚"缓冲室"，让想离婚的夫妇在最终决定离婚之前冷静地思考一下。
East China's Jiangsu province is planning to equip its marriage registration offices with "buffer zone" rooms to help divorcing couples to think calmly before making the final decision to end their marriage.

缓和紧张状况 ease the tension
中国为缓解两国的紧张局势做出了努力。
China tried to ease the tension between the two countries.

换乘站 transfer stop; interchange station
这里是十号线的换乘站。
This is the transfer stop for line 10.

换汇潮 currency exchange boom
人民币对美元汇率跌至5年来最低位，引发了中国内地换汇潮，管理机构不得不加强干预以减轻资本外流压力。
The renminbi's fall to a five-year low against the US dollar has triggered a currency exchange boom on the Chinese mainland, forcing the regulator to strengthen intervention to ease capital outflow pressure.

黄昏恋 romances among the elderly; twilight romances
随着婚恋观的转变，黄昏恋也日渐为社会接受。
With changing views on marriage and love, romances among the elderly are being accepted by society.

黄金单身族 golden single
如果你是月可支配收入为8000元及以上的单身人士，那么你才符合我国"黄金单身族"的标准。
If you are single with monthly disposable income of 8,000 yuan or more, then you are qualified to be called a "golden single" in China.

黄金热 gold rush
春节7天假期中，"黄金热"和全球股市动荡推动国内黄金售价一天一涨。
A "gold rush" during the week-long Lunar New Year holiday and chaos in the global stock market have pushed the price of gold up on a daily basis in China.

黄金时段 prime time
然而，他们一起新合作的动作片恐怕很难在电视黄金时段播出。
But their latest action film might have trouble finding a place on prime time TV.

黄金投资者 gold bug
有些人属于"黄金投资者"。他们告诉大家要买黄金抗通胀。
Some people are "gold bugs". These are investors who say people should buy gold to protect against inflation.

黄色预警 yellow alert

北京市国土资源局和气象局联合发布地质灾害黄色预警,房山、门头沟、怀柔、平谷、石景山及密云部分浅山地带发生泥石流、崩塌、滑坡等地质灾害的可能性较大。
Beijing Municipal Bureau of Land and Resources and Beijing Meteorological Bureau jointly issued the yellow alert for possible geological disasters of mudslides, cave-in and landslip in mountainous areas in the districts of Fangshan, Mentougou, Huairou, Pinggu and Shijingshan, as well as Miyun County.

灰发离婚 grey divorce

50岁以上夫妻分道扬镳的数量空前多,美国正处于"灰发离婚"变革的阵痛中。
America is in the throes of grey divorce revolution as married couples over the age of 50 split up in unprecedented numbers.

灰色技能 gray skills

一项2298人参与的调查显示,70.7%的人认为喝酒、奉承等"灰色技能"在职场中非常重要。
A survey of 2,298 people showed that 70.7% people consider "gray skills", which refer to special social skills including drinking and flattering, important at work.

灰色经济 gray economy

莫斯科汽车维修业多半仍属灰色经济,但总的来说,服务水平在缓慢提高。
Although more than half of Moscow's car repair businesses still operate in the gray economy, services in general are slowly improving.

灰色收入 gray income; off-the-books income

这项政策的初衷是强制医院消灭"灰色收入"。
The policy was intended to press hospitals to eliminate gray income.

灰市 gray market [未经商标拥有者授权而销售该品牌商品的市场渠道。所售商品都是真品,只不过是一种"非正式"的渠道,介于white market(合法的交易市场)与black market(黑市)之间]

分析人士指出,在中国,iPad 2在"灰市"的价格可能上涨。苹果中国网络营销店表示,最新款的平板电脑已经售罄。
In China, the price of iPad 2 on the "gray market" may rise, analysts said. Apple's Chinese online store says it has sold out of the new tablets.

灰犀牛 grey rhino

灰犀牛不是随机的突发事件,而是在一系列预警和明显征兆之后爆发出来的问题。灰犀牛袭击时,极具爆发力,且不可阻挡。

Grey rhinos are not random surprises, but problems that break out after a series of warnings and visible evidence. When the grey rhino attacks, its power is explosive and unstoppable.

恢复营业 resume operations
东风本田、东风日产等日本在华合资汽车企业本周三依然处于停工状态，不过很多其他日资企业已经恢复营业。
Japanese automobile joint ventures in China, including Dongfeng Honda and Dongfeng Nissan, kept their production facilities closed on Wednesday, but many other Japanese businesses resumed operations.

徽章热 pin craze
继世博护照热之后，又掀起徽章热。世博徽章在那些乐于收集世博会纪念品的游客当中掀起热潮。
After Expo passports, comes the pin craze. Expo pins have taken visitors, who are eager to collect souvenirs of the mega fair, by storm.

回流移民 returning emigrants
这篇文章叙述回流移民的经历，特别是20世纪80年代离开爱尔兰90年代又回国的移民们的遭遇。
The article recounted the experiences of returning emigrants, focusing in particular on those who left Ireland in the 1980s and returned in the 1990s.

回收火箭 recycled rocket
美国太空公司SpaceX创造历史，首次实现将一枚回收火箭再度送入太空，此后其一级火箭在大西洋的一艘无人船上着陆。
US space firm SpaceX made history as it launched a recycled rocket back into space for the first time and then landed its first stage on a drone ship in the Atlantic Ocean.

回收流动性 soak up liquidity
去年年初开始，中国已9次上调存款准备金率，以回收流动性。
Since the beginning of last year, China has raised the bank reserve requirement nine times to soak up liquidity.

回头客 returning customer
有一点可以肯定，如果饭店回头客多，那这家店一定不错。
One thing is for sure, if a restaurant has a lot of returning customers, then it is a

good one.

汇款单 money order
他每月汇款200元给妹妹。这样，妹妹就能继续上学。
He sends 200 yuan a month to his sister through money orders. With the money, she can stay in school.

汇率 exchange rate
中国将会加强外汇管理，保持国际收支平衡和汇率的稳定。
China will improve foreign exchange administration and maintain balance of payments and exchange rate stability.

汇率微调 rate fine-tuning
人民币汇率可能进行微调。
RMB rate fine-tuning is possible.

汇率中间价 central parity rate
在中国即期外汇市场，人民币的定价可以依照交易当日的汇率中间价上升或下调一个百分点。
In China's foreign exchange spot market, the yuan is allowed to rise or fall by 1 percent from the central parity rate each trading day.

贿选 buy votes
国际足联首次承认过去的世界杯主办权竞选过程中存在"贿选"。
FIFA has acknowledged for the first time that votes were bought in past World Cup hosting contests.

婚检 premarital health checkups
据北京市卫生部门官员介绍，北京的准夫妻婚检率不足10%。这导致过去5年内，出生缺陷发生率不断增加。
Less than 10% of unmarried couples in Beijing get premarital health checkups, and this has led to an increase in birth defects over the past 5 years, according to a Beijing health official.

婚介所 matrimonial agency
据估计，在各种婚介所登记求偶的北京人可能多达百万人次。
As many as one million Beijingers seeking spouses have registered with matrimonial agencies, according to estimates.

婚礼式颁证 wedding-style registration
在我国，新人结婚时一直存在"轻登记、重婚宴"的现状。为改变这一情况，民政部正考虑在民政局婚姻登记处推广"婚礼式颁证"。

Wedding receptions have long been overvalued compared with the registration process in China. To change that, civil departments are considering wedding-style registrations at civil affairs bureaus.

婚恋交友网；鹊桥网 match-making website
中国政府成立了一家婚恋交友网站，帮助成千上万名繁忙却孤单的政府职员在工作中寻找爱情。

China's central government has set up a match-making website to help thousands of busy but lonely government workers find love at work.

婚奴 marriage slave
一位姓曾的男士称，现在结婚花费十分昂贵，在花钱举办完结婚仪式和婚宴后生活陷入了困境，他感觉自己成了一名"婚奴"。

A man surnamed Zeng said it is quite expensive to get married and he felt like a "marriage slave" who fell into trouble in life after spending a lot of money on his wedding ceremony and banquets.

婚前单身派对 stag/hen night
这对明星夫妇在举行婚前单身派对时必须保持低调，以免给随时准备出击的狗仔队提供报道素材。

Known in Britain as hen night (for the bride) and stag night (for the groom), it is clear that the celebrity couple must keep a low profile to avoid giving fodder to the ever-ready paparazzi.

婚前同居 premarital cohabitation
数据显示，过去10年间该市婚前同居率由13%上升至20%。

Figures show that premarital cohabitation in the city increased from 13 percent to 20 percent during the past decade.

婚前协议 prenuptial agreement
婚前协议的内容可能不尽相同，但是普遍都包括离婚或婚姻破裂时财产分配以及配偶赡养方面的条款。

The content of a prenuptial agreement can vary widely, but commonly includes provisions for division of property and spousal support in the event of divorce or breakup of marriage.

婚外恋 extramarital affair
调查显示76.6%的答卷者反对婚外恋，19.1%的人则认为婚外恋可以理解。
The survey shows that 76.6 percent of the respondents are opposed to extramarital affairs, while 19.1 percent said they are understandable.

婚姻保险 marriage protection insurance
婚姻保险宣传册上的一个案例说，如果丈夫花50万元买一份50年期的保险，这份保险到期时如果婚姻还在持续，那么他们将获得400万元的收益。
An example on a booklet about marriage protection insurance says if a husband pays 500,000 yuan to buy a 50-year-term policy, the yield will be 4 million yuan if the marriage is still alive when the term ends.

婚姻状况证明 marital status certificate
民政部取消了不必要的婚姻状况证明。
The Ministry of Civil Affairs canceled unnecessary marital status certificate.

混改方案 mixed-ownership reform plan
我国第二大移动运营商中国联通的117亿美元的混改方案获得证监部门批准后，联通旗下两个上市公司的股价飙升。
The $11.7 billion mixed-ownership reform plan of China Unicom, the country's second-largest mobile carrier, has been approved by the country's securities authority, causing shares of its two listed units to skyrocket.

混合所有制 diversified ownership; mixed ownership
混合所有制是中国各银行的发展趋势，但是发展起来仍需时间。
Mixed ownership will become a type of trend for Chinese banks, though it will take time.

混合所有制改革 mixed-ownership reform
我国已选定31家国有企业进行第三批混合所有制改革，以将更多民间资本引入国企。
China has picked a group of 31 State-owned enterprises for the third round of SOE mixed-ownership reform, aiming to bring more private capital into the state sector.

混合项目 mixed-gender events
国际奥委会宣布，2020年东京奥运会的田径、游泳、乒乓球以及铁人三项的男女混合项目已获得批准。
Mixed-gender events in athletics, swimming, table tennis and triathlon have been approved for the Tokyo 2020 Olympic Games, the IOC has announced.

活禽交易 live poultry trade
新型禽流感H7N9的出现迫使中国多个城市开始捕杀活禽并禁止活禽交易。
The new bird flu strain H7N9 has prompted the slaughter of live fowl and bans on the live poultry trade in several cities in China.

活跃用户 active users
新浪微博宣布，截至2017年3月底，其月活跃用户数达3.4亿，在活跃用户总数方面超过了美国的"推特"。
Sina Weibo has announced it had 340 million monthly active users as of the end of March 2017, overtaking US-based Twitter in active user totals.

火箭军 Rocket Force
中国军队改革继续推进，建立了解放军火箭军和战略支援部队。
China's military reform continues, with the establishment of the PLA Rocket Force and the PLA Strategic Support Force.

火星模拟基地 Mars simulation base
当地政府称，我国将在青海建立国内首个火星模拟基地。
China will establish the country's first Mars simulation base in Qinghai, the local government said.

货币操纵国 currency manipulator
商务部部长表示，由于进口的大幅度增长，3月份中国的贸易逆差可能"破纪录"，同时他警告说，如果华盛顿方面将中国定义为货币操纵国，北京将"予以反击"。
The country will probably see a "record trade deficit" in March due to surging imports, the Minister of Commerce said, while warning that Beijing will "fight back" if Washington labels China a currency manipulator.

货币供应量 measure of money supply
广义的货币供应量（即M2）包括流通货币以及全部储蓄存款。
The broad measure of money supply, M2, covers cash in circulation and all deposits.

货币回笼 withdrawal of money from circulation; withdrawal of currency from circulation
去年，货币回笼增加了。
Last year saw an increased withdrawal of money from circulation.

货币战 currency war

从韩国到印尼和印度,各国货币政策机构正准备让本币贬值,因为日元下跌导致他们的经济竞争力下降,并被拖入一场决策者口中的"货币战"。

From South Korea to Indonesia and India, monetary authorities are preparing to let their currencies weaken as a falling Japanese yen makes their economies uncompetitive, and drags them into what some policymakers are calling a "currency war".

货币政策 monetary policy

作为世界第二大经济体,我国努力平衡增长与风险防范之间的关系,决定在2018年继续实施稳健中性的货币政策。

China has decided to maintain a prudent and neutral monetary policy in 2018 as the world's second largest economy strives to balance growth and risk prevention.

货到付款 cash on delivery

您可选择现在付款或者货到付款。

You can choose to pay now or cash on delivery.

获得感 sense of benefit

注重保障和改善民生,人民群众获得感增强。

We gave particular attention to ensuring and improving living standards, helping Chinese people gain a stronger sense of benefit.

饥不择食 eat whatever one can catch
阿根廷官员在海拔2800多米(9300英尺)的山洞里发现了戈麦斯先生。他靠吃剩余的食物和可以吃的一切东西活了下来,"饥不择食"的他甚至吃下了老鼠。
Mr Gomez was found in a mountain shelter at an altitude of more than 2,800m (9,300ft) by Argentine officials. He survived by eating leftover supplies and whatever else he could catch, even including rats.

饥饿营销 hunger marketing
苹果公司长期遵循的"饥饿营销"策略受到了行业内的质疑。
Apple's long-term "hunger marketing" strategy has sparked questions from inside the industry.

机场建设费 airport construction fee; airport tax
自9月1日起,机场建设费将在机票内收取,乘客无须另购机场建设费。
Starting September 1, passengers will no longer have to pay the airport construction fee at the airport, as it will be included in the ticket itself.

机动车排放标准 automobile emission standards
北京市将从2月1日起提高机动车排放标准,使其成为全国最严格的排放标准,北京市环保局称该标准实施后机动车污染有望减少40%。
The capital will raise its automobile emission standards on Feb. 1, making them the strictest in the nation in a move that the Beijing Environmental Protection Bureau said is expected to reduce auto pollution by 40 percent.

机动车行驶证 road-worthiness certificate
根据草案规定,2.0升以下小排量车的车船税将会减少,车主需要提交缴纳车船税证明才能办机动车行驶证。国内87%的车辆为2.0升以下的小排量车。
According to the draft law, taxes on vehicles with engines smaller than 2.0 liters, which account for 87 percent of China's cars, will be reduced and vehicle owners should submit tax certificates in order to qualify for a road-worthiness certificate.

机构重叠 organizational overlapping
不能小看政府部门的机构重叠现象。

Organizational overlapping is not something to be taken lightly.

机构改革 institutional reform; institutional restructuring
机构改革精简政府部门，人少了，办事效率高了。
Institutional reforms have led to a more streamlined government of fewer people and greater efficiency.

机构投资者 institutional investor
此次由世界银行主办的研讨会旨在吸引更多的机构投资者来到中国。
This World Bank seminar aims to bring more institutional investors to China.

机密；保密事件 hush-hush affair
早在两人关系还处于保密状态之时，就有报道透露两人计划在不同的城市举办至少3场婚礼。
Earlier when their relationship was still a hush-hush affair, there were leaked reports that the couple planned to throw at least three weddings in different cities.

机译 machine translation（MT）
机译是一种自动将文本从一种语言转换为另一种语言的技术。
Machine translation (MT) is a technology that automatically translates text from one language to another.

鸡蛋碰石头 strike a rock with an egg; attack someone stronger than oneself
打他的正手就像是拿鸡蛋碰石头。反手是他的弱点。
Attacking his forehand is like striking a rock with an egg. His backhand, however, is his vulnerable point.

积分落户制度 points-based household registration (hukou) system
北京市有关部门公布了积分落户制度和居住证管理办法草案，公开征求社会意见。
Beijing authorities released two draft regulations on a points-based household registration (hukou) system and residential permit to solicit public opinions.

积水路段 waterlogged road section
北京遭遇近年来罕见的暴雨，因此市中心13个积水路段暂时禁止车辆通行。
Thirteen waterlogged road sections in downtown Beijing had been temporarily closed to traffic, as the capital was hit by heavy rainfall rarely seen in years.

积习难改 Old habits die hard.
积习难改。他抽了30年的烟，恐怕一下子戒不掉。
Old habits die hard. He's been smoking for 30 years, I'm afraid he cannot give it

up immediately.

积压产品 inventory surplus; overstocked commodity (inventory)
他刚接手这个厂时，厂里有员工12000人，积压产品和债务很多。
When he first took over the factory, it had a staff of 12,000 people, with huge inventory surpluses and mounting debts.

积压航班 flight backlog
周二，欧洲很多航班在停飞数天后首度飞上蓝天，但交通混乱状况远未结束：伦敦机场仍然关闭，积压航班数量非常大且呈上升趋势。
Many European flights took to the skies Tuesday for the first time in days but the travel chaos was far from over: London's airports remained shut; a massive flight backlog was growing.

基本药物 essential medicine
本月，卫生部所列出的基本药物中，近半数药物的零售价将下调12%。
Retail prices of almost half of the drugs on the Ministry of Health's essential medicines list will be slashed by 12 percent this month.

基层代表 grassroots delegates
更多基层代表参加了中国共产党第十九次全国代表大会。
The 19th National Congress of Communist Party of China featured more grassroots delegates.

基层民主 democracy at the grassroots level; grassroots democracy
扩大基层民主是发展社会主义民主的基础。
Extending democracy at the grassroots level is the groundwork for developing socialist democracy.

基层社区 grassroots community
国务院鼓励大学生拓宽就业渠道，考虑去基层社区、中西部地区以及中小企业就业，或自主创业。
The State Council encouraged college students to broaden their job searches and consider working in grassroots communities, the central and western parts of China or small and medium-sized enterprises, or start their own businesses.

基层选举 grassroots election
每5年举行一次的基层选举，是我国选举过程中最基层、也是唯一进行直接选举的层面。

The grassroots election, held every five years, is the lowest and only level of China's electoral process where direct elections are allowed.

基层组织 grassroots organization
我们将健全基层自治组织和民主管理制度，完善公开事务制度。
We will improve grassroots self-governing organizations, their democratic management system and the system of information release.

基础产业 main industry
自19世纪初期第一批美国人穿越密西西比河到此定居以来，农业一直是爱荷华州的基础产业。
Agriculture has been Iowa's main industry since the state's first settlers crossed the Mississippi River in the early 1800s.

基础设施 infrastructure
今后5~10年，中国在西部基础设施建设和环境保护方面会有重大突破。
China will make major breakthroughs in infrastructure construction and environmental protection in its vast western areas in the next five to ten years.

基础四国 BASIC countries
"基础四国"（即巴西、南非、印度和中国）呼吁按照公平、共同但有区别的责任以及各自能力的原则达成巴黎气候协议。
BASIC countries, namely Brazil, South Africa, India and China, called for a Paris climate agreement in accordance with the principles of equity and common but differentiated responsibilities and respective capabilities.

基尼系数 Gini coefficient; Gini index
城乡区域收入分配差距持续缩小，中等收入群体持续扩大，基尼系数下降，每年新增城镇就业已连续4年保持1300万人以上。
Income gaps between urban and rural areas and between different regions have been narrowing, middle-income group expanding, and Gini coefficient dropping. More than 13 million new urban jobs have been created every year for four consecutive years.

基因工程 genetic engineering
中国的基因工程产业开始于20世纪80年代后期，比其他一些国家晚了20年。
China's genetic engineering industry didn't get started until the late 1980s, two decades later than it did in some other countries.

基因库 gene bank
基因库到年底将建成并投入运行。
The gene bank will be up and running by the end of the year.

基因突变 genetic mutation
大约1%的白种人因基因突变，体内不存在趋化因子受体。因此，艾滋病毒（HIV）无法侵入这些人的细胞。
The AIDS virus, or HIV, is not able to enter the cells of about 1 percent of Caucasians, who do not have chemokine receptors due to genetic mutation.

基准利率 benchmark rate
中国工商银行上海各支行已取消首套房贷利率8.5折优惠政策，恢复执行首贷基准利率。
ICBC's Shanghai outlets have stopped issuing mortgage loans with 15% discounts and have reverted to benchmark rates for first-time home purchasers.

缉毒队 narcotics squad
缉毒队需要更多的人手和财力支持。
The narcotics squad needs more men and money.

激光导航 laser navigation
激光导航是对我们综合配件系列的极大加强。
Laser navigation is a powerful addition to our line of integrated accessories.

激励和制约体系 system of incentives and disincentives
对现代企业来说，建立健全激励和制约机制很重要。
For a modern enterprise, establishing and perfecting a system of incentives and disincentives is important.

激烈竞争 cut-throat competition; fierce competition
激烈的竞争导致工人大量失业，市场萎缩。
The consequence of cut-throat competition is massive unemployment and market shrinkage.

吉利钱 lucky money
美国财政部铸印局局长奥利雅尔宣布发售该局2018年狗年"吉利钱"，以庆祝即将到来的中国农历狗年。
Leonard Olijar, director of the US Bureau of Engraving and Printing, announced the release of the bureau's lucky money of the Year of the Dog 2018 to celebrate

the upcoming Chinese Lunar Year of the Dog.

极地旅游 trips to the polar regions
极地旅游近年来在中国呈现出了爆发式的增长。
Trips to the polar regions have witnessed explosive growth in China in the past few years.

极端天气 extreme weather
民政部周四表示,我国南方五省本周遭遇极端天气,已导致至少24人死亡、4人失踪。
At least 24 people have died and four are missing after extreme weather hit five provinces in South China this week, the Ministry of Civil Affairs said on Thursday.

极限运动 extreme sports; X-sports
挑战、奋斗、成功,甚至放弃都是极限运动的一部分。
The challenges, the struggles, the successes, and even the giving up are all a part of extreme sports.

即时退税 real-time tax refund
在米兰马尔彭萨机场、慕尼黑机场和赫尔辛基机场这3个机场,我国消费者现在可在手机上享受即时退税服务,为他们节省退税到卡所需的数周等待时间。
Chinese shoppers can now enjoy a real-time tax refund service via their mobile phones at three airports: Milan Malpensa, Munich and Helsinki, saving them weeks of waiting time if receiving refund by card.

即席讲话 make an impromptu speech; speak impromptu; off-the-cuff remarks
总统在晚会上发表了即席讲话。
The President made an impromptu speech at the party.

即印相片(拍立得)instant photo
他有一个别致的拍立得相机。
He has a fancy camera that takes instant photos.

急功近利 be eager for instant success and quick profits
许多企业急功近利,没有长远的发展规划。
Many enterprises are so eager for instant success and quick profits that they don't even have a long-term development plan.

集福卡 lucky card collection
电商巨头阿里巴巴集团公布其红包战略,并推出"集福卡"活动为抢红包游戏增添乐趣。
E-commerce giant Alibaba Group unveiled its hongbao strategy and came up with a "lucky card collection" campaign to spice up the game.

集思广益 draw on collective wisdom of the people
通过集思广益,董事长决定将建新厂的计划推迟一年。
Drawing on the collective wisdom of the people, the president decided to postpone plans for setting up a new plant for a year.

集体承包 be contracted to collectives; collective contract
国有土地、山地、草地、荒地、滩涂、水面,都可以承包给个人或者集体作为农业生产之用。
Land, mountains, grassland, barren land, sand and mud banks, and water surfaces owned by the State may be contracted to individuals or collectives for agricultural production.

集体合同 collective contract
中华全国总工会周四表示,集体合同作为工人和雇主之间有效协商机制的一部分,有助于缓解最近中国部分地区出现的劳资纠纷。
Collective contracts as part of an effective negotiation mechanism between workers and employers will help mitigate labor unrests that have hit parts of the country recently, the All China Federation of Trade Unions (ACFTU) said on Thursday.

集体婚礼 group wedding ceremony
集体婚礼将在周日举行。
The group wedding ceremony will be held on Sunday.

集体建设用地 collectively owned land parcels
国土部、住建部鼓励全国各大城市利用集体建设用地建设租赁住房,这是增加住房租赁市场供应的又一项举措。
Land and housing authorities are encouraging large cities across China to set up housing projects for tenants using collectively owned land parcels, in one more measure to increase supplies for the residential leasing market.

集体经济 collective economy
乡镇企业是集体经济的一种形式。
The township enterprise is a form of collective economy.

集体所有用地 collectively owned land
有关国有土地上房屋征收与补偿条例生效后,立法部门正忙于修订土地管理法,以防止农村集体所有用地上的强制拆迁。
Legislators are busy revising the Land Administration Law to curb forced demolitions on "collectively owned" rural land after an updated housing demolition regulation on State-owned property took effect.

集体所有制 collective ownership
一夜之间涌现出了大批私有制和集体所有制采矿企业。
Many mining enterprises under private and collective ownership mushroomed overnight.

集团消费 institutional spending
他们在缩减集团消费方面提出了一些新建议。
New measures have been suggested for curbing institutional spending.

集中供暖 central heating
如果平均气温连续5天低于5℃,或遭遇暴雪、强风天气,北京市就将于今冬提前启动集中供暖。
Beijing's central heating is likely to be switched on early this winter, when the average temperature plunges below 5℃ for five consecutive days or when a heavy snowfall or high wind hits the city.

集装箱公寓 container apartment
这种18平方米的"集装箱公寓"一天的租金是8元,这种集装箱还可改造成移动厕所、厨房、办公室、车库等。
The daily rent for this 18-square-meter container apartment is eight yuan. They can also be refitted as mobile restrooms, kitchens, offices and garages.

集装箱运输船 container freighter
这艘6万吨级集装箱运输船属于世界大船之一。
The 60,000-ton container freighter is among the largest in the world.

集资 raise money; raise funds
自8月以来,全国各地学生一直在为水灾灾民集资捐款。
Since August, students across the country have been raising money for flood victims.

挤兑 bank run
2月19日,两位高层领导人间的分歧导致挤兑事件,群众提取银行金额达75亿美元。

On February 19, the dispute between the two senior leaders led to a bank run of $7.5 billion.

计划单列市 city with independent budgetary statuses
中国允许外资进入计划单列市，股权最高限制是65%。
China allows foreign funds to flow into cities with independent budgetary statuses, with the maximum stock share set at 65 percent.

计划外投资 off-plan investment
有了这笔计划外投资，这家公司可以开展一项新业务。
The company will start a new business with the off-plan investment.

计价器 meter
我告诉出租车司机，我进去拿行李时他不用关计价器。
I told the taxi driver to leave the meter running while I ran in to pick up my luggage.

计时工资 pay by the hour
这家企业同意实行计时工资制，员工们因此感到高兴。
To the delight of employees, this company has agreed to pay them by the hour.

计算机集成制造系统 computer integrated manufacturing system (CIMS)
联想集团的计算机集成制造系统为亚洲一流。
Legend Group's computer integrated manufacturing system is among the best in Asia.

记过 get a demerit
在上周比赛中参与斗殴的3名球员都受到记过处分。
All three players got a demerit for fighting on the pitch last week.

记名投票 disclosed ballot
记名投票意味着投票人必须在选票上被选举人名字的旁边写下自己的名字。
Disclosed ballot means that the voter's name shall be written down on the ballot beside the one who stands for election.

记者席 press box
届时记者席将配备可以上网的电脑。
By then, every press box will be equipped with a computer connected to the internet.

纪念封 commemorative envelope
中国为纪念同苏里南建交30周年发行了一套纪念封。

A commemorative envelope was issued celebrating the establishment of diplomatic relations with Suriname thirty years ago.

纪念演唱会 tribute concert
35个迈克尔·杰克逊粉丝俱乐部联合起来要求取消杰克逊纪念演唱会，称将于10月举办的这场演唱会注定会失败。
A group of 35 Michael Jackson fan clubs have joined forces to lobby for the cancellation of a Michael Jackson tribute concert, saying the October event is "doomed to fail".

纪念仪式 memorial service
人们在主体育馆举行了一个纪念仪式，到场的有8万名观众。
A memorial service was held at the main stadium in front of an audience of 80,000.

纪念邮票 commemorative stamp
中国邮政发行中国共产党第十九次全国代表大会纪念邮票一套2枚，小型张1枚。
China Post issued a set of commemorative stamps marking the 19th National Congress of the Communist Party of China. The set consists of two stamps and a stamp sheetlet.

纪实文学 reportage
他们指控这家报纸有种族偏见，刊载了那篇反映20世纪70年代移民生活的纪实文学。
They accused the paper of racial bias in running the reportage on immigration in the 1970s.

纪委 disciplinary inspection commission
大家猜测他有麻烦了，因为纪委人员找他谈了话。
People assume he is in trouble because he has been summoned for an interview with members of the disciplinary inspection commission.

技能交换 skill trading
赶集网发言人王京（音）介绍称，该网站北京站点每天发布的"技能交换"新帖约有50条。
According to Wang Jing, a spokeswoman for ganji.com, the site sees about 50 new posts daily for "skill trading" in Beijing.

技术成果商品化 commercialization of technological achievements
高科技企业一定要加速技术成果商品化。
High-tech enterprises must speed up the commercialization of technological achievements.

技术创新 technological innovation
中国信息高速公路的发展将以技术创新为龙头。
Technological innovation will play a key role in China's information superhighway development.

技术改造 technological upgrade; technological upgrading
为了推进技术改造,企业再次向政府伸手要钱。
Enterprises again asked the government for money to support their technological upgrading effort.

技术工人;技工 skilled laborer
技术工人少得可怜。
Skilled laborers are hard to come by.

技术密集产品 technology-intensive product
1~11月期间,技术密集产品的出口占总出口量的59%。
Technology-intensive product exports accounted for 59 percent of total exports from January to November.

技术下乡 give farmers tips on farming techniques
他们通过提供免费咨询服务达到技术下乡的目的。
They gave farmers tips on farming techniques through free consulting services.

技术移民 skill immigration
过去几年中,技术移民在移民业务中占很大比例。
In previous years, skill immigration took up a large portion of their business.

技术转让 technology transfer
德国是欧洲对华技术转让最多的国家,截至2017年5月,中国从德国引进技术合同金额累计768.2亿美元。
Germany ranks the top among European countries in terms of technology transfer to China. As of May 2017, China signed with Germany a total of 76.82 billion dollars worth of technology transfer contracts.

季节工 seasonal worker
新疆棉区今年大丰收,估计需要100万名季节工采摘棉花。
Cotton fields in Xinjiang are having a good harvest this year, and may need a million seasonal workers to pick cotton.

季节性调价 seasonal price adjustment
每年秋天空调的降价属于季节性调价。
The drop in air conditioner prices that comes every autumn is a seasonal price adjustment.

既成事实 fait accompli
可是他毕竟对事故做了善后处理,那是既成事实,无法更改。
His handling of the aftermath of the incident produced a fait accompli that could not be undone.

既得利益集团 vested interest group
研究人员和立法人士均表示,为了践行(包容性增长)这一理念,就需要限制既得利益集团,并促成各项法律的有效实施。
To implement the concept of inclusive growth will require restricting vested interest groups and effective law enforcement, researchers and legislators said.

寄售 commission sale; consignment sale
大到全部收藏品,小到单个纪念币,我们均为您提供寄售服务。
We offer a commission sale for people who wish to buy entire collections or single coins.

寄宿家庭 home stay
寄宿家庭可以让你居住在外国人家中感受外国文化。
A home stay provides the opportunity to experience foreign culture while living in a foreign home.

加班费 overtime pay
一项网络调查显示,中秋十一长假期间加班的很多员工都没有拿到加班费。
Many employees who worked over the Mid-Autumn Festival and National Day holiday failed to receive their overtime pay, an online survey has found.

加大污染治理力度 strengthen pollution control
政府必须加大污染治理的力度。
The government must strengthen pollution control.

加价功能 price-hiking function
上海市交通运输委员会紧急约谈叫车服务公司滴滴出行,敦促其平台在两天内撤销加价功能。

Shanghai Municipal Transportation Commission held an urgent meeting with ride-hailing company Didi Chuxing, urging its platform to eliminate the price-hiking function within two days.

加密 encrypt
无线硬件开发商可以用该软件为他们的产品加密。
This software enables wireless hardware developers to encrypt their products.

加名税 name-adding tax
在财政部、国家税务总局联合发布通知后,地方税务机关必须退还已征收的加名税。
Following the joint regulation by the Ministry of Finance and the State Administration of Taxation, the name-adding taxes imposed by local tax authorities should be refunded.

加塞儿 cut lines; cut the line
加塞儿的人不受欢迎。
People who cut lines are frowned upon.

加息 rate hike
美国联邦储备局将基准利率上调了25个基点,这是美联储2016年唯一一次加息。
The US Federal Reserve raised benchmark interest rate by 25 basis points, the only rate hike in 2016.

加息周期 interest rate hike cycle
专家表示,除了最近出台的措施外,也不排除会提高利率。我们已经进入加息周期。
Despite the latest move, interest rate hikes cannot be ruled out, said an expert. We have entered an interest rate hike cycle.

家谱 family tree; genealogy
新发现的哺乳动物化石是目前所知中生代时期最小的动物化石,代表了哺乳动物家谱中一个新的分支。
The newly discovered mammal fossil is the smallest in size known from the Mesozoic Era, and represents a new branch on the mammalian family tree.

家庭暴力 domestic violence; family violence; domestic abuse
人们普遍认为伴侣间施虐是"个人私事",这正是反家庭暴力运动面临的巨大挑战之一。
One of the greatest challenges facing the domestic violence movement is the widespread perception that spousal abuse is a "private matter".

家庭暴力限制令 domestic violence restraining order
艾梅伯·希尔德申请对强尼·德普发出家庭暴力限制令。
Amber Heard filed for a domestic violence restraining order against Johnny Depp.

家庭财富 household wealth
瑞信发布的报告称,按照以往的发展速度,到2015年,中国的家庭财富总量将不止翻番到35万亿美元。
China's household wealth is set to more than double to $35 trillion by 2015 if the country maintains its historic growth rates, according to a report by Credit Suisse.

家庭财务 household financing
汇丰银行近日发布的一项全球调查显示,63%的中国内地女性受访者表示她们是家庭财务的决策者,而男性受访者只有58%做出相同的回答。
Sixty-three percent of female respondents on the Chinese mainland said they were in charge of household financing, while only 58 percent of male respondents said so, according to a latest global survey by HSBC.

家庭出身 family background
他的犯罪与家庭出身没有任何联系。
His criminal act has nothing to do with his family background.

家庭寄养 family foster care
尽管民政部在2003年颁布了鼓励家庭寄养儿童的管理暂行办法,但家庭收养在中国仍处于起步阶段,人们通常会想到把孤儿送进孤儿院。
Although the Ministry of Civil Affairs issued a regulation to encourage families to take in foster children in 2003, family foster care is still new in China, where the tradition of the orphanage has been the rule.

家用电器 household electrical appliance
由于有利可图,国内家用电器制造商开始投入更多资源生产更多的空调。
Since air conditioner manufacturing has been profitable, many domestic household electrical appliance manufacturers have been attracted to devote more resources to make more air conditioners.

家长作风 play the authoritarian parent
每次我要求和谁外出时,妈妈就开始耍家长作风,命令我几点之前必须回家。
Whenever I asked to go out with someone, my mother would play the authoritarian parent, ordering me to be back home by a certain hour.

家政服务人员 domestic helper
（香港人力代理）总会称，香港大约需要10万名家政服务人员，随着香港人口的老龄化，5年后这一缺口可能会扩大至50万。
Hong Kong is in need of about 100,000 domestic helpers, and the gap will likely increase to 500,000 in five years with the graying of its population, the chamber said.

家政服务业 home services industry
我国政府日前公布了在全国范围内促进家政服务业发展的指导方针。
The Chinese government announced guidelines designed to boost the development of the home services industry across the country.

家族企业 family firm
无论放到哪里，这个家族企业都称得上是最好的。
It is the best family firm you'll see anywhere.

家族式管理 family-run management
以勤奋和强抗压能力著称的中国企业家应该研究一下西方管理学了，因为他们的公司正处于扩大时期，旧的家族式管理模式不再适应目前以市场为导向的商业模式。
It is time for Chinese entrepreneurs, who are well known for their diligence and ability to handle pressure, to study western management because their companies are growing larger and the old family-run management style is no longer suitable for the market-oriented business model.

夹心层 sandwich class
"夹心层"既达不到申请廉价住房的标准，又买不起商品房。
Sandwich class does not meet the requirements for budget homes, nor can they afford commercial housing.

甲醇汽车 methanol-fueled car
中国工信部决定从本月开始在3个省级地区开展甲醇汽车试点工作，这标志着中国作为世界第二大经济体对推动绿色经济增长的决心。
China's industrial authority said that it will introduce trials for methanol-fueled cars in three provincial level regions starting this month, signaling the world's second largest economy's resolution to boost greener economic growth.

甲骨文 inscriptions on oracle bones
甲骨文是中国现存最早的书写形式之一。

Inscriptions on oracle bones represent one of the earliest forms of writing in China.

假唱 lip-synch
对她假唱的指责始于她去年的巡回演出。
Lip-synching accusations began with her concert tour last year.

假钞 counterfeit note; counterfeit money
20美元的假钞是最常见的，不过100美元的假钞也越来越多。
The most common counterfeit note is the $20 bill, but more and more counterfeiters are passing $100 lookalikes.

假发票 fake invoice
中国公安部门将于周三起开展为期30天的行动，追捕假发票诈骗案件的犯罪嫌疑人。
China's police departments will launch a 30-day campaign starting Wednesday to hunt down fugitives who are suspected of having committed a crime known as fake invoice fraud.

假后综合征 post-holiday syndrome
一想到又要回到单调的上班生活，许多人都会患上假后综合征。
With the gloomy prospect of returning to work, many people could suffer post-holiday syndrome.

假结婚 bogus marriage
加拿大官员在识别假文件和假结婚案例时越来越熟练了。
Canadian officials are becoming more skilled at spotting fake documents and bogus marriages.

假冒产品 counterfeit product
市长承诺将坚决打击假冒产品。
The mayor has vowed to crack down on counterfeit products.

假日出游 holiday getaway
住在北京的外籍人士开始加入创纪录的假日出游大军。
Expats living in Beijing are joining the record number of Chinese people who will be making the great holiday getaway.

假释 get/be released on parole
对于女犯来说，提请医疗假释得到批准要相对容易些。
It is relatively easy for women prisoners to get released on parole for medical

treatment.

假摔 diving/simulation（一个球员为了令对方球员得到黄牌、红牌或为了博取任意球和点球而假装受伤倒地，此动作近似跳水，故英文称为diving）

虽然很多人对假摔行为嗤之以鼻，但它其实也是足球比赛的一部分。

As much as it may be unappealing to many, diving is just a part of the game of soccer.

价格波动 price fluctuation

国际市场的石油价格波动受诸多因素影响。

Price fluctuations in the international oil market are influenced by a number of factors.

价格操纵 price manipulation; price rigging

证监会正在调查一起股票价格操纵案。

The China Securities Regulatory Commission is investigating possible stock price manipulations.

价格反弹 price rebound

西瓜价格的反弹让瓜农看到了一线希望。

The price rebound of watermelons has given farmers a ray of hope.

价格改革 pricing reform

北京和河北在其价格改革实施意见中提出"到2020年竞争性领域和环节价格全部放开"。

According to their pricing reform plans, Beijing and Hebei will lift the cities' price controls in competitive sectors by 2020.

价格欺诈 price cheating; price gouging

2011年初，国家发改委官员表示，在他们调查的所有城市中，家乐福都涉嫌价格欺诈。

In early 2011, an official at NDRC, said that in all the cities they investigated, Carrefour stores were suspected of price cheating.

价格脱离价值 divergence between price and value

在股市上，股票价格出奇高涨是司空见惯的事。这种情况被称为股票的价格脱离了其价值。

In the stock market, it's quite common to see exorbitantly high prices for some stocks. It's called a divergence between price and value.

价格违法行为 price violation
国务院周一宣布将修改相关处罚规定，进一步打击价格违法行为，以应对通货膨胀。
The State Council, China's cabinet, said Monday it will revise penalties to further crack down on price violations in order to tackle inflation.

价格战 price war
最近正在上演的电商价格战或许可以暂时促进销量，但同时也引发消费者担忧，恐会因此导致市场混乱。
An ongoing price war between Chinese online retailers may have temporarily spiked sales, but it has also triggered concerns among consumers over potential market disruptions.

价格震荡 price gyration
石油和天然气供应中断可能会加剧能源价格震荡。
Disruptions to oil and gas supplies may add to energy price gyrations.

驾车过失杀人 vehicular manslaughter
人民法院周日早上发表声明称，这个年轻人对其酒后驾驶和驾车过失杀人罪供认不讳。
The young man pled guilty to drunk driving and vehicular manslaughter, the People's Court said in a statement Sunday morning.

驾驶证互认换领 driving license reciprocity
驾驶证互认换领对推进经济合作、文化交流、人员往来具有重要意义。
Driving license reciprocity is of great significance in promoting economic cooperation, cultural and personnel exchanges.

驾驶证使用规定 regulations on driving licenses
公安部修订的驾驶证使用规定加强了对司机闯红灯的处罚力度，同时新司机发生严重事故的也将对发证机关进行处罚。
The Ministry of Public Security's amended regulations on driving licenses increase the penalties for motorists who run red lights, as well as authorities who issue licenses to new drivers who cause serious accidents.

架空 make someone a figurehead; deprive someone of his authority while keeping him in office
感到自己开始被架空，他就辞职了。
He resigned when he felt he was beginning to be made a figurehead.

歼-20隐形战机 J-20 stealth fighter
两架歼-20隐形战机在广东珠海航展上进行了60秒的飞行表演。
Two of J-20 stealth fighters performed a 60-second flypast at the Zhuhai air show in Guangdong province.

间接选举 indirect election
间接选举杜绝了选举中的不正之风,至少目前如此。
Indirect elections put an end to foul play, at least for now.

监督部门 watchdog organization; supervisory committee
价格调整须经过行业监督部门批准。
Any price change must be approved by the industry's watchdog organization.

监护权 custodial care (of a child)
果然,法院把男孩的监护权判给了母亲。
As expected, the court gave custodial care of the boy to the mother.

检测试剂 test reagent
中国疾控中心周三表示,H7N9禽流感检测试剂已发放至全国各个流感监测点。
Test reagents for the H7N9 avian influenza virus have been distributed to all flu monitoring sites across the country, China's center for disease control said on Wednesday.

检察机关 procuratorial organ
检察机关也免不了受到腐败指控。
Procuratorial organs have not been free from corruption allegations either.

减肥药 diet pill; slimming drug
因担心会增加心脏病的风险,15种含有西布曲明的减肥药已经在全国范围内被召回。
Fifteen weight-loss products containing the drug sibutramine have been recalled across the country over concern that the diet pills could lead to an increased risk of heart disease.

减负 alleviate someone's burden
大多数学校支持少留作业,给学生减负。
Most schools support less homework for students to alleviate their burdens.

减排 emission reduction
中国所做的碳减排承诺是科学和实际的。

China's commitment on carbon emission reduction is scientific and practical.

减速玻璃 decelerating glass
汽车装有减速玻璃窗，能预防乘客晕车。
The car is equipped with decelerating glass windows that keep passengers from getting carsick.

减刑 have one's sentence commuted
听到儿子的刑期由两年减为一年的消息，母亲不由喜极而泣。
Overwhelmed with happiness after learning that her son had had his two-year sentence commuted to 12 months, the mother cried.

减刑和假释 commutation of sentences and parole
最高人民法院发布了有关办理减刑和假释的法律规定，列出具体规定以防止不公正的减刑行为。
The top court has issued a revision to the regulation on seeking commutation of sentences and parole, specifying the circumstances to prevent unjust reduction of prison time.

减员 downsize; cut payroll
减员一直是政府机关为提高效率而采取的一项措施。
Downsizing has been one of the measures taken by government institutions to improve efficiency.

减员增效 downsize for efficiency; cut payroll to improve efficiency

剪彩 cut the ribbon
公司的总经理和市长一起为这次活动正式开始剪了彩。
General Manager of the company, together with the mayor, cut the ribbon to officially open the event.

见不得人的勾当；私底下交易 under-the-table deal
他为人正派，从不干见不得人的勾当。
He is a man of integrity. He never gets involved in any under-the-table deal.

建立外交关系（建交）establishment of diplomatic relations
中国外交部长王毅在北京与巴拿马副总统兼外长德圣马洛举行会谈。会谈后，两国外长签署了两国建立外交关系的联合公报。
Chinese Foreign Minister Wang Yi held a meeting in Beijing with Isabel de Saint Malo, Panama's vice president and foreign minister, and they signed a joint

communique on the establishment of diplomatic relations.

建设公债 public bonds for construction
他建议发行建设公债，以加快中国西部道路的建设。
He proposed to issue public bonds for construction to accelerate road building in China's western areas.

建设社会主义法治国家 build a socialist country under the rule of law

建设社会主义物质文明和精神文明 promote socialist material progress and cultural advancement

建设社会主义新农村 build a new countryside with socialist characteristics; build the socialist new countryside

建设性战略伙伴关系 constructive, strategic partnership
中国希望同美国建立建设性战略伙伴关系。
China seeks a constructive, strategic partnership with the United States.

建设有中国特色的社会主义 build socialism with Chinese characteristics
全面建设小康社会，加快推进社会主义现代化，为开创中国特色社会主义事业新局面而奋斗。
We will build a well-off society in an all-round way, speed up socialist modernization and work hard to create a new situation in building socialism with Chinese characteristics.

建议零售价 suggested retail price
产品的建议零售价可能随进口税的改变而变化。
Suggested retail prices are subject to changes caused by varying import duties.

建筑面积 floor space
这些建筑总面积22万平方米，周围的绿地面积有3万平方米。
The buildings have a total floor space of 220,000 square meters, with green areas totaling 30,000 square meters.

健康带菌者 healthy carrier
除了19个确诊病例外，还有一名学生被诊断为"健康带菌者"，也就是被感染了霍乱病毒但是却没有表现出症状。但是，"健康带菌者"可以把病毒传染给他人。
In addition to the 19 confirmed cases, one student was diagnosed as a "healthy carrier", or a person who was infected with the cholera bacteria but displays no

symptoms. However, "healthy carriers" can transmit the bacteria to others.

健康证 health certificate
在与对乙肝病毒携带者的歧视斗争了2年之后，一位大学毕业生终于拿到了允许他从事食品行业的健康证。
A university graduate who fought discrimination against Hepatitis B virus (HBV) carriers for two years has received a health certificate allowing him to be employed in the food industry.

健康指标 health index
国务院发布的《"健康中国2030"规划纲要》提出，我国主要健康指标应接近高收入国家相关指标。
The State Council issued an outline of the country's 2030 health plan, which indicates that China's major health indexes should be similar to those in high income countries.

健走 fast walking
社交网络应用QQ发布的调查显示，健走因低门槛、低成本成为2016年中国人最常进行的运动。
A survey by social networking app QQ has unveiled that fast walking topped all exercise activities as the most popular exercise in China in 2016 due to its accessibility and low cost.

渐进式延迟退休年龄 progressively raise the retirement age
"十三五"规划（2016—2020年）提出渐进式延迟退休年龄，以缓解国家的养老金压力和劳动力短缺。
The 13th Five-Year Plan (2016-20) proposes progressively raising the retirement age to help address the country's pension pressure and labor shortage.

"僵尸"电脑 "zombie" computer
入侵者可激活Conficker蠕虫病毒等恶意代码来窃取数据，或使被感染的电脑受黑客控制，进而产生大量的"僵尸"电脑以用于犯罪。
Malicious code such as Conficker can be triggered to steal data or turn control of infected computers over to hackers amassing "zombie" computers for criminal ends.

"僵尸粉" zombies
"僵尸粉"是指那些可以在网上只花4元就能买1000个的虚假粉丝。
"Zombies" are artificial followers that can be bought and sold online for as little

as 4 yuan a thousand.

"僵尸企业" zombie company
我国约有7.51%的工业企业是"僵尸企业",钢铁行业的"僵尸企业"比例最高。
Around 7.51 percent of China's industrial businesses are "zombie companies" and it is the steel sector that has the highest proportion of such companies.

"僵尸"手机 "zombie" phone
我们可以把染了病毒的手机比作"僵尸"手机,它会偷偷向你的朋友和同事发送带有病毒链接的信息,然后把他们的手机都变成"僵尸"手机。之后,这些手机又会发展出更多的"僵尸"手机。
We can compare an infected cell phone to a "zombie" phone. It will secretly send virus-linked text messages to your friends and colleagues and turn their phones into "zombies", which will later create more "zombie" phones.

讲诚信,反欺诈 honor credibility and no cheating
"讲诚信、反欺诈"将成为今年房地产行业的口号。
"Honor credibility and no cheating" will be the motto for the real estate industry this year.

讲排场;摆阔气 extravagance
暴发户的常见特征是讲排场、摆阔气。
Extravagance is often a trait of the nouveau riches.

讲义气 loyal; faithful to friends
不管怎样,那家伙还算够义气,不像那帮在他背后捅刀子的人。
For all his sins, the guy is at least loyal, unlike those who stabbed him in the back.

降杠杆 deleveraging
企业降杠杆被列为供给侧结构性改革的五大任务之一。
Corporate deleveraging has been listed as one of the five major tasks of supply-side structural reform.

降税 tariff cut
我国消费者迎来了澳大利亚和韩国进口商品的新一轮降税。
Chinese consumers welcomed a new round of tariff cuts on imported products from Australia and South Korea.

降速门 slowdown drama
苹果公司承认,该公司确实基于电池性能放缓了iPhone的速度。在遭到多起诉讼和外国政府的调查之后,苹果公司就"降速门"发布道歉信。
Apple admitted that it was indeed slowing down iPhones based on the performance of their batteries. After multiple lawsuits and investigations by foreign governments followed, Apple published a letter of apology for the slowdown drama.

降息 reduction of interest rate
美国银行今年的第五次降息将会刺激经济的复苏。
The reduction of interest rates by US banks for the fifth time is expected to give an impetus to its economic recovery.

交叉感染 transmission of viruses from patient to patient
改善医院的空气质量对于防止病人间病毒交叉感染十分重要。
It is very important to prevent the transmission of viruses from patient to patient by improving the air quality in hospitals.

交叉销售 cross sale
在与中国银行家的座谈会上,弗里曼说他相信交叉销售是提高银行利润的核心驱动力,交叉销售是指向现有客户推销额外的产品及服务的销售方式。
Freeman said during a roundtable discussion with Chinese bankers that he believes cross sale—selling additional products or services to established customers—could be a core driver in increasing banks' profits.

交换意见 compare notes
我们想就白天谈判的情况交换一下意见。
We'd like to compare notes on what we've discussed during the day.

交会对接 dock with; rendezvous and docking; space docking
神舟十号飞船计划将于周四中午左右与天宫一号对接,天宫一号是在2011年发射升空的目标飞行器兼太空飞行器。
The Shenzhou X spacecraft is scheduled to dock with the Tiangong-1, a target orbiter and space module sent to space in 2011, around noon on Thursday.

交火 exchange of fire
第一轮交火后,一位韩国国防部新闻发言人说:"目前形势稳定。我方回击后,朝方没有进一步回应。我们依然保持警戒。"
After the initial exchange of fire, an ROK Defense Ministry spokesman said, "The situation is now stable. After we fired back, there was no further response from the DPRK. We are still on alert."

交流学者 exchange scholar
I-F-S 国际文化交流学院的主要培训对象是各国大使馆人员和交流学者。
I-F-S-Studies International mainly provides training for staff in foreign embassies and for exchange scholars.

交通补助 travel allowance
我们每天给您200元,其中包括交通补助。
We give you 200 yuan per day, travel allowance included.

交通干线 traffic artery
长安街就是横穿北京心脏地带天安门广场的交通干线。
Chang'an Avenue is the main traffic artery running through Tian'anmen Square in the heart of Beijing.

交通违法人员 traffic violators
一份官方文件指出,将通过媒体平台公开公示交通违法人员的姓名,以提高安全意识。
The names of traffic violators will be made public via media outlets to increase awareness of safety, according to an official statement.

交通文明 road civility
北京市在新闻发布会上公布了常见的"十大交通陋习",希望能够提高市民的"交通文明"意识。
Beijing released top 10 of commonly seen bad driving habits at a press conference in the hope of raising awareness of "road civility".

交通协管员 traffic warden
交通协管员有责任执行涉及非法停车的相关法规。
Traffic wardens are responsible for enforcing the law relating to illegal parking.

交通指数 Traffic Performance Index
交通指数用0到10的数字来衡量交通拥堵程度,0为通畅,10为最严重。
Traffic Performance Index measures congestion on a scale of zero(smooth)to 10(snarled).

交易费 transaction fee
在国内股市持续低迷后,我国两大证券交易所将交易费调降30%左右。
China's two major stock exchanges lowered their transaction fees by around 30

percent after a continued slump in the country's stock market.

交易税费转嫁 shift the tax increase to the buyer
刘女士说:"卖家当然会把税费转嫁给买方,这会把房价推向新高。"

"Sellers will definitely shift the tax increase to the buyer, which will push the home price to a new high," said Ms. Liu.

浇冷水 throw cold water on
她抗议道:"我来找你是征求意见的,不是让你给我浇冷水的。"

"I didn't come to get cold water thrown on me," she protested. "I came to you for advice."

胶囊公寓 capsule apartment
他正在拍卖其胶囊公寓的5年专利使用权。这种公寓是他毕生的成就,自去年4月以来就得到了国际媒体的关注。

He is auctioning a five-year patent to his life's work—the capsule apartments that have been capturing the international media attention since last April.

铰接式公共汽车 articulated bus
世界最长铰接式公共汽车在巴西首次亮相。这种公共汽车可容纳250名乘客,车身长28米,宽2.6米,采用的燃料是从大豆中提取的生物柴油。

The world's longest articulated bus makes debut in Brazil. The bus has a capacity of 250 passengers, is 28 meters long, 2.6 meters wide, and powered with biodiesel made from soybeans.

脚踩两只船 sit on the fence
更差劲的是脚踩两只船,不向着任何一方说话,也不反对任何一方。

Worse still are those who sit on the fence and refrain from speaking for or against either party.

脚踏实地 be down to earth
有些人爱表决心唱高调,而其他人则脚踏实地,仅仅表示会按时完成任务。

Some were full of high sounding vows while others sounded more down to earth, saying simply they would get the job done on time.

叫座 be a big box office draw; be a big draw at the box office
《超人归来》有望成为今年暑期又一部叫座的影片。

Superman Returns promises to be another big box office draw this summer.

教书育人 impart knowledge and educate people
教书育人是教师义不容辞的职责。
It is the sworn duty of teachers to impart knowledge and educate people.

教育规划纲要 education plan
国家发布的未来十年教育规划纲要提到的中国教育体制改革目标包括了普及学前教育和承诺扫除文盲两项工作。
Universal preschool education and a pledge to eliminate illiteracy are among the reforms of China's education system published in the national education plan for the next decade.

教育体制 education system
教育体制问题是中国教育发展过程中的一个困扰。
Education system is a problem that plagues China's development of education.

阶梯电价 tiered pricing for electricity
国务院周三宣布,中国会调整天然气价格机制,推行居民用电阶梯价格,以实现节能减排的目标。
China will adjust the natural gas pricing mechanism and push forward tiered pricing for household electricity, as part of its efforts to save energy and cut emissions, the State Council said Wednesday.

接受妥协 accept a compromise
他们在谈判中做了妥协。
They accepted a compromise in the negotiation.

接种疫苗 vaccinate
人们首次接种麻疹疫苗是什么时候?
When were people first vaccinated against measles?

接踵而至 on one's heels
短暂的幸福之后,灾难接踵而至。
Disaster comes on the heels of transitory happiness.

揭幕战 opening game
在周五世界杯揭幕战中,南非队西菲韦·查巴拉拉的进球使东道主的南非之旅有了完美的开端。之后,墨西哥队拉法埃尔·马克斯的进球将与东道主南非队的比分扳为1比1。
Rafael Marquez's score earned Mexico a 1-1 draw with host South Africa in the

opening game of the World Cup Friday after Siphiwe Tshabalala had given the host nation a dream start.

街谈巷议 gossip; rumor
口蹄疫成了街谈巷议的热门话题。
Foot-and-mouth disease has become a hot topic for gossip.

节假日轮流值班 holiday rotation
这个岗位要求隔周值班，节假日也要轮流值班。
This position requires every other weekend and holiday rotation.

节能的 energy-saving
长安街各地下通道都安装了节能型照明灯。
Energy-saving lights are installed in the underground passages on Chang'an Avenue.

节能型轿车 energy-efficient car
市政府出台政策，鼓励消费者购买节能型轿车。
The municipal government issued policies to encourage consumers to buy energy-efficient cars.

节日团聚 festival reunion
节日团聚对年轻人来说成本过高。
Festival reunions are too costly for the young.

节水农业 water-saving agriculture
给我举一个节水农业的例子吧。
Give me an example of water-saving agriculture.

劫持人质 hostage-taking
中国政府周一强烈谴责马尼拉发生的一名前任警察劫持中国游客的事件，并要求菲律宾政府对此进行彻查。
The Chinese government Monday strongly condemned the hostage-taking of Chinese tourists by a former police officer in Manila and demanded the Philippine government thoroughly investigate the incident.

劫机 hijack an airplane
恐怖分子劫持了一架客机，机上有260名乘客。
Terrorists hijacked an airplane with 260 people on board.

结汇 settlement of foreign exchange deals; settle a foreign exchange account

结汇将按照专门的结算结汇规则进行办理,该规则对所有交易成员都有效。

The settlement of foreign exchange deals is governed by specific Clearing and Settlement Rules, which are binding to all members.

结婚誓词 marriage vow

民政部表示,引入结婚誓词的目的是提升新人的共同责任意识和对婚姻法的认识。

Introducing the marriage vow, the Ministry of Civil Affairs (MCA) says, is aimed at improving new couples' sense of mutual responsibility and their awareness of the Marriage Law.

结算货币 settlement currency

截流 dam; damming

官员们说,长江三峡截流将不会影响当地的景观。

The damming of the Three Gorges will not spoil the local scenery, officials say.

解除好友关系 unfriend

"unfriend"是一个动词,意思是在Facebook等社交网站上与某人解除好友关系。

The word "unfriend" is defined as a verb that means to remove someone as a "friend" on a social networking site such as Facebook.

解除劳动关系 sever labor relation

公司可以跟严重违纪的员工解除劳动关系。

The firm can sever labor relation with those who severely break certain rules.

解放生产力 emancipate the productive forces

中国的改革是为了解放生产力。

The Chinese reform is aimed at emancipating the productive forces.

解雇金 severance pay

解雇员工是一个艰难的决定,因为公司和雇员之间的关系紧密,而且还要支付高额解雇金。

Laying off workers is a tough decision because of the strong relation with workers and the high severance pay.

解铃还须系铃人 Whoever caused the trouble should solve it; it is better for the doer to undo what he has done.

戒毒所 drug rehabilitation center
他被送进了戒毒所，在那里待了6个月。
He was sent to a drug rehabilitation center, where he stayed for six months.

金边债券 gilt-edged bonds
金边债券由具备长期盈利能力且可以连续支付债券持有者利息的公司发行。
Gilt-edged bonds are issued by a company that has demonstrated the long-term ability to earn a good profit and pay its bond holders interest without interruption.

金蝉脱壳 slink off; escape like a cicada by casting off its skin
我把大衣留在床上，为的是让他以为我仍在熟睡，拿了汽车钥匙，金蝉脱壳，溜之大吉了。
I left my overcoat on the bed to make him believe I was still asleep, took the car key, and slunk off.

金降落伞 golden parachute
金降落伞指公司和高管之间签订的一份协议，详细写明雇佣关系终止时高管能获得一大笔利益补偿。
A golden parachute is an agreement between a company and an upper executive employee specifying that the employee will receive significant benefits if employment is terminated.

金牌崇拜 gold obsession; obsession with gold medals
这种金牌崇拜心理必须祛除。否则，中国可能会成为拿了很多金牌但在体育方面仍处弱势的国家。
This gold obsession has got to stop. Otherwise, China may become a nation that wins a lot of gold medals but is still weak in sports.

金球奖魔咒 Ballon d'Or curse
过去数年的经验表明，凡是在世界杯前一年获得金球奖的球员都会在世界杯比赛中失利。这就是大家所说的"金球奖魔咒"。
The trend from the previous years suggests that the player who wins the Ballon d'Or in the year before the World Cup will fail at the tournament, which is widely known as the Ballon d'Or curse.

金融反腐 corruption fight in financial sector
我国正加大金融反腐力度。
China is strengthening corruption fight in the financial sector.

金融服务区 financial services park
按照该计划,金盏乡将被打造成金融服务区,旨在吸引为跨国公司和银行企业提供后台服务的公司。
Under the plan, Jinzhan township will be transformed into a financial services park aimed at companies that provide back-up services for multinational companies and banking corporations.

金融寡头 financial oligarchy; tycoon
普京再次向俄罗斯金融寡头们发起了进攻。
Putin again attacked Russia's financial oligarchies.

金融科技 fintech
一份最新报告显示,随着中国创新企业数量迅速上升,英国可能失去全球领先金融科技中心的地位。
The UK is at risk of losing its reputation as the world's leading fintech center as the number of innovative companies in China is rising rapidly, according to a new report.

金融市场退出机制 financial market exit mechanism
我国将推进金融市场退出机制的常态化和规范化,建立适合我国国情的法律体系。
China will promote normalization and standardization of the financial market exit mechanism and the upcoming legal system will be in line with China's conditions.

金融危机 financial crisis
中国经济已经摆脱了亚洲金融危机的影响。
China's economy has freed itself from the impact of the Asian financial crisis.

金融中心 financial center
伦敦是世界三大金融中心之一。
London is one of the world's three financial centers.

金融自由化 financial liberalization
新政策的实施旨在为金融自由化作准备。
The new policies have been put in place in preparation for financial liberalization.

金色十年 golden decade
由于金砖国家致力于开启第二个"金色十年",因此对这些国家来说,交流治国理政经验十分重要。
It is important for BRICS countries to exchange governance experiences as the bloc strives to usher in its second "golden decade".

金砖+ BRICS plus
在金砖国家外长会晤记者会上,中国外交部长王毅介绍了"金砖+"的概念。
At a news conference for the meeting of the BRICS Ministers of Foreign Affairs, Chinese Foreign Minister Wang Yi introduced the concept of "BRICS plus".

紧急状态 emergency; state of emergency
美国乔治亚州宣布6个沿海县进入紧急状态,之前的飓风造成了那里600万美元的财产损失。
The American State of Georgia declared a state of emergency in six coastal counties after a hurricane caused $6 million in property damage.

紧迫感 sense of urgency
男篮首节便落后对手15分,最终没能扭转败局。教练赛后说:"我们缺乏紧迫感,受到了惩罚。"
"We were punished for lacking a sense of urgency," said the men's basketball coach whose team had trailed by 15 points at the start of the first quarter and never recovered.

紧俏 in short supply;(commodities)sell well
五一长假期间火车票紧俏。
Train tickets were in short supply during the Labor Day holidays.

紧俏产品 commodities in short supply and highly sought after
这种车型曾一度紧俏。
This type of car was once commodities in short supply and highly sought after.

紧缩银根 tight money policy; monetary restraint
某些经济学家认为,紧缩银根会阻碍经济的发展。
Some economists think that monetary restraint hinders the development of the economy.

紧张局势 tension
中东地区的紧张局势是被讨论的话题之一。
Tension in the Middle East was one of the topics discussed.

紧追 close on one's heels; thunder on one's trail
银行劫匪开车逃跑,警察在后面紧追不舍。
The bank robbers rode off with the police close on their heels.

进口税 import duty; import tariff
中国入世后,汽车的进口关税将逐年下降。
The import tariff on cars will decrease year by year after China enters the WTO.

进行战略性调整 make strategic readjustment
公司目前正在进行战略性调整。
The company now is making strategic readjustment.

进修班 crash course class for further studies
自从1999年以来,该银行先后举办进修班19期,参加培训的各级职员达2574人。
Since 1999, the bank has held 19 crash course classes for further studies, training 2,574 workers at various levels.

近海地区 offshore area
江苏农民在其大片近海地区种植耐盐性的蔬菜,已能获利。
Farmers in Jiangsu have been able to profit from growing salt-resistant vegetables in its vast offshore areas.

近海钻探 offshore drilling
据报道,近海钻探已获得成功。
Offshore drilling has reportedly been a success.

近日点 perihelion
今晨,地球到达近日点,即每年地球距离太阳最近的轨道位置。
This morning the Earth reached its perihelion, the point on its annual orbit that is closest to the sun.

近水楼台先得月 A waterfront pavilion gets the moonlight first. / The one nearer the waterside sees the moon first. / have the convenience to do something
英语里类似的谚语:
A baker's wife may bite of a bun.
A brewer's wife may drink of a tun.
A fishmonger's wife may feed of a conger.
But a servingman's wife may starve for hunger.

禁飞 ban on flying activities
为加强国庆前安保工作,北京近日已扩大了"禁飞"范围,鸽子和风筝也在其中。
Beijing has widened a ban on flying activities to include pigeons and kite flying in its latest efforts to beef up security ahead of the National Day celebrations.

禁飞区 no-fly zone
法国举办2016欧洲杯期间,10个球场和24支球队的全部训练场都设立了禁飞区。
No-fly zones were declared over all 10 stadiums as well as training grounds for the 24 teams at Euro 2016 in France.

禁渔期 fishing ban; fishing moratorium
为了使鱼类得以繁衍下去,每年将有两个月的禁渔期。
A two-month fishing ban is imposed every year to allow the fish to reproduce.

京津冀一体化 Beijing-Tianjin-Hebei integration
京津冀一体化的最大受益者并非河北或天津,而是北京区县的远郊地区。
The outer suburbs in Beijing's districts and counties benefit the most from the Beijing-Tianjin-Hebei integration, rather than Hebei or Tianjin.

京剧票友 amateur Peking Opera singer
慈禧太后也是一个忠实的京剧票友。
The Empress Dowager was an avid amateur Peking Opera singer as well.

经济发展模式 economic development model
城市化将引发国内需求的突破性增长,帮助推进经济发展模式的转变。
Urbanization will trigger the explosive expansion of domestic demands and help the transformation of economic development models.

经济繁荣 economic boom
目前经济繁荣的动力是科技。
Science and technology are behind the current economic boom.

经济封锁 economic blockade
中国政府不赞成对中东国家进行政治孤立或经济封锁。
China is not in favor of political isolation or an economic blockade of any Middle Eastern country.

经济复苏 economy witnesses a recovery; economic recovery
美国联邦储备委员会声明说,美国经济在4月下旬和5月份稍有复苏。
The US economy witnessed a modest recovery in late April and May, the US

Federal Reserve said.

经济杠杆 economic lever; economic leverage
银行将决定利率的高低,也就是说银行控制货币政策。这就意味着政府掌握的经济杠杆就只剩下预算政策了。
The bank will determine the interest rates and, in effect, dictate the monetary policy, leaving budgetary policy as the only economic lever in the hands of the State.

经济过热 overheated economy
加强宏观调控有助于抑制经济过热。
Strengthening macro-regulation will help cool the overheated economy.

经济滑坡 economic downturn
同时,因为德国持续的经济滑坡,很多德国企业都需要从海外注入资金。
Meanwhile, due to a continuous economic downturn in the country, a number of German businesses need capital injection from abroad.

经济技术开发区 economic and technological development zone
浦东是个规模庞大的经济技术开发区。
Pudong is a huge economic and technological development zone.

经济林 cash crop trees
新疆维吾尔自治区鼓励农民种植经济林。
The Xinjiang Uygur autonomous region is encouraging farmers to plant cash crop trees.

经济全球化 economic globalization
随着经济全球化的加速,简化贸易已成为国际贸易领域的普遍要求。
With the acceleration of economic globalization, trade facilitation has become a common call in international trade.

经济适用殡葬 affordable burial
宁波北仑区为平息民众对殡葬费用飙升的不满,将面向低收入者推出"经济适用殡葬"。
Low-income earners in Beilun, Ningbo, will get affordable burials amid complaints of soaring funeral costs.

经济适用住房 affordable housing
我们将改进和规范经济适用房制度。

We will improve and standardize the system of affordable housing.

经济逃犯 economic fugitive
公安部的一名官员透露,中国有150多名经济逃犯仍在美国逍遥法外,这些人大多数是贪官或正面临腐败控诉的嫌疑人。
More than 150 economic fugitives from China, most of whom are corrupt officials or facing allegations of corruption, remain at large in the US, according to an official from the Ministry of Public Security.

经济特区 special economic zone
深圳是中国最早建立的经济特区之一。
Shenzhen was one of the first special economic zones established in China.

经济头脑 a head for business; business sense
杰克有经济头脑。他虽然年轻,但不久就会有所建树。
Jack has a head for business. Young as he is, he'll soon make a mark for himself.

经济危机 economic crisis
南非和津巴布韦两国部长结束了为期两天的会谈,南非将帮助津巴布韦解决经济危机。
Ministers from South Africa and Zimbabwe ended the two-day talks with South Africa promising to help solve the economic crisis in Zimbabwe.

经济萧条 depression; slump
经济萧条时期,成年男子每10人中就有4人失业。
During the depression, four out of ten male adults were out of work.

经济效益 economic returns
国家统计局最新统计表明,这一年头5个月里工业企业已取得了良好的经济效益。
According to the latest statistics released by the National Bureau of Statistics, industrial enterprises recorded good economic returns during the first five months of the year.

经济走廊 economic corridor
中国和巴基斯坦表示,将建立经济走廊,进一步推进两国的经济往来。
China and Pakistan said on Wednesday they will set up an economic corridor to further connect their two economies.

经受住历史考验 stand the test of history
此次动车追尾重大事故的调查结果将"经受住历史考验"。
The investigation into the fatal train crash will offer a result that could "stand the

test of history".

经营管理不善 mismanagement; poor management; poor operation and management
多数国企亏损的祸首是经营管理不善。
Mismanagement is a major culprit in the most unprofitable State-owned enterprises.

经营性公墓 commercial cemetery
根据周一通过的殡葬管理办法规定,政府将限制经营性公墓的开发,并推进公益性公墓的建设。
According to the regulation on funeral and interment management passed on Monday, the government will restrict the development of commercial cemeteries while promoting the construction of social welfare cemeteries.

惊悚片 thriller
妮可·基德曼与西恩·潘联袂主演的惊悚片《翻译风波》首映之后便以2280万美元的可观票房收入勇夺本周票房冠军。
Nicole Kidman and Sean Penn's *The Interpreter* translated into solid box-office as the thriller debuted with $22.8 million to top the weekend.

精简会议 have fewer but shorter meetings; cut down on meeting length and frequency
提高机关办事效率要从精简会议入手。
To improve office efficiency, it is a good start to have fewer but shorter meetings.

精简开支 cut costs
在全球经济滑坡的形势下,芯片巨人英特尔公司也不得不精简开支。
Faced with a world economic recession, even the chip giant Intel had to cut costs.

精简政府机构 government streamlining; streamline government organs
海南省2月19日宣布省级政府机构的精简改革已经完成。
Hainan province announced February 19 that the process of government streamlining was completed at the provincial level.

精品酒店 boutique hotel
跟传统的标准化酒店不同,精品酒店,也叫生活时尚酒店或设计师酒店,内设各种不同等级的奢侈设施。精品酒店的布置通常独特亲切,让旅客有机会探究当地文化。
Unlike the traditional standardized hotel, a boutique hotel—also known as a

lifestyle hotel or designer hotel—contains luxury facilities of varying degrees in unique or intimate settings with the opportunity to explore the local atmosphere.

精神病强制收治 compulsory mental health treatment
多位法律界人士提醒，中国目前的精神病强制收治体制的漏洞有可能造成正常人被送入精神病院。
Members of the legal profession have warned that the loopholes in China's current system of compulsory mental health treatment are at risk of forcing healthy people into psychiatric hospitals.

精神食粮 nourishment for the mind
读书吧，书是精神的食粮。
Read books. Books are nourishment for the mind.

精神损失费 mental damage compensation
他收到了一封信，信中要求他赔偿5万元精神损失费。
He received a letter asking him to pay a mental damage compensation of 50,000 yuan.

精神支柱 spiritual strength; spiritual pillar
许多中国人把儒道当作自己的精神支柱。
Many Chinese draw spiritual strength from Confucianism and Taoism.

精准扶贫 targeted poverty reduction
精准扶贫要做到因地制宜。
Targeted poverty reduction should follow local characteristics.

精准医疗 precision medicine
国家卫计委和科技部宣布，我国科学家将拟定"精准医疗"计划。
The National Health and Family Planning Commission and the Ministry of Science and Technology have announced that Chinese scientists will draw up a precision medicine project.

精子库 sperm bank
我国的精子库本就面临捐献者不足的问题，而二孩政策或许将加剧精子库资源紧张。
China's sperm banks are already facing a shortage of donors, and the two-child policy may put more pressure on the institutions.

警戒水位 danger (water) level; warning (water) level
8月末安徽省境内河水预计将超过警戒水位1米。

In Anhui province, the river is expected to rise to 1 meter above the danger level by the end of August.

净就业前景指数 net employment outlook
全球就业服务公司表示，2016年第一季度调整后的美国净就业前景指数为+6。
The global employment services company said its seasonally adjusted US net employment outlook was plus-6 for the first quarter in 2016.

净资本 net capital
中国银监会表示，一家信托公司的净资本不能少于其风险资本总额，也不能少于其净资产的40%。
The China Banking Regulatory Commission (CBRC) said that a trust company's net capital should not be less than the sum of its all risky capital, as well as no less than 40 percent of its net assets.

竞业禁止协议 non-compete agreement
竞业禁止协议是合同法中的条款，通过劳动合同和保密协议规定合同中的一方（通常指雇员）不得进入或创建与原另一方（通常是雇主）范围相同的企业或交易。
According to Labor Contract and Confidentiality agreement, a non-compete agreement, is a term used in contract law under which one party (usually an employee) agrees not to enter into or start a similar profession or trade in competition against another party (usually the employer).

竞争机制 competitive mechanism
我们应当建立竞争机制，营造竞争环境。
We should set up a competitive mechanism to create a competitive environment.

竞争优势 competitive edge
起初我们没有任何竞争优势可谈，但经过我们的努力后，现在情况良好。
We didn't have any competitive edge to speak of at first, but we worked hard and are now in good shape.

敬老院 nursing home
一个典型的敬老院，其人数一般在500人左右，而老人的年龄都在60岁以上。
A typical nursing home houses around 500 people aged 60 years and older.

敬业精神 be (a) professional; professionalism
迈克尔·乔丹不仅才华出众，还很有敬业精神。他训练刻苦，每场比赛都全力以赴。
Michael Jordan was not only an exceptional talent, but also a true professional. He worked hard and brought his best to every game.

境外非政府组织 overseas NGOs
我国通过了史上首部境外非政府组织管理法，以便于这些组织在大陆合法运营，同时打击任何可能危及国家安全的活动。
China adopted its first-ever law on overseas non-governmental organizations (NGOs) to facilitate their legal operations on the mainland but to combat any activity that might harm national security.

境外服务器 foreign server
约90%的黄色网站都使用境外服务器，这些服务器大都设在美国。
About 90 percent of pornographic websites in China use foreign servers, mostly based in the United States.

境外投资 outbound investment
中国政府会继续鼓励境外投资，同时吸引外来投资。
The Chinese government will continue encouraging outbound investment while attracting foreign investment.

镜像站点 mirror site
在服务器提供商公然受到政治压力后，维基解密网站也关闭了。但该网站称目前已在全球建立750个镜像站点，这意味着目前已经曝光的信息仍然可以从网上获得。
The WikiLeaks website was also shut down after the apparent political pressure on service providers, but WikiLeaks said there were now 750 global mirror sites meaning the data so far released remained readily available.

纠纷调解车 dispute mediation bus
北京首辆，也是全国首辆公交纠纷调解车周二首次亮相北京街头，驶上道路，解决公交车上的纠纷。
A dispute mediation bus, the first of its kind not only in Beijing but the whole of China, fired up its engine for the first time on Tuesday and hit the road to solve problems that flare up on public buses.

酒后驾车 drunk driving
禁止酒后驾车。

Drunk driving is forbidden.

酒精呼气测试 breath alcohol test
警察在闻到该驾车男子身上的酒气后要求对其进行酒精呼气测试，这时该男子一口咬住了警察的左手。
When the policeman asked the driver to take a breath alcohol test after smelling alcohol on him, the man bit the policeman's left hand.

酒精浓度 alcohol concentration
当汤斯维尔市的司机被拦下来做酒精测试，登记的酒精浓度为零时，他们就有机会抽代金券。
When Townsville drivers are pulled over for breath alcohol test and register a nil reading of alcohol concentration, they are given the opportunity to go into the draw for the coupons.

酒肉朋友 fair-weather friend
有困难的时候，这些酒肉朋友就不见了。
In times of need, fair-weather friends are nowhere to be found.

九年义务教育 nine-year compulsory education
中国从1978年开始实行九年义务教育政策。
In 1978, China introduced the nine-year compulsory education system for children.

旧车报废 scrapping of old cars
随着中国的机动车数量持续攀升，旧车报废也成为大城市迫切需要解决的问题，废旧汽车回收是为了确保交通安全，减少机动车污染。
As China's automobile count continues to soar, the scrapping of old cars has become an urgent issue for major Chinese cities to ensure traffic safety and reduce automobile pollution.

救济；救济品 relief
当地慈善组织将救济物资运送给水灾灾民。
The local charity organization sent relief to the flood victims.

救援黄金时间 golden window
周三，搜救幸存者的工作进入第四天，搜救部队仍使用生命探测仪和搜救犬在废墟中寻找生命迹象。在被称为最适宜救援的72小时"黄金时间"过去后，出现幸存者的希望日渐渺茫。
The hunt for survivors entered its fourth day Wednesday, with troops still searching

the ruins with life detectors and sniffer dogs. Hopes are fading after the end of the 72-hour "golden window" for survivors, considered the optimum time for rescue.

救助基金 rescue fund; bailout fund
中国有可能向欧洲提供救助基金。
China may offer rescue funds to Europe.

就地取材 obtain materials from local sources; use local resources; do...with local materials
建雷峰塔时靠的是就地取材。
Leifeng Tower was built purely with local materials.

就业机会 job opportunity; job opening
今年的毕业生更乐意在媒体单位寻求就业机会。
This year's graduates prefer scrambling for job opportunities in the media.

就业歧视 employment discrimination
北京将采取一系列措施为应届大学毕业生增加就业机会,同时打击一切非法职业介绍机构和就业歧视。
Beijing will launch a series of measures to increase employment opportunities for this year's college graduates and to fight any illegal job agency and employment discrimination.

就业预警机制 job alert system
我们国家应该有一个更好的就业预警机制来帮助学生在大学里选择专业。
The country should have a better job alert system to help students choose their major in college.

就业振兴计划 job-creation package
总统计划于周四推出3000亿美元的就业振兴计划。
The president plans to lay out a $300 billion job-creation package on Thursday.

拘留 take into custody
警方拘留了罪犯。
The police took the criminal into custody.

居家养老服务 home-based care service
中国将重点发展居家养老服务,以应对日益严重的人口老龄化问题。
China will prioritize more home-based care services for its growing aged population.

居民委员会 residential committee; neighborhood committee
广东省第一次居民委员会选举是在肇庆举行的。
It was in Zhaoqing that Guangdong province's first election of residential committee members was held.

居民消费价格指数 consumer price index (CPI)

居住用地 residential land
居住用地的供应量会增加，低收入家庭住房工程将成为地方政府议事日程的重中之重。
Residential land supply will increase and low-income housing projects will top local governments' agendas.

举办城市 host city
平昌是2018年冬季奥运会的举办城市。
Pyeongchang is the host city for the 2018 Winter Olympic Games.

举报网站 tip-off website
继最高人民法院开通举报网站之后，中国大陆各省级人民法院也已全部开通了类似网站，收集针对腐败法官的检举信息。
All provincial courts on the Chinese mainland have launched websites to collect tips against corrupted judges, following the launch of a tip-off website by the Supreme People's Court（SPC）.

举手表决 vote by show of hands
全国人民代表大会已经不采用举手表决的投票方式了。
Voting by show of hands is no longer done in the National People's Congress.

具有深远的影响 have a far-reaching impact on
这项改革牵涉到很多地区，将对全国的经济发展产生深远影响。
This reform involves many areas and will have a far-reaching impact on the economic development of the whole country.

聚焦 focus on
未来北京还将继续迁移一些不利于其发展的产业，聚焦于首都功能。
In the future, Beijing will continue to relocate industries viewed as unhealthy to its development and focus on its role as the country's capital.

（出租车）拒载 refuse to take passengers
有人抱怨一些出租车司机拒载。
There have been complaints about taxi drivers refusing to take passengers.

捐款滥用 misuse of donations
在近期捐款滥用丑闻曝光后,公众对红十字会的信任度大幅下跌。
The Red Cross Society's credibility has already plummeted after a recent scandal involving the misuse of donations.

捐献器官 donated organs
捐献器官将在国内所有民用机场享有优先登机权。
Donated organs will have priority when it comes to boarding airplanes at all civil airports in China.

决策机构 policy-making body; decision-making organ
董事会是公司的最高决策机构。
The board of directors is the highest policy-making body in a company.

决堤 break the banks; breaching of the dyke
中国南方一带上周突降暴雨,导致河流决堤,暴雨引发的山体滑坡致使公路和铁路系统中断。
Heavy rain across a swathe of southern China over the last week has caused rivers to break their banks and landslides cut off road and rail links.

决定性竞选 runoff
前华沙市长周日赢得了波兰总统大选中一次决定性竞选的胜利。
Warsaw's former mayor won Poland's presidential runoff vote Sunday.

决定性胜利 decisive victory
汶川地震灾后恢复重建实现了既定目标,并取得决定性胜利。
The post-quake reconstruction effort in Wenchuan, Sichuan province has achieved its goals and registered a decisive victory.

决斗;单挑 PK (player killing)
在"超级女声"比赛中,PK 指的是两名歌手竞争,只有一人有机会胜出。
In the case of the "Super Voice Girl" singing competition, PK refers to the contest between two singers of which only one can win.

绝杀球 last-gasp goal
美国队凭借对阵阿尔及利亚队时的绝杀球,成功晋级第二轮。
The US booked their place in the 2nd round with a last-gasp goal against Algeria.

绝食抗议 hunger strike
180名阿富汗人在美国拘留所绝食,以抗议美军的虐待。

180 Afghans at the US detention facility were on a hunger strike to protest alleged mistreatment.

军备竞赛 arms race
美国政府坚持发展反导弹防御计划,这将引发一场新的全球军备竞赛。
The US government's insistence on developing an anti-missile defense shield would trigger a new global arms race.

军费预算 military budget
十二届全国人大五次会议新闻发言人傅莹表示,2017年中国军费预算增幅在7%左右。
China will raise its military budget by around 7 percent in 2017, said Fu Ying, spokeswoman for the Fifth Session of China's 12th National People's Congress.

军服 military uniform
多款军服亮相"9·3"纪念抗日战争暨世界反法西斯战争胜利70周年阅兵彩排。
Several types of military uniforms were displayed at the rehearsal of the military parade which will commemorate the 70th anniversary of the victory of the Chinese People's War of Resistance against Japanese Aggression (1931- 45) and the end of World War II on Sept 3.

军火走私 arms smuggling
军火走私数额有几十亿美元之巨。
Arms smuggling is a multibillion dollar business.

军事扩张 military expansion
中国没有军事扩张的计划,发展国防是出于本国安全考虑。
China has no plan for military expansion as its development of national defense is for its own security.

军事演习 military drill; military exercise
最近几周,中国人民解放军进行了一系列军事演习,演练两栖作战能力。
The People's Liberation Army conducted a series of military drills over the past few weeks to fine-tune its capabilities of amphibious operations.

军售合同 arms-sale contract
中俄已签署两份军售合同,中方将从俄罗斯购买战斗机和潜艇。
China and Russia signed two arms-sale contracts in which China will buy Russian fighter jets and submarines.

军训 military training (for high school and college students)
大学第一个月非常特别，因为我们有3周时间参加军训，在山里度过。
The first month of university life was quite special because we spent three weeks in the hills going through military training.

竣工仪式 completion ceremony
联合国教科文组织驻北京办事处的一名行政官员参加了这座教学楼的竣工仪式。
An administrative officer of UNESCO's Beijing Office attended the completion ceremony of the classroom building.

开标 bid opening
开标日期作了调整,以便竞标者能有足够的时间作准备。
Bid openings have been rescheduled to allow bidders more time to prepare.

开除某人的公职 get somebody expelled from public office
他的所为也许不是什么滔天大罪,但足以被开除公职。
What he did may not have been a serious crime, but it was enough to get him expelled from public office.

开发新产品 develop new products
该化学纤维公司正开发新产品以谋求更大的市场份额。
The chemical fiber company is trying to gain a bigger market share by developing new products.

开放边境 open the border
10月31日,巴基斯坦和印度达成协议,同意为运输救济物资开放双方边境。
Pakistan and India agreed on Oct. 31 to open the border to allow the transportation of relief goods.

开放低空空域 open low-altitude airspace
中国明年将开放低空空域,允许私人飞机使用1000米以下空域,无须军方批准。
China next year will open its low-altitude airspace to allow private planes to fly no higher than 1,000 meters without approval from the air force.

开放式基金 open-ended fund
开放式基金在未来5年内将会成为中国股市的主流。
Open-ended funds will become the mainstream in the Chinese stock market within five years.

开工率 rate of construction
日本住房开工率6月份下降了。
In June, the rate of construction of housing decreased in Japan.

开光 consecration
由中国佛教协会主办的玉佛的开光仪式在北京灵光寺举行。

A consecration ceremony for a jade Buddha statue was held by the Chinese Buddhist Association in Beijing's Lingguang Temple.

开卷考试 open-book exam
学生更喜欢开卷考试，他们认为闭卷考试会比较难。
Students prefer open-book exams because they think they're easier than closedbook tests.

开门红 a good start
国家统计局发布的数据显示，2016年一季度国民经济实现"开门红"。
China's economy had "a good start" in the first quarter of 2016, data released by the National Bureau of Statistics showed.

开小灶 give extra help (as a favor)
期终考试临近，老师正忙于给班上的后进学生开小灶。
As the final examination draws near, the teacher is busy giving extra help to those students who lag behind others.

开夜车 burn the midnight oil; work late into the night
许多考生在备考期间开夜车学习。
Many students are burning the midnight oil to prepare for the examination.

开足马力 put into high gear; go full steam
开足马力的话，这些新汽船每小时能航行40海里。
The new steamers can cover 40 nautical miles per hour going full steam.

侃大山 chew the fat; chatter
这位影星同网友们侃起了大山，畅谈因特网、伊拉克局势及他自己的私人生活。
The movie star chewed the fat with cyber surfers, talking about the internet, Iraq, and his personal life.

侃爷 big talker
北京人嘴贫善侃，故有"侃爷"之称。
Beijingers love to talk and are sometimes referred to as "big talkers".

看病难、看病贵，上学难、上学贵 the difficulty and high cost of getting medical treatment and receiving education
要着力解决看病难、看病贵，上学难、上学贵的问题。
We should put more effort in dealing with the difficulty and high cost of getting medical treatment and receiving education.

看守政府 caretaker government
荷兰女王要求首相在大选成立新政府之前组建看守政府。
Dutch Queen called on the Prime Minister to form a caretaker government until a new cabinet is formed after the general election.

康复中心 recuperation center; rehabilitation center
当地医院的康复中心技术一流,医院因此也远近闻名。
The local hospital is known for having a first-rate recuperation center.

抗日战争 War of Resistance against Japanese Aggression
中国政府发布了纪念中国人民抗日战争暨世界反法西斯战争胜利70周年活动标识。
A logo marking the 70th anniversary of the victory of the Chinese People's War of Resistance against Japanese Aggression (1931-45) and the end of World War II has been revealed by the Chinese government.

抗生素滥用 overuse of antibiotics
中国卫生部出台计划进一步抑制抗生素滥用,包括限制抗生素的品种和使用比率,惩治滥用抗生素的医生。
China's health authority announced plans to further curb the overuse of antibiotics, including setting caps for the variety and use ratio of antibiotics, and punishing doctors found to misuse antibiotics.

抗议照会 note of protest
一架挪威海军飞机近距离掠过俄罗斯北方舰队指挥官乘坐的直升机,险些造成危险。俄罗斯外交部已就此事件向挪威政府递交了抗议照会。
The Russian Foreign Ministry has sent a note of protest to Norway after a Norwegian naval plane flew dangerously close to a helicopter carrying Russia's Northern Fleet Commander.

抗震鉴定 anti-earthquake evaluation
所有的公共建筑每5年都要经过严格的质量检查,其中包括抗震鉴定。
All public buildings will be subject to stringent quality tests, including an anti-earthquake evaluation, every five years.

考研 take entrance exams for graduate schools
每年有50%~60%的大学毕业生选择考研或出国。
Every year, 50 to 60 percent of university graduates choose to take entrance exams for graduate schools or go abroad.

靠山 backer; patron
有人做靠山,这个年轻人终于得到了他觊觎已久的职务。
With someone as a backer, the young man got the position he'd coveted for a long time.

科班训练 professional training
中央戏剧学院将开办相声科班。
The Central Academy of Drama will offer professional training for cross-talkers.

科幻小说 science fiction; science-fiction novel
他的处女作曾高居科幻小说排行榜首位。
His first novel topped the best-seller list for science fiction.

科技富豪 tech billionaire
《福布斯》发布了2017年科技富豪榜。这张年度榜单上的名字并不让人意外,惊人的是这100位科技富豪的资产净值总额高达1.08万亿美元。
Forbes has put out its annual Richest In Tech list for 2017. The names on the list won't surprise you but what's shocking is that these 100 tech billionaires have a combined net worth of $1.08 trillion.

科普 science dissemination; dissemination of science
很多市民参加了由市政府组织的科普宣传周活动。
Many citizens attended the Science Dissemination Week organized by the municipal government.

科学发展观 Scientific Outlook on Development
科学发展观是坚持以人为本,全面、协调、可持续的发展观。
The Scientific Outlook on Development means putting people first and aiming at comprehensive, coordinated and sustainable development.

科学素养 scientific literacy
中国具备基本科学知识的公众人数正在增长,但科学素养仍处于低水平。
The proportion of people in China with basic scientific knowledge is growing but scientific literacy is still low.

可比价格 comparable prices
1至7月份广州市国内生产总值按可比价格计算,比上年同期增长了12.4%。
The GDP of Guangzhou, from January to July, increased 12.4 percent over the same period last year at comparable prices.

可采储量 recoverable reserves
石油专家相信中国石油的可采储量大大高于目前已知的储量。
Oil experts believe that China's recoverable oil reserves are far greater than those that are known to exist now.

可持续城镇化 sustainable urbanization
支持可持续城镇化——在中国，城镇化取得了卓越的成就，但同时也面临着严峻的挑战。
Supporting sustainable urbanization—In China, the trend toward urbanization has been both remarkable and challenging.

可持续发展 sustainable development
他心里装的是如何实现企业可持续发展。
Sustainable development for the company was what on his mind.

可持续消费 sustainable consumption
根据中国连锁经营行业协会发布的报告，中国超过七成的消费者已具备一定程度的可持续消费意识。
More than 70 percent of Chinese consumers, to some extent, understand the idea of sustainable consumption, according to a report released by the China Chain Store and Franchise Association.

可见度；能见度 visibility
随着污染的减少，北京市大气能见度有很大提高。
With less pollution, visibility in Beijing has improved considerably.

可降解塑料袋 bio-degradable plastic bag
可再利用的绿色包装比可降解塑料袋得到更多认可。
Reusable bags got the nod over the bio-degradable plastic bags.

可燃冰 flammable ice
全球各地都有大量的可燃冰，但目前还不能作为能量来源进行开采。
Flammable ice exists in vast quantities around the world but so far isn't producible as an energy resource.

可入肺颗粒物 particulate matter (PM)
专家称，长时间呼吸空气中的颗粒物，特别是直径小于2.5微米的可入肺颗粒物（PM2.5）对人体健康危害很大。
Longtime exposure to particulate matter especially the particulate matter smaller

than 2.5 micrometers（PM2.5）which can go directly to the alveoli of the lungs is a major health hazard.

可替代能源汽车 alternative energy vehicle
全球汽车大佬齐聚2016北京国际车展之时，大笔资金正在涌入中国的可替代能源汽车市场，电动汽车、插电式混合动力车以及燃料电池车均属于可替代能源汽车。
As global auto executives gathered for the 2016 Beijing Auto Show, a torrent of money is pouring into the nation's alternative energy vehicle market, which includes electric vehicles, plug-in hybrids and fuel-cell cars.

可行性研究 feasibility study
越南政府允许香港有关组织在越南中部建立一个石油精炼厂进行可行性研究。
The Vietnamese government has allowed a Hong Kong-based group to conduct a feasibility study for an oil refinery in central Vietnam.

可再生能源 renewable source of energy; renewable resource
瑞士政府通过了一项新能源政策，以鼓励瑞士居民使用可再生能源。
The Swiss government approved a new energy policy to encourage the Swiss to use renewable sources of energy.

可再生资源回收 renewable resource recycling
北京市今年计划将300个社区垃圾回收站纳入"可再生资源回收日"活动中，以鼓励人们在住所附近的地区参与垃圾回收。
Beijing plans to involve 300 community rubbish recycling stations in a "Renewable Resource Recycling Day" this year, to encourage people to recycle rubbish near their homes.

可载人无人机 passenger-carrying drone
国内无人机制造商亿航在2016年拉斯维加斯消费电子展上发布了全球首款可载人无人机。这款无人机或将帮助人们实现自动中短途日常飞行的夙愿。
Chinese drone maker Ehang unveiled the world's first passenger-carrying drone at the 2016 Consumer Electronics Show in Las Vegas, which might help achieve the long-standing dream of automated short-to-medium-distance everyday flights.

可支配收入 disposable income
对于住公房的中国人来说，总收入中的可支配收入占比比较高。
With housing taken care of by employers, the disposable income of some Chinese is relatively large in proportion to total income.

可转换债券 convertible bond
可转换债券的市价往往会随等值的普通股的市价波动而波动。
The market value of a convertible bond tends to fluctuate with the market value of an equivalent number of shares of common stock.

克扣工资 unreasonable deductions from paychecks
要求各地人力资源和社会保障部门为工资被拖欠或不合理克扣的工人提供举报投诉渠道。
Local human resources and social security departments were asked to provide a complaints' procedure for workers to report if their wages have been delayed or unreasonable deductions have been taken from their paychecks.

客队 visiting team
德国队对于对手客队而言具有主场优势。
Germany had home field advantage against its opponents, the visiting teams.

客座教授 guest professor
他作为客座教授在北京大学授课。
As a guest professor, he gives lectures at Peking University.

课外培训 extracurricular/after-school training
北京的一项调查发现,受采访的小学四年级、五年级的学生中,有92%接受过课外培训。课外班价格高昂,有父母甚至哀叹他们养的不是孩子而是"烧钱机器"。
A survey in Beijing found that 92 percent of the Grade 4 and Grade 5 pupils interviewed received extracurricular training. The cost of after-school classes is extremely expensive and some parents even lamented that what they were raising were not children but "cash burners".

空巢家庭 empty-nest family
空巢家庭(子女离家后老年人独自生活的家庭)数量未来几年将有所增加。
There will be an increase in empty-nest families (households in which elderly people live alone after their children left home) in the next few years.

空巢青年(独自生活的青年) empty-nest youths
一项调查显示,我国20~39岁的空巢青年数量已超过2000万,大部分空巢青年生活在大城市。
China has over 20 million empty-nest youths aged 20 to 39, and most of them live in major cities, according to a survey.

空城 ghost town
中国主要的制造业中心东莞被评为春节期间国内第一大空城。
China's major manufacturing hub Dongguan was rated China's top ghost town during the Spring Festival.

空间站 space station
"发现"号机组人员的任务之一是向国际空间站输送补给。
One of the missions for the Discovery's crew is to deliver supplies to the international space station.

空降兵 paratrooper
6月进行的军事演习调动了600名空降兵。
Six hundred paratroopers were deployed in the military exercise in June.

空难 plane crash
空难中共有78人丧生,包括4名机组成员。
Seventy-eight people, including four crew members, died in the plane crash.

空怒族 air rage tribe
航班延误在中国已成常态。过去两个月发生了至少8起愤怒的乘客围堵在登机口抗议的事件。这些愤怒的乘客甚至有了一个新称呼:"空怒族"。
The constant flight delays in China have seen mobs of angry passengers mount at least 8 protests at departure gates in the last 2 months. There is even a new phrase for the rampaging hordes: "air rage tribe".

空气净化器 air purifier
国家质检总局称,国内市场上销售的空气净化器中,有1/4的产品不合格。
A quarter of air purifiers sold on the domestic market are substandard, according to the General Administration of Quality Supervision, Inspection and Quarantine.

空气末日 airpocalypse; airmageddon
上个月持续相当长一段时间的严重污染天气在上周又报复性回归了一天,网友将其戏称为"空气末日"。
A prolonged bout of heavy pollution over the last month, which returned with a vengeance for a day last week—called the "airpocalypse" or "airmageddon" by internet users.

空气污染 air pollution
北京的空气污染有渐渐减轻的迹象。
There are signs that air pollution is decreasing in Beijing.

空气污染物 air pollutant
相关空气污染物还包括有毒污染物，比如汞和二氧化碳。
Air pollutants of concern include toxic air pollutants such as mercury and greenhouse gases.

空气浴 air bath
时髦的市民健身活动还包括所谓的空气浴，即到乡间呼吸一下新鲜空气。
Other trendy health exercises for urban dwellers include the so-called air bath, breathing fresh air in villages.

空气质量 air quality
中国国家气象局称，北京当天空气质量下降至罕见的5级"重度污染"，能见度非常低。
China's national weather bureau gave the air quality a rare 5 rating—"heavily polluted"—and low visibility.

空气质量监测 air quality monitoring
由于标准不同，北京市环保局和美国驻华大使馆公布的北京市空气质量监测数据经常存在差别，这也引发了有关PM2.5标准和PM10标准的首次公开大讨论。
The public debate on PM2.5 and PM10 first began when air quality monitoring results released by Beijing Municipal Environmental Protection Bureau and the US Embassy in Beijing often differed based on the different measurements.

空前绝后 surpass the past and the future; unique
三峡工程在中国水利工程建设史上是空前绝后的。
The Three Gorges Hydro-Power Project surpasses the past and the future in China's water power construction.

空铁列车 sky train
我国首列空铁列车在南京下线，我国成为继德国和日本后，第三个掌握空铁列车技术的国家。
China's first sky trains came off the assembly line in Nanjing, with China becoming the third country to master sky train technology, after Germany and Japan.

空头支票 empty promise
开空头支票对他们来说是司空见惯的事。
Empty promises from them are nothing unusual.

空域拥堵 air traffic congestion
民航官员表示，中国将开通10条空中单向通道，以治理严重的空域拥堵和航班延误问题。

China aims to handle its serious air traffic congestion and flight delays by opening 10 one-way air passages, civil aviation officials said.

空中楼阁 castle in the air; daydream
现实些,不要指望中彩票,那是空中楼阁。

Be realistic. Don't count on winning the lottery. That's a castle in the air.

空置率 vacancy rate
在珠三角一带主要的经济和贸易中心广州,甲级写字楼空置率降至6年来最低水平。

The vacancy rate of Grade A offices in Guangzhou, a major economic and trade hub along the Pearl River Delta, hit its lowest level in six years.

空中上网服务 in-flight WiFi services
中国三大航空公司——中国东方航空公司、中国南方航空公司和中国国际航空公司已获批提供空中上网服务。

Three major Chinese airlines, including China Eastern Airlines, China Southern Airlines and Air China, have been approved to provide in-flight WiFi services.

恐怖片 fright flick; horror movie; horror film
出乎大家的意料,派拉蒙影片公司出品的一部小成本恐怖电影《鬼影实录》在午夜场放映两周后,在扩大规模放映的第一个周末就蹿升到了第五位。

To everybody's surprise, a micro-budgeted fright flick *Paranormal Activity* from Paramount rose to No. 5 in its first full weekend after two weeks of midnight-only screenings.

恐怖威胁等级 terror threat level
英国首相特雷莎·梅宣布将该国的恐怖威胁等级从"严重"提升至最高级别"危急"。

British Prime Minister Theresa May announced that the country's terror threat level has been raised from "severe" to "critical", its highest level.

恐怖袭击 terrorist attack
伦敦议会大厦外发生恐怖袭击事件,造成4人死亡,至少40人受伤。

A terrorist attack outside the Houses of Parliament in London has left four people killed and at least 40 others injured.

恐归族 home-fear group
春节临近,很多人急切盼望着回家与亲人团聚,但与之相反,一些被称为"恐归族"的人们却对于回家有着深深的顾虑。

In contrast to the mass enthusiasm for returning home for family union during the upcoming Spring Festival, there are some, becoming known as the "home-fear group", who have deep reservations about going back home.

恐慌购买 panic buying
虽然专家表示日本核辐射不会影响美国民众健康,但防辐射药物主要供应商表示,由于恐慌购买,药品已经断货。
Major suppliers of pills that provide protection from radiation say they're out of stock due to panic buying, even though experts say that the Japanese nuclear catastrophe poses no health threat to Americans.

控股公司 holding company; controlling company
作为柯尼卡美能达集团的一分子,该公司拥有与控股公司相同的经营理念及构想。
Being one of the members of Konica Minolta Group, the company has the same management philosophy and visions with the holding company.

控球率 possession percentage
我从没有看到控球率是多少,但两队相差一定很悬殊。
I never saw what possession percentage was, but it had to be lopsided.

口蹄疫 foot-and-mouth disease
口蹄疫是一种由病毒感染引起的偶蹄动物共患的急性接触性传染病。
Foot-and-mouth Disease (FMD) is an acute, highly contagious picornavirus infection of cloven-hoofed animals.

扣帽子 put a label on
不要给别人乱扣帽子。
Do not put labels on others at will.

枯水季节 dry season
枯水季节时这条河几乎断流。
The river barely flows in the dry season.

哭穷 complain about not being rich enough; pretend to be poor
一般人都认为足球俱乐部财大气粗,但俱乐部老总却常常向足协哭穷。
Football clubs are believed to be rich, but in front of the Football Association, club presidents keep going on complaining about not being rich enough.

苦果 a bitter pill to swallow
你犯了错,苦果你自己吃。
You made the mistake yourself. It is a bitter pill for you to swallow.

夸大 play up
在工作面试时她夸大了自己的经验。
She played up her experience during the job interview.

跨行取款收费 fees on withdrawing cash from other banks' ATMs; fees on interbank withdrawal
中国多家银行已将跨行取款收费上调至每笔4元,是之前收费金额的两倍。
Chinese banks have doubled the fees on withdrawing cash from other banks' ATMs to four yuan per withdrawal.

跨境平行交易 cross-border parallel trading
香港特别行政区政府已经开始打击婴儿配方奶粉的跨境平行交易,以保证当地商店的奶粉供应。
The government of the Hong Kong Special Administrative Region has cracked down on cross-border parallel trading in infant milk formula to ensure local stores don't run out of stock.

跨年晚会 new year countdown party
据预计,在新加坡滨海湾举办的跨年晚会今年将吸引更多的观众,这一地区的几处关键修缮工程已完工,将呈现给观众更多亮点。
The New Year Countdown party at Singapore's Marina Bay is expected to draw in a bigger crowd this year, with the completion of key developments in the area and more vantage points on offer.

跨业公司 conglomerate
随着中国加入世界贸易组织,更多的国际跨业企业会来到中国。
With China joining the World Trade Organization, more international conglomerates are coming to China.

跨越式发展 leapfrog development
他敦促黑龙江省政府和人民利用黑龙江独特的潜能实现跨越式发展。
He has urged the provincial government and people in Heilongjiang to tap its unique potentials for "leapfrog development".

快递 express delivery
随着外国快递公司的加入,更大的快递业市场大战在中国就要打响了。
A bigger market war is underway in China as foreign express delivery firms join the fray.

快递公司 courier company
我国快递公司泄露用户个人信息或面临最高5万元罚款及吊销许可证的处罚。
Chinese courier companies might face fines of up to 50,000 yuan and license revocation for leaking customers' personal information.

快捷图标 short-cut icon
如果你愿意，可以使用默认的快捷图标。
You can use a default short-cut icon if you wish.

快速反击 rapid counter-attack
巴拉圭主帅拉尔多马·马蒂诺表示，如果想成功晋级世界杯四分之一决赛，就一定要小心日本的快速反击和死球威胁。
Paraguay coach Gerardo Martino has highlighted Japan's rapid counter-attacks and dead-ball prowess as two areas his side will need to address if they are to progress through to the quarter-finals of the World Cup.

快速反应部队 rapid-response force
经过多年训练，中国人民解放军陆军武装直升机部队已转变成一支强大的快速反应部队。
After years of training, the Chinese People's Liberation Army has developed its Armed Helicopter Corps into a powerful, rapid-response force.

快速响应码 Quick Response code
快速响应码在广告界已经使用多年了，有一部分美国丧葬机构开始将其用于墓碑。
Quick Response codes (QR code) have been used in advertisements for years, and a handful of American funeral homes began attaching them to gravestones.

快讯 news flash; flash
快讯简要播报当日新闻。
A news flash tells brief stories about what happens today.

宽带接入 broadband access
一位专家建议电信商家要对目前火热的宽带接入网络投资持慎重态度，投资前应做好进一步的市场分析。
An expert has advised telecom market players to be cautious amid the current enthusiastic investment mood in broadband access networks, saying that closer market analyses should be done before investments are made.

宽限期 grace period
李先生说，45天的宽限期还是不够。

Mr. Li said that the 45 days grace period is not long enough.

宽严相济 tempering justice with mercy
对修正案草案所做的修改将有助于依照"宽严相济"的政策对国家的刑法体系进行重组。
The changes to the draft amendment will help restructure the country's system of criminal law in accordance with its policy of "tempering justice with mercy".

矿难 coal mine accident
6起矿难中共有222个相关负责人被惩处。
A total of 222 people were punished for being responsible for 6 catastrophic coal mine accidents.

亏本生意 a losing proposition
电子商务对许多企业来说都成了亏本生意。
E-commerce for many firms turned out to be a losing proposition.

困境儿童 children in difficulty; children living in difficulty
困境儿童包括因家庭贫困导致生活、就医、就学等困难的儿童,因自身残疾导致康复、照料、护理等困难的儿童,以及因家庭监护缺失或监护不当遭受虐待、遗弃、意外伤害的儿童。
Children in difficulty include children who grow up in poverty and thus have poor access to medical treatment or education, children who have difficulty in receiving rehabilitation and nursing due to their disabilities, and children who are subject to abuse, abandonment, or accidental injuries for lack of or improper family custody.

扩大内需 expand domestic demand
中国人民银行行长表示中国将继续执行扩大内需的政策方针。
The governor of the People's Bank of China said that China would stick with the policy of expanding domestic demand.

扩招 scale/enrollment expansion
过去几年,高校掀起了一阵扩招的热潮。然而,许多学校只关注于规模的扩大,却忽视了教学质量的改善。
The past years have witnessed a frenzied expansion of colleges and universities. Many schools, however, have just focused on scale expansion, but neglected quality improvement.

L型走势 L-shaped growth
我国经济运行将是L型的走势,深层次的问题还将持续,也会出现新的挑战。
China's economy will tend towards L-shaped growth as deep-rooted problems persist and new challenges emerge.

垃圾处理 garbage treatment
新垃圾处理基地日处理能力达5000吨。
The new garbage treatment plant is capable of treating 5,000 tons of waste per day.

垃圾短信 spam message
中国移动表示3月15日之前他们每天收到大约4000条关于垃圾短信的投诉。
China Mobile said it had received about 4,000 complaints each day over spam messages before March 15.

垃圾分类 garbage sorting
上海绿化管理部门通过与支付宝合作来激发年轻人对垃圾分类的兴趣。
Shanghai's greenery authorities teamed up with Alipay to spur interest in garbage sorting among young people.

垃圾焚烧 waste incineration
北京市政府的官员昨日仍然表示他们会在今年内推进该计划,建造更多的垃圾焚烧厂。
Beijing government officials said yesterday they will proceed with plans to build more waste incineration plants this year.

(发送)垃圾邮件 spam
根据新规定,未经互联网用户同意而发送商业广告等垃圾邮件是非法行为。
According to the new regulation, it is illegal to spam internet users with unsolicited commercials.

垃圾债券 junk bond
垃圾债券是一种高风险、低信用评估的非投资债券,其回报率因而较高。
A junk bond is a high-risk, non-investment-grade bond with a low credit rating. Consequently, it usually has a high yield.

拉锯战 seesaw battle
警察总长提名拉锯战凸显泰联盟间分裂。
Seesaw battle over police chief nomination reflects coalition rift in Thailand.

拉链车 zipper truck
山东省会济南启用"拉链车"在交通高峰期转换潮汐车道,缓解道路拥堵。
The capital of Shandong province, Jinan, started using a "zipper truck" to alternate traffic lanes during rush hours and ease congestion.

拉选票 seek a vote
禁烟令的支持者们正在州内拉选票。
Smoking-ban backers are seeking votes in the state.

拉闸限电 power rationing
寒潮导致多地拉闸限电。
Cold wave causes power rationing in several regions.

啦啦队 cheerleaders; cheerleading squad
篮球比赛场间休息时,啦啦队活跃起来。
Cheerleaders perform during the breaks at basketball matches.

蜡雕 wax sculpture; wax carving
出乎人们意料,蜡雕作品在展销会上销售一空。
Wax sculptures sold well at the artifacts fair, to the surprise of many.

蜡染法 batik
蜡染技术相当复杂,几句话讲不清。
Batik involves complicated techniques. It cannot be explained in a few words.

蜡像馆 wax museum
参观伦敦,不要忘记去看看有名的蜡像馆。
Don't miss the city's famous wax museum when you visit London.

来电显示欺诈 caller ID spoofing; call laundering
美国威斯康星州和其他许多州的监管机构不断接到人们对"来电显示欺诈"行为的投诉。
Regulators in Wisconsin and many other states are hearing a significant jump in complaints about what is often called "caller ID spoofing" or "call laundering".

来料加工 process materials supplied by clients
这个加工区的大多数工厂从事来料加工业务。
Most plants in this Processing Zone process materials supplied by clients.

来世；下辈子 next life
我们只能来世再见了。
We can only meet in the next life.

蓝筹股 blue chip
投资者下午购入蓝筹股和科技股，使得总体指数在午间震荡之后上升。
Investors bought both blue chips and technology stocks in the afternoon session, driving the major indices up after a midday swing in trading.

蓝领工人 blue-collar worker
蓝领工人指的是体力劳动者，有别于办公室工作的白领阶层。
Blue-collar workers do physical work, in contrast to white-collar workers who work in offices.

蓝色经济 blue economy
一位中国官员表示，中国倡导"蓝色经济"发展，在推动可持续发展的同时，优化传统海洋产业，壮大新兴海洋产业。
China calls for the development of a "blue economy" to optimize the traditional marine sector and speed up the development of emerging marine industries while promoting sustainability, a Chinese official said.

蓝色经济通道 blue economic passage
为推进"一带一路"倡议下的海洋合作，我国提出建设3条连接亚洲与非洲、大洋洲、欧洲和其他地区的海上"蓝色经济通道"的方案。
China has put forward plans for three ocean-based "blue economic passages" that will connect Asia with Africa, Oceania, Europe and beyond, in a bid to advance maritime cooperation under the Belt and Road Initiative.

澜湄合作机制 Lancang-Mekong Cooperation（LMC）mechanism
澜沧江—湄公河合作机制的创建可以说是水到渠成，有利于充分发挥地缘相近、人文相亲、经济互补性强的优势。
The Lancang-Mekong Cooperation (LMC) mechanism comes as a natural result of our existing cooperation, and will take full advantage of our close geographic proximity, traditional friendship and complementary economies.

烂摊子 mess
仅仅两年,王就把这家国有企业搞垮了。现在他被解职,留下个烂摊子得等新领导来收拾。
In only two years, Wang ran the State firm into the ground. Now he's been sacked, leaving a mess for a new leader to clean up.

滥发纸币 excessive issuance of bank notes
滥发纸币导致了通货膨胀。
Excessive issuance of bank notes led to inflation.

滥用职权 abuse of power
因滥用职权,两名警官去年被解职。
Two officers were removed last year for abuse of power.

浪子回头金不换 It's never too late to change.
俗话说,浪子回头金不换。他出狱两个月后开了个杂货店,开始了新的生活。
Turning over a new leaf, he opened a grocery store two months after being released from prison. It's never too late to change, as they say.

劳保 labor insurance
私营企业的劳保问题越来越突出。
Labor insurance is increasingly a problem in private enterprises.

劳动合同制 labor contract system
中国于20世纪80年代中期试行劳动合同制,在20世纪90年代扎根并推广开来。
China first experimented with the labor contract system in the mid-1980s. It took hold in the 1990s.

劳动合同终止协议 labor termination agreement; employment termination agreement
该公司同意提高赔偿金额之后,大部分被裁员工都已在周二的最后期限之前同意签署劳动合同终止协议。
Most of the laid-off employees of the company agreed to sign labor termination agreements before a Tuesday deadline after the company agreed to boost their compensation.

劳动力供给 labor supply
中国虽然存在人口老龄化问题,但由于未来至少40年内劳动力供给充足,因此中国仍将能够保持发展势头。

Although facing an aging population, China will be able to maintain its development thanks to a sufficient labor supply for at least the next 40 years.

劳动力过剩 labor surplus
劳动力过剩增加了就业压力。
A growing labor surplus led to increased pressure on the employment market.

劳动力流动 movement of labor
户口制度妨碍了劳动力的流动。
The household registration system hinders the movement of labor.

劳动密集型产业 labor-intensive industry
中国加入世贸组织之后，劳动密集型产业即刻受益。
After China entered the WTO, labor-intensive industries reaped the benefits immediately.

劳动模范 model worker
理所当然，劳模会在会议期间受到很多优待。
Model workers enjoy a lot of preferential treatment during conferences, and they deserve it.

劳动年龄人口 working-age population
2015年，中国劳动年龄人口遭遇现代史上最大跌幅。
China's working-age population saw its largest decline in modern China's history in 2015.

劳动者素质 quality of the workforce
西部开发要注重劳动者素质的提高。
It is important to improve the quality of the West's workforce in developing the region.

劳力输出 labor export; export of labor
中国劳力输出前景看好。
Prospects are good for labor exports from China.

劳务派遣工 contractor
该草案还包括以下条例：劳务派遣单位及用工单位在协商劳务派遣工的工资时应遵守"同工同酬"的原则。
The bill also includes an article requiring agencies and employers to follow the principle of "equal pay for equal work" when negotiating payment for their

contractors.

老大难问题 long-standing problem
污水处理一直是"老大难"问题。
How to deal with polluted water has been a long-standing problem.

老调重弹 beat a dead horse
我知道我已说了好几遍,我并不想老调重弹。但是,我真的觉得我们应该重新考虑一下。
I know I've already said this several times, and I don't mean to beat a dead horse, but I really think we should reconsider this.

老漂族 elderly immigrants
随着越来越多的老年人离开故土,跟随子女来到城市落脚,老漂族成为热门话题。
Elderly immigrants become a hot topic as more and more elderly are leaving their hometown, and settling down in cities with their children.

老爷车 vintage car
显然许多婴儿潮一代的加拿大人都对老爷车情有独钟,他们年轻时是买不起这样的车的。
It is evident that many Canadian baby boomers are indulging in vintage cars they could not afford when they were young.

老一套 the same old trick; the same old story
这位教练的训练方式总是老一套。队员们怀疑他到底有没有新东西。
This coach always makes the team practice the same old trick in training. Players wonder if he has anything new.

老字号 time-honored brand
有关人士提醒那些"老字号"要加快行动,在国外市场进行品牌和商标注册,以免被竞争对手抢注。
The time-honored brands are being warned to hurry up and register those brand names and trademarks in foreign markets, before rivals effectively steal them.

勒索软件 ransomware
一种名为"想哭"的勒索软件空前地席卷了150多个国家,感染电脑超过30万台,全球响起网络安全警钟。
The unprecedented spread of a ransomware dubbed WannaCry has swept across more than 150 countries and infected more than 300,000 computers, setting off

alarm bells for global internet security.

累犯 third-time offender—a criminal who has broken the law multiple times
作为累犯,他的刑期更长。
As a third-time offender, he got a longer term in prison.

冷冻卵子 egg freezing
富有争议的冷冻卵子在中国引发了越来越多的关注。错过最佳生育年龄的中国女性越来越多,这项新技术据称可以给这些女性带来新希望。
Controversial egg freezing gains rising attention in China. This new technology is said to be bringing new hope to the growing number of women in China who miss out on the optimal age to conceive a child.

冷锋;冷空气 cold front
由于冷空气导致气温骤降,中国北方的居民们不得不重新换上厚厚的冬装。
Residents of North China have to get their heavy jackets out with a cold front closing in and temperatures set to drop dramatically.

冷战思维 Cold War mentality
人们指责美国外交政策决策者有冷战思维。
The US foreign policy-makers were accused of displaying a Cold War mentality.

离婚协议书 divorce settlement
大多数夫妻会先行签订离婚协议书。无法在财产分配或子女监护等问题上达成一致时,他们才采取法律手段。
Most try to sign a divorce settlement by themselves first. After failing to reach an agreement on issues such as the division of property or custody of children, they turn to legal resolution.

离境退税政策 departure tax refund scheme
北京今年有望实施离境退税政策,以吸引境外游客扩大消费。
Beijing may implement a departure tax refund scheme this year to help increase spending by overseas visitors.

礼品回收 gift-recycling
收到昂贵、又不想要的节日礼品的人们开始找礼品回收产业帮他们处理这些不想要的东西。
Recipients of expensive, but unwanted holiday gifts are turning to "gift-recycling" businesses for help to get rid of the things they don't want.

礼尚往来 Kindness deserves reciprocation./ Kindness should be reciprocated.
礼尚往来嘛！他送了我DVD影碟，我就送他两盘中国古典音乐CD。
I gave him two classical Chinese music CDs for the movie on DVD he had sent to me as a present. Kindness deserves reciprocation.

理财产品 wealth investment product
中国银行监管机构银监会公布了新措施，以加强银行理财产品的监管。
The China Banking Regulatory Commission (CBRC), the nation's banking regulator, unveiled new measures to improve regulations over banks' wealth investment products.

理论与实践相结合 put theory into practice
理论只有与实践相结合才会发挥作用。
Theory works only when it is put into practice.

理想雇主 preferred workplace/employer
韩国就业门户网站Job Korea对1146名大四学生进行的调查中，三星连续第二年被选为韩国大学生的理想雇主。
Samsung was selected as the preferred workplace for a 2nd straight year in a survey of 1,146 college seniors, done by Job Korea, a recruitment portal of South Korea.

力挫 beat the hard way; defeat
中国1比0力挫阿根廷队，爆了开赛以来最大的冷门。
China beat Argentina 1 : 0 the hard way, causing the greatest surprise since the beginning of tournament.

力所能及 within one's power; to the best of one's ability
要什么我都会给你搞到，当然了，得在我力所能及的范围内。
I will get anything you want for you. Within my power, that is.

力争上游 aim high; strive for the best
力争上游才会成功。
Winners are those who aim high.

历史遗留问题 problem left over from history
我们提倡用和平方式解决历史遗留问题。
We advocate solving problems left over from history in a peaceful way.

立法听证会 legislative hearing
由全国人大常委会法律委员会召开的我国个人所得税减除标准立法听证会举行。

The legislative hearing, held by the Law Committee of the National People's Congress (NPC) Standing Committee, was on the adjustment of personal income tax deduction criterion.

立法真空 legislation vacuum
完善立法体制，杜绝立法真空是我们的目标。
Our objective is to perfect the legislation system and prevent a legislation vacuum.

立体快巴 straddling bus
今年5月在第十三届北京国际科技产业博览会上首次展出的立体快巴将可能成为解决交通问题的一条出路。在不久的将来，这种新型车将在北京门头沟区进行试运行。
The straddling bus, first exhibited on the 13th Beijing International High-tech Expo in May this year, may be one possible answer to the traffic problem. In the near future, the model is to be put into pilot use in Beijing's Mentougou District.

立体农业 three-way farming economy
这是一座集旅游、种植、水产养殖为一体的庄园，人称"立体农业"。
This is what is called a three-way farming economy with the integration of tourism, crop planting, and aquaculture.

立于不败之地 remain invincible; be in an invincible position
每家公司都想在目前竞争日益激烈的市场中立于不败之地。
All companies would love to remain invincible in today's increasingly competitive marketplace.

利改税 tax-for-profit reform
企业一部分利润过去要上缴国库，现在以税收的形式缴纳。这就是利改税。
Companies used to hand over a certain percentage of their profits to State coffers. Now they pay in the form of taxes. This is the tax-for-profit reform.

利好因素 feel-good factor
市场调查公司总经理尼克·莫恩说："这会带来利好因素，但不太可能会让人们对自己的钱袋更有信心。"
"It may provide a feel-good factor, but it's unlikely to make people feel any more confident about their own finances," said Nick Moon, the managing director of the polling group.

利率走廊 interest rate corridor
中国人民银行副行长表示，中国正在探索建立利率走廊。

China is exploring the creation of an interest rate corridor, said vice-governor of the People's Bank of China.

利益共同体 community of shared interests
中英两国正变得越来越相互依赖,成为利益共同体。
China and Britain are increasingly interdependent and becoming a community of shared interests.

连锁反应;骨牌效应 domino effect; chain effect
你玩过多米诺骨牌吗?一个骨牌倒了会推翻下一个骨牌,它又会推翻下一个。这叫作骨牌效应,也就是连锁反应。
Have you ever played dominoes? One chip falls, another topples, then another. It's called the domino effect, or chain effect.

联合国儿童基金会青年教育使者 special advocate for education by the United Nations Children's Fund (UNICEF)
歌手、演员、TFBOYS成员王源被联合国儿童基金会任命为青年教育使者。
Chinese singer and actor Wang Yuan, a member of the pop band TFBOYS has been appointed as a special advocate for education by the United Nations Children's Fund (UNICEF).

联合竞标 joint bid
吉利汽车总裁在一次新闻发布会上称,公司将参与此次联合竞标,但他并未透露国内任何一家投资机构的名称。
Geely's chief executive was quoted at a news conference as saying the company would make the joint bid but did not disclose the name of any local investor.

廉价商店 discount store; discount shop
超市有时被看作是廉价商店。
Supermarkets are sometimes seen as discount stores.

廉价市场 bargain center; bargain market
二手市场是个廉价市场。
A second-hand market is a bargain center.

廉政建设 keep oneself as a clean government; build a clean and honest government; strive for a clean government
廉政建设是各级政府部门的奋斗目标。
Governments at all levels should strive to keep themselves as a clean government.

廉政准则 code of ethics
中共中央周二颁布了党员领导干部廉政准则。
The Communist Party of China (CPC) Central Committee issued a code of ethics for CPC cadres to follow Tuesday.

恋父情结 Electra complex
西格蒙德·弗洛伊德相信所有女儿都无意识地想和父亲同眠,他称此为"恋父情结"。与之相对的是男子的"恋母情结"。
Sigmund Freud believed that all daughters unconsciously want to sleep with their fathers. It is what he called the Electra complex, which he believed to be the female counterpart to the Oedipus complex in males.

良性循环 virtuous cycle
中国的国民经济保持了持续、快速和健康的发展。如果能继续在良性循环中前进,中国将很快成为世界最强的经济体之一。
China's national economy has maintained sustained, rapid, and sound growth. If this virtuous cycle continues, it will soon be one of the strongest economies in the world.

两岸直接"三通"(通邮、通航、通商)the three direct cross-Straits links, namely mail, transportation, and trade
两岸直接"三通"的呼声日益高涨。
The proposal to strengthen the three direct cross-Straits links, namely mail, transportation and trade, is gaining momentum.

两败俱伤 Both sides suffer losses.
在这次边界武装冲突中,双方两败俱伤。
Both sides suffered losses in the border armed conflict.

两个确保(确保国有企业下岗职工的基本生活;确保离退休人员的基本生活,保证按时足额发放基本养老金)two guarantees (to guarantee the basic livelihood of the laid-off workers from State-owned enterprises and to guarantee the basic livelihood and timely and full payment of basic pensions for all retirees)

两个文明一起抓 place equal emphasis on material progress and spiritual development
我们应该两个文明一起抓,也就是说,在建设社会主义物质文明的同时,我们不能忘记与之同等重要的社会主义精神文明建设。

We should place equal emphasis on material progress and spiritual development, that is, when building a socialist material civilization we should not neglect the socialist spiritual civilization since both are of equally great importance.

两条腿走路 walk on two legs
英语口语和英文写作同等重要，因此，在英语学习中，二者应得到平衡发展。用中国话来说，这种保证平衡的做法叫作"两条腿走路"。
English learners must attempt to strike a balance between spoken English and written English in their studies, as both are equally important. In Chinese, this sort of balancing act is referred to as "walking on two legs".

两学一做 Two studies, one action
"两学一做"，基础在学，首先要学好党章。党章是党的根本大法，是全面从严治党的总依据和总遵循，也是全体党员言行的总规矩和总遵循。
The foundation of the "two studies, one action" campaign is to study. We must further our study of the Party Constitution. The Party Constitution is the fundamental law of the Party, the key basis and principle in exercising Party discipline and guiding Party members' behavior.

两者不可兼得 You can't have your cake and eat it too./ can't have it both ways
我既想去看电影又想参加聚会，可是它们被安排在同一个晚上。我知道两者不可兼得了。
I wanted to see the movie as well as go to the party. But they were scheduled for the same night so I knew I couldn't have it both ways.

亮底牌 show one's hand/cards
他是谈判高手，总是最后亮底牌。
He's a smart negotiator. He's always the last to show his hand.

谅解备忘录 Memorandum of Understanding（MoU）
摩洛哥外贸银行—非洲银行与中国国家开发银行签署谅解备忘录，以促进双边贸易和投资。
Morocco's BMCE Bank of Africa (BOA) and the China Development Bank (CDB) have inked a memorandum of understanding (MoU) to enhance bilateral trade and investment.

量子卫星 quantum satellite
中国科学院表示，我国科学家已成功接收世界首颗量子卫星"墨子号"传回的首批数据。
The first batch of data from the world's first quantum satellite "Micius" was received by Chinese scientists, the Chinese Academy of Sciences said.

劣迹艺人 tainted star
广电总局日前下令，各电视台和其他媒体机构停止播出涉吸毒、有嫖娼行为的"劣迹艺人"参与录制的节目。
The State Administration of Press, Publication, Radio, Film and Television has ordered TV stations and other outlets to stop broadcasting material featuring "tainted stars" who use drugs or visit prostitutes.

劣质产品 shoddy goods; substandard goods
在这场仍在进行的行动中，他们将继续同中国政府保持合作，打击生产和出口劣质产品的行为。
They will continue to cooperate with the Chinese government in the ongoing campaign against the production and export of shoddy goods.

猎头公司 head-hunting company
一直以来，美国和欧洲国家的猎头公司锁准的对象是中国、印度、墨西哥、巴西和其他一些发展中国家。
Head-hunting companies in America and Europe have been targeting China, India, Mexico, Brazil, and other developing countries.

临床试验 clinical trial
在志愿者身上进行的临床试验将在近期开展。
Clinical trials on volunteers would start in days.

临界点 tipping point
美国发布的一份报告称，地球轨道上太空垃圾的数量已经达到"临界点"，有撞击风险，而后可能产生更多碎片，威胁宇航员和人造卫星的安全。
The amount of debris orbiting the Earth has reached "a tipping point" for collisions, which would in turn generate more of the debris that threatens astronauts and satellites, according to a US study released.

临时停职 provisional suspension
国际足联道德委员会下令国际足联主席布拉特临时停职90天。
FIFA's Ethics Committee has imposed a 90-day provisional suspension on FIFA President Sepp Blatter.

临时主教练；代理教练 interim coach
真不可思议！作为代理教练，他取得了5胜2平仅负1场的佳绩。
As an interim coach, he has managed to make an incredible record of five wins, two draws and only one loss.

零和博弈 zero-sum game
这是一场零和博弈，因为一个发展中国家的收益正是另一个发展中国家的损失。
It is a zero-sum game, because what one developing country gains will be at the direct expense of another.

零和冷战思维 zero-sum Cold War mentality
他呼吁双方今后摒弃零和冷战思维，创造更美好的未来。
He called for both sides to abandon the zero-sum Cold War mentality for a better future.

零排放车辆 zero-emission vehicle
除了提高公共交通运行效率外，改用零排放的车辆应该是北京所有司机的终极目标。
Apart from accelerating the public transport efficiency, switching to zero-emission vehicles should be the ultimate goal for all drivers in Beijing.

零团费旅游 free-of-charge tour
目前，旅行社多提供"零团费"甚至"负团费"香港游业务。
The current offerings include free-of-charge tours or even negative-charge tours to Hong Kong.

零星抵抗 scattered resistance
利比亚政府军的坦克和狙击兵进行了零星抵抗，但是几乎没有迹象表明反对派力量遇到了任何有组织的抵抗。
Libyan government tanks and snipers put up scattered resistance but there was little sign that the rebel offensive was meeting any coordinated opposition.

领事保护 consular protection
去年，外交部处置领事保护案件7万多起。
The Ministry of Foreign Affairs handled more than 70,000 cases of consular protection last year.

领土归属 territorial entitlement
两国在这些岛屿的领土归属问题上存在分歧。
The two countries differ over territorial entitlement to the islands.

领土完整 territorial integrity
我们绝不允许任何人侵犯中国的主权和领土完整。
We will never allow anybody to encroach upon China's territorial integrity and sovereignty.

领土坐标 territorial coordinates
中国政府公布了钓鱼岛及其附属岛屿的领海基点和基线等领土坐标。
Chinese government announced territorial coordinates—base points and baselines—for waters off the Diaoyu Island and its affiliated islands.

另起炉灶 make a fresh start
新教练想另起炉灶,带来了自己的人马。
The new coach, hoping to make a fresh start, brought in his own people.

溜须拍马 fawn on
他说他不会为求及格而溜须拍马奉承老师。
He says he isn't the one who hopes to pass the exam by fawning on the teacher.

留存指纹 collect fingerprints
我国将开始在选定的口岸留存入境外国人的指纹和面部图像信息。
China will start to collect fingerprints and capture facial images of foreign passport holders entering China at selected ports.

留任官员 holdover
他是前内阁中的留任者。
He is a holdover from the last administration.

留守儿童 left-behind children
根据民政部的信息,我国农村留守儿童人数为902万。
China has 9.02 million left-behind children in the countryside, according to a statement from the Ministry of Civil Affairs.

留学签证 student visa
根据澳大利亚移民和边境保护局宣布的最新留学签证政策,2016年7月1日起,年满6岁的中国小学生可申请赴澳大利亚留学,其父母可申请陪读。
From July 1, 2016, Chinese pupils from the age of six can apply to study in Australia and their parents can apply to accompany them, according to the latest student visa policy announced by the Department of Immigration and Border Protection in Australia.

流动儿童 migrant children
一份报告指出,截至2014年,我国九年义务教育阶段流动儿童在父母现居住地公办学校就读的比例仅为80%。
Only 80 percent of migrant children who qualify for nine-year compulsory education in China as of 2014 could attend public schools where their parents live, according to a report.

流动人口 migrant population
我国流动人口占总人口的18%。
China's migrant population accounts for 18 percent of China's overall population.

流动医院 mobile clinic
由中国医药卫生事业发展基金会捐赠的100所"流动医院",迄今以来已使中国边远地区的3000多万名农牧民受益。
A hundred "mobile clinics" donated by the China Health & Medical Development Foundation (CHMDF) have to date benefited over 30 million villagers and herdsmen in the remote areas of China.

流感集中爆发 flu outbreak
北京疾控中心表示,目前流感暴发率居于5年来最高水平。
Beijing Center for Disease Control and Prevention said the flu outbreak rate is at its highest level in five years.

流量不清零 rollover data service
三大电信运营商于2015年10月1日起推出"流量不清零",即未使用流量不会在月底清零。
China's three major telecom operators launched rollover data services on Oct 1, 2015, meaning unused data at the end of the month will no longer just disappear.

流通股 tradable share
上市公司必须向流通股股东提供保证书。
Listed companies are required to provide guarantees to holders of tradable shares.

流行文化 pop culture
这位画家从美国流行文化中汲取灵感。
The painter gets inspiration from the American pop culture.

录取分数线 minimum enrollment mark; lowest mark for admission
北京大学的录取分数线有一年在全国是最高的。
The minimum enrollment mark of Peking University was once the highest in the country.

路演 road show
代表团在美国东海岸进行路演,向美国观众宣传中国是理想的旅游目的地。
The delegation is staging a road show along the East coast of the United States to promote China as an ideal destination for American tourists.

露天烧烤 outdoor barbeque
北京正着手整治非法露天烧烤,以减少路边空气和噪音污染。
Beijing is stepping up efforts to reduce illegal outdoor barbeques, to cut down on roadside air and noise pollution.

乱收费 arbitrary charge; illegal charge
我们要采取有效手段制止乱收费。
We need to take effective measures against arbitrary charges.

轮流(坐庄) in turn; rotate
国际足联正式宣布,从2010年开始,世界杯将由各大洲轮流主办。
The Federation of International Football Association has announced that the World Cup will be hosted in turn by each continent from 2010.

轮流停电 rolling blackout
东京电力公司宣布,计划在东京和周边城市实行轮流停电。
Tokyo Electric Power Co(TEPCO) had reported that it would schedule rolling blackouts in Tokyo and surrounding cities.

轮值主席 rotating chairman
作为安理会轮值主席,中国鼓励所有参与者采取灵活合作的态度,通过协商达成一致。
As the Security Council's rotating chairman, China encouraged all parties to take a flexible and cooperative attitude in order to reach a consensus through negotiation.

轮作 crop rotation
我国将扩大耕地轮作休耕制度试点规模,促进农业绿色发展。
China will expand its trials of crop rotation and fallow systems as part of efforts to facilitate the green development of agriculture.

论资排辈 give priority to seniority
我们要杜绝教师队伍中论资排辈提级的现象。
We should put an end to the practice of giving priority to seniority in the promotion of teaching staff.

螺旋式下降 spiral downward
美国股市周四暴跌,股市抛售已长达4天。决策者未能成功治愈全球经济停滞,导致市场走向呈螺旋式下降。
US stocks plunged on Thursday, extending a sell-off to four days, as policymakers' failure to arrest global economic stagnation sent markets spiraling downward.

裸官 naked official
中共中央发布了针对"裸官"的新管理规定,裸官指家属都已移居国外的官员。
The Central Committee of the Communist Party of China has released new restrictions governing "naked officials", or those whose family members have all gone abroad.

裸婚 naked marriage
裸婚的意思是新婚夫妇没有房、没有车、没有钻戒或盛大的婚礼仪式的现象。
Naked marriage means newly-weds without a house, car, diamond ring or grand wedding ceremony.

裸捐(死后将全部财产捐出) donate one's entire fortune to charity after one's death
这位中国著名企业家和慈善家已承诺死后将全部财产捐出,即"裸捐"。
The well-known Chinese entrepreneur and philanthropist has pledged to donate his entire fortune to charity after his death.

落地签 visa-on-arrival
共有47个国家和地区给予我国公民个人签证免签、落地签待遇。
A total of 47 countries and regions have introduced visa exemptions or visa-on-arrival policies for Chinese private citizen passport holders.

旅游保证金 travel deposit
380多名北京游客正寻求市旅游委的帮助,希望取回此前交给旅行社的"旅游保证金"。
More than 380 tourists in Beijing are demanding help from the city's tourism commission to get back their travel deposit handed to a travel agency.

旅游扶贫 lift poverty-stricken people out of poverty through tourism; poverty alleviation through tourism
未来5年内,我国将通过发展旅游使1200万至1400万贫困人口脱贫。
China will lift 12 to 14 million poverty-stricken people out of poverty in the next five years through tourism development.

绿地覆盖率 green coverage rate
该地区绿地覆盖率从以前的6.8%上升到现在的15.3%。
The green coverage rate of the area has risen from 6.8 percent to the current 15.3 percent.

绿化 afforestation
根据该省政府10年绿化计划,该省将植树80万公顷。
Under a 10-year afforestation plan drawn up by the provincial government, the province will plant trees on 800,000 hectares of land.

绿化面积 afforested area; greening space
目前,三北防护林已完成一期和二期的造林计划,新造林面积达1.851亿公顷。
Currently, the first and second phases of the "Three North Shelterbelts Project" have been completed, resulting in a newly afforested area of 185.1 million hectares.

绿卡 green card
在美国他曾申请过绿卡,不过没有成功。
While in the US, he sought to get a green card but failed.

绿色奥运,科技奥运,人文奥运 Green Olympics, Technology Olympics and Cultural Olympics; Environment-friendly Olympics, Technology-empowered Olympics and culture-enriched Olympics

绿色包装 green packaging
包括国家邮政局在内的10个中央政府部门联合发布了快递行业指导意见,目标是到2020年将生物降解绿色包装材料的应用比例提高到50%。
Ten central government departments including the State Post Bureau have jointly issued guidance for the express delivery industry, with the aim of increasing the application ratio of biodegradable green packaging materials to 50 percent by 2020.

绿色产品 green product
贴有绿色食品标签的蔬菜售价较高。
Vegetables with a "green product" label fetch higher prices.

绿色金融 green finance
国务院宣布决定建立绿色金融试验区,推动绿色金融产业升级。
The State Council announced its decision to set up pilot zones for green finance to support its industrial upgrading.

绿色金融改革创新试验区 pilot zones for green finance reform and innovations
国务院宣布建设绿色金融改革创新试验区。
The State Council announced it is setting up pilot zones for green finance reform and innovations.

绿色就业 green job (green employment)
截至去年底,全市新开发绿色就业岗位约有2.45万个。
Some 24,500 green jobs have been created by the end of last year.

绿色能源 green energy
中国对绿色能源,尤其是太阳能的需求每年递增30%。
The demand in China for green energy, solar power in particular, increases 30 percent every year.

绿色农业 green agriculture
美国科学家指出,绿色农业可能实际效益更高。
The American scientists say that green agriculture might in fact be more efficient.

绿色烟花 green fireworks
为使因烟花燃放禁令而受影响的市场恢复活力,制造商纷纷努力研发"绿色烟花"。
Manufacturers are working to develop green fireworks in an effort to rejuvenate the market hurt by firework display bans.

绿色账户 green account
上海"绿色账户"活动旨在普及垃圾分类知识、鼓励再生资源回收、倡导低碳生活方式、助力绿色文化传播。
The green account activity in Shanghai aims to popularize the idea of garbage sorting, encourage recycling of renewable resources, promote low-carbon lifestyle, and spread the green culture.

马拉松热 Marathon fever
"马拉松热"正席卷中国。2015年11月8日,全国6个城市共有约7.5万名参与者在参加马拉松赛事。
Marathon fever has swept across China, with about 75,000 participants running in marathon competitions in six cities on Nov 8, 2015.

霾天气预警系统 weather warning system for smog
中国气象局首次推出霾天气预警系统,将细颗粒物PM2.5作为发布预警的重要指标之一。
China's meteorological authority has introduced a new weather warning system for smog which will use readings of PM2.5, a particle pollutant, as one of the major indicators.

买断工龄 buyout
《纽约时报》于周一称,为应对广告收入下滑,该报将以买断工龄或解雇的形式裁减100个新闻部门岗位。
The *New York Times* said on Monday it would cut 100 newsroom jobs through buyouts or layoffs as it tried to counter the lost advertising revenue.

买方市场 buyer's market
现在是买方市场,鸡蛋到处都是。质量差的鸡蛋恐怕卖不出去,更别提卖高价了。
With eggs galore, it's now a buyer's market. Eggs of poor quality can hardly be sold, let alone fetch a high price.

买官卖官 buy or sell official posts
8名中国共产党官员因"买官卖官"被查处。
Eight Communist Party of China (CPC) officials have been punished for buying or selling official posts.

买一送一 two-for-one; buy one, get one free
消费者受到打折和买一送一的诱惑,周末都涌向了百货公司和商场。
Shoppers, lured by discounts and two-for-one offers, packed department stores over the weekend.

卖点 selling point
他们发现电影制作者们并不试着去理解音乐家,而只是把他们的音乐作为一个卖点。
They discovered the filmmakers were not trying to understand the musicians, but merely using their music as a selling point.

脉冲星导航卫星 pulsar navigation satellite
我国成功发射了世界上第一颗X射线脉冲星导航卫星。
China successfully launched the first X-ray pulsar navigation satellite in the world.

满意度 satisfaction rate
调查显示,电信用户满意度仍然不高。
Satisfaction rates among telecom subscribers remained low, according to samples.

满座;爆满 full-house
根据夏洛蒂·勃朗特1847年的爱情小说《简·爱》改编的话剧今年早些时候登上了国家大剧院的舞台。这部剧在6月份演出的时候,10个晚上都是场场爆满。
Charlotte Bronte's 1847 love story *Jane Eyre* was adapted for the stage earlier this year at Beijing's National Center for the Performing Arts. The new adaptation played to full-houses for ten nights in June.

漫话;闲话 shoot the breeze; chatter
闲话少说,现在我们言归正传。
Enough chatter, let's get to the point.

漫游(服务) roaming service
现在很多国家都开通了国际漫游服务。
International roaming service is now available in many countries.

慢镜头 slow motion
老虎捕猎的慢镜头动作真漂亮。
The tiger, hunting in slow motion, is a beautiful creature to watch.

慢就业 delayed employment
随着就业市场的竞争一年比一年激烈,越来越多的应届大学毕业生选择"慢就业"。
With the job market becoming increasingly competitive every year, a growing number of fresh university graduates are opting for "delayed employment".

忙音 busy signal; busy tone
他的电话简直是个热线,什么时候打过去都是忙音。
His telephone is literally a hotline—whenever you call him, you get a busy signal.

盲目点赞党 blind liker
"盲目点赞党"指给你微博或微信朋友圈所有的帖文点赞,却连帖文内容都没读过的人。
Blind liker refers to someone who "likes" all your posts on Weibo or WeChat Moments without even reading them.

盲目改造 blind reconstruction; blind rebuilding
国家文物局局长反对盲目改造旧城。
The nation's cultural relics chief is opposed to the blind reconstruction of old city towns.

盲目投资 blind investment
他盲目投资了5个矿,均颗粒无收。
He made five blind investments in mines, without getting any return whatsoever.

猫腻 something fishy; under-the-table deal; underhanded conduct
看那俩人的样子,他感觉他们有什么猫儿腻。
By the look of them, he could tell something fishy was going on between the two.

毛利 gross proceeds
毛利看起来不错。
Gross proceeds look good.

冒牌服务中心 phony service center; dodgy service center
自从该公司生产的笔记本电脑近日在中国爆出质量问题后,一些冒牌服务中心开始积极地面向该品牌的问题电脑用户招徕生意。
After a quality problem involving laptops produced by this company was recently exposed in China, some phony service centers are lapping up business from the brand's troubled users.

贸易壁垒 trade protectionism; trade barrier
地区贸易壁垒已阻碍了中国出口的增长。
Regional trade protectionism has hindered China's efforts to increase exports.

贸易逆差 trade deficit
美国对中国的贸易逆差仍在加大。
The US trade deficits with China continue to grow.

贸易失衡 trade imbalance; imbalance of trade
在二十国集团峰会上,各方可能就解决贸易失衡指示性方针的基本原则达成共识。

It is likely to reach an agreement on the basic principle of indicative guidelines on trade imbalance at the G20 Summit.

贸易顺差 trade surplus
调查中有40%的经济学家预测今年中国全年的贸易顺差将达到1500亿元。
Among the economists interviewed, 40 percent of them estimated that the trade surplus of China would reach 150 billion yuan this year.

贸易战 trade war
新一轮贸易战阴云笼罩，因为最近的谈判没有取得一点进展，又告破裂。
A new round of trade war is looming since the latest negotiations have ended without making any progress.

贸易自由化 trade liberalization
美国把中国香港特别行政区看作贸易自由化进程之天然伙伴。
The United States looks on the Hong Kong Special Administrative Region（SAR）of China as a natural partner in the move toward trade liberalization.

帽子戏法 hat trick
足球比赛里独中三元的人被称作上演帽子戏法。
In soccer, one who scores three goals in a match is said to have had a hat trick.

眉毛胡子一把抓 do lots of things all at once; go about several tasks all at once
问题要一个一个回答，不要眉毛胡子一把抓，不然你会乱套。
Answer questions one by one. You'll lose yourself if you try to answer them all at once.

煤转化产业 coal conversion industry
业内人士估计，中国将在2020年建成全球最大的煤（清洁）转化产业。
China is expected to develop its coal conversion industry into the world's largest by 2020.

美食节 gourmet festival
在中国旅游交易会上，"成都美食节"的举办有望吸引5万名以上的食客。
The Chengdu Gourmet Festival will be held during the China Tourism Trade Fair, which is expected to attract more than 50,000 people.

门儿清 well-informed
去问他，他对会上发生的一切都门儿清。
Ask him. He's well-informed about all the goings on at the meeting.

蒙上阴影 overshadow
他父亲在事故中受伤的消息给他参加新工作的第一天蒙上了阴影。
The news that his father had been hurt in an accident overshadowed his first day in his new job.

弥补；补偿 atone for
我该怎样做才能弥补对你造成的感情伤害呢？
How can I atone for hurting your feelings?

迷彩服 army fatigues
将军像往常一样身着迷彩服出席了晚会。
The general, in his usual army fatigues, attended the party.

迷你睡眠仓 mini hotel
西安咸阳国际机场T3航站楼的"迷你睡眠仓"于周二开始运营。
The mini hotel in the Terminal 3 of Xi'an Airport opens for business Tuesday.

密码疲劳 password fatigue
很多人都在经历"密码疲劳"，记住大量密码已经成为他们日常生活的一部分。
"Password fatigue" is the feeling experienced by many people who are required to remember an excessive number of passwords as part of their daily routine.

蜜罐里长大 be born and bred with a silver spoon in one's mouth
爸爸总说我是蜜罐里长大的。
My father always says that I was born and bred with a silver spoon in my mouth.

免费乘车 free ride
峰会期间，当地政府提供免费的公共交通出行。
The local government offers free ride of public transport during the summit.

免费通过 free passage; be exempted from road tolls; scrap toll charge; go toll-free
包括机场高速在内的北京所有高速公路将在国庆长假期间对小客车免收通行费。
All of Beijing's highways, including the airport expressways, will give free passage to small passenger cars during the National Day holidays.

免费退货 free-of-charge return
苹果公司取消了一直以来在香港和澳门特别行政区实行的免费退货政策，此举显示了这家科技巨头打击黄牛靠其最新发布的机型牟取暴利的决心。
Apple has scrapped its longstanding free-of-charge return policy in Hong Kong

and Macao SARs, in a sign of the tech giant's determination to deter scalpers from making a quick buck on its newly launched handsets.

免税商店 duty-free shop
免税商店过时了。过去只能在免税商店买到的东西现在在别处也能买到。
Duty-free shops have had their time. Now you can buy things that used to be sold only in duty-free shops at other stores.

免押金 deposit waiver
国内共享单车初创企业ofo正在上海试点对符合条件的用户免押金,观察人士称,此举将进一步加剧共享单车行业已然激烈的竞争。
Chinese bike-sharing startup ofo Inc is testing deposit waivers for qualified riders in Shanghai, a move observers said would further intensify the already heated competition in the sector.

勉强度日 eke out a living; (live) a hand-to-mouth existence; make ends meet
对村里的乡亲来说,这些打工者或许挣了大钱。可是在上海,一个月500元不过能勉强度日罢了。
To folks back home in the villages, these laborers may be making a lot of money. But 500 yuan a month in Shanghai is a hand-to-mouth existence.

面试筛选程序 interview-screening process
美国驻华使馆将采取多项措施简化对中国公民入境审理的流程,比如简化面试筛选程序、在广州新建领事馆以及扩大现有的领馆办事处。
Several steps, such as reducing the interview-screening process, building a new consulate in Guangzhou and expanding current offices, are being taken by the US embassy to ease the entry process for Chinese visitors.

面条外交 noodle diplomacy
美国副总统乔·拜登近日访问中国时在北京一家饭馆点的炸酱面和其他小吃现在受到食客们的追捧。那顿饭也被冠以"面条外交"的美名。
Black bean sauce noodles and other delicacies served at one Beijing eatery are being snapped up by customers eager to order the dishes eaten by US Vice President Joe Biden on a recent visit, a meal dubbed "noodle diplomacy".

面子工程 face job
美国有线电视新闻网日前报道不少中国企业"租借"白种人老外撑门面,报道中把这种现象称为"面子工程"。

The CNN website has targeted a phenomenon called "face job" in which Chinese companies "rent" white foreigners.

面子消费 face consumption
这类消费行为不是为了实际需要，而只是出于炫耀和满足消费者的"面子"的目的，因此被称为"面子消费"。

These purchases, which are not for practical needs, but merely to show off and gratify the owners' vanity, are called "face consumptions".

秒杀 seckilling
用了几秒钟时间，仅仅花费1.1元人民币，杭州大学生杨江明就成为四川成都一套价值80万元住宅的主人了。这处房产是用鼠标"秒"到的，这种新生的网络现象被称为"秒杀"。

Within seconds, and for just 1.1 yuan, a university student from Hangzhou, Yang Jiangming, was the owner of an 800,000 yuan apartment in Chengdu, Sichuan province. The property was his at the click of a mouse, thanks to a new online phenomenon called "seckilling".

民调持平 too-close-to-call poll
此次大选中，双方民调持平，且摇摆选民不多。

The race is marked by too-close-to-call polls and a dearth of undecided voters.

民航发展基金 Civil Aviation Development Fund
根据征收、使用和管理民航发展基金的临时办法规定，从本月开始，乘坐国内航班的旅客每次将支付50元基金。

According to the interim measures on collecting, using and managing the Civil Aviation Development Fund, passengers flying on domestic flights will pay 50 yuan per trip, starting this month.

民间交流 people-to-people communication
这位教授呼吁中国和其他国家展开更多民间交流，以在国际社会营造更积极的国家形象。

The professor called for more people-to-people communication between China and other countries to help create a more positive image of the country in the international community.

民间借贷 private lending
中国政府正考虑建立民间借贷活动的监控系统。

The Chinese government is considering establishing a monitoring system for private lending activities.

民间投资 private investment
中央政府近日发布关于进一步鼓励民间资本在更多关键领域投资的指导意见。
The central government released guidelines on further encouraging private investment in a wider range of key industries.

民间艺人 folk artist
作为一个民间艺人,他从未料到自己会闻名全国。
As a folk artist, he never expected to get national recognition.

民间智库 private think tank
据《人民日报》报道,华南某省已批准注册首个民间智库,为官员在关键问题的决策上提供帮助和建议。
A province in South China has approved the first registered private think tank to help and advise officials on key issues, the *People's Daily* reported.

民间资本 private capital
民间资本已经被允许投资连锁药店。
Private capital to fund chain drugstores has been allowed.

民间组织;社会组织 civil society; non-governmental organization
政府将简化注册手续、加强监督力度、鼓励社会组织发挥更大的作用。
The government will encourage civil societies to play a greater role by simplifying registration while beefing up supervision.

民生 people's livelihood
他在主旨演讲中强调了改善民生的重要性。
He highlighted the importance of improving people's livelihood during his keynote speech.

民事诉讼 civil procedure
根据中国的民事诉讼法,法院将在几天内做出正式答复。
The court is expected to give a formal reply in a few days, according to China's civil procedure law.

民以食为天 people regard food as their primary need

民意病毒 public opinion virus
网络操控或"民意病毒"危害了互联网的健康发展并可能会影响公众情绪、误导民意,可能会激化或放大社会矛盾。

Internet manipulation, or "public opinion viruses", harmed the healthy development of the internet, and could affect public emotions and mislead public opinion, which could intensify or magnify social conflicts.

民意测验 opinion poll
民意测验表明挪威人愿意不再纠缠新王妃的过去。
An opinion poll confirmed that Norwegians were ready to forget the new princess' past.

民营企业 privately-run enterprise
越来越多的北京人喜欢在民营企业就职。
More and more Beijingers prefer jobs with privately-run enterprises.

民政 civil affairs
北京民政局为管理老房子的公务人员提供培训。
The Civil Affairs Bureau of Beijing provides training for civil servants who are managing old houses.

民主党派、工商联与无党派人士 non-Communist parties, federations of industry and commerce, and personages without party affiliation

民族凝聚力 national cohesion
我们必须提高经济实力,提高民族凝聚力。
We must make China economically stronger and enhance national cohesion.

民族区域自治 regional autonomy of ethnic minorities
随着民族区域自治的全面实施,平等和团结互助的社会主义民族关系不断稳定增强。
With the all-round implementation of the system of regional autonomy of ethnic minorities, the socialist ethnic relationship, which features equality, solidarity, and mutual assistance, has been steadily improving.

民族文化大省 province with rich ethnic culture
这个民族文化大省每年吸引海外游客几万人。
This province with rich ethnic culture attracts tens of thousands of visitors from overseas.

民族优越感 ethnocentrism
民族优越感会导致我们歪曲其他民族文化。
Ethnocentrism leads us to make false assumptions about other cultures.

M

名额分配 slot allocation
国际足联理事会就一项关于2026年世界杯参赛名额分配的提案达成一致。2026年世界杯决赛阶段比赛将有48支队伍参赛。
The FIFA Council agreed on a proposed slot allocation for the World Cup 2026, which will witness 48 teams in the finals.

名人代言 celebrity endorsement
中国广告法修订建议的重点之一就是要让明星代言人对他们所代言的产品担负更多的责任。这些修订是为了加强对名人代言和名人广告的管控。
One of the highlights of the proposed changes to Chinese Advertisement Law includes making celebrity spokespersons more responsible for the endorsement deals they take on. These changes were made to strengthen controls over celebrity endorsements and advertising.

名人堂 Hall of Fame
前休斯敦火箭队中锋姚明被提名入选奈史密斯篮球名人堂，成为首个获此殊荣的中国球员。
Former Houston Rockets center Yao Ming has been nominated for the Naismith Memorial Basketball Hall of Fame, becoming the first Chinese player to receive the honor.

名人效应 celebrity charm
利用名人效应，企业经常请影视体育明星为他们拍广告。
Taking advantage of celebrity charm, enterprises often hire movie stars and sports stars to be featured in their ads.

名誉教授 honorary professor
著名的生物学家布莱恩·史密斯先生已经被我们大学聘为名誉教授。
Brian Smith, the famous biologist, has been engaged as honorary professor by our university.

明文规定 stipulate in explicit terms
公司有明文规定，产妇可休假4个月。
The company has stipulated in explicit terms that four-month maternity leaves are allowed.

冥想区 meditation area
南京理工大学图书馆新设计的信息共享空间设立了冥想区和站立学习区，学生可以在这里看书、眺望窗外或者只是冥想。

A meditation area and a stand-only studying area are parts of the newly-designed information sharing space of the library at Nanjing University of Science and Technology, where students can read, look out of the window, or simply meditate.

摸着石头过河 grope across the river by feeling the way; test each step before taking it; advance cautiously

中国在改革伊始就采取了坚定而谨慎的策略,用总设计师邓小平的话说叫作"摸着石头过河"。

In the Chinese reform, a determined but cautious approach had been adopted from the beginning. To quote from Deng Xiaoping, the chief architect of the reform, it is called "groping across the river by feeling the way".

模拟测试 practice test; mock test; simulated exam

高考前,学生们参加模拟测试的次数可能多达3次。

Before the National College Entrance Exam, students may have taken as many as three practice tests.

模拟装置 simulator

这是一个实时空间模拟装置,让您感受三维宇宙。

This is a real-time space simulator that lets you experience the universe in three dimensions.

摩天大楼热 skyscraper fervor

有网友表示,席卷全国的摩天大楼热或与经济研究专家安德鲁·劳伦斯一个相当有争议的理论有关。该理论指出,世界最高楼的建成往往紧随经济衰退出现。

The skyscraper fervor spreading across the country is linked with a controversial theory by economic researcher Andrew Lawrence, according to netizens, which shows that the world's tallest buildings often rise in the wake of economic downturns.

磨洋工 dawdle along

公司聘请心理学家与那些容易磨洋工的职员交谈。

The company has hired psychologists to talk to those who tend to dawdle along at work.

抹黑 stain someone's (good) name; bring shame on

电信海报警告说:自己欠费,自己"抹黑"。

Deferring payment of your mobile phone fee stains your own good name, warns a telecom poster.

末日论者 doomster
马尔萨斯是最早的末日论者。许多人认为他的预测过于悲观。
Malthus was the original "doomster". Many feel his predictions are overly pessimistic.

末日时钟 Doomsday Clock
"末日时钟"的分针将保持在距离午夜3分钟的位置。其设计的初衷是为了让世人以简单直观的方式来估算人类灭绝的可能性。
The minute hand of the Doomsday Clock, designed to give the world an easy way to gauge the likelihood that our species will destroy itself, will remain at three minutes to midnight.

没收犯罪收益 confiscate criminal proceeds
一旦中国与美国、澳大利亚达成协议,非法资产犯罪收益便可被冻结并没收。
Once the agreement between China, America and Australia is reached, illegal assets and those criminal proceeds can be frozen or confiscated.

莫失良机 take full advantage; make hay while the sun shines; strike while the iron is hot
公司派你出国培训,你可不要错失良机,要好好提高一下业务能力。
Now that you've been selected to go abroad for training, you should take full advantage of this opportunity to improve yourself professionally.

默片;无声电影 silent movie
奥斯卡颁奖典礼重温了电影对于许多人的特殊意义,好莱坞表现出了对其历史的钟爱,将最佳影片奖和其他四个奖项给了默片《艺术家》。
Hollywood showed some love for its history at the Oscars, giving its best film award and four others to silent movie *The Artist* in a ceremony that recalled why the cinema is special to so many people.

母乳喂养 breastfeeding
世界卫生组织推荐母乳喂养为最佳哺育方式,因为母乳能为婴儿提供他们健康成长和发育所需的营养。
Breastfeeding is recommended by the WHO as the best way to provide infants with the nutrients they need for healthy growth and development.

母婴设施 mother-and-child facilities
到2020年底,全国所有主要公共场所,如交通枢纽、大型购物中心和医院,应配置用于哺乳或换尿布的母婴设施。

All major public places in China, such as transportation hubs, big shopping malls and hospitals, should be equipped with mother-and-child facilities used for breast-feeding or diaper changing by the end of 2020.

木马（一种黑客程序）Trojan Horse

当心！祝福新年的电子卡片可能是一种木马程序。

Watch out! That New Year's electronic greeting card may be a Trojan Horse.

目标飞行器 target spacecraft

项目发言人称，天宫一号将作为空间交会对接的目标飞行器，完成交会对接试验。

The program spokesman said that Tiangong-1 will serve as a "target spacecraft" for rendezvous and docking experiments.

目无法纪 in defiance of the law (or standards of discipline, regulations); defy the law (or standards of discipline, regulations)

他目无公司法纪，对上级多次的警告充耳不闻，挪用公款5万元。

He was found to have misappropriated 50,000 yuan for personal purposes, in defiance of company regulations and repeated warnings from his superiors.

募捐活动 donation activity

大规模的募捐活动在中国非常普遍，但有时举办方式并不恰当。

Campaign-style donation activities are very common in China, but inappropriate.

幕后操纵 pull the strings behind the scenes

虽然逮捕了3个人，但幕后操纵者依然在逃。

Although three were arrested, the person pulling the strings behind the scenes is still at large.

睦邻友好关系 neighborly and friendly relations

各成员国在共同关心的领域进一步发展睦邻友好关系，包括将共同边界建设成为永久和平友好的边界。

The member states aimed at the further development of neighbourly and friendly relations in areas of mutual interest, including to turn mutual borders into borders of lasting peace and friendship.

慕课 MOOC

慕课，即大规模在线开放课程，是一种通过互联网实现广泛参与和开放接入的课程模式，始于西方。

MOOC (Massive Online Open Course)—which involves widespread participation and open access through the internet—was initiated in the West.

N

拿手项目 forte; specialty
他的拿手项目是网球。她的强项是乒乓球。
Tennis is his forte. Her specialty is ping-pong.

拿原则和群众利益换人情 seek personal favors at the expense of principles and public interests
政府官员被告诫不可拿原则和群众利益换人情。
Government officials are told not to seek personal favors at the expense of principles and public interests.

奶嘴男 mama's boy; mummy's boy; mother's boy
"奶嘴男"指到了应该独立生活的年纪却还对母亲过度依赖的男人。
Mama's boy is a term for a man who is excessively attached to his mother at an age when men are expected to be independent.

耐用品 durable goods
根据周四发布的政府数据,美国11月份收到的耐用品订单仅上升了0.2%,低于预期水平。
The US orders for durable goods edged up 0.2 percent in November, weaker than expected, according to government data released Thursday.

男闺蜜 bromeo
吉姆不是我的男朋友,他顶多算我的男闺蜜。
Jim is not my boyfriend. He is my bromeo at most.

男女同工同酬 equal pay for equal work without regard to sex
几十年来,世界各地妇女一直在为男女同工同酬而斗争。
For decades, women worldwide have been fighting for equal pay for equal work without regard to sex.

南北对话 South-North dialogue
中非论坛将推动中非友好合作关系在新世纪中进入新的阶段,并对南南合作与南北对话起积极的促进作用。

The China-Africa forum will push Sino-African friendship and cooperation to a new stage in the next century and have a positive impact on South-South cooperation and South-North dialogue.

南海仲裁案 South China Sea arbitration case
中国与菲律宾的关系因菲律宾前总统阿基诺三世提出的南海仲裁案降至冰点。
The ties between China and the Philippines were frozen by the South China Sea arbitration case brought by former Philippines president Benigno Aquino III.

南水北调工程 South-North Water Diversion Project（SNWD）
湖北省的499位村民永远告别自己的家乡，成为第一批为中国的南水北调工程外迁的移民。
Bidding farewell to their hometown for good, 499 villagers in central China's Hubei province left their homes, becoming the first group to relocate to make way for China's South-North Water Diversion Project（SNWD）.

难民营 refugee camp
他没有忘记难民营的苦难。近两年虽然大有作为，但依旧谦逊、勤俭。
He remembers the days at the refugee camp, so he remains humble and frugal even though he's had nothing but success in the past two years.

闹洞房 horseplay at wedding
《中国青年报》的调查显示，约70.7%的年轻人表示应抵制低俗"闹洞房"，因为它有违伦理。
About 70.7% of young people said they would boycott vulgar horseplay at weddings as it violates ethical standards, a survey by *China Youth Daily* showed.

闹情绪 be disgruntled
两天过去了，她仍在闹情绪。
She remained disgruntled two days later.

内幕交易 insider trading
光大证券因内幕交易被证监会处以罚款5.23亿元。
China Securities Regulatory Commission has fined Everbright Securities 523 million yuan for insider trading.

内向型经济 domestically-oriented economy
从1998年开始，欧洲内向型经济已明显活跃起来。
The European domestically-oriented economy has become noticeably more animated since 1998.

能源安全 energy security
该委员会将负责拟订国家能源发展战略,审议能源安全,协调能源领域国际合作。
The commission will be responsible for drafting national energy development plans, reviewing energy security and coordinating international cooperation.

能源强度 energy intensity
我们重申到2035年将总能源强度降低45%,到2030年将可再生能源在地区能源构成中的比例提升1倍的期望目标,在亚太地区实现可持续、有韧性的能源开发。
We reaffirm our aspirational goals to reduce aggregate energy intensity by 45 percent by 2035 and double renewable energy in the regional energy mix by 2030 to achieve sustainable and resilient energy development within the Asia-Pacific.

能源危机 energy crunch
近几个月来国内许多地区出现的电力短缺预示着将可能出现数年来最严重的能源危机,有关经济增长会因此受阻的担忧也在加剧。
Power shortages that gripped many parts of the country in recent months could herald the worst energy crunch in years amid growing concerns that economic growth may suffer.

逆回购 reverse repurchase
中国人民银行开展了1300亿元的逆回购操作,操作期限为7天。
The People's Bank of China (PBOC) conducted seven-day reverse repurchase (repo) agreements worth 130 billion yuan.

逆商 adversity quotient
现在不少机关干部和公务员教育背景很好,但是缺乏实践经验。他们智商很高,但是"逆商"偏低。
Many government officials and civil servants nowadays have good educational backgrounds, but lack practical experience. Their intelligence quotient is high but their adversity quotient is comparatively low.

逆行 drive the wrong way
按照新规定的扣分办法,在高速公路上倒车、逆行、(穿越中央分隔带)调头的司机也将面临更严厉的处罚——直接扣掉12分。
Under the amendment, motorists who reverse or drive the wrong way or make a U-turn on highways will also receive the harsher 12 demerit points.

逆周期因子 countercyclical factor
中国外汇交易中心表示,我国正在考虑在人民币对美元汇率中间价报价模型中引入逆周期因子。

China is considering introducing a "countercyclical factor" to adjust the way it calculates the yuan's daily reference rate against the dollar, according to a statement by the country's foreign exchange trading system.

年度考核 annual assessment
国家公务员局做出规定，连续两年年度考核为"不称职"等级的公务员将被辞退。

China's State Administration of Civil Service stipulated that civil servants who were evaluated as "incompetent" for two consecutive years in the annual assessment would be dismissed.

年关焦虑症 year-end panic/anxiety
"年关焦虑症"指的是年关将至而产生的自责和恐慌心理，通常由年度收入不佳、工作和家庭压力引起。

Year-end panic refers to the self-reproach and overall feeling of panic brought about by the approach of the year's end, often due to a poor financial year and pressure from work and family.

年会恐惧症 year-end party phobia
虽然很多员工很喜欢参与年会活动，但也有些员工患上了"年会恐惧症"。

While many employees enjoy the activities, some suffer from "year-end party phobia".

年末促销 year-end promotion
热衷打折货的购物者在年末促销中涌入北京市的几大珠宝商店，黄金珠宝的销量在周末增长幅度超过30%。

Gold jewelry sales jumped more than 30 percent over the weekend in Beijing, as bargain shoppers swarmed the city's major jewelry stores on year-end promotions.

年夜饭 Lunar New Year's Eve dinner
年夜饭是春节最重要的大餐。近年来，越来越多的中国人过年选择到饭店去吃团圆饭，以免去在家做菜的麻烦。

Lunar New Year's Eve dinner is the most important meal of the Spring Festival. In recent years, more and more Chinese choose to go to a restaurant to have the family reunion dinner to avoid the trouble of cooking at home.

年终奖 year-end bonus
在通货膨胀率高达4.4%的情况下，只有两成员工认为今年的年终奖会比去年丰厚。

Only 20 percent of employees expect their year-end bonus will be more generous than last year's, while the inflation mounted to 4.4 percent.

年终总结 year-end summary
许多白领发愁写不出好的年终总结,于是求助于代写机构。
Worried about preparing a favorable year-end summary, many white-collar workers are approaching ghostwriting agencies for help.

尿布外交 diaper diplomacy
英国威廉王子和妻子凯瑟琳的儿子乔治小王子首次海外出访,在新西兰和澳大利亚率先开展"尿布外交",引来全球瞩目。
Prince George, son of Britain's Prince William and his wife, Catherine, has caught the attention of the world and led a trend of "diaper diplomacy" during his first foreign visit to New Zealand and Australia.

凝聚力 cohesive force
中国共产党依靠其凝聚力确保国家统一、安定和繁荣。
The Communist Party of China, with its cohesive force, holds the country together, ensuring stability and prosperity.

扭亏为盈 turn a losing company/business around; turn around a losing company/business into a profitable one
有了投资,加上运气,我们希望这个长期亏损的老厂大约在两年内扭亏为盈。
With new investment and luck, we hope to turn this age-old losing company around in two years.

农村电网改造项目 projects to upgrade rural power grids
该地区的农村电网改造项目已经完成。
Projects to upgrade rural power grids in this region have been completed.

农村剩余劳动力 surplus rural laborer/labor
多达4000万的农村剩余劳动力在待业。
Up to 40 million surplus rural laborers are waiting for jobs.

农村学生专项计划 special college enrollment plan for students from rural areas
我国将继续推行农村贫困学生专项计划。
China will continue to implement a special college enrollment plan for students from impoverished rural areas.

农药残留物 pesticide residue
自由市场上出售的蔬菜和水果农药残留物经常超出国家规定的标准。

The amounts of pesticide residue on vegetables and fruit sold in free markets often exceed the limits set by national regulations.

女性专用车厢 women-only compartment; women-only passenger car
针对近日报道的多起"猥亵"案件,《广州日报》近期在微博上发起一个调查,询问人们地铁有无必要开设女性专用车厢,约2/3的调查参与者认为有必要。
Guangzhou Daily recently launched a survey on its micro blog about the necessity to open women-only compartments after reports of several molestation cases. Around two in three respondents ticked "yes".

虐童 abuse children; child abuse
又一名浙江幼师因网络上的虐童照片而被拘留。
A second preschool teacher has been detained over online images that appear to show her abusing children in Zhejiang province.

OTT内容 over-the-top (OTT) content
注：OTT 意指互联网企业越过运营商，发展基于开放互联网的各种视频和数据服务业务，微信就是典型的OTT 应用。Over the top原为体育用语，指"过顶传球"。
电信服务提供商称微信及其他OTT内容服务商应为产生过量的数据流量支付费用，这些流量有时会导致信号渠道拥堵。
Telecom service providers allege that WeChat and other over-the-top (OTT) content service providers should pay for generating excessive data flows, sometimes leading to traffic jams in signaling channels.

欧式英语 Euro-English
一项研究认为，英国脱欧或将催生"欧式英语"，即一种为欧洲大陆社会的文化和需求量身打造的新型语言。
Britain's exit from the European Union may give rise to "Euro-English"—a new language tailored to the cultures and needs of continental European societies, according to a study.

欧亚大陆桥 Eurasia Land Bridge
欧亚大陆桥将欧洲、中亚、俄罗斯和中国东北联系起来。
The Eurasia Land Bridge links Europe, Central Asia, Russia and northeastern China.

欧元区 euro zone
注：欧元区是指欧洲联盟成员中使用欧盟的统一货币——欧元的国家区域。目前，欧元区共有18个成员国，包括德国、法国、意大利、荷兰、比利时、卢森堡、爱尔兰、希腊、西班牙、葡萄牙、奥地利、芬兰、斯洛文尼亚、塞浦路斯、马耳他、斯洛伐克、爱沙尼亚，以及拉脱维亚。
希腊如果还不能形成重振经济的严肃方略，将被逐出欧元区。
Greece will be out of the euro zone if they cannot find a way to get economy into shape.

欧洲货币一体化 European monetary integration
欧洲各国为了促进经济交流与合作，实现了欧洲货币一体化。
European countries have carried out European monetary integration to improve economic exchange and cooperation.

扒手 pickpocket
扒手似乎多了起来。警方上周再次提醒市民购物时提防扒窃。
Last week, police again warned shoppers to be wary of pickpockets, whose numbers seem to be on the rise.

拍板；定夺 the final decision rests with...; have the final say (or last word); make the final decision
请注意这不过是个人观点，最后还要经理定夺。
Please note that this is a personal opinion. The final decision rests with the manager.

拍卖 put something under the hammer; sell something at auction; auction something
北京中贸圣佳国际拍卖有限公司打算在6月21日的春季拍卖会上拍卖钱锺书的书信。
Sungari International Auction in Beijing intends to put letters written by Qian Zhongshu under the hammer on June 21 as part of its spring collection.

拍卖成交价 hammer price
这个价格包括卖家在拍卖成交价基础上支付的10%的佣金，比一年前在法拉利总部一场类似拍卖会中创下的拍卖纪录高出了近200万欧元。
The price, which includes a 10 percent buyer's premium on top of the "hammer price", is nearly 2 million euros more than the previous record set at a similar auction at Ferrari's headquarters a year ago.

排水系统 drainage system
人们开始质疑，一个城市的现代化进程是否是以牺牲基础设施建设如排水系统为代价。
Questions were being raised about whether a city's push for modernization came at the expense of sacrificing basic infrastructure such as the drainage system.

排污许可证 pollutant discharge license
根据一项改革后的排污政策，国内所有固定污染源须在2020年前获得排污许可证。
A revamped pollutant discharge policy requires all stationary sources of pollution

in China to have discharge licenses by 2020.

盘点；评估 take stock
瞎忙了6个月，我们该盘点一下，找出解决问题的办法。
After six months of aimless work, it's time to take stock of the situation and figure out what we need to do to fix things.

旁观者效应 bystander effect
有些人可能会把路人的反应归结为"旁观者效应"这种社会心理现象。还有些人，特别是在中国的那些熟悉"彭宇案"的人会认为可能更深层次的原因是人们担心救助会招致同样的后果。
Some may cite the social psychological phenomenon of "bystander effect". Others, especially those in China familiar with the case of Peng Yu, may consider the fear of repercussions as a result of offering aid to be a more likely root cause.

跑龙套 play a bit role; utility man
跑了多年的龙套后，周的努力终于有了结果，他把握机会成了明星。
After playing bit roles for years, Zhou's hard work eventually paid off and he got the break he needed to become a star.

跑题；离题 off topic
请尽量不要跑题。
Please try not to get off topic.

跑腿服务 errand service
随着全国多地迎来高温天气，人们对跑腿服务的需求迅速攀升。
The demand for errand services has soared along with the high temperatures that have hit many parts of China.

泡吧 kill time at a bar
他白天忙工作，下了班就泡吧。
He is busy with work during the day. After work, he kills time at bars.

泡沫经济 bubble economy
美国的新泡沫经济反映在股价上。
The new bubble economy in the United States is reflected in stock values.

泡沫浴 bubble bath
泡沫浴有安抚作用，让人放松。洗个泡沫浴，感觉一下。

A bubble bath is soothing and relaxing. Take one. See how it feels.

配股 allotment of shares
根据新规定,只有近3年平均收益与资产比等于或高于6%,企业方可申请配股或者发行新股。
According to the new regulations, companies applying for the allotment of shares or the offering of new shares must ensure that their average earnings to asset ratio in the past three years is 6 percent or more.

棚户 shacks (in the slum area); families that live in shacks
大火烧毁了贫民区大约1500个棚户,但还没有伤亡报告。
The huge blaze destroyed about 1,500 shacks in the slum area but there were no reports of any deaths or injuries.

棚户区改造 rebuild shanty areas
我们将努力确保保障性住房、棚户区改造,以及自住的中小套型住宅用地占到全部土地供应的70%以上。
We will strive to guarantee that land used for low-income housing, for rebuilding shanty areas and for self-occupied small-or-medium-sized houses accounts for more than 70 percent of the overall supply.

碰头会 brief meeting
演出开始前,演员们和工作人员开了个碰头会,以确保万无一失。
Before the show, performers and staff held a brief meeting to make sure that everything was going according to plan.

碰一鼻子灰 be snubbed; be rebuffed
她想邀请他参加自己的婚礼,没想到碰了一鼻子灰,而且是断然拒绝。
She wanted to invite him to her wedding, but got snubbed—in fact, he flatly refused.

批评风暴 blamestorming
全世界的报纸都在报道,在持续低迷的全球经济的背景下,近日"批评风暴"正在盛行。
Newspapers around the world are reporting that there is a lot of "blamestorming" going around these days in the face of a still-weak global economy.

皮包公司 bogus company
这家皮包公司的办公地点结果是一处被抹去房间号的普通民宅。
The bogus company's location turned out to be an ordinary residential apartment

with the room number removed.

偏方 folk remedy
自有偏方以来，苹果醋就被誉为包治皮肤和头发类疾病的良药。
For as long as there have been folk remedies, apple cider vinegar has been touted as a cureall for all kinds of skin and hair problems.

偏科 do (much) better in some courses than in others; unbalance between arts and science subjects; good at some courses and not others
从考试结果看得出你偏科。这可不是好兆头，应该纠正，保持各学科均衡发展，不然高考会有麻烦。
Your tests show you did much better in some courses than in others. It's not a good sign. You should change it by keeping a balance between both, or there'll be trouble when it's time to take college entrance examinations.

片面追求升学率 attach undue/too much importance to the ratio of high-school/middle-school graduates enrolled by universities; place undue/too much emphasis on the proportion of students who move on to higher-level schools
许多学校片面追求升学率，不重视学生的身体素质，只要他们能考上大学就万事大吉。
Many schools attach too much importance to the ratio of middle-school graduates enrolled by universities. So they care nothing about the physical well-being of students as long as they are able to be admitted by a university when they graduate.

骗婚 marital fraud
中国在2015年底之前建立了全国婚姻登记网上数据库，以提高办事效率，防止骗婚行为。
China established a nationwide online database for marriage registration by the end of 2015 to enhance efficiency and prevent marital fraud.

飘窗 bay window
他喜欢坐在新房子的飘窗边上，边看书边欣赏楼下花园的美丽风景。
He likes to sit beside the bay window in his new house and read books while enjoying the beautiful view down in the garden.

票房惨败 box office flop
这部影片遭遇票房惨败，在国内的票房收入不到3000万美元。
The film was a box office flop, earning less than $30 million domestically.

贫二代 poor second generation
同时涌现出的"富二代"与"贫二代"在中国媒体上引发了热议。
The simultaneous emergence of the "rich second generation" and "poor second generation" has triggered a heated debate in the Chinese media.

贫富差距 gap between the rich and the poor; wealth gap
贫富差距有加大的危险。许多人不愿这种情况发生。
The gap between the rich and the poor is threatening to widen. It's something a lot of people don't want to see happen.

贫困线 poverty line
按人均收入1天1美元的国际通行标准和购买力评价折算,中国的贫困线应该为年收入924元人民币,那么,中国农村的贫困人口仍有7580万。
Converted from the purchasing power of the international standard of one dollar a day, China's poverty line should be set at an annual per capita income of 924 yuan. Thus there are still 75.8 million rural people below the poverty line.

贫铀弹 depleted uranium bomb
据说,他们还投下了几枚贫铀弹,那东西对环境危害极大。
They are also said to have dropped a few depleted uranium bombs, which are extremely harmful to the environment.

品牌忠诚度 brand loyalty
中国豪华出境游游客的明显特征为年轻、自主、品牌忠诚度高。
Youth, self-reliance and brand loyalty are the defining characteristics of luxury outbound travelers in China.

品质革命 quality revolution
国务院首次提出推动"品质革命",以满足发展需求和改善国内消费品产业的薄弱环节。
In meeting the demand for development and improving the weak links in China's consumer goods industry, the State Council proposed promoting a "quality revolution" for the first time.

乒乓外交 Ping-Pong Diplomacy
乒乓外交指的是20世纪70年代中美乒乓球运动员间的文化交流。它标志着中美关系开始和解。
Ping-Pong Diplomacy refers to the cultural exchange of table tennis players between the United States and China in the 1970s. This marked the beginning of a

thaw in China-US relations.

平仓 close a position
法规未就证券公司是否有权强行平仓做出明确规定。
The law does not specify whether a securities company has the right to forcibly close a position.

平等、互利、互相尊重主权和领土完整 equality, mutual benefit, mutual respect for sovereignty and territorial integrity

平等互利原则 principles of equality and mutual benefit
国与国之间必须在平等互利的原则上建立外交关系。
Diplomatic relations between countries must be conducted under the principles of equality and mutual benefit.

平均主义 leveling-off; equalitarianism
平均主义束缚人的积极性。
The leveling-off of distribution hinders people's initiative.

平稳过渡 smooth transition
他赞扬了他们为香港回归的平稳过渡所做的工作。
He praised them for all that they'd done to make Hong Kong's return to the motherland a smooth transition.

平抑物价 price rollback; price control; stabilize commodity prices
物价指数自去年9月以来首次停止上涨，说明政府平抑物价措施初见成效。
The government's price rollback measures began to work as the consumer price index stopped increasing for the first time since last September.

评分机 scoring machine
在奥运会拳击比赛中，由评分机给拳手打分。运动员、教练员均认为评分机更公正。
In Olympic boxing, scoring machines are used. Players and coaches alike think this is a fairer system.

评头论足 make wanton comments (on someone)
她乐意穿什么就穿什么，你凭什么对人家评头论足？
She may wear whatever she pleases. Who do you think you are to make such wanton comments?

凭证式国债 certificate T-bonds
这是今年发行的第一批凭证式国债。
This is the first batch of certificate T-bonds that's been issued this year.

迫降 emergency landing
飞机迫降在莫斯科机场前不久,孩子出生了。
The baby was born shortly before the plane made an emergency landing at Moscow Airport.

破发(跌破发行价) fall on its first day of trading; fall on debut
中国最大的风轮机制造商华锐风电集团在上海开盘后首日便破发,新能源产品的竞争日趋激烈,使人们担心股票价格被高估。
Sinovel Wind Group Co, China's biggest maker of wind turbines, fell on its first day of trading in Shanghai as rising competition for clean-energy products fueled concern that the company's shares may be overvalued.

破土 break ground for construction
那座新桥下个月破土动工。
The new bridge will break ground for construction next month.

剖腹产 Caesarean section
因为难产,她必须得做剖腹产手术。
It was a difficult birth. She had to have a Caesarean section.

扑杀 cull
为防止这种致命病毒的进一步传播,当地政府已扑杀了疫区周围3000米范围内的50余万只家禽。
Local governments have culled more than 500,000 poultry within a 3-kilometre radius of the outbreak sites to prevent the spread of the deadly virus.

普法 enhance one's awareness to abide by the law; disseminate knowledge of the law; increase awareness of the law
为提高学生遵纪守法的意识、维护校园治安秩序,实验小学举办了一系列普法知识讲座。
In order to enhance students' awareness to abide by the law and the campus regulations, the Experimental Primary School gave a series of lectures on law.

普及九年制义务教育 make nine-year compulsory education universal

普及科普知识,传播科学思想,倡导科学精神 popularize scientific and

technological knowledge, spread scientific thought and advocate scientific spirit

普通高等教育 regular higher education
为了给更多的学生接受普通高等教育的机会,中国从去年开始扩大高校招生范围。
China began to expand college enrollment last year to give more school learners opportunities to receive regular higher education.

Q

70年土地使用期 70-year term of land use
住宅70年土地使用期到期后,业主可续期,不需申请,没有前置条件,也不影响交易。
When the 70-year term of land use for residential buildings ends, owners can renew the lease without applying, and no preset conditions are set, and it will not affect any transactions of the property.

妻管严 henpecked
亦舒的短篇小说《错先生》,描述的是"妻管严"男士的生活。
Mr. Wrong, a short novel written by Yi Shu, describes the lives of henpecked men.

欺骗消费者 play foul with buyers
某国际品牌家具的零售商坚称没有欺骗消费者,但承认职员的销售策略"有误"。该品牌最近涉嫌高价出售低质假冒洋货。
A retailer of international brand furniture, which has recently been suspected of selling poor-quality fake foreign products at high prices, has insisted it does not play foul with buyers but has admitted "faults" in its employees' sales tactics.

欺上瞒下 deceive superiors and delude subordinates
欺上瞒下的公职人员必须被清除出去,否则廉政建设就无从谈起。
Civil servants who deceive superiors and delude subordinates must be gotten rid of before clean government can be talked about.

旗帜鲜明 clear stance; clear-cut position; clear stand
《南方日报》旗帜鲜明地支持国企改革。
South Daily took a clear stance on the reform of State-owned enterprises—it supported them.

乞讨儿童 child beggar
自该网络活动(随手拍照解救乞讨儿童)发起以来,预计已有6名乞讨儿童成功被警方解救。
An estimated six child beggars have been successfully rescued by police thanks to the online campaign.

企业改制 restructuring of enterprises
企业状况的千差万别,决定了企业改制形式必须多样化。
Different conditions call for different approaches in the restructuring of enterprises.

企业降杠杆 corporate deleveraging
企业降杠杆被列为供给侧结构性改革的五大任务之一。
Corporate deleveraging has been listed as one of the five major tasks of supply-side structural reform.

企业文化 corporate culture
创造性是我们企业文化的核心。
Creativity is the central point of our corporate culture.

企业形象 corporate image (CI)
老板们现在远比过去关心企业形象。
Bosses care about their corporate image much more now than before.

启动基金 initial funding
政府宣布将投入25万美元的启动基金,推动政府部门和企业发展环保型燃料。
The government has announced initial funding of $250,000 to boost government and industry action to help develop environment-friendly fuels.

起步价 flag-fall price
上海市的出租车起步价白天由3000米10元上调至11元。
The flag-fall price of a taxi in Shanghai, which covers the first three kilometers of a trip, has risen to 11 yuan from 10 yuan during the daytime.

气候变化合作 collaboration on addressing climate change
7月10日第五轮中美战略与经济对话第一天,中美在华盛顿就气候变化合作方面的五个新的行动计划达成一致。
China and the United States agreed to five new initiatives for collaboration on addressing climate change in Washington, DC, on July 10, the first day of the fifth round of the China-US Strategic and Economic Dialogue.

气候融资 climate financing
发展中国家提出的2015年中期融资目标意在确保发达国家承诺的到2020年前实现每年1000亿美元的气候融资能够到位。
Developing countries have submitted a proposal for a mid-term financing target for 2015, which is meant to ensure that the $100 billion a year in climate financing that developed countries have pledged to provide by 2020 in climate financing is

guaranteed.

气候协议 climate agreement
《巴黎协定》是《联合国气候变化框架公约》内的气候协议,自2020年起应对温室气体减排、适应和融资。
The *Paris Agreement* is a climate agreement within the *United Nations Framework Convention on Climate Change* (UNFCCC) dealing with greenhouse gas emissions mitigation, adaptation and finance starting in the year 2020.

气荒 gas shortage
能源分析家们把这次几十年来罕见的严重"气荒"归咎为国内"天然气市场的垄断"。南方低温和暴风雪天气致使天然气消耗居高,从而使得此次"气荒"更加严重。
Energy analysts have blamed the country's "monopolistic natural gas market" for one of the most serious gas shortages in decades, made worse by high gas consumption amid freezing temperatures and snowstorms in the south.

气象监测 meteorological monitoring
易受洪水和地质灾害侵袭的地区需要加强气象监测。
Meteorological monitoring in areas prone to flood and geological disasters needs to be strengthened.

气象灾害 meteorological disaster
北京的气象灾害防治条例草案将霾列为气象灾害。
Beijing included smog as a meteorological disaster in its draft of a prevention and control regulation.

弃权;不投票 abstention from voting
尽管弃权票占了很大的比例,莫桑比克总统仍然很乐观,相信他所领导的政党将在大选中获得60%的选票。
Mozambican President was optimistic that his ruling party might scoop 60 percent of the votes in the general elections despite a high percentage of electors opting for abstention from voting.

汽车共享/共享汽车 car sharing
交通运输部发布了指导意见,以改善对迅速发展的汽车共享业的管理。
The Ministry of Transport issued guidelines to improve management of the burgeoning car-sharing industry.

汽车尾气 vehicle exhaust
尽管科学家们对于汽车尾气在大城市PM2.5来源中所占确切比例尚未达成一致意见，但他们一致认为汽车尾气是主要的空气污染源。

Although scientists have not agreed on an exact percentage of vehicle exhaust's contribution to PM2.5 in big cities, they do agree it is a major source of pollution.

汽车限购 curb the purchase of vehicles
由于全国上下对污染和交通堵塞的担忧日趋严重，另外8个城市可能会在今年宣布实行私用汽车限购政策。

Eight more cities are likely to announce policies this year curbing the purchase of vehicles for private use, as worries about pollution and traffic congestion rise around the country.

汽车租赁 car rental
大多数汽车业内人士认为，由于用车需求的大幅增长，汽车租赁市场将迅速发展起来。

Most industry insiders believe the car rental market will develop quickly because of the soaring demand.

契税 deed tax
所有土地、房屋的买卖、抵押、赠与和交换均需要缴纳契税。

A deed tax can be levied on the sale and purchase, mortgage, gift and exchange of land and buildings.

器官捐献 organ donation
我们需要检验该医疗机构在器官捐献和器官移植方面的标准操作程序。

We need to check the medical institutions' standard operating procedures (SOP) for organ donations and transplants.

器官移植 organ transplant
器官移植涉及很多有争议的道德问题。

The concept of organ transplants involves many controversial ethical issues.

器官转运 organ transportation
我国卫生、公安和交通运输部门日前联合建立人体器官转运绿色通道，以实现转运时间最小化，挽救更多患者。

China's health, police and transportation authorities have jointly established a green passage for human organ transportation to minimize delivery times and help more patients survive.

牵线搭桥 act as a go-between

法国牵线搭桥,帮两个国家解决了争端。

Acting as a go-between, France helped the two countries resolve their differences.

签售会 signing session

这个小说家取消了下周在南京的签售会。

The novelist canceled the signing session in Nanjing next week.

前怕狼后怕虎 be over cautious; fear the wolf in front and dread the tiger behind

遇事先考虑个人的利益、前怕狼后怕虎的干部,很难创造性地开展工作。

Cadres who think of their own interests first and who are over cautious can hardly be expected to be creative at work.

前沿科学 frontline sciences

第三届中美前沿科学研讨会在美国加州贝克曼学术中心举行,共有70多位中美科学家参加。

The Third Sino-US Frontline Sciences Seminar was held in the Bakerman Academic Center in California. More than 70 Chinese and American scientists attended it.

潜伏期 incubation period

感染后的潜伏期大概持续10至14天。

The incubation period lasts approximately 10-14 days after contact.

潜伏特工 sleeper agent

美国一家联邦法院周四判处一名在押基地组织潜伏特工八年以上徒刑。这名特工承认与9·11恐怖袭击事件据称的幕后主谋有联系。

A US federal judge Thursday sentenced a convicted al-Qaida sleeper agent who admitted having contact with the alleged mastermind behind the Sept. 11 terrorist attacks to more than eight years in prison.

潜亏 hidden loss

知情者说该公司潜亏不少。

Insiders say the company has many hidden losses.

潜逃疑犯 fugitive suspect

随着中国官方不断加大力度追踪潜逃犯罪嫌疑人,一名潜逃在外七年有余的嫌犯于近日向警方自首。

A fugitive suspect who had been at large for more than seven years has turned himself in amid Chinese authorities' intensifying efforts to track down suspected criminals who have avoided justice.

遣返贪官 repatriate corrupt officials
卡梅伦·克里表示，中美检察官"在想办法遣返腐败官员或返还非法所得财产方面"有"不错的合作"。
Cameron Kerry said that "there's good cooperation" between Chinese and US prosecutors "in finding ways to repatriate corrupt officials or ill-gotten assets".

歉收 crop failure
假种子、劣质种子是歉收的元凶，使3个县6000多名农民受害。
Fake and shoddy seeds are the biggest culprits for the crop failure, which hit more than 6,000 farmers in three counties.

枪手 ghostwriter
北京市一位26岁的兼职枪手称，他对枪手产业的发展并不感到惊讶。他当枪手已有5年了，从中获得了"可观的利润"。
A 26-year-old, part-time ghostwriter in Beijing says he is not surprised about the growing industry, from which he had drawn "decent profits" for half a decade.

枪支管控 gun control
周末的枪击事件再次引发了严格枪支管控的呼声。
The shooting spree over the weekend reignited calls for tougher gun control.

强化班 intensive-training class
校园里，暑期强化班的广告铺天盖地。
Too many advertisements for summer intensive-training classes are posted on the campus.

强化环境管理规范 tighten up environmental management regulations
目前欧盟新成员国正在加强环境管理规范。
Now the new EU member states are tightening up their environmental management regulations.

强降雨 torrential rain
湖南省连日强降雨，导致长江主要支流湘江水位上升。
Days of torrential rain in central China's Hunan province raised the water level of the Xiangjiang River, a major tributary of the Yangtze River.

强迫购物 forced shopping
计划赴香港旅游的北京游客在参加旅游团时将不会被强迫购物及支付附加费用。
Beijingers who plan to travel to Hong Kong SAR of China will be able to join tours without forced shopping and extra charges.

强迫婚姻 forced marriage
英国去年共调查了400起强迫婚姻案件,目前正在深入调查是否有些辍学的女孩子是被迫离开学校去结婚的。
Britain investigated 400 cases of forced marriages last year and is also looking into whether some girls who have vanished from schools were taken out of schools to be married against their will.

强权外交 power diplomacy
他嘲弄说,美国没有外交,只有强权外交。
The United States has no diplomacy except for power diplomacy, he quipped.

强硬路线 hard line
总统采取强硬路线对恐怖主义作战,受到舆论赞扬。
The president was praised by the media for taking a hard line on the war against terrorism.

强制拆迁 forced demolition
法律专家呼吁修订我国有关土地征收的法规,以减少强制拆迁引发的争议。
Legal experts have called for a revision of the country's laws on land seizure, in a bid to ease tensions over forced demolitions.

强制性标识 mandatory labeling
中国立法者开始审议修订的食品安全法,内容包括强制性标识转基因食品。
Chinese lawmakers began to consider a proposed revision to the country's Food Safety Law, including mandatory labeling of GM food.

抢镜头;抢戏 scene stealing
休·杰克曼说:"我觉得不会有演员担心被抢镜头这种事,如果真有人担心,那就犯傻了。毕竟拍戏是演员们集体完成的。"
"I don't think any actor ever worries about the whole thing of scene stealing. If they do, it's stupid. Basically it's a team sport, you know." said Hugh Jackman.

抢跑;抢跳 false start; jump the gun
抢跑差点让他错失了这次比赛的机会。
A false start almost ruined his chances at the event.

抢票插件 ticket purchasing plug-in
工信部要求各类浏览器提供商停用火车票抢票插件。
Web browser providers were ordered by the Ministry of Industry and Information Technology to stop providing train ticket purchasing plug-ins.

巧防御 Smart Defense
北约秘书长安诺斯·福格·拉斯穆森于2011年2月首次提出了"巧防御"的理念，以应对这个跨大西洋联盟所面对的财务紧缩问题，以及美国与其欧洲盟国之间日益扩大的防御能力差距。这种差距是因为多年来欧洲缩减国防支出导致的。
The Smart Defense notion was first broached by NATO Secretary-General Anders Fogh Rasmussen in February 2011 in response to the financial constraints facing the transatlantic community and the yawning gap in defense capabilities between Washington and its European allies as a result of reduced European spending on defense for years.

巧实力 smart power
美国正以"巧实力"策略解决利比亚和叙利亚问题。
The United States is taking a "smart power" approach to dealing with Libya and Syria.

翘尾因素 tail-raising factor
中国央行周二的经济分析报告指出，由于翘尾因素逐渐减小，中国价格上行压力将减弱，但仍存在通胀风险。
China's price pressures are easing due to the weakening tail-raising factors, but inflationary risks still exist, said China's central bank Tuesday in an economic analysis report.

侵吞公款 embezzlement of public funds
他指出，打击腐败的重点在于查处侵吞公款。
He identified the key target for the crackdown on corruption as the embezzlement of public funds.

亲子环 parent-child bracelet
为防孩子在世博园游览期间与父母走散，上海世博园专门提供了"亲子环"。
The Shanghai Expo Park provides parent-child bracelets to prevent kids wandering off when they tour around the park.

禽流感 avian influenza
我国农业部一名专家表示，H7N9禽流感病毒或由候鸟带入国内。

Migratory birds may have carried the H7N9 avian influenza virus into China, an expert with the country's agricultural ministry has said.

青花瓷 blue and white porcelain

江西馆的外形类似于一个巨大的青花瓷容器,描绘出了江西作为无数人才和丰富的自然源之乡的特殊魅力。

The pavilion, resembling a huge blue and white porcelain container, depicts the peculiar charm of Jiangxi as home to a myriad of talents and natural resources.

清洁能源 clean energy

为加强中美在清洁能源方面的合作,科技部和美国能源部将在北京举办论坛。

To further strengthen Sino-US cooperation on clean energy, the Ministry of Science and Technology and the US Department of Energy will jointly host a forum on the subject in Beijing.

清算中心 clearing house

清算公司在确保交易按时高效实施方面发挥着重要作用。

Clearing house corporations play a key role in ensuring that executed trades are settled within a specified period of time and in an efficient manner.

情绪性进食 emotional eating

一项新的研究发现,"情绪性进食"是造成澳大利亚肥胖问题加剧的重要因素。

Emotional eating is playing a substantial role in fuelling Australia's obesity epidemic, according to a new research.

情绪中暑 emotional sunstroke

警方表示,随着气温的升高,城市里"路怒"也随之增多。这种现象被称为"情绪中暑"。警方称,夏季司机更易怒,小小的摩擦会迅速升级为暴力事件。

Rising temperatures are being accompanied by rising levels of road rage in the city, police said. In a phenomenon they've dubbed "emotional sunstroke", police say that drivers are more irritable in summer and that minor incidents can quickly escalate into violence.

晴空颠簸 clear air turbulence

海南航空某航班在从成都飞往北京途中遭遇严重晴空颠簸,造成30人受伤。

Thirty people were injured after a Hainan Airlines plane was rocked by severe clear air turbulence while flying from Chengdu to Beijing.

求大同,存小异 seek common ground on major questions while reserving differences on minor ones

双方仍应求大同，存小异，扩大合作。
The two parties must continue to seek common ground on major questions while reserving differences on minor ones, so as to further expand cooperation.

球门范围内射门 shot on goal
在一场精彩的进攻展示中，梅西共有8次球门范围内射门，其中有6次正对球门。
In a stunning attacking display, Messi attempted eight shots on goal, including six on target.

区别对待 deal with each situation on its own merits
坚持区别对待、有保有压，不搞一刀切，不搞急刹车。
We must continue to deal with each situation on its own merits, encourage growth in some sectors and discourage it in others as the situation requires, and refrain from taking a uniform approach to different situations or putting on the brakes without good reason.

区域电商发展指数 regional e-commerce development index
中国发布了首个区域电商发展指数，该指数以浙江著名的小产品生产中心义乌命名。
China introduced its first regional e-commerce development index named after the famed small commodity production center of Yiwu in Zhejiang province.

区域经济 regional economy
美国对东南亚国家联盟（东盟）地区实行的新举措将会对这一地区产生更大的影响，尤其是对区域经济影响最大。
New US policies toward the Association of Southeast Asian Nations (ASEAN) will lead to a greater influence in the region, especially in regional economies.

取得进展 make headway
教育改革几乎没有取得什么进展。
Little headway has been made in educational reform.

去产能 reduce excessive capacity
我国将继续去除钢铁和煤炭行业多余产能，并将去产能范围扩大到能源行业。
China will further reduce excessive steel and coal production capacity and extend capacity cutting efforts to energy sectors.

圈阅 read and circle
这份备忘录经政府最高官员圈阅。
The memorandum was read by and circled among the highest-level governmental

officials.

权力下放 delegate power (to the lower levels)
中央权力下放使得地方积极性得到充分发挥。
Delegating power has given full play to local enthusiasm.

权钱交易 backroom deal; power-for-money deal
这一大批富人中，既有通过自己的才能和勤劳致富的个体商人，也有勾结官吏通过权钱交易发财的人。
The rich population consists of private business owners that got rich from their talent and diligence as well as people who gained wealth through collusion with officials in backroom deals.

权为民所用，情为民所系，利为民所谋 exercising power for the people, showing concern for them and working for their interests
党在任何时候都把群众利益放在第一位，同群众同甘共苦，保持最密切的联系，坚持权为民所用、情为民所系、利为民所谋，不允许任何党员脱离群众，凌驾于群众之上。
At all times the Party gives top priority to the interests of the people, shares weal and woe with them, maintains the closest possible ties with them, and persists in exercising power for them, showing concern for them and working for their interests, and it does not allow any member to become divorced from the masses or place himself or herself above them.

全部付清 pay in full
账单必须在本月底之前全部付清。
The bill must be paid in full by the last day of this month.

全家福 family photo
峰会将打破20年来元首身穿举办国当地特色传统服饰拍摄"全家福"的惯例，永远不再执行。
The summit packed away for good the two-decade tradition of having the group-pose for a "family photo" in some garb representative of the host country.

全面禁止和彻底销毁核武器 complete prohibition and thorough destruction of nuclear weapons
中国始终支持全面禁止和彻底销毁核武器。
China has long stood for the complete prohibition and thorough destruction of nuclear weapons.

全球创新指数 Global Innovation Index
全球创新指数显示，中国在多个指标上的表现强劲，在全球前25个创新经济体中排名上升，从25位升至22位。
China has moved up the list of the world's top 25 innovative economies, rising three notches from 25 to 22, with strong performance in several indicators, according to the Global Innovation Index (GII).

全球多边贸易 global multilateral trade
我们要积极参与区域经济合作和全球多边贸易。
We must take an active part in regional economic cooperation as well as global multilateral trade.

全球伙伴关系网 global partnership network
中国已与全球60多个国家建立伙伴关系，中国的全球伙伴关系网已基本成形。
As China has forged partnerships with more than 60 countries around the world, China's global partnership network has basically taken shape.

全球治理体制 global governance system
中国需努力抓住机遇，妥善应对挑战，以建立一个更加公平的全球治理体制。
China needs to seize the opportunities and cope with the challenges to build a fairer global governance system.

全身扫描 full-body scanning
全身扫描技术在机场的推广目前正在白宫进行讨论，这一技术的广泛使用引来了保护隐私拥护者的激烈批评，他们把全身扫描称为"虚拟裸体搜查"。
The wide use of full-body scanning at airports now being discussed at the White House has set off hot criticism from privacy advocates who call it a "virtual strip search".

全天候（服务）round-the-clock (service) ; 24-hour (service)
如今，许多网络公司纷纷为用户提供全天候服务，想方设法鼓励用户多上网。
Nowadays, many internet corporations are providing round-the-clock services to encourage consumers to spend more time surfing the internet.

全天候朋友 all-weather friends
中国和津巴布韦是"真正的全天候朋友"，中津传统友谊源远流长，历久弥坚。中津两国不仅要做政治上的好朋友，还要做发展中的好伙伴。
China and Zimbabwe, with their traditional friendship both having a long history and growing ever stronger now, are "real all-weather friends". They should not

only be good friends on politics but also be good partners on development.

全天监测 around-the-clock surveillance
上海以及东部省份黑龙江、辽宁、山东、江苏、浙江和福建的监测站受命对空气和海水中的放射性物质进行全天监测。
Monitoring stations in Shanghai as well as those in the eastern provinces of Heilongjiang, Liaoning, Shandong, Jiangsu, Zhejiang and Fujian were ordered to conduct around-the-clock surveillance of radioactive substances in the air and sea water.

全网络售票 online-only ticket sale
故宫博物院宣布将取消现场售票，开始实施全网络售票。
The Palace Museum announced it will stop selling onsite tickets and start online-only ticket sales.

全要素生产率 total factor productivity(TFP)
政府智囊团的一位资深专家表示，中国应采取措施应对全要素生产率下滑态势。
China should take actions to cope with its falling total factor productivity (TFP), a senior expert with a government think tank said.

全域旅游 all-for-one tourism
政府工作报告呼吁完善旅游设施和服务，大力发展乡村、休闲和全域旅游。
The Government Work Report called for improved tourist facilities and services, and for a big push to develop rural tourism, recreational tourism and all-for-one tourism.

全院表决 floor vote
即使该政策通过了美国参议院的全院表决，仍需得到众议院通过，才能经由总统签字生效。
Even if the measure passed a floor vote in the Senate, it needs to get approval from the House before it could reach the president for being signed into law.

全职爸爸 stay-at-home dad
一位人口统计学家估计，在家照顾小孩的全职爸爸人数去年在全美达到了近200万。
Based on one demographer's estimate, the number of stay-at-home dads who are the primary caregivers for their children reached nearly 2 million in the US last year.

拳头产品 competitive product; knock-out product
政府在财税、信贷、投资等方面也将出台优惠政策，旨在培育和发展一批环保业的拳头产品和骨干企业。
The government will launch preferential policies in finance, revenue, credit, and investment to develop a set of competitive products and backbone enterprises in the environmental protection industry.

劝诱消费；诱导消费 induced consumption
诱导消费的成功之处在于抓住了消费者的心理需求。
Success of induced consumption lies in meeting the psychological demand of consumers.

群发短信 mass texting
国内三大电信运营商去年6月做出统一规定，同一手机号码1小时内群发短信数超过200条，1天内超过1000条，该号码的短信功能将被暂停1周。
An agreement among the country's three main mobile network operators last June stipulated that if the number of mass texting from a phone number reaches 200 within an hour or 1,000 within a day, the phone's message service will be suspended for a week.

群面 group interview
群面往往采取小组讨论解决问题的形式，每一位应聘者的表现都会被记录下来。
Group interviews take the form of group problem-solving sessions where each candidate's contributions are noted.

群众工作 mass work
他号召（领导干部）更加重视群众工作，称群众工作是社会管理的基础性、经常性、根本性工作。
He called for greater efforts in mass work, calling it a basic, regular, and essential task of social management.

群众路线 the mass line
我的小小成绩来源于走群众路线，听群众意见，做符合大多数人利益的事。
I attribute the little success I have had to taking the mass line, listening to the views of the masses, and doing what's best for the majority.

绕岛巡航 island patrol
我国空军近期在训练期间组织进行绕岛巡航，着力提升维护国家主权和领土完整的能力。
A Chinese air force formation conducted island patrols recently during a training exercise with an aim of improving the ability to safeguard national sovereignty and territorial integrity.

绕圈子 beat about the bush
不要绕圈子。直说吧，是你干的吗？
Don't beat about the bush. Did you do it?

热岛效应 tropical-island effect
植树造林可缓解城市所谓的"热岛效应"。
Tree planting can alleviate the so-called "tropical-island effect" in the city.

热核弹头 thermonuclear warhead
发射原子弹的火箭弹头叫作原子弹头，又称热核弹头。
The warhead of a missile designed to deliver an atom bomb is called an atomic warhead or a thermonuclear warhead.

热门歌曲 top song
帕瓦罗蒂在其告别演唱会的每一站都演唱了34首热门歌曲，这些歌曲标志着他44年演唱生涯的顶峰。
At each stop of his farewell tour, Pavarotti performed 34 of his top songs——marking the peak of his 44-year singing career.

热污染 thermal pollution
这家工厂已投资1800万元用于热污染处理。
This factory has spent 18 million yuan on the treatment of thermal pollution.

热指数 heat index
在筹备了一年之后，上海气象局近日向大家推出了最新开发的、基于"热指数"先进模型的天气预报系统。
After a year's preparation, the Shanghai Metrological Bureau recently announced

its newest weather forecast system, which is based on the advanced model of Heat Index.

人才保障房 social security housing for talents
浙江省省会杭州将供地200多万平方米，用于建设人才保障房，这些人才包括艺术家、企业家甚至政府官员，他们可以用市场价一半的价格购买这些房子。
Hangzhou, the capital city of East China's Zhejiang province, will provide more than 2 million square meters of social security housing for talents, including artists, entrepreneurs, even government officials, who can buy these houses for half the market price.

人才流失 brain drain
中国应该解决人才流失这一有碍西部大开发的严重问题。
China should curb the brain drain that is jeopardizing the country's western development campaign.

人才培养机制 talent development scheme
调查报告显示，民众认为官僚作风是大学存在的第二大问题，其他对大学教育的不满意见包括人才培养机制落后、创新教育不足以及学术剽窃现象。
The bureaucratic manner in universities ranks second among public concerns, other unsatisfactory opinions like the poor talent development scheme, the poor innovative education and the plagiarism showed up in the survey report.

人才战 rivalry/competition for talents
许多公司以及人力资源方面的专家参加了在天津举办的21世纪人才战研讨会。
Many companies and experts in human resources attended the seminar held in Tianjin on rivalry for talents in the 21st century.

人道主义救援 humanitarian relief
他们的主要任务是保护中国船舶及船员的安全，以及保护联合国世界粮食计划署等国际组织运送人道主义救援物资船舶的安全。
Their major task is to protect the safety of Chinese ships and crew on board as well as ships carrying humanitarian relief materials for the international organizations such as the United Nations World Food Program.

人工繁殖 artificial breeding
中国计划通过人工繁殖增加金丝猴数量。金丝猴是中国独有的稀缺物种。
China plans to increase the number of golden monkeys, a rare species native to China, by way of artificial breeding.

人工降雨（雪）cloud seeding
中国计划到2020年，通过人工降雨（雪）作业年增加降水600亿吨。
By 2020, China plans to increase precipitation by 60 billion tons annually via cloud seeding.

人工智能 artificial intelligence (AI)
AlphaGo开发团队证实，近日在网上以60胜战绩横扫中国顶尖围棋手柯洁等围棋高手的神秘棋手Master是最新版的人工智能程序AlphaGo。
The mysterious "Master" that has scored 60 victories against elite Go players online, including China's top player Ke Jie, is the latest version of artificial intelligence program AlphaGo, its development team confirmed.

人工智能应用 artificial intelligence application
我看到了云服务以及人工智能应用的潜在价值。
I see the potential of cloud computing service and artificial intelligence application.

人际传播 human-to-human transmission; interpersonal transmission
世界卫生组织发言人克里斯蒂安·林德梅尔重申，尚未观察到中东呼吸综合征冠状病毒在韩国具备可持续的人际传播能力与社区传播能力。
Christian Lindmeier, a spokesperson of the World Health Organization reaffirmed that sustained human-to-human transmission and community transmission of Middle East respiratory syndrome coronavirus in South Korea had not yet been observed.

人口负增长 negative population growth (NPG)
上海是我国唯一保持人口负增长的城市。
Shanghai is the only city in China to maintain a negative population growth rate.

人口红利 demographic dividend
中国人口红利消失的拐点已在2012年出现，将对经济增长产生显著影响。
China's demographic dividend has been disappearing since 2012, which will have a significant impact on economic growth.

人口老龄化 aging population
中国正面临人口老龄化以及老龄化带来的社会问题。
China is confronting an aging population and the social problems that go with it.

人口普查员 census taker
我国已经为下一轮全国人口普查招募了650万人口普查员。
China has recruited 6.5 million census takers for the next national census.

人口素质 quality of population
提高西部人口的整体素质是一项长期而又紧迫的任务。
Improving the overall quality of the western population is a long-term and yet pressing task.

人类命运共同体 a community of shared future for mankind
我们呼吁,各国人民同心协力,构建人类命运共同体,建设持久和平、普遍安全、共同繁荣、开放包容、清洁美丽的世界。
We call on the people of all countries to work together to build a community of shared future for mankind, to build an open, inclusive, clean, and beautiful world that enjoys lasting peace, universal security, and common prosperity.

人类乳头瘤病毒（HPV）human papilloma virus
首个人类乳头瘤病毒（HPV）疫苗获准在中国大陆使用。
The first vaccine for the human papilloma virus has been licensed for use on the Chinese mainland.

人脸识别技术 facial recognition technology
人脸识别技术的应用意味着每位乘客进站检票只需要5秒钟。
The application of facial recognition technology means it takes only five seconds for each passenger to check in.

人民币清算行 renminbi clearing bank
中国政府已决定指定某家已获批准的银行成为人民币清算行。
The Chinese authorities have decided to designate one of the approved banks to be the renminbi clearing bank.

人民对美好生活的向往 the people's aspirations to live a better life
把人民对美好生活的向往作为奋斗目标,依靠人民创造历史伟业。
We must regard as our goal the people's aspirations to live a better life, and rely on the people to move history forward.

人身攻击 personal attack
秘鲁总统呼吁总统候选人之间不要再搞人身攻击。
The president of Peru called an end to personal attacks among presidential candidates.

人身意外保险 personal accident insurance
中国保险监督委员会近日称,它将努力完善当前的旅游人身意外保险制度。
The China Insurance Regulatory Commission（CIRC）said recently that it would

try to perfect the present tourist personal accident insurance system.

人体彩绘 body-painting
在这家新开张的维他命水"闪店"中,顾客可以尽享人体彩绘和商标设计活动。
In the newly launched Vitaminwater pop-up shop, customers can indulge in body-painting and label-designing activities.

人为失误 human error
俄方调查人员周一表示,波兰总统及随行95人搭载的苏联制造的飞机并未发现技术上的故障,其坠毁的原因可能是人为失误。
Russian investigators suggested human error may have been to blame in the plane crash that killed the Polish president and 95 others, saying Monday there were no technical problems with the Soviet-made plane.

人员流动率 turnover rate
随着经济复苏和职位的增加,雇员的期望值在升高,这同时也影响了人员流动率。
Employees' expectations have been rising as the economy recovers and the number of available positions increases, which affects turnover rates.

任意球 free kick
贝克汉姆独特的任意球把英格兰队送进了四分之一决赛。
Beckham's trademark free kick nudged England into quarterfinals.

熔断机制 circuit-breaker mechanism
设计不良的股市熔断机制实施数日后就被叫停。
The ill-designed stock market circuit-breaker mechanism was removed just days after being put in place.

入户摸底调查 door-to-door interview
入户摸底调查在全国人口普查之前开展。每10年进行一次的全国人口普查将于11月1日正式开始。
The door-to-door interviews precede the nationwide population census, which officially starts on November 1 and is held once every 10 years.

入境禁令 travel ban
一个由3名法官组成的联邦上诉委员会一致拒绝恢复美国总统特朗普有针对性的入境禁令。
A three-judge federal appeals panel unanimously refused to reinstate US President Donald Trump's targeted travel ban.

入境限制 ban on entry; entry ban
中国政府周二宣布，取消对艾滋病病毒携带者，以及患有性病、麻风病等疾病的外国人实行了20年的入境限制政策。
The Chinese government announced on Tuesday the lifting of the 20-year-old ban on entry for foreigners with HIV/AIDS, sexually transmitted diseases and leprosy.

入世议定书 Protocol on China's Accession to the WTO
德国总理默克尔在柏林表示，欧盟将履行《中国加入世界贸易组织议定书》第十五条条约义务。
German Chancellor Angela Merkel said in Berlin that the European Union will fulfill its obligations under Article 15 of the *Protocol on China's Accession to the World Trade Organization*.

入园难 kindergarten crunch
目前多数中国家长都感觉幼儿园"入园难"。
Most Chinese parents nowadays are aware of kindergarten crunch.

软资产 soft assets
已有证据表明，中国在提供机场、公路及工业区等硬资产方面很有优势。不过，相比而言，中国应该更加关注软资产。
China has proven to be very good at providing hard assets such as airports, highways and many industrial zones. But in contrast, more attention should be turned to soft assets.

弱肉强食法则 law of the jungle
弱肉强食法则不适用于人类社会。
The law of the jungle should not apply to human societies.

弱势群体 disadvantaged group
对弱势群体应给予特殊就业援助。
Special employment assistance should be given to members of disadvantaged groups.

S

三包服务（修理、更换及退货）repair, replacement and refund
该规定由中国质检总局出台，规定了汽车销售方对在中国生产和销售的私家车修理、更换及退货时应承担的责任。
The regulation, published by China's quality control authority, stipulates responsibilities on the part of sellers for the repair, replacement and refund of private cars manufactured and sold in China.

三大攻坚战（防范化解金融风险、精准脱贫、污染防治）three critical/tough battles(against financial risks, poverty and pollution)
坚决打好三大攻坚战，要围绕完成年度攻坚任务，明确各方责任，强化政策保障，把各项工作做实做好。
To fulfill our key annual tasks in fighting three critical battles, we need to make everyone involved clear about their responsibilities, strengthen policy implementation, and ensure that every element of work is done to good, solid effect.

"三废"综合利用 multipurpose use and recovery of three types of wastes (waste water, waste gas, solid waste)
"三废"的综合利用取得了令人瞩目的成果。
Notable results have been obtained in the multipurpose use and recovery of three types of wastes.

三个代表的重要思想（中国共产党应该始终代表中国先进社会生产力的发展要求，始终代表中国先进文化的前进方向，始终代表中国最广大人民的根本利益）
The important thought of Three Represents—The Party should always represent the development requirements of China's advanced social productive forces, the progressive orientation of China's advanced culture and the fundamental interests of the overwhelming majority of the Chinese people.

三公经费 the three public expenses
中央各政府部门和组织的公车购买使用、因公出国及公务接待等"三公经费"拨款预算为79.7亿元。
Departments under the central government and organizations that receive public

funds are planning to spend 7.97 billion yuan this year to buy and use cars, travel overseas and host meetings—collectively known as "the three public expenses".

三连冠 win for the third time in a row; three straight championships; three successive titles; three titles in a row

洛杉矶湖人队赢得NBA三连冠。

The Los Angles Lakers won the NBA championship for the third time in a row.

三亲婴儿 three-parent baby

研究人员利用一项备受争议的"三亲婴儿"技术，成功孕育出一名婴儿。

Researchers have successfully carried out the process of giving birth to a baby using a controversial "three-parent baby" technique.

三权分立 separation of executive, legislative and judicial powers

三权分立是民主制度不可分割的一部分。

The separation of executive, legislative and judicial powers is regarded as integral to democracy.

三天打鱼，两天晒网 work by fits and starts

琼斯做事三天打鱼，两天晒网，缺乏努力坚持的精神。

Jones works by fits and starts and lacks continuity in endeavor.

三网融合 tri-networks integration

备受期待的三网融合将在3至5年内覆盖中国的城市地区。

The much-anticipated tri-networks integration will cover China's urban areas in three years, five years at most.

"三严三实"（既严以修身、严以用权、严以律己，又谋事要实、创业要实、做人要实）the 3+3 initiative (be strict with oneself in self-cultivation, in the exercise of power, and in self-discipline, and act in good faith when performing official duties, taking initiatives, and interacting with others)

每一名党员干部都要坚守"三严三实"，拧紧世界观、人生观、价值观这个"总开关"，做到心中有党、心中有民、心中有责、心中有戒，把为党和人民事业无私奉献作为人生的最高追求。

Every Party-member official is required to adhere to the 3+3 initiative; maintain the right worldview, outlook on life, and values; be mindful of the Party, the people, their responsibilities, and the rules; and regard selfless contribution to the causes of the Party and people as their highest aspiration in life.

散户 private investor
经纪人说，监管机构即将降低硬通货B股的交易印花税，这一消息促使散户们在周一纷纷购进股票，两家交易所的股指因此上扬。
The news that regulators would cut the stamp duty on transactions of hard-currency B shares triggered private investors to buy on Monday, sending both bourses up, brokers said.

散伙饭 farewell dinner
他和同学一起吃了顿散伙饭，以纪念大学生活的结束。
He had a farewell dinner with his classmates to mark the end of university days.

桑拿天 sauna weather
这场降雨可能将持续至周六，在本周后几天将京城拖入"桑拿天"。
The rain could continue until Saturday, leading to "sauna weather" during the second half of the week.

扫黄 sex trade crackdown
央视暗访东莞卖淫嫖娼活动猖獗的报道播出后，东莞市公安局随即展开扫黄工作。
A sex trade crackdown was launched by Dongguan police after a CCTV undercover report revealed rampant prostitution business in the city.

扫黄打非（行动） crack down on pornography and illegal publications; crackdown on pornography and illegal publications
最近一次"扫黄打非"行动收缴淫秽DVD光碟数千张。
Thousands of pornographic films on DVD were seized in the latest crackdown on pornography and illegal publications.

扫码打赏 tipping by scanning a QR code
国内一线城市的餐厅现在流行让顾客"扫码打赏"，顾客可以扫服务员制服上的二维码来支付小费，每次的金额为3元或5元。
A growing trend in China's first-tier cities now gives customers the option to tip the waiters/waitresses in restaurants by scanning a QR code on their uniforms. The tip ranges between 3 and 5 yuan each time.

"四个全面"战略布局 the four-pronged comprehensive strategy
注："四个全面"具体为，全面建成小康社会、全面深化改革、全面依法治国、全面从严治党 comprehensively building a moderately prosperous society, comprehensively driving reform to a deeper level, comprehensively governing the

country in accordance with the law, and comprehensively enforcing strict Party discipline
按照高质量发展的要求,统筹推进"五位一体"总体布局和协调推进"四个全面"战略布局,坚持以供给侧结构性改革为主线,统筹推进稳增长、促改革、调结构、惠民生、防风险各项工作。
Heed the requirement that development must be high quality; coordinate efforts to pursue the five-sphere integrated plan and the four-pronged comprehensive strategy; continue to regard supply-side structural reform as our main task; coordinate all work to maintain stable growth, promote reform, make structural adjustments, improve living standards, and guard against risk.

杀手锏 trump card
对墨西哥的来料加工企业来说,靠近美国无疑是它们与中国企业竞争的杀手锏。
Proximity to the United States is the trump card for Mexico's "maquiladora" factories in their competition from Chinese factories.

山寨应用 fake app
被植入恶意软件的"山寨应用"正在日益威胁着毫无防备的手机用户。
Fake apps installed with malicious software are posing a growing threat to unsuspecting mobile phone users.

闪崩 flash crash
英镑"闪崩"导致英镑在几分钟内暴跌6%。
The Pound "flash crash" sees sterling plunge 6% within minutes.

擅离职守;擅自缺勤 absent without leave; absent without official leave
在美国总统奥巴马周三召开新闻发布会后几小时,共和党众议院发言人约翰·博纳就指责他在讨论削减债务问题时擅离职守。
A few hours after President Obama's press conference Wednesday, Republican House Speaker John Boehner accused him of being "AWOL"—absent without leave—on the debt-reduction debate.

商标侵权 trademark infringement
网上有关商标侵权的指控越来越多,其中一些是合法的,指控对象主要是那些对这个领域的法规不十分了解的网络用户。
Claims of trademark infringement are increasingly common on the internet. Some of these claims are legitimate complaints, made against Web users who do not fully understand this area of the law.

商品房 commercial residential building
全国商品房销售价格持续升高。
Prices of commercial residential buildings throughout the country keep rising.

商品房空置 leave commercial houses unsold; unsold commercial housing/houses
由于前些年房产开发商的过度开发,北京市有大量的商品房空置。
Over-development in the past few years has left many commercial houses unsold in Beijing.

商品房预售 presale of commercial residential houses
目前实行的预售制允许开发商在建筑完工之前出售房屋。此次改革将使南宁成为中国首个禁止商品房预售的城市。
The existing presale system allows developers to sell residential houses prior to the completion of construction. The reform would make Nanning China's first city to ban the presale of commercial residential houses.

商业不正当行为 business misconduct
中国中央电视台的3·15晚会在每年的3月15日国际消费者权益日举行,因此得名。晚会的目的是揭露商业不正当行为,保护消费者权益。
China Central Television's（CCTV）"3·15 Evening Gala" is so called because it is broadcast every March 15, international consumer rights day. The program aims to reveal business misconduct and help consumers fight for their rights.

商业贷款 commercial loan
目前银行的商业贷款有3种担保方式。
At present, banks provide three guarantees for commercial loans.

商业贿赂 commercial bribery
根据该解释,医务人员如果接受制药公司销售部门和医疗器械供应商的贿赂,或是利用开处方的职务便利帮助厂家促销药品牟利,均会面临商业贿赂的指控。
Under the interpretation, medical staff face being charged with commercial bribery if they receive bribes from sales agents of pharmaceutical companies and suppliers of medical equipment, or if they help promote pharmaceutical products through their prescriptions for the benefits.

商业间谍 industrial espionage
这4人的受贿行为将面临至少5年的刑期,而商业间谍罪的最高刑期可达7年。
The four face jail terms of at least five years for bribery, and the maximum penalty

for industrial espionage is seven years.

商业养老保险 commercial pension insurance
国务院发布加快发展商业养老保险的意见。
The State Council released a guideline to speed up the development of commercial pension insurance.

商业遥感卫星 commercial remote-sensing satellite
我国成功将国内首个商业遥感卫星吉林一号发射升空,标志着我国在航天遥感技术方面迈出了重要一步。
China launched "Jilin-1", the country's first commercial remote-sensing satellite, marking an important step in the development of remote-sensing space technology.

赏花游 flower tour/trip
北京市政府推出了192个赏花点,从3月至5月,人们在这些景点可进行"赏花游",欣赏桃花、木兰、杏花和迎春等春花。
The Beijing municipal government released a list of 192 areas in the capital where spring blooms, including peach, magnolia, apricot and winter jasmine, can be enjoyed for flower tours from March to May.

赏月航班 moon-viewing flight
某旅游服务提供商透露,随着中秋节临近,"赏月航班"的预订量大增。
As Mid-Autumn Festival approaches, bookings for moon-viewing flights have soared, according to a travel service provider.

上海金基准价 Shanghai Gold Benchmark Price
我国是全球最大的黄金生产国、进口国和消费国,上海金基准价将有助于我国获得与其地位相当的定价权。
The Shanghai Gold Benchmark Price will help China gain a pricing power that matches its position as the world's top producer, importer and consumer of the precious metal.

上海五国机制 the "Shanghai Five" mechanism
俄罗斯总统普京评论说,上海五国机制为发展成员国之间的关系创造了良好的氛围,并为各个领域的合作奠定了基础。
Russian President Putin said the "Shanghai Five" mechanism has created a favorable atmosphere for developing relations among its member states and laid the foundation for cooperation in all fields.

上了一个新台阶 improve considerably; reach a new level; reach a higher stage of development

韩国认为中国纺织品质量已经跃上一个新台阶。
Republic of Korea thinks that the quality of Chinese textiles has improved considerably.

上门服务 door-to-door service

对体积大的产品，您可以选择自己送修，也可以利用我们提供的上门服务。
You may choose to bring large-size products here for repair yourself, but you can always take advantage of our door-to-door service.

上座率 occupancy rate

由于上座率较低，中国铁路部门即将暂时停运京沪高铁部分路段上的两对动车。
China's railway authority is about to suspend two pairs of bullet trains on part of the Beijing-Shanghai high-speed railway because of their low occupancy rate.

少年犯 juvenile delinquent

这个少年犯承诺如果得到宽大处理，他一定会改过自新。
The juvenile delinquent promised that he would turn over a new leaf if he could be given lenient punishment.

社保费率 social security premium rate

广东、云南、甘肃、贵州、江苏、上海和天津均下调了企业所缴的社保费率，以发展实体经济。
Guangdong, Yunnan, Gansu, Guizhou, Jiangsu, Shanghai and Tianjin have reduced the social security premium rate on companies' behalf, in a drive to develop real economy.

社保基金 social security fund

国务院发文表示，将把国有企业和金融机构国有股权的10%划转给全国社会保障基金理事会和小型地方国有企业。
Ten percent of State-owned equity, including shares of State-owned enterprises and financial institutions, will be transferred to the National Council for Social Security Fund and smaller, local State-owned companies, the State Council announced in a document.

社会保障税 social security tax

中国财政部正考虑开征社会保障税，以缩小收入分配中存在的巨大差距。
China's Ministry of Finance is considering levying a social security tax in an effort to narrow the wide gap in income distribution.

社会保障体系 social welfare system
政府智囊机构中国发展研究基金会表示,中国计划在2020年前投入5.74万亿元人民币用于建设覆盖城乡的社会保障体系,提高人民的生活水平。
China plans to invest 5.74 trillion yuan by 2020 in building an all-round social welfare system to enhance people's livelihoods, according to the China Development Research Foundation, a government think-tank.

社会公平正义 social justice
政府将继续努力促进社会的公平正义。
The government will continue to work hard to promote social justice.

社会力量办学 education sponsored by non-governmental sectors; running of schools by non-governmental sectors
新疆社会力量办学已取得了明显的进展。
Education sponsored by non-governmental sectors in Xinjiang has made much progress.

社会信用体系 social credit system
我国首个社会信用体系示范区将在长三角地区筹建,涵盖上海、江苏、安徽以及浙江等地区,旨在推广良好信用的益处。
The first demonstration zone of social credit system in China, aimed to promote benefits of good credit, is planned for the Yangtze River Delta region, encompassing Shanghai municipality, Jiangsu, Anhui and Zhejiang provinces.

社会舆论 public opinion
迫于社会舆论压力,这位副部长星期一辞职了。
Pressured by public opinion, the vice minister quit Monday.

社会治安 public security
互联网带来的变化和人口的自由流动让生活更便利,同时也给社会治安的维持带来新的挑战。
While changes brought by the internet and the free flow of people have made life more convenient, they also pose new challenges in maintaining public security.

社会主义市场经济 socialist market economy
不断增强我国经济实力、科技实力、综合国力,让社会主义市场经济的活力更加充分地展示出来。
We will increase China's economic and technological strength, and composite national strength, so as to better demonstrate the vitality of the socialist market economy.

社交媒体审查 social media check; social media screening
特朗普政府计划将社交媒体审查扩大至赴美的中国公民。
The Trump administration is moving to expand social media checks to cover Chinese citizens traveling to the US.

社区服务 community service
北京市政府将进一步为发展社区服务提供新的优惠政策。
The Beijing municipal government will bring about new preferential policies for the development of community services.

社区矫正 community correction
社区矫正近日被载入刑法修正案,成为中国惩罚罪犯的一种方式,并将于5月1日起开始实施。
Community corrections will become a means of punishing criminals in China starting May 1, following the program's inclusion in the latest Amendment to the Criminal Law.

射手榜 top scorer list
伊瓜因和已被淘汰出局的斯洛伐克队球员罗伯特·维特克一同登顶射手榜。
Higuain and the now departed Slovakia's player Robert Vittek, lead the top scorer list.

涉水车辆 waterlogged vehicle
对涉水车辆进行赔付时,我们只赔付清理发动机和更换零部件、电子元件以及内部零件产生的费用。
When we settle claims on waterlogged vehicles, we only pay to clean the engine, as well as change parts, electronic components and interior components.

涉性广告 sexually suggestive ad
涉性广告及其他不良广告不仅严重误导消费者,损害人民群众的健康,而且污染社会环境,败坏社会风气,还直接影响广播电视的社会公信力。
Sexually suggestive ads and other bad ads not only mislead consumers seriously and harm public health, but are socially corrupting and morally depraving, and discredit the radio and TV industry.

申请破产保护 file for bankruptcy protection
这家公司总裁表示不久后将申请破产保护。
The company's CEO said the company would soon file for bankruptcy protection.

申诉权 right to petition
申诉权是法律赋予公民的基本权利。

The right to petition is a basic legal right granted to citizens.

身份管理 identity management
决定草案提出身份管理政策，要求网络用户向网络或电信运营商等服务商提供真实的身份信息。
The draft decision proposes the adoption of an identity management policy requiring internet users to identify themselves to service providers, including internet or telecommunications operators.

身份红利 status dividend
有人担心，官员跳槽可能是获取身份红利的一种途径，可能导致市场不公平竞争、权力寻租和腐败现象。
Some people worry that officials' job-hopping may be a way to obtain a status dividend, which may result in unfair competition in the market, rent-seeking and corruption.

身份困境 identity dilemma
分析人士指出，中国应更妥善处理"身份困境"。一方面我们身为发展中国家，另一方面要求中国在全球事务中扮演更重要角色的外部压力也日益加大。
China should better handle its identity dilemma, caused by its status as a developing country conflicting with increasing external pressure for it to exert a greater global role, analysts said.

深港通 Shenzhen–Hong Kong Stock Connect
深港通的启动将为国内和国际金融市场注入积极能量与自信。
The launch of Shenzhen-Hong Kong Stock Connect will inject positive energy and confidence into domestic and international financing markets.

深空门 Deep Space Gateway
双方在澳大利亚阿德莱德发表的联合声明表示，将在月球轨道以及表面的科学探索任务中进行合作，其中包括建立"深空门"空间站。
In a joint statement, signed in Adelaide, Australia, the two agencies declared their intention to cooperate on organizing scientific missions on the lunar orbit and on the moon surface, including building the Deep Space Gateway station.

审美疲劳 aesthetic fatigue
经过一周的游历，我或多或少有些审美疲劳了。
After a week of traveling around seeing the sights, I was more or less in a mode of aesthetic fatigue.

深潜技术 deep-dive technology
"蛟龙"号让中国成为掌握深潜技术的国家之一。
Jiaolong has enabled China to join the ranks of countries with deep-dive technology.

审时度势 size up the situation
这位官员说:"台湾当局应该审时度势得出正确的结论,即赞同'一个中国'的原则。"
"Taiwan authorities should size up the situation and reach the right conclusion, that is, to subscribe to the one-China principle," the official said.

审议 deliberate on
陪审团花了5天时间来审议此案。
The jury spent five days deliberating on the case.

渗透、颠覆和分裂活动 infiltrative, subversive and splittist activities
一位退休了的政府官员做了有关如何在当前形势下挫败各种敌对势力渗透、颠覆和分裂活动的报告。
A retired former official gave a lecture on how to thwart the infiltrative, subversive and splittist activities by various enemy forces today.

生产者责任延伸 extended producer responsibility
国务院印发生产者责任延伸制度推行方案,以更好地保护资源和环境。
The State Council has issued China's extended producer responsibility plan in order to better protect resources and the environment.

生命共同体 community of shared life
我们要认识到,山水林田湖是一个生命共同体。
We should realize that the country's mountains, rivers, forests, land and lakes form a community of shared life.

生前契约 pre-planned funeral arrangement contracts
上海一些墓园试行推出"生前契约"。
Cemeteries in Shanghai are running trials on pre-planned funeral arrangement contracts.

(产品)生命周期分析 Product LCA (Life Cycle Assessment)
产品生命周期分析是对产品在整个使用寿命中对环境造成的影响进行评估。
Product life Cycle Assessment (LCA) evaluates the effects a product has on the environment over the entire period of its life.

生死关头的 do-or-die
这支部队面临着和敌人的生死决战。
The force faces a do-or-die clash against the enemy.

生态补偿机制 mechanisms for ecological compensation; ecological compensation mechanisms
来自湖北省的人大代表呼吁加快生态补偿机制的立法工作，以更好地为国家保护环境提供支持。
National lawmakers from Central China's Hubei province have called for drafting laws on ecological compensation mechanisms to better support the country's efforts to protect the environment.

生态财富 ecological wealth
我们将加强荒漠化、石漠化治理，积累更多生态财富，构筑可持续发展的绿色长城。
We will address the spread of desertification and stony deserts to accumulate more ecological wealth and build a green Great Wall of sustainable development.

生态红线 ecological red line
我国已发布一份意见，要求在禁止开发区域附近划定"生态红线"，这项国家倡议预计将于2020年前完成。
China has issued a guideline calling for an "ecological red line" around areas where development is prohibited, with the nationwide initiative expected to be completed by 2020.

生态环境损害赔偿 ecological and environmental damage compensation
中共中央办公厅和国务院办公厅联合印发了《生态环境损害赔偿制度改革方案》。到2020年，我国计划建立高效的综合损害赔偿制度以保护和改善我国的生态系统。
The General Office of the Communist Party of China Central Committee and the General Office of the State Council jointly issued a reform plan for the ecological and environmental damage compensation system. By 2020, China aims to establish an efficient comprehensive damage compensation system to protect and improve the country's ecosystem.

生态农业；绿色农业 environmentally friendly agriculture; green agriculture
郊区农民正在从生态农业中获益，他们种植的无污染蔬菜市场售价较高。
Suburban farmers are benefiting from environmentally friendly agriculture by growing pollution-free vegetables that fetch higher prices at the market.

生态友好型安葬 eco-friendly burial
去年12月民政部发布指导意见要求各地政府出台生态友好型安葬补贴政策之后，非传统安葬方式可能会更加普及。
Non-traditional burial practices may become even more popular following a Ministry of Civil Affairs guideline released last December that encourages local governments to roll out policies to subsidize eco-friendly burials.

生物护照 biological passport
常规检测方法能测出是否体内有违禁药物，与此不同的是，"生物护照"监测器是对血液指标进行监控，可以从变化中看出是否被人为干预。
Unlike conventional tests, which can detect the presence of a banned substance, the biological passport monitors swings in blood parameters that may indicate manipulation.

生物识别数据 biometric data
生物识别数据和签证申请表格上填写的信息将被保存在申根地区签证信息系统的中央数据库中，保存期限为59个月。
Biometric data and information provided on the visa application forms will be stored in the Schengen Area's Visa Information System's central database for 59 months.

生物识别信息 biological identification data
出入境管理法草案首次提出，允许公安部和外交部根据出入境管理的需要，建立一个留存境外游客的指纹等人体生物识别信息的系统。
The draft law on entry and exit procedures, for the first time, allows the Ministry of Public Security and the Ministry of Foreign Affairs to put in place a system to gather biological identification data, such as fingerprints, on foreign visitors.

生育登记服务制度 birth registration service system
新的"生育登记服务制度"以为想要孩子的夫妇提供更多便利，改善服务为宗旨。
The new birth registration service system aims to provide more convenience and improve the service for couples wanting children.

生育旅游 birth tourism
美国宪法第十四条修正案规定，不论他们的父母来自哪个国家，在美国国土上出生的小孩都会自动成为美国公民。由此引出了赴美国"生育旅游"的现象，而且这一现象似乎有扩大的趋势。
Due to the Fourteenth Amendment to the US Constitution, children born on US soil

automatically become US citizens, regardless of where their parents hail from. Hence the phenomenon of US birth tourism, which appears to be a growing trend.

生源 student pool
人口出生率下降，接受素质教育存在困难，以及出国留学门槛降低等诸多因素导致中国高校生源不断减少。
A number of factors, including a declining birth rate, difficulties in obtaining quality education, and easier access to overseas universities, have combined to drain the student pool of Chinese universities.

生殖健康 reproductive health
首次全国范围的调查显示，中国青少年对婚前性行为的态度变得更开放，但是他们对生殖健康和安全性行为的知识却相对缺乏。
Youths in China are becoming more open about premarital sex, but their awareness of reproductive health and safe sex remains relatively low, the first-ever extensive nationwide survey on the subject suggests.

失联航班 missing flight
失联航班MS804失踪时正从巴黎飞往开罗，机上有乘客和机组人员共66人。
The missing flight MS804 was travelling from Paris to Cairo with 66 passengers and crew when it vanished.

失落的十年 lost decade
哈佛大学一位经济学教授说："这真是失落的10年。我们以为美国的每一代人都会越过越好，但你看现在，中等家庭的日子比20世纪90年代晚期还要惨。"
"This is truly a lost decade," an economics professor at Harvard said. "We think of America as a place where every generation is doing better, but we're looking at a period when the median family is in worse shape than it was in the late 1990s."

失学辍学率 dropout rate
国务院办公厅发布通知，要求进一步控制学生失学辍学率，确保义务教育的实施。
The General Office of the State Council has issued a circular requiring efforts to control the dropout rate of students to ensure the implementation of compulsory education.

"十三五"脱贫攻坚规划 poverty alleviation plan for the 13th Five-Year Plan period
《"十三五"脱贫攻坚规划》坚持精准帮扶与区域整体开发有机结合，以革命老区、民族地区、边疆地区为重点。
The poverty alleviation plan for the 13th Five-Year Plan period (2016-20)

maintains the nation's precision-poverty relief measures while implementing regional development strategies, with a focus on old revolutionary bases, as well as ethnic minority and border areas.

实干家 man of action
他是个实干家。他的领导作风就是自己做表率。
He's a man of action. He leads by example.

实际年龄 chronological age
近日一份关于中国人健康状况的报告称,中国人的身体状况平均比实际年龄老8.2岁,健康状况堪忧。
A recent report on Chinese health revealed that the average Chinese person is 8.2 years older than his or her chronological age, a sign of poor health.

实践是检验真理的唯一标准 Practice is the sole criterion for testing truth.

实名购票制 ID-based ticket booking system
新的实名购票制度实行之后,春节回家过年的旅客在火车站候车的时间可能要延长了。
People returning home for Spring Festival can expect lengthy delays at train stations after the introduction of a new ID-based ticket booking system.

实名举报 real-name reporting; real-name whistleblowing
监察部门应该采用实名制举报方式,而且为了保护举报人,不应将举报信息公之于众。
Supervision departments should apply real-name reporting and should not make public the reporting information so as to protect informants.

实名举报者 real-name whistleblower
日前一项新草案提议,监察机关应对举报政府腐败行为的实名举报者予以回复。
A new draft law has proposed that discipline authorities are required to reply to each real-name whistleblower while reporting corruption in the government.

实名认证 real-name authentication
阿里巴巴宣布将针对其中国站的企业及个人用户推出实名认证,以加强反欺诈措施。
Alibaba announces it will implement real-name authentication for corporate and individual users on its China site to improve anti-fraud measures.

实时到账 real-time account settlement
多家银行已开始提供大额转账实时到账业务。
A number of banks have introduced real-time account settlement for large transfers.

实体书店 brick-and-mortar bookstore
亚马逊在西雅图为爱书人士开设了首家实体书店。
Amazon opened its first ever brick-and-mortar bookstore for bibliophiles in Seattle.

实现突破 make a breakthrough
我国第一条化纤生产线出口印度尼西亚,实现了行业突破。
The first production line for chemical fibers exported to Indonesia made a breakthrough in the industry.

食品安全 food safety
任何未能履行责任的政府部门都将受到严惩。迟报、漏报、瞒报食品安全事故的相关责任人都将被问责。
Any governmental department that fails to fulfill its duty should be seriously punished. Responsible persons concerned with late, left-out and concealed reports on food safety accidents will be called to account.

食物中毒 food poisoning
陕西省政府表示,周一该省两个市的200多名学生在饮用学校的早餐奶之后出现食物中毒的症状。
More than 200 students had symptoms of food poisoning on Monday after drinking school breakfast milk in two cities of northwest China's Shaanxi province, provincial authorities said.

世界观 outlook on the world
树立正确的名利观,需要我们不断提高世界观和人生观。
To establish a correct view on fame and gain, we must constantly elevate our outlook on the world and life in general.

世界记忆名录 Memory of the World Register
甲骨文成功入选联合国教科文组织"世界记忆名录",成为第十三个成功入选的中国文献遗产。甲骨文是中国发现最早的文献材料。
Ancient oracle bone inscriptions—the earliest documentary evidence found in China—became the 13th Chinese documentary heritage inscribed on the UNESCO Memory of the World Register.

市场化制度 market-driven system
采用市场化制度会进一步增加贸易和投资机会。
The adoption of a market-driven system would further increase opportunities for trade and investment.

市场疲软 sluggish market
目前市场疲软，更糟糕的是消费者信心受挫。
This is a sluggish market. Even worse, there's also a dent in consumer confidence.

市场占有率 market share
我们希望增加在北京的市场占有率。
We would like to increase our market share in Beijing.

市盈率 price/earning (P/E) ratio
作为一个自由市场，中国香港特别行政区对上市公司的市盈率没有限制。
As a free market, Hong Kong SAR of China sets no restrictions for companies to go public in Hong Kong in terms of P/E ratio.

市值 market capitalization
7月5日，市值巨大的中国银行在上海证交所上市。
Bank of China, with its large market capitalization size, was listed on the Shanghai Stock Exchange on July 5.

事假 casual leave
根据调查，在过去3个月中，1%的人经常请病假或事假，5%的人偶尔请个假，30%的人至少请过一次假。
According to the survey, one percent has been taking the sick or casual leave very often, 5 percent occasionally and 30 percent at least once in the past three months.

事业单位 government-funded public institutions
为提高公共服务质量，我国将对事业单位进行整改。
China is set to reshape its government-funded public institutions to improve public services.

试点项目 pilot project
该试点项目由欧盟提供资金。
The pilot project is funded by the European Union.

试管婴儿 test-tube baby
一名中国医生呼吁推广试管婴儿技术。
Test-tube baby technology should be popularized, a Chinese doctor said.

试航 sea trial
周三，中国第一艘航母低调出海试航，开启了它在中国国旗下的处女航。
China's first aircraft carrier set out on a low-profile sea trial Wednesday, its first

journey under the Chinese national flag.

试映 test screening
他解释说在试映结束后，这些年轻的会员观众提出了十分宝贵的建议。
He explained that after the test screening, the young audience members made very valuable suggestions.

试运行 trial operation
武广（武汉至广州）高速铁路将于12月20日开始试运行。线路开通后，两地间的运行时间将10小时缩短至3小时。
The Wuhan-Guangzhou high speed railway, which will shorten travel time from ten hours to three, will start a trial operation on December 20.

视频购物服务 video-shopping service
电子商业巨头——阿里巴巴集团控股有限公司，将于下个月推出一项视频购物服务。
The e-commerce giant Alibaba Group Holding Ltd will launch a video-shopping service next month.

视频监控 surveillance camera
北京市中小学视频监控系统即将纳入全市整体的安全监控平台。
Surveillance camera systems at primary and middle schools in Beijing will soon be integrated into the city's overall security monitoring platform.

适度从紧的财政政策 moderately tight fiscal policy
从短期看，中国将可能坚持实行适度从紧的财政政策。
For the short term, China is likely to stick to a moderately tight fiscal policy.

适销对路的产品 marketable product
尽管利润不高，这些产品都适销对路，为他挣来了他的第一个百万。
Although the profit margins were small, these were marketable products. They made him a million dollars—his first million in fact.

收费公路债券 toll road bond
根据财政部和交通运输部发布的一份官方文件，我国将发行地方收费公路债券，以规范地方政府的收费公路融资行为。
China will issue local toll road bonds to standardize local government's financing for toll roads, according to an official statement released by the Ministry of Finance and Ministry of Transport.

收购兼并 merger and acquisition
电视行业收购兼并不断。
Merger and acquisition among TV producers has been hectic.

收入分配 income distribution
中国必须改革收入分配制度,以便让全体13亿国民享受到国家改革开放所带来的成果。
The country's income distribution system should be perfected so that all 1.3-billion Chinese could enjoy the fruit of the country's reform and opening-up drive.

手机转账 money transfer via mobile banking
为应对来自互联网金融服务越来越激烈的竞争,我国五大商业银行将开始提供手机银行转账免费服务。
China's five biggest commercial lenders will start providing free money transfers via mobile banking in a bid to tackle increasing competition from internet finance services.

首次代币发行 Initial Coin Offerings
因市场迅速扩大引发金融风险担忧,我国相关机构叫停首次代币发行。首次代币发行是新出现的一种融资形式,科技创业公司面向投资者发行自己的数字货币,或"代币",来获取资金。
Chinese authorities ordered a ban on Initial Coin Offerings (ICOs), a nascent form of fundraising in which technology start-ups issue their own digital coins, or "tokens", to investors to access funds as the rapidly expanding market spawned concerns over financial risks.

首次公开发行股票 initial public offering (IPO)
纳斯达克股市要求首次公开发行股票的公司必须连续两年实现超过100万美元的税前利润。
The NASDAQ market requires initial public offering (IPO) companies to have a pre-tax revenue over $1 million for two years of consecutive operation.

首次置业者 first-home buyer
中国人民银行(央行)称,各商业银行应该制定差别化的信贷政策,保证首次置业者的房贷需求。
The People's Bank of China (PBOC), the central bank, said that commercial banks should put in place a differentiated credit policy to guarantee housing loans to qualified first-home buyers.

首付贷 down payment loan
随着一线城市房价急剧升温,首付贷也火了。房产中介和P2P平台是提供首付贷的主力。

Given the jump in home prices in first-tier cities, the so-called "down payment loans" are in great demand. Property agencies and P2P platforms have become a driving force by offering loans for down payments.

首航 maiden voyage
能容纳800名乘客的超级游船将于明年首航。

A super ferry capable of carrying 800 passengers is set to make its maiden voyage next year.

首期付款 down payment
很多年轻人买房时都是父母亲帮他们付大部分的首期付款。

Normally parents pay most of the down payment when young people are buying a new apartment.

首日封 first-day cover
芬兰邮政局周二发行了以上海世博会芬兰馆"冰壶"为主题的邮票和首日封。

The Finnish Post Tuesday issued stamps and a first-day cover featuring Finland's pavilion "Kirnu" in Shanghai World Expo.

受挤压的中产阶层 Squeezed Middle
英国数百万中低收入家庭的生活水平因高通胀、薪资停涨和政府财政紧缩政策而不断下降。英国工党将该群体称为"受挤压的中产阶层"。

Dubbed the "Squeezed Middle" by the Labour Party, millions of low-or-middle-income families have seen their standard of living eroded by a toxic mix of high inflation, stagnating pay and government austerity measures.

输入型通胀 imported inflation
由于美元发行失控,国际商品价格持续上涨,中国正面临输入型通胀的危机,这导致的不确定性给公司造成巨大困难。

Because the United States' issuance of dollars is out of control and international commodity prices are continuing to rise, China is being attacked by imported inflation. The uncertainties of this are causing firms big problems.

熟年离婚 late-life divorce
有关"熟年离婚"难以忽视的真相:这对名人夫妇在结婚40年后宣布离婚,这反映出熟年离婚呈上升趋势,但这事儿真有那么糟糕吗?

An inconvenient truth about late-life divorce: The separation after 40 years of the celebrity couple reflects an increasing trend for splitting up in old age—but is it such a bad thing?

树洞帖 tree hole post
脑子里藏着这个秘密，我每天都在受煎熬。或许我应该去发个树洞帖，也好让自己松口气。
I am living in hell with this secret in my mind, maybe I should try to put it into a tree hole post and give myself a break.

数据泄露 data breach
社交媒体巨头脸书的大量用户数据被政治利用的消息传出后，欧盟和英国议会要求脸书就数据泄露一事作出说明。
European Union and British lawmakers demanded that Facebook should clarify data breach following revelations that personal data was massively misused for political purposes.

数码专辑 digital-only album
环球音乐集团近日赶制出数码专辑，为日本地震和海啸罹难者募捐。专辑中收录有加拿大著名流行歌手贾斯汀·比伯和爱尔兰摇滚乐队U2等众多明星的歌曲。
Canadian pop sensation Justin Bieber and Irish rockers U2 are among the artists being featured on a digital-only album being rushed out by Universal Music to raise funds for Japan's earthquake and tsunami victims.

数字电影 digital film
在过去5年中，国家保证了每个住户超过20户的村子都能收到卫星广播信号。今天很多村子也能收到多套广播和电视节目。同时，现在还有64万个村子能享受到数字电影放映服务。
During the past five years the country ensured that satellite broadcasting signals reached every village with more than 20 families, and today many villages are able to receive many radio and TV programs. Meanwhile, digital film screening services now are available in 640,000 villages.

数字鸿沟 digital gap
中国需要进一步消除城乡间的"数字鸿沟"。
The "digital gap" between urban and rural China needs to be further bridged.

数字货币 digital currency/money
央行宣布将争取早日推出数字货币。

China's central bank announced that it will try to issue digital currency as soon as possible.

数字钱包 digital wallet
微信宣布将开始对每笔从数字钱包提现到用户个人银行账户的交易收取0.1%的费用。每笔交易最少收取0.1元。
WeChat said that it will start to charge a fee of 0.1% for each transfer from its digital wallet to users' personal bank accounts. The minimum charge for each transfer is 0.10 yuan.

数字人才 digital talent
基于美国职场社交平台领英用户数据的一份报告显示,过去三年中,成都、苏州、南京、武汉以及西安五个二线城市在数字人才库方面表现出明显优势,不过,上海、北京、深圳、广州,以及电商巨头阿里巴巴总部所在地杭州依然是数字人才数量最多的五个城市。
Five second-tier cities-Chengdu, Suzhou, Nanjing, Wuhan and Xi'an-displayed an obvious advantage in their digital talent pools over others in the past three years, although Shanghai, Beijing, Shenzhen, Guangzhou, and Hangzhou, which is the base of e-commerce behemoth Alibaba, remain the five leading cities in this area, according to the report based on user data by LinkedIn, a US-based networking website.

双重感染 co-infection
中国卫生部周二发布了对抗艾滋病病毒和结核菌双重感染的方案细节。
China's Health Ministry Tuesday detailed a plan to fight co-infection of HIV and tuberculosis(TB).

双重国籍 dual citizenship
我父母出生在英格兰,他们说我因此可以兼有英国和加拿大国籍。这可能吗?此外,双重国籍对我将来究竟有没有好处?
My parents were born in England, and they say I may be a citizen of Britain as well as Canada. Is that possible? Also, how will it help me in the future to have dual citizenship?

双创人才 innovative and entrepreneurial talent
对于"双创人才",北京将给予优惠政策。"双创人才"包括一定规模创业投资的初创公司、投资团队以及投资公司,高新技术企业以及文化产业市场领军者。
Beijing will give priority to what it calls "innovative and entrepreneurial talent", which includes startups with a certain level of investment, investors and investment

companies, high-tech companies and market leaders in the cultural industry.

双轨制 twin-track approach
分析人士指出,日本新内阁对华关系选择了"双轨制",对安全问题十分谨慎,但很愿意在经济领域实现合作。

Japan's new administration has opted for a twin-track approach in its dealings with Beijing, showing caution on security issues but wishing to be cooperative in the economic field, analysts said.

双开(开除党籍、开除公职)be expelled from the CPC and removed from public office
中共中央政治局会议决定给予令计划开除党籍、开除公职处分。

Ling Jihua has been expelled from the Communist Party of China (CPC) and removed from public office, according to a decision made at a meeting of the Political Bureau of the CPC Central Committee.

双控行动 double control actions
"十三五"时期,我国将实行双控行动,促进绿色可持续发展。

During the 13th Five-Year Plan (2016-20), China will implement double control actions to propel green and sustainable development.

双刃剑 double-edged sword
出名是把双刃剑。表面上看出名是好事,但是如果处理不好,就会变坏事。

Being famous is a double-edged sword. It seems to be something wonderful, but not for those who cannot handle it.

双一流 "Double First-Class" initiative
教育部、财政部和国家发改委联合发布了入选我国"双一流"建设方案的高校名单。

The Ministry of Education, the Ministry of Finance and the National Development and Reform Commission jointly released a selected list of universities and colleges, which will participate in the country's construction plan of "Double First-Class" initiative.

双引擎 two engines
中国经济不会出现硬着陆,因为未来我们的经济增长由政府改革和市场"双引擎"驱动。

China's economy is not heading for a hard landing, as there are two engines for China's economic growth in the future: the government reforms and the market.

双赢局面 win-win situation/outcome
他拒绝签署协议,结果把一个双赢局面变成了个对大家都不利的局面。
By refusing to sign the agreement, he turned a win-win situation into a no-win situation for all.

水荒 water scarcity
世界水日的主题集中在淡水资源可持续利用的不同方面,包括水资源清洁状况以及水荒。
The focus of the World Water Day has been on a different aspect of freshwater sustainability, including sanitation and water scarcity.

水货 smuggled goods
他保证以后不卖水货了。不过,这话他过去也说过。
He promised to stop selling smuggled goods, but then again, he had said that before.

水利工程 water conservancy project
如果中国西南部没有修建水库和其他水利工程,那么干旱发生的时间会更早,损失也将更大。
Without the reservoirs and other water conservancy projects in Southwest China, the drought would have happened earlier and resulted in more loss.

水陆两栖飞机 amphibious aircraft
我国研发的"鲲龙"AG600飞机进行首飞。这是全世界在研最大的水陆两栖飞机。
China's homegrown AG600, codenamed Kunlong, took to the skies for its maiden flight. This is the world's largest amphibious aircraft in production.

水土流失 soil erosion
水土流失严重是该地区最主要的环境问题。
This region is plagued by serious soil erosion, which is its top environmental problem.

水污染治理项目 water clean-up projects
2017年上半年中国启动了近8000个水污染治理项目,预计总投资6674亿元人民币。
China launched nearly 8,000 water clean-up projects in the first half of 2017 with projected total investment of 667.4 billion yuan.

水涨船高 When the river rises, the boat floats high.
由于油价上涨,工厂提高了批发价格,零售价也随之提高。水涨船高嘛。

Retail prices rose as factories raised wholesale prices to offset increasing fuel costs. When the river rises, boats have to float high, naturally.

水质 water quality
从今年1月15日起,首都将通过网络向社会公布饮用水水质信息。水质信息每季度公布一次,公布内容包括硝酸盐含量、硬度及浑浊度。
Starting from Jan. 15 the capital will release information on drinking water quality to the public online every three months, including concentration levels of nitrate, the degree of hardness and turbidity.

税收法定 statutory taxation
中国立法法修正案草案强调税收法定。
Statutory taxation was underlined by a draft revision to China's Legislation Law.

税收改革 tax overhaul
美国总统特朗普赢得其任内最大的胜利,共和党人推动通过了自20世纪80年代以来最彻底的税收改革。
US President Donald Trump secured the biggest win of his presidency as Republicans passed the most sweeping tax overhaul since the 1980s.

税收减免 tax break
文件要求政府部门采取税收减免和油价优惠政策以鼓励消费者购买小排量汽车。
The notice urged government departments to use tax breaks and preferential oilpricing policies to encourage consumers to buy small displacement cars.

税收起征点 tax threshold
领退休金的人的纳税起点是6000美元。
The tax threshold for a pensioner is $6,000.

睡眠障碍 sleep disorder
约有38%的中国人受睡眠障碍困扰,其中大约30%患有失眠,4%患有睡眠呼吸暂停症,这两种是最常见的睡眠障碍症状。
About 38 percent of Chinese people suffer from sleep disorders, with about 30 percent having insomnia and 4 percent suffering sleep apnea—the two most common forms of sleep disorders.

硕博连读 successive postgraduate and doctoral program
硕博连读通常需要花6年时间。
The successive postgraduate and doctoral program of study will usually take six years.

司法独立 judicial independence
为本国或家庭成员中的有罪之人辩护求情是人之常情，但司法独立应得到全面尊重，在法律面前应做到人人平等。

It's human nature to plead for a criminal who is from the same country or the same family, but judicial independence should be fully respected and everyone should be equal before the law.

司法解释 judicial explanation; judicial interpretation
根据中国最高人民法院发布的司法解释，父母为子女购买房产且产权登记在自己子女名下的，即使在子女婚后仍属于其个人财产。

A house bought by parents and registered under their child's name remains the personal property of the child even after the child gets married, according to a judicial explanation issued by China's Supreme People's Court.

司法拍卖 judicial sale; judicial/court auction
中国拍卖协会副秘书长欧阳树英周四表示，此次网拍违反了司法拍卖的有关法律法规，并称此举会扰乱市场秩序。

Ouyang Shuying, deputy secretary-general of the China Association of Auctioneers, said on Thursday the online auctions violated laws and regulations on judicial sales, and warned that such activities could disturb the market order.

司法巡查 judicial inspection
第一轮司法巡查中，巡视组发现问题242个，提出整改建议122条。

In the first round of the judicial inspections, the inspection teams found 242 problems and issued 122 guidelines to correct them.

丝路基金 Silk Road Fund
中国将出资400亿美元成立丝路基金，推进基础设施和资源发展，改善历史悠久的丝绸之路沿线的产业合作和金融合作。

China will contribute $40 billion to set up Silk Road Fund that will boost infrastructure and resource development while improving industrial and financial cooperation along the centuries-old Silk Road trading routes.

丝路精神 Silk Road spirit
丝路精神是人类文明的伟大遗产，其核心是和平合作、开放包容、互学互鉴、互利共赢。

The Silk Road spirit is a great heritage of human civilization, with peace and cooperation, openness and inclusiveness, mutual learning and mutual benefit at its core.

私募股权投资 private equity investment
普华永道在报告中指出，在投资者寻求科技领域高增长投资机会的推动下，中国私募股权投资创历史新高。

China's private equity investment surged to a record high as investors pursued high-growth opportunities in technology, PricewaterhouseCoopers said in a report.

私募债 privately raised bond
中国证监会将加快筹建独特的全国性场外交易市场，并建立中小企业私募债发行试点，以鼓励对小企业的财务支持。

China's capital market regulator is encouraging financial support for small businesses by accelerating the launch of a unique national over-the-counter market and a pilot program for issuing privately raised company bonds.

四个意识（政治意识、大局意识、核心意识、看齐意识）consciousness of the need to maintain political integrity, think in big-picture terms, follow the leadership core, and keep in alignment
必须增强政治意识、大局意识、核心意识、看齐意识，自觉维护党中央权威和集中统一领导，自觉在思想上政治上行动上同党中央保持高度一致。

We must strengthen our consciousness of the need to maintain political integrity, think in big-picture terms, follow the leadership core, and keep in alignment. We must work harder to uphold the authority and centralized, unified leadership of the CPC Central Committee, and closely follow the Central Committee in terms of our thinking, political orientation, and actions.

四个自信（道路自信、理论自信、制度自信、文化自信）confidence in the path, theory, system, and culture of socialism with Chinese characteristics
全党要更加自觉地增强道路自信、理论自信、制度自信、文化自信，既不走封闭僵化的老路，也不走改旗易帜的邪路，保持政治定力，坚持实干兴邦，始终坚持和发展中国特色社会主义。

Our whole Party must strengthen our confidence in the path, theory, system, and culture of socialism with Chinese characteristics. We must neither retrace our steps to the rigidity and isolation of the past, nor take the wrong turn by changing our nature and abandoning our system. We must maintain our political orientation, do the good solid work that sees our country thrive, and continue to uphold and develop socialism with Chinese characteristics.

四合院 courtyard dwellings; quadrangle dwellings
外国游客喜欢北京的四合院。
Foreign tourists love Beijing's courtyard dwellings.

夙敌 arch-rival
韩国在乒乓球、篮球、足球以及其他体育项目上都是中国的"夙敌"。
Republic of Korea is China's arch-rival in table tennis, basketball, soccer and other sports.

速成班 crash course
他要去参加一个法语速成班。
He will get a crash course in French.

随身携带行李 carry-on luggage
此次劫机事件后,上海机场的乘客们过安检的时候,需要脱鞋、解皮带,打开随身携带行李接受仔细检查的概率增加了。
The hijacking means passengers in Shanghai are now more likely to be asked to remove shoes and belts and to open carry-on luggage for thorough searches.

随选优惠券 on-demand discount coupon
消费者可以在地铁站内、商场、超市内的维洛卡自助终端机打印随选优惠券。
On-demand discount coupons are available from Velo vending machines installed in subway stations, shopping malls and supermarkets.

损人利己 seek benefits at the expense of others
他不是损人利己的人。我认为他会是个合格的公务员。
He's not one who seeks benefits at the expense of others. I think he'd make a good civil servant.

缩减资产负债表(缩表)reduce the balance sheet
美国联邦储备委员会维持基准利率不变,但宣布将缩减其4.5万亿美元的资产负债表,向结束宽松的货币政策又迈进了一步。
US Federal Reserve kept its benchmark interest rate unchanged, but announced that it would start reducing its $4.5 trillion balance sheet, a further step to end the loose monetary policy.

缩小……间的距离 narrow the gap between
他们计划缩小进出口的差额。
They planned to narrow the gap between imports and exports.

T

她经济 She-conomy
一些报告指出,"她经济"正在崛起。
The "She-conomy" is on the rise, as pointed out by more than a few reports.

胎教 fetal education
传统的胎教提倡吃好、保持情绪稳定、多接触艺术等高雅文化以及保持生活环境和谐。
The traditional fetal education advocated eating well, keeping an emotional balance, maximizing exposure to "high culture" such as art, and maintaining a peaceful environment.

太空加油 in-orbit refueling
2017年4月27日,我国货运飞船天舟一号与天宫二号空间实验室完成首次"太空加油"。
China's Tianzhou-1 cargo spacecraft and Tiangong-2 space lab completed their first in-orbit refueling on April 27, 2017.

太空经济 aerospace economy
神舟九号飞船的成功发射表明中国的经济基础建设和科技发展已经取得了很大进展,中国已经做好开发太空经济的准备。
The successful launch of the Shenzhou Ⅸ spacecraft indicates China's economic infrastructure and technology have made great progress and the country is ready to explore aerospace economy.

太空垃圾 space trash; space junk; space debris
据估计,目前有数百万块太空垃圾漂浮在太阳系中。
It is estimated that millions of pieces of space trash are now floating through the solar system.

太空游客 space tourist
软件设计师查尔斯·西蒙易在2007年4月7日成为了第五位太空游客。
Charles Simonyi, a software architect, became the fifth space tourist on April 7, 2007.

贪多嚼不烂 bite more than one can chew
学习是个循序渐进的过程,要一点一点提高。耐心些,贪多嚼不烂。
Learning is a step-by-step process. You make progress little by little. So be patient. Don't try to bite more than you can chew.

贪内助 corrupt spouse
在许多涉及贪腐官员的案件中,"贪内助"已成为一个引人注目的现象。这些官员的配偶被曝牵涉贪污腐败,通常助其配偶收受贿赂,或利用配偶职务之便牟取不法利益。
"Corrupt spouse" has already become a noticeable phenomenon in a number of cases involving corrupted officials. The spouses of officials found to be involved in corruption have often helped their partners take bribes, or take advantage of their spouses' positions to make illegal profits.

摊牌 put one's card on the table
我们摊牌吧,不要兜圈子了——我们有证人说在星期五的晚会上看到了你。
Let's put our cards on the table. No more beating around the bush—we have witnesses who saw you at the party Friday night.

滩长制 coast chief
浙江省将推行滩长制来治理污染和非法捕鱼。
Zhejiang province is to appoint coast chiefs to fight pollution and illegal fishing.

谈判的筹码 bargaining chip
巴西把扩大农业出口作为新一轮谈判的筹码。
Brazil uses its increase of agricultural exports as a bargaining chip for the new round of negotiation.

弹劾 impeach
韩国宪法法院的法官们一致赞成议会弹劾朴槿惠的决定。朴槿惠成为韩国历史上首位被罢免的民选总统。
Judges at the South Korea's constitutional court unanimously upheld Parliament's decision to impeach Park Geun-hye. Park has become the country's first democratically elected leader to be forced from office.

弹性工资 flexible pay
在弹性工资问题上,同资方的谈判陷入僵局。
Negotiation with the employer has come to a standstill on the subject of flexible pay.

弹性退休金制度 flexible pension system
中国某政府机构透露将适时向中央机构提出更灵活的弹性退休金制度,在促进就业和减少养老金支付压力之间取得平衡。
A Chinese government agency has revealed that it will propose a more flexible pension system to central authorities at an appropriate time to keep a balance between employment and expected shortfall in retirement payments.

探明储量 verified deposit; verified reserve
美国探明的石油储量占世界总量的2.8%。
The verified deposits of oil in the US account for 2.8 percent of the world's total.

探亲假 home leave
她单位每年允许有10天探亲假。
Home leave in her organization is 10 days a year.

探月工程 lunar exploration program
我国探月工程将向民营企业开放,以加速航天技术创新,打破航天工业壁垒。
China will open its lunar exploration program to private enterprises in an attempt to boost technological innovation and break the barriers in the space industry.

碳补偿市场 carbon offsets market
澳大利亚周一在建立碳补偿市场方面又迈出了新的一步。碳补偿市场将对农民、护林员、土地所有者在温室气体减排方面的努力进行奖励。
Australia on Monday moved closer to setting up a carbon offsets market that would reward steps by farmers, foresters and landholders to reduce greenhouse gas emissions.

碳交易 carbon exchange
建立碳交易中心是未来的必经之路。
Setting up carbon exchange centers is the way we must go in the future.

碳排放 carbon emission
一项报告发现,全球最富裕的10%人口的碳排放量占全球碳排放总量的一半。
The world's richest 10% population are responsible for half of all carbon emissions, a report found.

碳排放交易 carbon emission trading
中国国家发展和改革委员会批准在京、津、沪、渝、鄂、广6个另外的地区建立碳排放交易计划试点。
China's National Development and Reform Commission approved pilot carbon

emission trading schemes in six other areas: Beijing, Tianjin, Shanghai, Chongqing, Hubei and Guangdong.

碳税 carbon tax
"碳税"是中国正在考虑要实行的市场机制之一,该机制的实行将提高现有包括汽油、电力、煤炭和天然气等在内的化石能源的价格。

Carbon tax, one of the market mechanisms that China is considering adopting, will raise the current energy price from fossil fuel sources, including gasoline, electricity, coal and natural gas.

套餐 set meal
我们推荐您从菜单中的各种菜品中选择一款套餐。

We recommend that you choose a set meal from the various dishes on this menu.

套话 empty talk; platitude
人们希望官员讲话平实些,少说套话、空话。

People would like to see officials talk plainly. No one likes to hear stale platitudes and empty talk.

套近乎 suck up to someone; cotton up to someone; curry favor with someone; polish the apple
他总和领导套近乎。

He's always sucking up to the boss.

特保关税 special protectionist tariff
美国对从中国进口的轮胎征收特保关税这一决定是严重的贸易保护主义措施,违背了其在二十国集团峰会上所做出的承诺。

The US decision to impose special protectionist tariffs on tire imports from China is grave trade protectionism and goes against its commitments made at the Group of 20 summit.

特别提款权 Special Drawing Rights
人民币被正式纳入国际货币基金组织特别提款权货币篮子。

The RMB was formally included in the International Monetary Fund's Special Drawing Rights basket.

特惠关税 preferential tariff
根据中国和泰国等5个国家的经济发展情况,日本将把这些国家从特惠关税制度中移除。

Japan will remove five countries, including China and Thailand, from a preferential tariff framework in light of their economic development.

特写镜头 close-up (shot)
特写镜头露出了女演员眼角的皱纹,她略显疲态。
A close-up shot of the actress reveals wrinkles round the eyes and a slight sign of fatigue.

特许税 franchise tax
众议院以420比2通过提案,废除联邦特许税。
The bill to revoke the federal franchise tax was passed by 420∶2 in the House of Representatives.

特种债券 special bonds
此外,发行长期特种债券也可以筹集资金。
In addition, issuing long-term special bonds may also raise funds.

踢皮球 pass the buck; shift responsibility onto someone else
在中国,工作推诿叫"踢皮球"。
In China, those who pass the buck are said to "kick the ball" to other people.

提前大选 early/snap general election
英国下议院批准首相特雷莎·梅提出的提前大选后,竞选活动已经展开。
Campaigning is under way after the British House of Commons approved Prime Minister Theresa May's call for an early general election.

提现服务费 service fee for cash withdrawal
即时通讯应用微信对用户收取提现服务费。
Instant messaging app WeChat charges service fee from customers for cash withdrawals.

替班司机 temp driver; substitute driver
他找了份工作,当替班司机。
He got a job as a temp driver.

替补队员 bench player; second-string player; reserve; substitute
像所有运动员一样,姚明初进国家队也得打替补。
Like other players, when Yao Ming first made the national team, he had to start as a bench player.

替代国 surrogate country
2001年中国加入世贸组织签订的议定书第十五条规定,"替代国"做法在2016年

12月11日终止。
In accordance with Article 15 of the accession protocol signed when China joined the WTO in 2001, the surrogate country approach expires on December 11, 2016.

替代疗法 alternative treatment
由于这一测试只涵盖了66位患者,还需更大规模的研究才能确认这一研究发现。不过研究人员指出,太极拳有望成为对抗纤维性肌痛的替代疗法。
As only 66 patients were involved in the test, larger studies are needed to confirm the findings. But Tai Chi looks promising as an alternative treatment to fibromyalgia, the researchers noted.

替身演员 stuntman or stuntwoman; stand-in
本影片没用替身演员。
No stuntmen or stuntwomen were used in this film.

天气保险 weather insurance
中国将在年底前推出首个天气保险类别,帮助农民应对自然灾害带来的经济损失。
China may roll out its first weather insurance coverage before the end of the year to help farmers cope with economic losses from natural disasters.

天有不测风云 a bolt from the blue; out of the blue; Anything can happen.
他说:"天有不测风云。明天出门可能被汽车撞死,谁知道呢?"
"Anything can happen," he said. "You may be run over by a car tomorrow. Who knows?"

填海 land reclamation
因围填海项目导致海洋生态系统受到严重破坏,持续引发关注,2018年,我国将不再审批新的商业填海项目。
China won't approve new commercial land reclamation projects in 2018, amid rising concerns that such projects have led to severe damage of the marine ecosystem.

调整产业结构 make adjustment in the structure of industry; adjust the industrial structure
过去一年,我们大力调整产业结构。
Last year, we channeled great energy into making adjustments in the structure of industry.

贴片广告;随片广告 pre-movie advert; cinema advertising
根据《电影产业促进法(征求意见稿)》,中国电影院可能禁止在电影票上明示的电影放映时间之后放映贴片广告。
Cinemas in China may be prohibited from screening pre-movie adverts after the start time of each film printed on tickets, according to a draft law on movie promotion.

贴现率 discount rate （国家中央银行向民间银行贷款的利率，其调高或降低往往间接影响银行对客户所收取的利率）
这是自2006年6月以来贴现率首次上调。
It was the first increase in the discount rate since June 2006.

铁杆粉丝 die-hard fan; hard-core fan; avid fan; ardent fan
对奥普拉的铁杆粉丝们来说，能观看她脱口秀的时间不多了。周二，粉丝们在哈波演播室外面排长队感受着那份热度，期待能参与录制最后几期脱口秀。
Time is running out for Oprah's die-hard fans, and they were feeling the heat Tuesday as they waited in line outside Harpo Studios in the hopes of getting into one of the final shows.

铁路运行图 railway operation plan
中国铁路总公司表示，新的铁路运行图提高了我国客运和货运列车的运力。
A new railway operation plan has increased China's passenger and freight train capacity, according to China Railway Corp.

铁腕的 ironhanded
他是个铁腕人物，对政治对手从不手软。
He's always had an ironhanded grip on power and dealt with political foes without mercy.

庭前会议 pretrial conference
据律师介绍，颇受关注的马航MH370航班诉讼案庭前会议主要关注证据交换并明确各方的诉讼请求和意见。
A pretrial conference in the high-profile litigation related to Malaysia Airlines Flight 370 was focused mainly on exchanges of evidence and clarifying appeals and opinions of the parties, a lawyer involved in the litigation said.

庭审 try (or hear) a case in court; court hearing
他说庭审时会说出全部真相。
He said he will tell everything when the case is heard in court.

停产 suspend operations
污染严重的小型造纸厂已被勒令无限期停产。
Small and heavily polluting paper mills were suspended operations indefinitely.

停车换乘停车场 Park & Ride site
格里姆斯顿酒吧P+R（停车换乘）停车场已挂牌出售，指导价为5.5万英镑。
Grimston Bar Park & Ride site has been put up for sale with a guide price of £55,000.

通风廊道 ventilation corridors
北京正计划建立通风廊道网络系统，以促进空气流通，吹走雾霾和污染物。
Beijing is planning to build a network of ventilation corridors to facilitate air flow and blow away smog and pollutants.

通缉名单 wanted list
新疆公安厅发布11名在逃犯罪嫌疑人的通缉名单，鼓励人民群众提供线索。
The Xinjiang Public Security Department released a wanted list of 11 suspects, encouraging residents to provide information.

通商口岸 trading port
与上海的长江隔江相望的南通是中国最早的通商口岸之一。
Nantong, across the Yantze River from Shanghai, was one of China's earliest trading ports.

通胀挂钩债券 inflation-linked bond
香港特区政府周一宣布将于6月发行第二批通胀挂钩债券，以缓解港人所面对的逐渐增加的通胀压力。
The Hong Kong SAR government announced Monday it would launch the second round of inflation-linked bond in June to help ease a mounting inflation tension on the residents.

通胀恐慌 inflation fear
10月份的消费价格同比上涨4.4%，创25个月以来的新高，引起了通胀恐慌。周三准备金率提高之后，进一步实行货币紧缩政策的可能性增大。
Consumer prices surged 4.4 percent year-on-year in October, a 25-month high, stoking inflation fears and making further monetary tightening more likely following Wednesday's reserve ratio hike.

通胀预期 inflation expectation
国务院明确指出，在今年余下的几个月中，政策将着力"在促进增长、均衡调整经济发展、以及管理通胀预期之间取得平衡"。
The State Council made it clear that in the remaining months of this year, the policy focus would be to "balance the relationship between boosting growth, rebalancing the economy and managing inflation expectations".

同胞竞争障碍 sibling rivalry disorder

兄弟姐妹之间打闹很正常，但如果争吵走向极端，且持续时间过长，则有可能预示着同胞竞争障碍。

Brothers and sisters fighting is nothing new, but when the rivalry goes to extreme lengths and continues for a long time, it may be a sign of sibling rivalry disorder.

同票同权 equal representation

全国人大常委会就该法修正案草案中提及的在人民代表大会中实现城乡居民"同票同权"进行了讨论。

China's Standing Committee of the National People's Congress discussed granting equal representation in people's congresses to rural and urban people, according to a draft law amendment.

统计造假 fraudulent data

深改组会议指出，官员要强化监督统计造假行为。

A meeting of a top Party reform group said officials must strengthen supervision over fraudulent data.

统一市场 single market

我们虽属欧洲统一市场，但不使用欧元。

We are in the European single market, but outside the euro.

头彩 jackpot; lottery jackpot

拉里中了头彩，他在自家地里发现了石油。

Larry hit the jackpot when he discovered oil on his land.

头号种子 top seed

作为世界排名第一的选手，他被列为美国网球公开赛头号种子。

As world number one, he was installed as the top seed for the US Open tennis tournament.

投标 bid for; tender for

参加这项工程投标的公司有30多家。

Over 30 companies placed a bid for this project.

投机性需求 speculative demand

随着主要城市住房交易量下滑，投机性需求得到明显遏制。同时，保障性住房建设也开始加快速度进行。

Speculative demands have been prominently checked with falling house trading in major cities. Construction of affordable housing also has picked up speed.

投资环境 investment environment
湖北省正在努力改善投资环境。
Hubei province is striving for an improved investment environment.

投资移民 investment immigration
近年来投资移民迅猛增长。
Investment immigration has grown rapidly in recent years.

图书漂流 bookcrossing
图书漂流指的是"将一本书留在公共场所让其他人捡走阅读,捡走书的人读后也会照做"的行为。
Bookcrossing is defined as "the practice of leaving a book in a public place to be picked up and read by others, who then do likewise".

涂色书 coloring books
《秘密花园:一本探索奇境的手绘涂色书》自2013年出版以来,在全球范围内共卖出约200万册。
Since the release of *Secret Garden: An Inky Treasure Hunt and Coloring Book* in 2013, it has sold about 2 million copies worldwide.

土地出让收入 land sale revenue
财政部表示,大部分土地出让收入用在了补偿及相关费用上,仅留下一小部分用作其他开支。
Most of China's land sale revenue went to compensation and related spending, leaving only a marginal sum to be used for other expenditures, according to the Finance Ministry.

土地沙化 desert encroachment; desertification
据介绍,全国每年因土地沙化造成的直接经济损失达540亿元。
It is said that the direct economic loss caused by desert encroachment nationwide is 54 billion yuan every year.

土地使用权到期 expiration of land use rights
土地使用权到期是关系到民众切实利益的全国性问题,该问题引发了民众的普遍关注。
Expiration of land use rights is a nationwide issue related to people's actual interests, and as such has drawn widespread public concern.

土豪 nouveau rich
中国大妈经常被描述成缺乏经济洞察力、跟风投资的土豪。

Chinese dama are often portrayed as nouveau rich with poor insight into the economy whose investment behavior resembles the herd instinct.

土十条（土壤污染防治行动计划）the 10-chapter soil pollution action plan

"土十条"是继旨在治理空气污染、水污染的行动计划之后，我国的第三个遏制污染的国家行动计划。该行动计划首次针对土壤退化问题提出了我国污染防治工作的目标。

The 10-chapter soil pollution action plan, China's third national action plan to curb pollution after the ones aimed at tackling air and water pollution, targets soil deterioration and advances the goal of China's pollution prevention and control work for the first time.

土特产 local specialty

到那儿之后不要忘了尝尝那儿的枣儿，当地的土特产。

While you're there, remember to try the dates, a local specialty.

团团转 be up to one's ears with work

他现在正忙得团团转，明天再和你谈。

He's up to the ears with work right now. He will talk to you tomorrow.

退耕还林还草 give up grain for green

耕作还是还林还草？土地沙化这么严重，对我们县来说没有别的出路，只有退耕还林还草。

Grain or grass? The desertification is so serious in our county that we can do nothing but give up grain for green.

退休金双轨制 dual pension scheme

网民呼吁废除长久以来一直在实行的"退休金双轨制"，在这个"双轨制"中，公务员和其他公有制企业人员所获得的养老金是非公有制企业人员的好几倍。

Netizens called for the scraping of the long-time "dual pension scheme", in which civil servants and other public employees were entitled to pensions several times the amount of citizens employed by non-public entities.

囤积居奇 hoard and profiteer; hoard for profiteering purposes

大蒜价格的疯涨主要是由一些人的囤积居奇引起的。

The price hike in garlic was mainly caused by hoarding and profiteering.

拖欠贷款者 loan defaulter

拖欠贷款者将有被列入黑名单的风险，信用也会丧失。

Loan defaulters are running the risk of getting blacklisted and losing their credit.

挖墙脚 swipe talents from others; cut the ground from under somebody's feet
据说，董事会一些成员曾私下要求猎头公司从别的公司雇员中物色人选，也就是我们汉语里所说的"挖墙脚"。
Members of the Board of Directors are believed to have privately asked headhunting agencies to swipe talents currently working for other companies, which is what we say in Chinese: cutting the ground from under somebody's feet.

外部环境 external environment
人们大多从外部环境找答案，难怪从来都找不到。实际上应当学着找找内因。
Most people seek answers from the external environment. Little wonder they never find it. In fact they should learn to look inward.

外国人居留证 residence permit for foreigners
对于那些在中国找到工作的外国人可以签发外国人居留证。
Foreigners granted work in China are issued a residence permit for foreigners.

外汇储备 foreign-exchange reserve
中国外汇储备量与一年前相比增加了1/3。
China's foreign-exchange reserves jumped by a third from a year earlier.

外汇掉期交易 Forex-swap
政府于4月24日正式推出人民币与外汇交易的外汇掉期交易市场。
The government officially launched a Forex-swap market for swapping the yuan and foreign currencies on April 24.

外交庇护 diplomatic asylum
没有人能够到美国寻求"外交庇护"，因为美国不承认这一国际法。
One cannot seek "diplomatic asylum" in the United States, which it does not recognize as a rule of international law.

外来物种 alien species
中国正受到超过400种入侵的外来物种的威胁，每年给中国造成的经济损失高达数十亿元。
China is threatened by more than 400 invasive alien species, which has caused

billions of yuan of economic losses.

外逃资本 flight of capital
中国金融监管机关已开始对非法外逃资本进行打击。外逃资本渠道是加勒比海域的避税区，如英属维尔京群岛和开曼群岛。
China's financial regulators have launched a crackdown on the illegal flight of capital via Caribbean tax havens, such as the British Virgin Islands and the Cayman Islands.

外向型经济 outward-oriented economy
该开发区以发展外向型经济为主。
This development zone focuses on the development of an outward-oriented economy.

外债余额 outstanding external debt
中国国家外汇管理局周三称，中国的外债余额（不包括香港特区、澳门特区和台湾省相关的）达到了5464.49亿美元。
China's outstanding external debt (excluding that of Hong Kong SAR, Macao SAR and Taiwan province) reached $546.449 billion, said the State Administration of Foreign Exchange (SAFE) on Wednesday.

完善国有资产管理体制 improve the management system of State-owned assets
完善国有资产管理体制，以管资本为主加强国有资产监管。
We will improve the the management system of State-owned assets and strengthen State-asset supervision by focusing on capital management.

完整预告片 full-length trailer
福克斯发布了该剧回归版的首部完整预告片，看到原班人马悉数回归，当年追剧的感觉又回来了。
Fox released the first full-length trailer for the revival series and seeing the original gang back together again brought all the feels.

玩不转 cannot/ be unable to manage; be beyond one's ability
许多事业单位官员业务上称职，但人际关系玩不转。
Many officials in public institutions have the competence business-wise. But they cannot quite manage interpersonal relations.

网购退货办法 refund policy for online shopping
国家工商总局发布网购退货办法草案，向社会公开征求意见。

The State Administration for Industry and Commerce issued a draft refund policy for online shopping. The policy was issued to solicit public opinion.

网红 online sensation; web celebrity; internet meme/hit/celebrity
这位中国游泳运动员搞笑的赛后采访和夸张的面部表情使她成为"网红"。
The Chinese swimmer's hilarious post-race interviews and exaggerated facial expressions have turned her into an online sensation.

网红经济 Wanghong economy/internet celebrity economy
网络红人们不仅进军时尚业,也正向网络游戏、旅游和母婴产品等行业发展,网红经济的整体规模正在不断扩大。
The overall size of the Wanghong economy is growing as cyber stars are going beyond the fashion industry and into online gaming, travel and baby products.

网恋 cyber romance; virtual love affair
她爱上了在网络聊天室的网友。这是典型的网恋。
She fell in love with someone from an internet chat room. This is a typical case of cyber romance.

网络安全事件应急预案 emergency response plan for internet security incident
我国发布了网络安全事件应急预案。
China released an emergency response plan for internet security incidents.

网络出版 online publishing
网络出版听起来吸引人,但是,涉足网络出版的多家传统出版社赚到钱的确实没有几家。
Though many traditional publishers have tried their hands on online publishing, which sounds attractive, to be sure, few have made any money from it.

网络恶作剧 online/web hoax
少林寺在中国以武僧闻名,该寺住持最近成了一起网络恶作剧的受害者,该寺网站的首页被换成了一张伪造的忏悔书。
The abbot of the Shaolin Temple, a Chinese monastery famous for its martial monks, fell victim to an online hoax in which the front page of the temple's website was replaced with a fake letter of remorse.

网络二手货市场 online flea market
专家表示,随着网络购物的发展,网络二手货市场还有继续发展的空间,但还应出台更多的监管措施来保护消费者权益。
Experts say the online flea market is expected to grow further as online shopping

continues to develop, but more regulation is needed to protect the rights of consumers.

网络反恐演习 anti-online terror drill
上海合作组织成员国在中国沿海城市厦门举办了首次网络反恐演习。
Member states of the Shanghai Cooperation Organization held their first anti-online terror drill in the Chinese coastal city of Xiamen.

网络攻击 cyber attack
包括WPP、俄罗斯石油公司、默克和AP穆勒-马士基集团在内的一些国际大公司已证实遭到大规模网络攻击，此次网络攻击还使乌克兰政府和银行的关键公共设施陷入瘫痪。
Some of the world's largest companies including WPP, Rosneft, Merck and AP Moller-Maersk have confirmed that they have been hit by a large-scale cyber attack that also took critical government and bank infrastructure in Ukraine offline.

网络间谍 cyber spy
在指控中国网络间谍试图入侵在美中国专家和国防承包商的电脑时，美国网络安全专家未能提供足够的证据。
American cyber-security experts failed to provide sufficient evidence when accusing Chinese cyber spies of trying to break into computers belonging to China specialists and defense contractors in the United States.

网络借贷 P2P lending
中国银监会等四部委联合发布了系列管理条例，旨在加强对我国迅猛发展的网络借贷行业的监管。
China's banking watchdog and three other ministries jointly issued a set of regulations to tighten supervision of the country's booming peer-to-peer (P2P) lending industry.

网络经济 cyber-economy
网络经济有泡沫经济的味道。
Cyber-economy smacks of the bubble economy.

网络礼节 netiquette; network etiquette
网络礼节不是一夜之间就能学会的。
Netiquette isn't something you learn overnight.

网络空间安全战略 cyberspace security strategy
国家互联网信息办公室发布了网络空间安全战略，倡导和平、安全、开放、合作、有序的发展目标。
China's top internet regulator released a cyberspace security strategy, advocating peace, security, openness, cooperation and order.

网络空间国际合作战略 International Strategy of Cooperation on Cyberspace
《网络空间国际合作战略》是中国就网络空间问题首度发布的战略。
International Strategy of Cooperation on Cyberspace is the first China has released regarding the virtual domain.

网络空间命运共同体 community of shared future in cyberspace
各国应该加强沟通、扩大共识、深化合作,共同构建网络空间命运共同体。
Countries should step up communication, broaden consensus and deepen cooperation, to jointly build a community of shared future in cyberspace.

网络募捐 online donation
由于公众不满其隐瞒家庭经济状况,一位父亲在为病重女儿发起的网络募捐中筹得的260余万元将退还捐赠者。
More than 2.6 million yuan raised in an online donation by a father for his seriously ill daughter will be returned to the donors following public outcry over his lack of honesty about the family's economic situation.

网络侵权 internet copyright infringement
国家版权局宣布,将建立公布侵权网站、移动终端应用以及其他平台的"黑名单",作为一项打击网络侵权的最新行动。
Blacklists naming websites, mobile apps and other platforms that violate copyrights will be created as part of the latest campaign to tackle internet copyright infringement, the National Copyright Administration said.

网络摄像机 webcam
拥有一架网络摄像机真够酷的。
It is really cool to have a webcam.

网络审查 censor the internet; internet censorship
微软公司董事长比尔·盖茨近日称,中国对互联网的审查"非常有限",在中国运营的公司应该遵守当地法律。
Microsoft Corp chairman Bill Gates has described Beijing's efforts to censor the internet as "very limited", saying corporations which operate in China should abide by the local law.

网络售彩 online lottery sale
财政部发布公告称,将禁止未经批准的网络售彩行为。
The Ministry of Finance issued an announcement saying it planned to ban unauthorized online lottery sales.

网络推手 internet marketer
通过让这些人成为公众注意的焦点这种手段,网络推手可能会获取巨额利润。
Internet marketers who stand to earn big money by thrusting them into the limelight.

网络围攻 online rioting
自周二大幅提高对商户的收费后,淘宝商城已连续经历了两拨网络围攻。淘宝商城是中国目前交易值最大的商家对客户(B2C)的在线商城。
Taobao Mall Co., China's current largest business-to-consumer (B2C) online marketplace by transaction value, has experienced two successive waves of online rioting since it significantly increased fees on online vendors on Tuesday.

网络文学 net literature; web literature
网络文学使年轻作家有机会把作品呈献给大批读者阅读、评论。
Net literature gives young writers a chance of having their writings read and critiqued by a wide range of readers.

网络虚拟财产 online virtual assets
深圳市发布《深圳市公安局公共服务白皮书》,成为广东省首个引入具体政策来保护居民网络虚拟财产的城市。
After publishing the *White Paper of Public Services of Shenzhen Public Security Bureau*, Shenzhen has become the first city in Guangdong province to introduce concrete policies to protect residents' online virtual assets.

网络议价师 net bargainer
"中间人"会代表你和网络经销商讨价还价,而他们则从差价中收取一部分作为报酬。这些人就是"网络议价师",他们提供的服务在中国快速发展的网购行业中日渐兴盛。
A middleman will—for a cut of the discount they get you—bargain on your behalf for lower prices with e-retailers. They are called "net bargainers", and the service is booming amid China's fast-growing online-shopping industry.

网络直播 online livestreaming
"主播"通过网络直播平台与观众互动。
People, who are called "hosts", speak to their audiences through online

livestreaming platforms.

网络治理 cyberspace governance
我们既要推动联合国框架内的网络治理,也要更好地发挥各类非国家行为体的积极作用。
Cyberspace governance under the framework of the United Nations should be advanced and non-state entities should play a better role.

网络主权 cyberspace sovereignty
他强调要尊重各国网络主权,维护和平安全的网络空间,促进开放合作,构建良好秩序。
He stresses respecting cyberspace sovereignty, maintaining peace and security in cyberspace, and promoting open cooperation and good order.

网络作家 cyberspace writer
中国的"网络作家"们正齐心协力地要求媒体公司提高工资,改善工作环境,并保证他们保留自己作品的所有权。
China's "cyberspace writers" are banding together to urge media companies to improve their pay and working conditions, and to ensure that they retain legal ownership of their work.

网上交易平台 online trading platform
上海交易所与波士顿咨询集团合作开发更先进的网上交易平台。
The Shanghai Exchange is cooperating with the Boston Consulting Group to develop a more advanced online trading platform.

网游监护 online guardianship (Parents' Guardian Project for Minors Playing Online Games)
有部分家长认为,申请网游监护的过程过于繁琐。
Some parents think the application process for the online guardianship is too complicated.

网游实名 real-name registration for online games
网游实名的要求旨在保障用户,特别是青少年的法律权益。
The requirement for real-name registration for online games is aimed at safeguarding the legal rights and interests of the users, especially the juveniles.

网游宵禁 online game curfew
网信办发布的《未成年人网络保护条例(草案征求意见稿)》规定对未成年人实

施"网游宵禁",这引起了社会的广泛关注。
The draft regulation on the online protection of minors, released for public opinions by the cyberspace authorities, stipulated an online game curfew for the minors, which has drawn wide public concern.

网约车 online car-hailing; online car-booking
中央政府发布了一项规定,给予网约车服务合法地位。
The central government released a regulation giving legal status to online car-hailing services in China.

旺季 busy season; height of the season
下半年通常是港口的旺季。
The second half of the year is usually the busy season for ports.

危房 dilapidated building
该市仍有大量危房需改造或者推倒重建。
There are still many dilapidated buildings to be renovated or rebuilt in the city.

危机意识 sense of crisis
他危机意识很强,强得也许过分。他说经常做失业的梦。
He has a heightened sense of crisis, perhaps too much so. He says that he often has the nightmare that he's out of a job.

危险驾驶 dangerous driving
驾驶过程中接打电话属于危险驾驶。
Making phone calls while behind the wheel is dangerous driving.

微博实名制 real-name microblogging registration
继北京和广州等其他大城市之后,上海周一也开始实行微博实名制。
Shanghai is going to require real-name microblogging registration on Monday, following similar moves adopted by other big cities such as Beijing and Guangzhou.

违法违规行为 foul play
根据交通委发布的规定,有违法违规行为的出租车驾驶员现在会面临3年不得从事该行业的处罚,极端违规行为或导致终身不得驾驶出租车。
According to rules announced by transport authorities, cabbies now face a ban of up to three years for foul play—or a lifetime ban in extreme cases.

违反合同 breach a contract; breach of contract
一方违反合同，另一方有权终止合同并要求赔偿。
If any party breaches a contract, the other is entitled to terminate the contract and claim compensation.

违约罚金 penalty for breach of contract
违约罚金高达数万美元。
Penalty for breach of contract runs to tens of thousands of dollars.

违章建筑 unapproved construction project
从4月1日起，政府将按照新规定对违章建筑予以打击，违章建设住房甚至会被断水断电。
From April 1, authorities can even cut off power and water supplies to rule breakers' homes under new regulations aimed at clamping down on unapproved construction projects.

唯利是图 have a money-only attitude; be bent solely on profits; seek nothing but profits; profits before everything; care only for money; be blind to all but one's own interest
她纳闷他如何能够主管旨在提高公众环保意识的杂志，因为他的商业理念就是唯利是图。
She wonders how he could run a publication aimed at raising the level of public awareness over environmental protection because he has a money-only attitude in business.

伪基站 pseudo base station
腾讯数据显示，伪基站发送的手机病毒感染了超过1100万台智能手机。
More than 11 million smartphones were infected by mobile viruses sent from the pseudo base stations, according to data released by Tencent.

伪科学 pseudo-science
虽然这期总结回顾是半娱乐的，但该运动组织强调它也有严肃目的，就是确保公众不要相信伪科学。
While the review is partly about entertainment, the campaign group stresses it also has a serious aim—to make sure pseudo-science is not allowed to become accepted as true.

伪造证据 give false evidence; falsify evidence
一个律师为一个有组织的犯罪团伙辩护时因为伪造证据，以及教唆他人作伪证而被判处有期徒刑两年半。

A lawyer was jailed for two years and a half for giving false evidence and inciting others to bear false witness in an organized crime gang trial.

尾气净化器 exhaust purifier
1968年，鲁弗斯·斯托克斯将尾气净化器申请了专利。
In 1968 Rufus Stokes patented an exhaust purifier.

委托投资 entrusted investment
我国七个省级地区已经开始将养老基金委托给全国社会保障基金理事会投资。地方养老金委托投资已正式启动。
Seven Chinese provincial-level regions have started entrusting their pension funds to the National Council for Social Security Fund for investment. Entrusted investment of local pension funds has been officially launched.

卫冕冠军 defending champion
卫冕冠军约翰·史密斯在上届奥运会上赢得拳击项目的金牌。
Defending champion John Smith won boxing gold at the last Olympics.

未偿贷款 outstanding loan
中国银监会小企业贷款负责人表示，截至7月末，小企业未偿贷款达到9.85万亿元，年同比增长26.6%。
Outstanding loans to small firms grew 26.6 percent year-on-year to hit 9.85 trillion yuan at the end of July, said an official in charge of financial services for small enterprises at the China Banking Regulatory Commission.

未删减版 uncut version
不管在哪个平台播出的电视剧，版本应该都是一致的，没有所谓的"未删减版"。
No matter what platforms the TV series will be broadcast on, the version should be the same, there is no such thing as an "uncut version".

文化创意产业 cultural and creative industry
文化创意产业已成为北京市的支柱产业之一，在2008年为全市GDP的贡献率达到11.4%。
The cultural and creative industry has become one of the pillar industries in Beijing, contributing 11.4 percent of the city's GDP in 2008.

文化旅游业 cultural tourism
一位意大利高级官员说，眼下在意大利举行的"中国文化年"活动将促进文化旅游业的发展，增进两个国家之间的相互了解。

The ongoing Chinese Culture Year in Italy will intensify cultural tourism and spread greater mutual awareness between the two countries, a senior Italian official says.

文化逆差 cultural deficit
进口影片的增加正是文化部副部长所说的中国面临的"文化逆差"的一方面。
The increase of imported films is part of what the vice-minister of culture called a "cultural deficit" facing the country.

文化渗透 cultural infiltration
文化渗透并不像听起来那么可怕。交流是相互的,文化渗透同时是反向文化渗透。
Cultural infiltration isn't as frightful a thing as it sounds. Exchanges are mutual; cultural influence must be happening in the other direction at the same time.

文化自信 cultural confidence
全国的文艺工作者要坚定文化自信,服务人民,为实现民族振兴而创造出更多激励人心和经典的作品。
Artists in the country should consolidate cultural confidence, serve the people and create more inspiring and classical works to revive the nation.

文物医院 Relic Hospital
国内水平最高的失修古文物保护修复中心,即民间所说的文物医院,近日在北京故宫启用。
Recently, a state-of-the-art conservation center to "treat" ancient cultural relics in disrepair, informally called the Relic Hospital, opened at Beijing's Palace Museum.

问责制 accountability system
新法规划定了各部门的职责,明确了反走私工作的考核和问责制度,制定了对于举报者的奖励和保护措施以及群众的参与机制。
The new regulation outlines departmental duties, an anti-smuggling assessment and accountability system, whistleblower rewards and protection, as well as grassroots participation.

卧铺客车 overnight bus; sleeper bus
周日发生的两起交通事故导致48人丧生,再次引发人们关注卧铺客车和搭载儿童的车辆的安全问题。
Two traffic accidents claimed the lives of 48 people on Sunday, renewing concerns over the safety of overnight buses and vans carrying children.

乌龙球 own goal
在此前进行的17场比赛中,乌龙球已出现5次,超过了C罗的4次进球。
Cristiano Ronaldo's four goals at the World Cup are closest to catching the five own goals scored after 17 games.

污染源普查 census of pollution sources
第二次全国污染源普查内容包括污染物种类、污染物排放量和污染治理设施运行情况等具体数据。
The second census of pollution sources included detailed data like pollutant types, emission amounts, and operation of equipment to reduce pollution.

污水处理 sewage treatment; sewage disposal
污水处理的方法多种多样。
Sewage treatment methods vary.

无车日 car-free day
今年无车日的主题是"选择健康环保的交通方式"。目前已有112个城市鼓励居民"绿色"出行。
The theme for the car-free day is to choose healthy and environment friendly ways of traveling. So far, 112 cities have encouraged residents to travel "green".

无多数议会 hung parliament
周五英国大选初步选举结果显示,没有政党赢得绝对多数选票,因此产生"无多数议会"。
The British general election has produced a "hung parliament" as no party wins an absolute majority, preliminary results showed Friday.

无风不起浪 There are no waves without wind./There's no smoke without fire.

无缝区域经济 seamless regional economy
参加亚太经合组织论坛的各国领导人周日表示他们将共同致力于建立一个无缝的区域经济。
Leaders of the Asia-Pacific Economic Cooperation (APEC) forum said Sunday that they are committed to building a seamless regional economy through joint efforts.

无固定期限合同 open-ended contract
新劳动合同法被认为是10多年来中国劳动制度领域最重要的变革。该法规定,为保护劳动者的合法权益,企业必须与劳动者签订合同,并鼓励签订无固定期限合同。

The new labor law is considered the most significant change in the country's labor rules in more than a decade. It makes mandatory the use of written contracts and encourages open-ended contracts to protect the legitimate rights and interests of workers.

无理由退货 unconditional returns
新修订的消费者权益保护法规定网购7天可无理由退货退款。
A newly revised Consumer Protection Law allows unconditional returns and refunds within 7 days after an online transaction.

无力偿付的公司 insolvent corporation
对于无力偿付的公司,法院将强制其申请破产。
The court will order insolvent corporations to file for bankruptcy.

无铅汽油 lead-free gasoline
像无铅汽油这样的新型燃料已经进入市场。
New fuels such as lead-free gasoline have appeared on the market.

无人超市 unmanned supermarket
亚马逊在美国开设其首家无人超市AmazonGo。国内电子商务巨头阿里巴巴效仿亚马逊,在杭州开设了两家没有收银员的杂货店。
Domestic e-commerce giant Alibaba opened two grocery stores with no cashiers in Hangzhou, following the example of Amazon, which opened its first unmanned supermarket AmazonGo in the US.

无人机驾照 drone certification
无人机在国内成了时兴的物件,越来越多的人也开始考虑考个无人机驾照了。
Drone is increasingly a popular item in China and with it, more and more people are considering getting a drone certification.

无人机紧急救援队 UAV emergency rescue team
我国首支无人机紧急救援队在北京成立。
China's first unmanned aerial vehicle (UAV) emergency rescue team was established in Beijing.

无人驾驶汽车 driverless vehicle
意大利一个工程师研究小组启动了被宣称为无人驾驶汽车最长行程的试车项目。
A team of Italian engineers launched what has been billed as the longest-ever test drive of driverless vehicles.

无人侦察机 spy drone
伊朗半官方的梅尔通讯社周三报道称,伊朗计划于近期展览截获的几架美国和以色列的无人侦察机。
Iran plans to display several US and Israeli spy drones it has taken possession of in the near future, the semi-official Mehr news agency reported Wednesday.

无人值守的 unattended
中国在"世界屋脊"珠穆朗玛峰脚下建成了首个无人值守地震台。
China has built its first unattended seismic monitoring station at the foot of Mount Qomolangma, the world's highest mountain.

无痛分娩 pain-free delivery
一名孕妇在请求进行剖腹产遭拒后自杀一事在全国引发公众热议,人们呼吁推广无痛分娩方式。
The suicide of a pregnant woman after her plea for a C-section was rejected has sparked a public outcry across China, with people calling for the promotion of pain-free delivery options.

无土栽培 soil-less cultivation
这些技术代表无土栽培科技取得重大突破。
These techniques represent a major breakthrough in the technology of soil-less cultivation.

无息贷款 interest-free loan
遇到意外资金困难,学生们可申请无息贷款。
An interest-free loan fund is available for students who find themselves in unforeseen financial difficulty.

无现金社会 cashless society
中国是世界上第一个使用纸币的国家,但到了几个世纪后的现在,随着移动支付的普及程度不断提高,一些分析师预测,中国或在未来10年成为首个无现金社会。
China was the first country in the world to use paper money, but centuries later, the soaring popularity of mobile payment has some analysts forecasting that it could become the first cashless society in the next decade.

无效进球 disallowed goal
周三在世界杯小组赛B组对阵西班牙的比赛中,伊朗的进球被判定为无效进球后,该队的一名工作人员被送进医院。
A member of the Iranian team's staff was hospitalized on Wednesday following the

disallowed goal in the World Cup Group B game against Spain.

无形资产 intangible asset
信用是无形资产。
Credit is an intangible asset.

无性繁殖 asexual reproduction
无性繁殖就是单亲繁殖，在植物中很常见，动物中则比较罕见。
Asexual reproduction is the formation of new individuals from the cell（s）of a single parent. It is very common in plants but less so in animals.

无烟工业 smokeless industry
旅游业有时又被称作无烟工业。
Tourism is sometimes referred to as a smokeless industry.

无烟环境 smoke-free environment
只有在试点城市政府以及法规的支持下，那里的人们才能最终享受到无烟环境。
Only with the support of the pilot cities' municipal governments and legislatures, can the people there finally enjoy smoke-free environments.

无法律约束力文件 non-legally binding document
为期两周的哥本哈根会议于周六在丹麦首都落下帷幕，并出台了一项有关气候变化的无法律约束力的文件。
The two week-long Copenhagen conference concluded Saturday in the Danish capital after producing a non-legally binding document on climate change.

500米口径球面射电望远镜 Five-hundred-meter Aperture Spherical Radio Telescope (FAST)
有着"中国天眼"之称的500米口径球面射电望远镜是世界上最大的单口径射电望远镜。
The Five-hundred-meter Aperture Spherical Radio Telescope (FAST), nicknamed "China's Eye of Heaven", is the world's largest single-aperture radio telescope.

5G商用 commercial use of 5G
第五代（5G）蜂窝网络可能最早于2020年投入商用。
The fifth generation (5G) of cellular networks may be put into commercial use as early as 2020.

五年之痒 five-year itch
一份婚恋报告显示，中国人在婚姻生活中，"七年之痒"已变成"五年之痒"，婚后3~5年就会出现婚姻危机。
The "seven-year itch" has turned into a "five-year itch" among Chinese couples who stand to experience a marriage crisis between three and five years after tying the knot, according to a marriage report.

"五位一体"（经济建设、政治建设、文化建设、社会建设、生态文明建设）Five-pronged overall plan (All-round economic, political, cultural, social, and ecological progress)

"五位一体"和"四个全面"相互促进、统筹联动，要协调贯彻好，在推动经济发展的基础上，建设社会主义市场经济、民主政治、先进文化、生态文明、和谐社会，协同推进人民富裕、国家强盛、中国美丽。
Mutually reinforcing and interconnected, the "Five-Pronged Overall Plan" and "Four-Pronged Comprehensive Strategy" need to be implemented on a coordinated basis. On the basis of promoting economic development, we must develop a socialist market economy, democracy, advanced culture, environmental culture, and harmonious society, and advance a coordinated effort to make our people prosperous, our nation strong, and our country beautiful.

武德 martial arts morality

一位综合格斗选手高调挑战一位太极拳师后，中国武术协会表示坚决反对"约架"行为，称该行为有违武德，涉嫌违法。
The Chinese Martial Arts Association said it absolutely opposes "arranged private fights" following a mixed martial arts fighter's high-profile challenge to a tai chi master, which it called a breach of martial arts morality and suspected violation of law.

物联网 Internet of Things

一些专家指出，中国的物联网还处在初级阶段，还得很长时间才能实现大规模发展，让公众享受其全部功能。
Some experts have said that China's Internet of Things was still in a very early stage, and it will take a long time for it to achieve large-scale development in order to let the public enjoy its full functions.

物业管理 property management; estate management

调解人敦促业主同物业管理公司通过协商解决纠纷。
Mediators urged house owners to settle disputes with property management companies through consultation.

误导性品牌 derivative trademark; copycat

其他业内观察人士认为,这种仿冒或误导性品牌对真正的奢侈品牌几乎没有影响,因为它们对准的是不同的消费群体。

Other industry watchers believe such copycats or derivative trademarks have little influence on real luxury brands because they target different consumer groups.

雾霾 fog and haze; smog

近几日北京持续被浓重雾霾笼罩,北京市场上防尘口罩和空气净化器的销量剧增。

The market for dust masks and air purifiers is booming in Beijing because the capital has been shrouded for several days in thick fog and haze.

雾霾津贴 smog subsidy

在一项调查中,约95%的受访者支持向雾霾天从事户外作业的劳动者发放"雾霾津贴"。

Some 95% of respondents to a survey support a "smog subsidy" for those who work outdoors on smoggy days.

雾霾净化塔 Smog Free Tower

雾霾净化塔据说每小时能够净化3万立方米的空气,捕捉并收集空气中至少75%的PM2.5和PM10雾霾颗粒。

The Smog Free Tower purportedly treats 30,000 cubic meters of air per hour, collecting more than 75% of PM2.5 and PM10.

雾炮车 mist cannon truck

两辆多功能抑尘车,也叫雾炮车,目前在外国使馆和奥运场馆集中的朝阳区作业。

Known as the multi-purpose anti-dust truck, two mist cannon trucks are now being used in Beijing's Chaoyang, a district home to foreign embassies and Olympic facilities.

夕阳产业 sunset industry
公众认为林业是夕阳产业，认识不到林业对提高生活水平的贡献，成为林业发展的主要障碍。
The perception of forestry as a sunset industry and low public awareness of its contribution to the standard of living are significant deterrents to forestry development.

西部片 Western/western film
追根溯源，最早的西部片是1903年出品的无声电影《火车大劫案》。
The Western film traces its roots back to *The Great Train Robbery*, a silent film released in 1903.

西电东送 West-East Electricity Transmission; transmit electricity from the western areas to the eastern areas
西电东送是西部大开发的重要工程。
The West-East Electricity Transmission is one of the key projects in developing the western regions.

西式管家 western-style butler
随着管家培训业兴起，不少教授"西式管家"艺术的培训学校和机构在华成立。
Specialized schools and institutes have been set up in China to teach the art of being a western-style butler as the sector starts to take off.

吸收游资 absorb idle funds
通过吸收游资建立投资公司，在理论上是个好主意。
Theoretically, it is a good idea to establish an investment company by absorbing idle funds.

希腊退出欧元区 Grexit
希腊于5月6日举行议会选举后组建新政府失败，这使得关于"希腊退出欧元区"的猜测越来越盛。
After Greece's national elections on May 6 left the country struggling to form a new government, speculations about "Grexit" kept rising.

习近平新时代中国特色社会主义思想 Xi Jinping Thought on Socialism with Chinese Characteristics for a New Era
中国共产党第十九次全国代表大会通过了关于《中国共产党章程（修正案）》的决议，将习近平新时代中国特色社会主义思想写入党章。
The 19th National Congress of the Communist Party of China(CPC) approved an amendment to the Party Constitution which enshrines Xi Jinping Thought on Socialism with Chinese Characteristics for a New Era.

洗钱 money laundering
5家公司被指控参与洗钱，涉及金额几百万美元。
Five firms were charged with money laundering involving millions of US dollars.

洗澡蟹 bathing-crabs
新华社一篇报道将部分只为获得一纸海外文凭、不认真对待学业的海外留学生定义为"洗澡蟹"。近年来，"洗澡蟹"式海归毕业回国后发现很难找到高薪的工作。
Some Chinese who study abroad only for an overseas diploma and have not taken their academic careers seriously are defined as "bathing-crabs" in a Xinhua report. "Bathing-crab" returnees have found it difficult to find a well-paid job when returning to China after graduation in recent years.

系统风险 systemic risk
只要政府保持相对高的经济增长，就能够及时有效地抑制系统风险。
Systemic risks could be well curbed as long as the country maintains comparatively high economic growth.

系统管理 system management
我是系统管理员。我负责网络设备和保证数据库的顺畅运转。
I'm a system management technician. I'm responsible for the smooth running of network devices and databases.

系统重要性国家 systemically important country
中国是25个系统重要性国家之一，法国、意大利、巴西等国也在此列，这些国家商定每5年至少进行1次强制性（金融系统）评估。
China is one of the 25 systemically important countries, including France, Italy and Brazil, which have agreed to mandatory assessments at least once every five years.

细菌耐药 antimicrobial resistance(AMR)
细菌耐药指细菌、真菌、病毒、寄生生物等微生物对于抗菌药物（包括抗生素、抗病毒药物和抗疟药物）的耐受性。
Antimicrobial resistance (AMR) is the ability of a microorganism (like bacteria, viruses, and some parasites) to stop an antimicrobial (such as antibiotics, antivirals and antimalarials) from working against it.

细菌战 germ warfare
二战中日本细菌战的中国幸存者和遇难者家属发誓将继续要求日本道歉并赔偿。
Chinese survivors and the families of victims of Japanese germ warfare in World War II vowed to continue their fight for an apology and compensation.

细则 bylaw
根据城市有关规定，居委会发布了宠物狗饲养细则。
In accordance with city regulations, the neighborhood committee issued a bylaw regarding the raising of dogs as pets.

下不为例 not to/must not be repeated; not to/must not be taken as a precedent
跳窗进教室怎么行？这次饶过你，下不为例。
I'll let you go this once, but entering the classroom through the window must not be repeated.

下岗职工 laid-off worker
要切实为下岗职工创造更多就业机会。
More substantial efforts should be made to provide more job opportunities for laid-off workers.

下降趋势 downturn
有迹象表明房价有下降趋势。
There is an evidence of downturn in the house prices.

下落 whereabouts
逃犯仍然下落不明。
The escaped prisoner's whereabouts is still unknown.

下水 hit the water; launch
我国首艘自主建造的001A型航空母舰在中国船舶重工集团公司大连造船厂下水。
China's first home-built aircraft carrier 001A hit the water in Dalian shipyard of the China Shipbuilding Industry Corp.

先发制人战略 preemptive attack
布什政府在反恐战争中采取先发制人的战略。
The Bush administration launched preemptive attacks in the war on terrorism.

先决条件 prerequisite; prior condition; precondition
几千年来洪水灾害一直侵扰中国,治洪是发展农业的先决条件,是政府的首要任务。
Destructive floods have been a part of the Chinese experience for thousands of years. Flood control tops the governmental agenda as a prerequisite for agricultural development.

先审后播 review-before-release system
分析人士表示,对于那些曾和海外同步推出正版美剧的国内网站来说,先审后播的制度会导致它们的点击量输给那些盗播网站。
For sites that were releasing legally authorized US shows in China simultaneously with their US counterparts, a review-before-release system means they'll lose page views to platforms distributing pirated copies, said analysts.

闲置地产 vacant property
目前中国闲置的房地产用地约1万公顷,其中因政府规划方案和司法查封而导致闲置的土地占55%。
The vacant property in China has reached about 10,000 hectares, and 55% of it was caused by the government's layout plan and the court's close rule.

闲置土地 land left idle; idle land
中国土地使用监管机构周四发布了一个黑名单,其中包括26宗闲置土地的开发商,以限制囤地投机行为。
China's land use watchdog released on Thursday a blacklist of 26 cases of land left idle by property developers to curb hoarding and speculation.

咸潮入侵 intrusion of saltwater; intrusion of tidal saltwater
当地水务局的官员称,该市的自来水供应不会受到持续干旱和随之而来的咸潮入侵的影响。
The city's tap water supply will not be undermined by the lingering drought and the consequent intrusion of saltwater, a local official from the water authority has said.

险胜 narrow victory; win narrowly; have a narrow lead over
英国脱欧阵营险胜不但让英国在欧盟的其他27个伙伴国震惊,也让包括中国在内的重要贸易伙伴讶异。

The narrow victory for the "Brexit" camp dismayed not just Britain's 27 partners in the EU but also important trading partners further afield, including China.

现场调查 on-scene investigation
专门负责调查各类猝死事件的不列颠哥伦比亚省法医服务处和加拿大皇家骑警队结束了对无舵雪橇赛道的现场调查。在温哥华冬奥会开幕的早晨，格鲁吉亚运动员诺达尔·库玛丽塔什维利在那里意外死亡。

The Coroners Service of British Columbia, responsible for the investigation of all sudden deaths, together with the RCMP (Royal Canadian Mounted Police), concluded their on-scene investigations on the luge track, where Georgian athlete, Nodar Kumaritashvili, died in the morning of the opening day of the Vancouver Winter Olympic Games.

现场演出 live performance
比起录音室专辑，我更喜欢听爵士大师们的现场演出录音。我喜欢听到观众疯狂地给大师们鼓掌、叫好，如痴如醉。
I prefer the recordings of live performances of Jazz masters to their studio recordings. I love to hear the audience cheer for them and go crazy.

现场招聘 on-site recruiting
四支工作组将与劳务输出省份在跨省劳务服务方面进行合作，一些企业还会参与现场招聘活动。
Four teams will cooperate with labor-exporting provinces on interprovincial labor services, and some enterprises will participate in on-site recruiting.

现场直播 be broadcast live; live broadcast
央视五套对2014年世界杯的所有比赛都进行了现场直播。
All the matches of the 2014 World Cup were broadcast live on CCTV 5.

现代海上作战体系 modern maritime combat system
海军将士们要全面贯彻党对军队绝对领导的根本原则和制度，坚定理想信念，弘扬光荣传统，大力推进科技创新，加快发展新型作战力量，着力构建现代海上作战体系。
Naval officers and soldiers should fully implement the Party's absolute leadership over the armed forces, be firm in ideals and convictions, and uphold the glorious traditions, while pushing for technological innovation, developing new types of battle forces, and building a modern maritime combat system.

现代医院管理 modern hospital management
我国应建立一个坚持以人民健康为中心、坚持公立医院的公益性、把社会效益放在首位的现代医院管理制度。
China should establish a modern hospital management system that adheres to putting people's health at the center and adheres to the nonprofit nature of public hospitals and putting the public's interest as a priority.

现代意识 modern thinking
令人惊奇的是，寺院的管理也受到了现代意识的影响。
Surprisingly, modern thinking has also influenced the management of the temple.

现货价格 spot price
在新产棉花的现货价格低于收购价格时，国家将向包括新疆维吾尔自治区在内的13个主要产棉区收储棉花。
The purchase will apply to the country's 13 major cotton production regions including Xinjiang Uygur autonomous region when spot prices of newly produced cotton are below the purchase price.

现货市场 spot market
石油产品现货交易市场——上海石油交易所于2006年8月正式开业。
The Shanghai Petroleum Exchange, a spot market for oil products, began its business in August, 2006.

现金补贴 cash subsidy
亚运会开幕前夕，广州市宣布取消免费乘坐公交的优惠政策，每个户籍家庭将领到150元的现金交通补贴。
Each household with permanent residence registration in Guangzhou will be offered 150 yuan in cash subsidies for commuting purposes after local authorities scrapped a move to make public transport free ahead of the Asian Games.

现金不足 be short of cash; be low on funds
因为现金不足，他没能买下那部笔记本电脑。
He didn't buy that notebook computer because he was short of cash.

现金奖励 cash rewards
北京市相关部门启动了一项通过提供现金奖励来鼓励车主少开车的活动，作为减少汽车排放的新举措。

In a new effort to reduce car emissions, Beijing authorities launched a campaign to encourage vehicle owners to drive less by offering cash rewards.

现款提货 cash-and-carry
加拿大安大略湖北部湾折扣花卉市场采取付现款提货的销售形式。
The Discount Flower Market is a cash-and-carry flower business in North Bay, Ontario, Canada.

现状 present situation; status quo
他直截了当的作风惹恼了一些安于社会现状的人。
His directness has annoyed some who seek to preserve the present social situation.

限广令 ban on all TV stations airing commercials; TV commercials ban
新闻出版广电总局近日颁布"限广令",规定在全国各电视台播出电视剧时,禁止插播广告。
The State Administration of Press, Publication, Radio, Film and Television has ordered a national ban on all TV stations airing commercials during TV dramas.

限制 cap; put a limit on
我们试图通过保持工资的低增长来限制成本。
We're trying to cap costs by keeping salary increases low.

陷入困境 be mired in
他陷入了债务困境。
He was mired in debt.

献礼工程 tribute project
建设这些所谓的"献礼工程"是为了向外界展示某个地区或整个国家所能取得的成就。一些地方官员还利用这些宣传彩头来谋求职位升迁。
These so-called tribute projects are intended to show the outside world what the particular region, or country in general, are capable of achieving. They have also been publicity ornaments used by local officials to boost their standing.

乡村振兴战略 rural revitalization strategy
大力实施乡村振兴战略。科学制定规划,健全城乡融合发展体制机制,依靠改革创新壮大乡村发展新动能。
We will make strong moves in the rural revitalization strategy. Plans will be well designed and the institutions and mechanisms needed to achieve integrated urban-rural development will be improved. We will rely on reform and innovation to build

powerful new growth drivers for rural development.

相亲 blind date
我和妻子是通过相亲相识的。
I met my wife on a blind date.

向钱看 put money/wealth above all; mammonism
做医生的如果都只向钱看,那就完了。
If doctors put money above all, it'll be terrible.

向宪法宣誓 pledge allegiance to the Constitution
我国最高立法机关通过了一项决定,国家机关工作人员正式就职时,要向宪法宣誓。
Chinese officials in State organs shall pledge allegiance to the Constitution when taking their posts, according to a decision adopted by China's top legislature.

消费革命 consumer revolution
中国正经历一场消费革命。阿里巴巴和京东等竞争者正让电商变得不仅高效而且充满娱乐性。
China is experiencing a consumer revolution. Alibaba and competitors such as JD.com are making e-commerce not merely efficient but entertaining.

消费税 consumption tax
日本的消费税是非常低的,与其到昂贵的免税店,还不如到廉价商店来得划算。
In Japan, the consumption tax is extremely low; you should buy things at the five and dime instead of a tax-free store with high prices.

消费信贷 consumer credit
在发达国家,消费信贷占银行贷款总额的20%至30%。
In developed countries, the consumer credit services account for 20 to 30 percent of the total loans of banks.

消费者购买力 consumer purchasing power
政策制定者们打算通过提高消费者购买力来刺激国内消费,从而保持国内经济的持续稳定发展。
To sustain the steady development of the national economy, policymakers aim to spur domestic consumption by increasing consumer purchasing power.

消极怠战 not using one's best efforts to win a match
国际羽联已对8名奥运会女子羽毛球双打选手提出指控,认为她们"消极怠战"。
The Badminton World Federation has charged eight female Olympic doubles

players with "not using one's best efforts to win a match".

消灭 stamp out
政府决心消灭犯罪。
The government is determined to stamp out crime.

消息灵通人士 well-informed source
"据消息灵通人士的话说""就不愿透露姓名身份的人士透露""一些人称"等这样有关消息来源的新闻伎俩已经被滥用。这些所谓的无名人士也许根本不存在。
Such journalistic gimmicks—such as "according to a well-informed source", "speaking on condition of anonymity" and "some say"—are ways overused in the media marketplace. Such sources may not exist at all.

小产权房 houses with limited property rights
小产权房是指占用集体土地搞建设，并向集体经济组织之外成员销售的住房。
Houses with limited property rights are homes built on collectively owned land but sold to buyers who are not part of the collective land ownerships.

小成本网剧 small-budget online series
在流媒体网站开播以来，《太子妃升职记》这部没有明星阵容的小成本网剧迅速俘获大批年轻粉丝，日播放量超过1000万。
Go Princess Go, a small-budget online series without a star cast, has become a hit among young Chinese since it was broadcast on a streaming website, with daily views crossing more than 10 million.

小程序 mini apps
国内互联网巨头腾讯控股有限公司发布"小程序"，该产品使用户无须下载和安装应用，即可在腾讯即时通信应用微信中与类似应用的服务进行互动。
Chinese internet giant Tencent Holdings Ltd launched "mini apps", which let users interact with app-like services within its instant messaging app WeChat, without having to download and install them.

小丑护理 clown care
这种"小丑护理"在以色列、美国、加拿大、欧洲和澳大利亚的医疗中心已经存在了很长时间，多见于儿童医院。
So-called clown care has long been used at medical centers in Israel, the United States, Canada, Europe and Australia, usually in children's hospitals.

小丑快递 clown express delivery
这位30岁的快递员3个多月前在上海成立了一家小丑快递公司,他在那一片已经算是个"名人"了。
The 30-year-old has been running his clown express delivery in Shanghai for more than three months and become a familiar figure within his district.

小道消息 grapevine; hearsay
那个故事是我听到的小道消息。
I heard the story on the grapevine.

小额贷款公司 micro-credit company
中国央行周二称,中国的小额贷款公司近年来增长迅猛。
Micro-credit companies mushroomed in China in recent years, China's central bank said Tuesday.

小金库 private coffer; slush fund
我们单位有个小金库,用于娱乐、体育以及其他活动。
My unit has a private coffer, which is used to fund entertainment and sporting activities, among other things.

小康之家 moderately prosperous family; well-off family
小康之家越多,社会越稳定。
The more moderately prosperous families there are, the more stable the society will be.

小目标 small target
中国地产大亨王健林表示:"先定一个能达到的小目标,比方说,先挣它1个亿。"
"Set a small target first, like earning 100 million yuan," Chinese real estate magnate Wang Jianlin said.

小排量汽车 small displacement car
政府鼓励消费者购买小排量汽车。
Consumers are encouraged by the government to buy small displacement cars.

小微企业 small and micro business
中国将通过提升对小微企业的服务以及使人民币在资本账户下可兑换,深化金融体制改革。
China will deepen the reform of its financial systems by improving services for small and micro businesses and making Renminbi convertible under capital accounts.

小意思 nothing to speak of; small token of one's appreciation
一点小意思，不足挂齿。
Don't mention it. It's nothing to speak of.

孝道 filial piety
该法的通过是为了维护60岁以上老年父母的合法权益，并传承中国传统的孝道。
The law was passed to protect the lawful rights and interests of parents aged 60 and older, and to carry on the Chinese virtue of filial piety.

校车安全 school bus safety
国务院法制办12月11日公布《校车安全条例（征求意见稿）》，面向社会各界征求意见。
A draft regulation on school bus safety management was made public on Dec 11 by the State Council, with the public invited to submit comments.

校园霸凌/欺凌 school bullying
为遏制校园欺凌，我国教育主管部门对此开展专项治理行动。
China's education authorities have launched a campaign to curb school bullying.

校园贷 campus loan
近日，在一些报道揭露了部分网络高利贷者要求大学生以自己的裸照为抵押办理贷款后，校园贷再度引发人们的担忧。
Concerns have been raised again about campus loans after reports revealed that some web-based loan sharks are demanding college students to provide nude photographs of themselves as collateral to borrow money.

校园文化 campus culture
20世纪60年代时吸毒是美国校园文化的一部分。
Drug taking was part of the US campus culture in the 1960s.

校园招聘 campus recruitment
我国电商巨头阿里巴巴集团宣布缩减校园招聘名额。
Chinese e-commerce giant Alibaba Group has announced a cut in its campus recruitment quota.

校园招聘会 on-campus job fair
他说，在最近的一次校园招聘会上，他和河北邯郸一家公司进行了接洽，这家公司为员工提供免费住宿。
He said that during a recent on-campus job fair he talked with a company in

Handan, Hebei province, that offers employees free housing.

笑柄 a laughing stock
他在派对上穿得像个超人,成了大家的笑柄。
Dressing up like Superman at the party made him a laughing stock.

笑气 laughing gas
中国学生林娜(化名)在美国学习期间吸食笑气成瘾,导致身体机能严重受损。
Chinese student Lin Na (not her real name) got hooked on laughing gas while studying in the US, resulting in serious injury.

协定关税 conventional tariff; agreement tariff
协定关税,即在关税谈判达成国际协约基础上制定的关税。
Conventional tariff is a tariff established through an international agreement resulting from tariff negotiations.

协助犬 assistance dog
三种来自日本的协助犬:两只导盲犬、一只助听犬和两只介助犬将演示如何帮助残疾人。
Three types of assistance dogs from Japan: two guide dogs, a hearing dog and two mobility dogs, will show how they help disadvantaged people.

协助自杀 assisted suicide
物理学家史蒂芬·霍金教授表示,如果他觉得自己无法再对这个世界做出任何贡献,而仅仅是别人的负担,那么他会考虑协助自杀。
Professor Stephen Hawking, the physicist, would consider assisted suicide if he felt he had nothing more to contribute to the world and was merely a burden, he has said.

协作 team up
那两个公司已经协作研制新型赛车。
The two companies have teamed up to develop a new racing car.

携号转网 shift from one operator to another without changing numbers; mobile number portability
该项目允许手机用户携号转网。
The program allows mobile users to shift from one operator to another without changing numbers.

泄洪 release flood waters
周三，战士兵们对华东地区内长江水位暴涨支流部分垮堤进行爆破泄洪，防止洪水淹没沿岸村庄。
Chinese soldiers Wednesday used explosives to blast part of a leaking dike so as to release flood waters on a swollen branch of the Yangtze River in East China, preventing the flooding of riverbank villages.

心电感应 telepathy; have spiritual communion
这两名运动员在一起配合了很长时间。他们好像知道对方什么时候做什么，有时简直就像有心电感应。
The two athletes have been playing together for a long time. They seem to know what the other is going to do and when he's going to do it. Sometimes it almost seems like they have telepathy.

心理干预 psychological intervention
该声明表示，它还就受灾地区的心理干预等问题咨询了有关专家。
It also consulted experts on issues of psychological intervention in disaster-stricken areas, the statement said.

心理素质 mental toughness
游泳对提高孩子的身体素质和心理素质都有帮助。
Swimming can help children improve health and develop mental toughness.

心理治疗 psychotherapy; counseling
寻求心理治疗，也就是心理咨询，在美国很普遍。
Seeking psychotherapy, or counseling, is commonplace in the US.

心照不宣 give tacit consent; tacit understanding
他们俩在会上心照不宣，都没有发言——你不说，我保持沉默。
Neither of them spoke at the meeting because they had earlier gave tacit consent—you say nothing; I keep mum.

新常态 new normal
我国发展仍处于重要战略机遇期，要增强信心，从当前我国经济发展的阶段性特征出发，适应新常态，保持平常心。
China is still in a significant period of strategic opportunity. We should boost our confidence, adapt to the new normal condition based on the characteristics of China's economic growth in the current phase and stay cool-minded.

新宠 new favorite
听说蟑螂又成了许多养宠物的人的新宠。

It's said that the cockroach has become the new favorite of many pet owners again.

新发行的股票 new issues
公司发言人则坚持说新发行的股票均符合有关法律法规。

The company spokesman, however, insisted that all new issues had been distributed in accordance with relevant rules and regulations.

新官上任三把火 A new official/boss lights three fires (after taking office)./A new broom wipes/sweeps clean.
俗话说,新官上任三把火,就是要让大家知道现在谁当家。

A new official lights three fires after taking office, as the saying goes, just to impress that he is the new boss.

新经济 new economy
当前我国发展正处于这样一个关键时期,必须培育壮大新动能,加快发展新经济。

This is the crucial period in which China currently finds itself, and during which we must build up powerful new drivers in order to accelerate the development of the new economy.

新经济增长点 new growth area in the economy
中国的环境保护产业有望成为新的经济增长点。

China's environmental protection industry is hopeful of becoming a new growth area in the economy

新零售 new retail
新零售的意思就是将实体店零售和网络零售的优势结合起来。用阿里巴巴创始人兼主席马云的话说,新零售就是让实体商业和虚拟商业的差别不复存在。

New retail is a term that roughly indicates a combination of the best in physical and online retail. In the words of Jack Ma, founder and chairman of e-commerce behemoth Alibaba Group Holdings Ltd, new retail is making the distinction between physical and virtual commerce obsolete.

新能源汽车 new energy vehicles (NEV)
我国将在全国启动新能源汽车使用特殊号牌政策。

China will issue special license plates for new energy vehicles in every city nationwide.

新生产业 infant industry
特许制度将继续保护被官方称为新生产业的汽车业。
A licensing system will continue to umbrella the motor industry, which is officially called "infant industry".

新时代 new era
经过长期努力，中国特色社会主义进入了新时代，这是我国发展的新的历史方位。
With decades of hard work, socialism with Chinese characteristics has crossed the threshold into a new era. This is a new historic juncture in China's development.

新兴11国 eleven emerging economies(E11)
注：11个全球新兴经济体，包括阿根廷、巴西、中国、印度、印度尼西亚、韩国、墨西哥、俄罗斯、沙特阿拉伯、南非和土耳其。
如不加速去杠杆化，可能会引发新兴11国的债务危机。
Debt crisis may erupt in the E11 (eleven emerging economies) countries, unless they make urgent de-leveraging efforts.

新兴市场 emerging market
小米会努力在明年进入更多的新兴市场，包括土耳其、俄罗斯和一些中东国家。
Xiaomi will try to enter more emerging markets including Turkey, Russia and some Middle Eastern countries next year.

新兴职业 new occupations
博主、陪跑员，以及无人机训练员等新兴职业使国内就业变得更加灵活。
New occupations, such as blogger, jogging buddy and drone trainer, are making employment more flexible in China.

新型大国关系 new type of major–country relations
中国将致力于同美方共同构建新型大国关系。
China is committed to working with the US to build a new type of major-country relations.

新型政党制度 new type of party system
中国共产党领导的多党合作和政治协商制度是从中国土壤中生长出来的新型政党制度。
The system of multiparty cooperation and political consultation led by the Communist Party of China (CPC) is a new type of party system growing from China's soil.

新秀 rising star; up-and-coming star
她被誉为当今美国最红的影坛新秀。
She is praised as the most promising rising star in America.

新中装 new Chinese-style outfit
国家主席习近平及夫人彭丽媛,以及到场贵宾均穿着丝质"新中装",这款服装的设计特别体现了中国悠久的历史和古老的传统。
President Xi Jinping, his wife Peng Liyuan and guests were all wearing new Chinese-style outfits made of silk and specially designed to represent China's rich history and old tradition.

薪酬改革 salary reform
央企负责人薪酬改革已经进行了10余年。
Salary reform for executives at State-owned enterprises has been underway for over a decade.

信贷支持 credit aid
对于某些房地产项目,政府要协调银行提供更加灵活的信贷支持。
For some real-estate projects, the government should coordinate banks to provide more flexible credit aid.

信任赤字 trust deficit
中美双边关系日益兴起,但仍然存在"信任赤字",国家主席习近平即将进行的美国之访对提升双边互信有着非常重要的作用。
President Xi Jinping's upcoming visit to the United States will provide a very important opportunity to enhance bilateral mutual trust, as a "trust deficit" exists that contrasts with booming bilateral ties.

信息安全法 information security law
在正在召开的全国人大会议上,有一份提案建议应尽快制定信息安全法。
A motion to the ongoing National People's Congress suggested that an information security law should be developed as soon as possible.

信息经济 information economy
国际数据公司报告称,瑞典的信息经济名列世界第一。
According to a report released by the International Data Company, Sweden ranks first in terms of information economy in the world.

信息经济示范区 information economy demonstration area
我国已批准在浙江成立首个国家信息经济示范区。

China has approved its first national information economy demonstration area in Zhejiang.

信息披露 information disclosure
一家信息披露违规的公司被上海证交所终止上市。
The Shanghai Stock Exchange said it had delisted a company for breaching rules on information disclosure.

信息时代 information era
现在是信息时代。西方知识界开始把未来几十年称作觉悟时代，或者说开化时代。从哲学意义上说，有了信息，人们当然就有希望更加开化。
Today is seen as the information era. The intelligentsia of the West talks about the next few decades as the age of consciousness, or enlightenment. With information, it is certainly hopeful that people will achieve a greater level of enlightenment, in the philosophical sense.

信息消费 information consumption
未来几年，中国将促进信息消费，这是刺激内需、推动经济增长举措的一部分。
China will bolster information consumption in the next few years as part of an effort to stimulate domestic demand and shore up economic growth.

信用紧缩 credit crunch
信用紧缩是防止信贷进一步增长的主要措施。
The credit crunch is primarily a measure to stop the further credit increment.

信用卡奴 credit card slave
他是一个有着8张银行卡的信用卡奴。
He is a credit card slave who holds eight bank cards.

信用扩张 credit expansion
信用扩张是中国在应对几十年来最严重的危机时所遇到的"没有预料到的困难"之一。
Credit expansion was one of the "unexpected difficulties" China had encountered in dealing with the worst crisis in decades.

信用评分系统 credit rating system
社交网络支付企业集团腾讯控股有限公司正在开发一种信用评分系统。这是该公司试图在国内利润丰厚的在线支付行业中，从主要竞争对手阿里巴巴集团控股有限公司手里抢夺市场份额的最新举措。
Tencent Holdings Ltd, the social networking-to-payment conglomerate, is

developing a credit rating system. This is the company's latest attempt to seize market share from archrival Alibaba Group Holding Ltd in China's lucrative online payment sector.

信用评级下调 credit downgrade
美国信用评级首次下调致使美国金融市场（华尔街）和美国政府（华盛顿）紧急着手应对新的世界秩序。
The first-ever credit downgrade of the US left Wall Street and Washington struggling to come to grips with a new world order.

信用危机 credit crisis
中国的银行应该是最早感受到信用危机并发出预警的部门。
Chinese banks should be aware of the credit crisis and send out alarms in the first time.

星级饭店 star-rated hotels
为维护全国1.5万家星级饭店的形象，我国计划加快建立星级饭店退出机制，将那些经营不善的星级饭店淘汰出局。
China is planning to accelerate a mechanism with which to strip poorly run hotels of their star rankings in order to protect the image of all the 15,000 star-rated hotels across the country.

刑讯逼供 extract confessions by torture; be tortured into confessing
中国司法机关正依法采取有效措施，防范和遏制刑讯逼供。
China's judicial organs are taking effective measures in accordance with the law to deter and prohibit extracting confessions by torture.

行使否决权 exercise the veto
这是4年来第一次行使否决权。
It was the first time in four years that anyone has exercised the veto.

行头 theatrical costume
他穿着与唱片封面上一模一样的行头前来赴会。
Attending the meeting, he wore the same theatrical costume as shown on the cover of the disc.

行为科学 behavioral sciences
应邀发言的还有王先生，他是研究精神病及行为科学的副教授。
Also invited to speak is Mr. Wang, an associate professor of psychiatry and behavioral sciences.

行为模式 behavior pattern
通过对少年犯行为模式的研究,她希望能指导学生知道如何避免与问题青少年交往。
By studying the behavioral patterns of juvenile delinquents, she hopes to be able to tip students on how to avoid mixing up with problem teenagers.

行政级别 administrative ranking
我希望可以取消高校的行政级别。
I hope that the administrative rankings of colleges will be removed.

行政拘留 administrative detention
一项拟将行政拘留执行年龄从16周岁降至14周岁的法律草案面临过度惩罚的担忧,同时也有谨慎的支持之声。
A new draft law that would change the minimum age for administrative detention from 16 to 14 has been met with both concerns of overcorrection and voices of support, albeit cautious.

行政审批 administrative approval
国务院将取消171个行政审批项目,同时将另外117个项目的审批权下放到下一级政府部门。
The State Council will remove 171 administrative approval items, while the power to approve another 117 items will be handed down to government departments at lower levels.

行政诉讼 administrative proceedings
对行政诉讼实施法律监督是我国法律赋予检察机关的职责。
Procurators are obliged by law to supervise administrative proceedings.

行政问责制度 executive accountability system

形成全方位、多层次、宽领域的开放格局 develop a pattern of opening up to the outside world that features reaching out in all directions, taking place at different levels, and covering wide-ranging fields

行走的钱包 walking wallets
日本和韩国都将中国游客视为经济增长的主要动力。西方媒体则把中国游客描述为"行走的钱包"。
Both Japan and South Korea see Chinese tourists as a major powerhouse to drive up their economies. They are described by Western media as "walking wallets".

幸福产业 happiness industries
国务院办公厅近日印发关于进一步扩大旅游、文化、体育、健康等产业消费的文件。上述产业与人民的生活质量和幸福感相关,被称为幸福产业。
The General Office of the State Council issued a document on further expanding consumption in the so-called happiness industries—tourism, culture, sport and health—that are related to people's quality of life and sense of well-being.

性别差距 gender gap
世界经济论坛表示,2017年,工作场所的性别差距有所扩大,这是自世界经济论坛2006年开始发布《全球性别差距报告》以来,差距首次扩大。
The workplace gender gap widened in 2017, the World Economic Forum said, for the first time since its *Global Gender Gap Report* was first published in 2006.

性价比 cost performance
性价比高的AMD处理器再加上捆绑DDR内存,可以让他们的产品在零售市场的份额上升30%。
The AMD processor with a high cost performance, plus the bound DDR RAM may increase their shares in the retail market by 30 percent.

性骚扰 sexual harassment
男上司的性骚扰案件正急速增加,这说明职业妇女已越来越清楚自己的权益。
Rapidly increasing sexual harassment cases against male bosses suggest women are more aware of their rights in the workplace.

雄安新区 Xiongan New Area
我国将设立对标深圳经济特区和上海浦东新区的河北雄安新区,作为又一经济引擎,推动京津冀协同发展。
China will develop the Xiongan New Area in Hebei, parallel to the Shenzhen Special Economic Zone and the Shanghai Pudong New Area, to serve as another economic engine and advance the coordinated development of the Beijing-Tianjin-Hebei region.

休病假 be on sick leave
他们随后又一同探望了那个已经休了半年多病假的同事。
They then went together to see their colleague who had been on sick leave for more than six months.

休闲业 leisure industry
仅仅几年前,休闲业在中国还是个不怎么为人所知的概念,而现在,休闲业已经成了一个普通话题。
The leisure industry, which was a largely unknown concept in China just a few years ago, has now become commonplace.

休学创业 starting business while suspending courses
教育部将发布新修订的高校学生管理规定，对弹性学制和休学创业等作出明确规定。
The Ministry of Education will release newly-revised college students management regulations, which will give explicit provisions on flexible study schedule and starting business while suspending courses.

修昔底德陷阱 Thucydides Trap
注："修昔底德陷阱"是由古希腊史学家修昔底德（Thucydides）阐述公元前5世纪发生在雅典和斯巴达两国之间的战争时提出来的理论。他认为，一个崛起的大国必然会挑战现有的大国，而现存大国也必然会回应这种威胁。双方面临的威胁多数以战争告终，而冲突的结果也会是灾难性的，两个强国都将走向衰落。
中国外交部部长表示，中美可以避开"修昔底德陷阱"和"金德尔伯格陷阱"，从长远角度共同规划双边关系。
China and the United States can sidestep the Thucydides Trap and the Kindleberger Trap and jointly chart bilateral ties from a long-term perspective, Chinese Foreign Minister said.

虚假宣传 deceptive advertising
广东某保健食品品牌及其产品代言人因涉嫌虚假宣传被北京一市民告上法庭。
A Beijing resident sued a Guangdong-based company producing dietary supplements, and its spokesman for deceptive advertising.

虚开增值税发票 write false value-added tax invoices
虚开增值税发票的现象要坚决制止。
The practice of writing false value-added tax invoices should be strictly forbidden.

虚拟超市 virtual supermarket
伦敦地铁站即将引进这种"虚拟超市"，把摆满百货商品的货架海报贴在地铁站台的墙上。
A "virtual supermarket" consisting of posters of shelves stocked with goods pasted on platform walls is set to be introduced at London underground stations.

虚拟现实 virtual reality(VR)
VR支付技术，也就是让用VR眼镜浏览虚拟现实购物中心的人不用摘眼镜就能支付。
The VR payment technology means people using virtual reality goggles to browse

virtual reality shopping malls will be able pay for purchases without taking off the goggles.

许可证制度 license-granting system
为了规范手机电池行业,我国将实行手机电池生产许可证制度。
The production license-granting system for mobile phone batteries will be introduced in order to regulate the industry.

续集病 sequelitis, sequel syndrome
皮克斯已找到治疗人们普遍对续集病感到恐慌的良方,动人的故事情节总是最佳良药。
PIXAR has found the prescription to treat all common fears of sequelitis. And the best medicine, as always, is good storytelling.

续签签证 renew one's visa
赴美签证失效不足4年的符合条件的中国非移民签证申请者可以续签签证而无须面谈。
Qualified non-immigrant Chinese applicants to the US can now renew their visas without undergoing another interview if their visas expired less than 48 months ago.

蓄洪工程 flood-storage project
由于受去冬今春恶劣天气的影响,该省堤防与蓄洪工程建设进展缓慢。
The embankment and flood-storage project in this province has slowed down due to bad weather conditions, which has been going on since last winter and this spring.

宣传视频 promotional video
发布在优酷网上的时长3分钟的中国共产党宣传视频在网络上走红。
A three-minute promotional video about the Communist Party of China released on youku. com has become a hot topic on the internet.

宣告破产 declare bankruptcy
作为下策,他准备宣告公司破产,从而避免归还8家债主的债务。
As a last resort, he is prepared to declare bankruptcy to avoid paying off debts owned to the eight creditors.

悬挂式单轨列车 mounted monorail train
国内最高速的悬挂式单轨列车在青岛中车四方下线,最高运行时速为70公里。
Chinese rail car manufacturer CRRC Qingdao Sifang has unveiled a prototype of a mounted monorail train with a maximum operating speed of 70 kilometers per

hour, the fastest of its kind in China.

选举权和被选举权 the right to vote and the right to be elected
每一位公民都有选举权和被选举权。
Each citizen has the right to vote and the right to be elected.

选举人团 Electoral College
每隔四年选出美国总统和副总统的团体就是美国的选举人团。
The United States Electoral College is the body that elects the President and Vice President of the United States every four years.

选美大赛 beauty pageant
匈牙利周五在布达佩斯举行了匈牙利"整容小姐"选美大赛。参赛者必须证明她们真正"动过刀子",仅注射肉毒杆菌或胶原蛋白是不算在整容范畴之内的。
The Miss Plastic Hungary beauty pageant was held Friday in Budapest, Hungary. To qualify for the pageant, the Hungarian residents had to prove they'd gone fully under the knife—mere Botox or collagen injections did not count.

炫富 flaunt wealth
中国的年轻学生在国外要保持低调,不要炫富。
Young Chinese should keep a low profile and avoid flaunting wealth abroad.

削减战略核武器会谈 strategic arms reduction talks (START)
建立全球导弹防御系统将使削减战略核武器会谈的成果化为乌有。
It will crumble the yields of strategic arms reduction talks (START) to dust by setting up the global missile protection system.

学分制 academic credit system
采用学分制可以使学生尽快完成学业。
Adopting an academic credit system enables students to finish their study as soon as possible.

学科带头人 academic leader; pace-setter in scientific research
为加速培养新一代高校优秀中青年学科带头人,该省决定实施"高校中青年学科带头人培养计划"。
That province decided to establish the Project of Nurturing Young and Middle-aged Academic Leaders in Universities to speed up the pace of fostering excellent new academic leaders in colleges.

学历教育 education with the record of formal schooling
国务院学位委员会明确了何谓学历教育。
The Degree Commission of the State Council defines education with the record of formal schooling.

学历造假 fabricate academic credentials
被指学历造假的官员已经被停职了。
The official who was accused of fabricating academic credentials has been suspended from office.

学前教育 preschool education
这对父母已经给孩子定下了严格的学前教育目标。他还只是个走路蹒跚的孩子，但父母却要他每天记住10个英文单词。
The parents have set strict goals for the child's preschool education. He's still a toddler and already they are asking him to memorize ten English words a day.

学区房 school district houses
生育政策放松也带火了"学区房"需求。
The loosened birth policy has ignited parent demand for xuequfang, literally school district houses.

学生减负 alleviate the burden on students
现在学生减负了，老师不需要改那么多作业，也轻松了。
As the burden on students has been alleviated, teachers are more relaxed too, not having so much homework to correct.

学术报告 academic report
这篇学术报告历数过去200年间的气候变化，并探讨了各种可能减缓地球变暖的办法。
This academic report lists major climatic changes in the past 200 years and discusses possible ways to slow global warming.

学术不端 academic misconduct
根据教育部发布的一系列规定，有学术不端行为的高等教育机构研究人员将受到校内通报批评甚至开除的处罚。
Researchers at institutions of higher education who commit "academic misconduct" will receive punishments ranging from notices of criticism circulated on campus to being fired, according to a series of regulations released by the Ministry of Education.

学术交流 academic exchange
学术交流给我们带来新观念,并让我们从新的视角审视旧的认识。有交流才有突破。
Academic exchanges offer new ideas and help put our old conceptions into better perspective. Exchange makes change.

学术评价体系 academic appraisal system
一位政协委员建议建立一个不过分注重学术论文和获奖数量的学术评价体系。

A CPPCC member called for the establishment of an academic appraisal system with less emphasis on quantity of academic papers and awards.

学术欺诈罪 academic fraud
一位全国人大代表在两会上提议,中国应设立"学术欺诈罪"来遏制造假行为。
China should make academic fraud a crime to curb dishonesty, a deputy of National People's Congress (NPC) proposed at the annual two sessions.

学术造假 academic cheating
政府应该确立更加严厉的规章制度防止学术造假。
The government should establish stricter regulations to prevent academic cheating.

雪花一代 snowflake generation
"雪花一代"指2010年之后成年的那代人。与以往几代人相比,他们被认为是适应能力更差且更易发怒的一代。
Snowflake generation refers to the young adults of the 2010s, who are viewed as being less resilient and more prone to taking offence than previous generations.

血荒 blood supply shortage
由于国内医院面临严重的"血荒",中国红十字会周六在北京组织献血活动,呼吁公众献血。
The Red Cross Society of China organized blood donations Saturday in Beijing, calling upon the public to donate, as China's hospitals cope with a severe blood supply shortage.

血库 blood bank
由于天气寒冷,加上甲型H1N1流感疫情的发展,前往街头流动献血车的人日趋减少,北京市血库库存量大幅下滑。
Beijing's blood bank has seen a dramatic decline in storage as fewer people visit the street blood donation buses due to the cold weather and A/H1N1 flu epidemic.

巡回大使 roving ambassador
托尼·布莱尔将在离开唐宁街后出任非洲和中东问题巡回大使,以期重塑其受损的声誉。

Tony Blair is to become a roving ambassador in Africa and the Middle East when he leaves Downing Street in an attempt to rebuild his tarnished reputation.

巡回医疗 medical tour
四川省各地的医院将为老年人开展巡回医疗等方面的服务。

Hospitals in Sichuan province will provide medical tour services for the elderly.

巡游揽客 cruise on the street for customers
交通部规定提供网约车服务的驾驶员不得上街巡游揽客。

The Ministry of Transport stipulates that drivers providing online ride-hailing services are banned from cruising on the street for customers.

徇私枉法 bend the law for personal gain
他承认有"过失",但拒不承认犯罪,还说徇私枉法的干部不止他一个。

He acknowledged some "wrongdoing" but denies any criminal charges, saying he's not the only one who bends the law for personal gain.

压倒性的一击 knockout blow
这名队员压倒性的一击让他赢了这场比赛。
The knockout blow of the player made him win the match.

压价竞争 competition by lowering of price; compete by lowering prices
让这家合资公司最担心的莫过于中国当地企业靠持续压价与之竞争。
What the joint venture firm feared the most was competition from local Chinese companies by continued lowering of price.

压力测试 stress test
据知情人士透露,中国银监会上个月指示银行进行新一轮压力测试,以评估楼市遭受最严重的冲击、房价暴跌60%的情况对银行产生的影响。
China's banking regulator told lenders last month to conduct a new round of stress tests to gauge the impact of residential property prices falling as much as 60 percent in the hardest-hit markets, a person with knowledge of the matter said.

压轴戏 the grand finale
中国综艺表演中,压轴戏通常都是最好的节目,或许是为了让观众高兴而归吧。
In Chinese variety shows, the last part of it is usually reserved for the best performance or the grand finale, presumably so that everybody can be sent home on a high.

亚健康 sub-health
长期长时间工作引起的疲劳会导致亚健康。
Fatigue caused by continued long working hours might lead to sub-health.

亚投行 Asia Infrastructure Investment Bank
英国已谋求作为创始成员国加入亚洲基础设施投资银行(亚投行)。
The United Kingdom has sought to join the Asia Infrastructure Investment Bank as a founding member.

亚文化 sub-culture
时至今日,老师们对内城青少年吸毒这一亚文化对青少年的影响还没有充分认识。
Teachers have yet to come to terms with the influence of the inner city sub-culture

of drugs on teenagers.

延迟退休 delay retirement age
有关官员表示:"相关政府部门只是在研究'延迟退休'的建议,暂时不会调整退休年龄。"

"Related government departments are only researching some proposals of delaying retirement age but it does not mean the current regulation on retirement age will be changed soon." the official said.

延期;拖欠 deferral
俱乐部的新东家宣布将在一周内足额支付拖欠的工资。这样,球员将拿到2月份的全部工资。

Players are to be repaid in full for wages lost during February as the club's new owners announced they would pay back wage deferrals within a week.

严厉斥责;抨击 lash out
这篇文章对社会上的不公平现象进行了猛烈抨击。

The article lashed out at social injustice.

严于律己,宽以待人 be strict with oneself and lenient towards others
总的来说,严于律己,宽以待人是个好准则。

Generally speaking, it is a good guideline to be very strict with oneself and lenient towards others.

研究生入学考试 postgraduate entrance examination; postgraduate qualification exam
周六参加今年研究生入学考试的人数达180万,又创新高。近几年大学毕业生就业状况不佳,报名考研的学生人数由此增加。

A record high of 1.8 million Chinese students sit this year's national postgraduate entrance examination on Saturday. Since landing a job after graduation has been difficult in recent years, the number of college graduates applying for graduate studies has increased.

验证码 verification code
为我国网购火车票的用户提供更好验证码的呼声越来越强,许多人担心目前的系统会导致春节出现一票难求的局面。

Growing calls are being made to create better customer verification codes for the purchase of railway tickets online in China, as many are concerned about the current system leading up to the Spring Festival buying rush.

赝品；冒牌货 shoddy substitute
故宫博物院一位发言人表示："官方网站上所展示的青花瓷器并不是受损的那一件。"否认了网上关于故宫博物院网站资料展示赝品的猜测。

"The porcelain plate shown on the official website is another piece." a spokesman for the Palace Museum said, dismissing speculation that the museum was presenting a shoddy substitute in its advertisements.

阳光产业 sunshine industry
生产有机肥是一个新兴的阳光产业，所有企业目前均盈利。

Organic fertilizer manufacture is a sunshine industry. All companies in the business are making money.

养老保险 endowment insurance
积极推进养老保险社会化管理，逐步做到退休人员与企事业单位相脱离。

Non-employer management of endowment insurance programs should be vigorously promoted so as to gradually shift responsibility for retirees from their former employers to society at large.

养老服务 elderly care service
国家开发银行每年将提供不少于100亿元的专项贷款，以支持社会养老服务体系建设。

China Development Bank will provide loans of no less than 10 billion yuan annually to help build a system to support the elderly care service industry.

养老金入市 invest money from pension funds into the country's capital markets
经批准，广东省尝试将大量非托管养老金投入资本市场。

Guangdong province won permission to try out investing money from its largely unmanaged pension funds into the country's capital markets.

遥感卫星 remote-sensing satellite
据报道，遥感卫星八号将于近日在山西太原卫星发射中心用长征四号丙运载火箭发射到太空。

The remote-sensing satellite Yaogan VIII will be sent into space in the coming days, according to reports. It will be launched aboard the Long March IV C from Taiyuan Satellite Launch Center in Shanxi province.

药驾 drug driving
专家指出，"药驾"危害甚至可能超过酒驾。大脑受药物作用影响，可能会导致反应和判断迟钝，从而酿成车祸。

Experts say drug driving can be more fatal than drunk driving, as drugs that act on the brain can impair one's reaction time and judgment, leading to traffic accidents.

药检 drug test; doping test

从经济角度看，28岁的莎拉波娃可能已成为体育史上最大的输家，她的未来收入估计减少1亿英镑。因为未通过药检，这位俄罗斯网坛明星最主要的赞助商耐克、保时捷和泰格豪雅都已停止与其合作。

Maria Sharapova, 28, could now become the biggest financial loser in sporting history, missing out on estimated future earnings of as much as £100 million. Her biggest sponsors Nike, Porsche, and TAG Heuer all moved to cut ties with the Russian tennis star after her drug test failure.

药品加成 markups on pharmaceuticals; medicine markups

全面推开公立医院综合改革，全部取消药品加成，协调推进医疗价格、人事薪酬、药品流通、医保支付方式等改革。

We will introduce overall reform in public hospitals nationwide, abolish all markups on pharmaceuticals, and make coordinated progress in reforming health care pricing, staffing and remuneration, medicine distribution, and models of health insurance payment.

药物滥用 abuse of medication

中国已在全国范围内建立起合理用药监测网，覆盖960家监测点医疗机构，防止医疗过程中的药物滥用。

China has established a nationwide monitoring network in 960 medical institutions to prevent the abuse of medication in the treatment of patients.

野鸡大学 diploma mill

教育部日前公布了1万余所正规海外院校名单，并提醒学生不要被"野鸡大学"忽悠。

The Ministry of Education has released a full list of over 10,000 accredited foreign universities for overseas study, and warns students against diploma mills.

业务审计 operational auditing

如果您有关于业务审计的文章和书籍，并认为于大家有益，请在会后与在座的诸位分享。

If you have an article or book related to operational auditing that would be of benefit to this audience, please share it with others after the meeting.

夜市 evening market; night fair
夏天夜市最旺,许多店铺拂晓还不关门。
Evening markets thrive in summer time, many staying open way after midnight.

"1+2+3"合作格局 "1+2+3" cooperation pattern
中国提出的中阿共建丝绸之路经济带和21世纪海上丝绸之路、构建"1+2+3"合作格局、加强产能合作等倡议得到了阿拉伯国家的积极响应。
China's proposed initiatives of jointly building the "Silk Road Economic Belt" and the "21st Century Maritime Silk Road", establishing a "1+2+3" cooperation pattern and industrial capacity cooperation, are well received by Arab countries.

一次性重估调整 one-off revaluation
中国人民银行周日称将不会对人民币汇率进行一次性重估调整。
The People's Bank of China (PBOC) said Sunday it will not conduct a one-off revaluation of the RMB (yuan) exchange rate.

一次性筷子 disposable chopsticks; throwaway chopsticks
老师鼓励学生不用一次性筷子。
Students are encouraged not to use disposable chopsticks.

一次性总付 lump-sum payment
在许多单位,职工如果有未休的年假,则可得到一笔一次性的总付补偿。
In many organizations, an employee is entitled to a lump-sum payment in compensation for any unused annual leave.

"一带一路"倡议 the Belt and Road Initiative
中国愿意同各国一道推进"一带一路"倡议,即"丝绸之路经济带"和"21世纪海上丝绸之路"的建设。
China is willing to work with other countries to promote the Belt and Road Initiative, or the constructions of the Silk Road Economic Belt and 21st Century Maritime Silk Road.

一个萝卜一个坑 One seed fills one hole./There is nobody to spare./one seed for one hole
恐怕你自己的活儿得自己干。一个萝卜一个坑,我没有多余人手。
I am afraid you have to see about the job yourself. I have no one to spare—my situation is one seed for one hole.

一棍子打死 no-second-chance; not give someone another chance
犯这点儿事就被学校开除,我认为学校做得不对。我认为学校不应该对学生采取一棍子打死的态度。

I don't think he should be expelled from school for a misconduct like that. The school shouldn't take a no-second-chance attitude to any student.

一国两制 one country, two systems

我们相信台湾终将会在一国两制的框架下回归，祖国终将实现统一。

We believe China will eventually achieve reunification with Taiwan under the "one country, two systems" framework.

一级市场 primary market

一级市场目前表现活跃。

The primary market is active right now.

一揽子购买 lump-sum purchase; basket purchase

此项一揽子购买协议总金额高达22亿美元。

The total sum of this lump-sum purchase reaches $2.2 billion.

一揽子计划 one-package plan

我们只能为你提供一揽子计划。

We only have one-package plan to offer you.

一揽子建议 a package of proposals

世贸组织成员国就将来全球农业贸易改革的一揽子建议达成了一致。

The WTO members agreed on a package of proposals for future reform of global farm trade.

一切向钱看 money-oriented

在20世纪80年代，一些人追求"一切向钱看"。

In the 1980s, some people took a money-oriented attitude.

一条龙 a full range of; end-to-end

我们的一条龙服务当然也包括送货，而且免费。

Our full range of services take care of delivery too, of course, and for free.

一头热 one's own wishful thinking

跟他结婚只是她一头热。她所有的朋友都认为她没戏。

Marrying him is only her own wishful thinking. None of her friends thinks she has a chance.

一线城市 first-tier city

中国一家顶级智库周日新发布的报告称，尽管经济快速发展、且拥有较好的投资环境,但由于生态环境问题,中国大多数一线城市都不宜居。
Most first-tier cities in China are barely suitable for living due to their poor ecological environment, despite rapid economic development and preferential regulations for investment, said a newly released report by a top Chinese think tank on Sunday.

一线员工 worker at the production line; frontline worker
节假日期间,一线员工仍然坚守工作岗位。
Workers at the production line manned their posts as usual during the public holiday.

一小时通勤圈 one-hour commuting circle
随着京津冀三地间道路交通网的建设,以北京为核心的"一小时通勤圈"正逐渐形成。
With the construction of the traffic network in the Beijing-Tianjin-Hebei region, a one-hour commuting circle is forming around Beijing.

医患纠纷 doctor-patient dispute
中国78%的医生不希望子女从医,医患纠纷和长年高压工作是主要原因。
Doctor-patient disputes and years of high-pressure work are the main reasons cited by 78% of doctors in China who do not want their children to become doctors.

医疗保险 medical insurance
城镇地区必须推行以养老、失业、医疗为重点的社会福利保险。
Social welfare insurance, particularly endowment, unemployment and medical insurance, must be made mandatory in urban areas.

医疗纠纷 medical dispute
目前,法院根据指定医疗人员的鉴定裁决医疗纠纷,但这些鉴定很少明示是谁做出的结论,或者该结论是怎么达成的,所以病人并不信服。
Currently the courts decide medical disputes based on the assessment of appointed health officials. But the assessments seldom indicate who made the conclusion or how it was arrived at, so patients are not convinced.

医疗游客 medical tourist
据估计每30个阿根廷人里就有1个人做过(整形)手术,这也使当地产生了世界上手术技巧最娴熟的一些整形医师,并因此吸引了大批医疗游客。
Estimates say that 1 in 30 Argentines has gone under the knife, making surgeons here some of the most experienced on the globe, attracting a large number of

medical tourists.

医疗制度改革 medicare system reform
中国在城镇医疗制度改革中取得了巨大进步,医药机构的管理也得到了加强。
China has made massive progress in urban medicare system reform and the management of medical organizations has been strengthened.

医事服务费 medical service fee
方案规定医事服务费将取代药品加成、挂号费及诊疗费。
A medical service fee will replace drug markups, registration and treatment fees, according to the plan.

依法履职 fulfilling legal duties
最高人民法院发文,落实保障司法人员依法履行职责的机制。
The Supreme People's Court published a document on improving the mechanism to protect judges and their associates in fulfilling their legal duties.

宜居城市 habitable city; livable city
中国社科院的一份报告称,包括北京、上海、广州在内的多个一线城市未能进入宜居城市榜单。
First-tier cities, including Beijing, Shanghai and Guangzhou, failed to make the list of habitable cities, according to a report by the Chinese Academy of Social Sciences.

移动支付 mobile payment
在一个手机用户超过7亿的国家,发展移动支付市场前景看好。
In a country with over 700 million mobile phone users, exploring the mobile payment market may appear lucrative.

疑似病例 suspected case
目前已有1例确诊病例,1例疑似病例。
There has been one confirmed case and one suspected case.

乙醇汽油 ethanol-added gasoline
我国首次设定了在全国范围内推广车辆使用乙醇汽油的时间表,这是我国清理污染、优化能源结构的部分举措。
China has for the first time set a targeted timeline to roll out the use of ethanol-added gasoline nationwide for cars, part of its efforts to clean up pollution and optimize the country's energy mix.

以房养老 house-for-pension
根据"以房养老"计划,你可以将自己的产权房抵押给保险公司或银行,后者将根据房屋价值和你的预期寿命,每月支付一定数目的养老金。
A house-for-pension program allows you to deed your house to an insurance company or bank, which will determine the value of your house and your life expectancy, and then grant you a certain amount of pension every month.

以房养老机制 house-for-pension scheme
文件指出,"政府将加快推进延税型养老保险制度,并探索发展以房养老机制"。
It was released in the document that "the government will accelerate the establishment of a tax-deferred pension insurance system and explore the house-for-pension scheme".

以理服人 convince through reason (and persuasion)
中国人相信以理服人,不相信以武力服人。
The Chinese people believe in convincing through reason, not force.

以人为本 people oriented; people foremost; people first
"以人为本"是我们企业文化的本质。
People orientedness is the essence of our corporate culture.

以身作则,廉洁奉公 set a good example by performing duties with honesty/honestly
主要领导干部要以身作则,廉洁奉公,忠于职守。
Top officials are asked to set a good example by performing public duties with dedication and honesty.

以市场为导向的 market-oriented
得益于以市场为导向的改革,中国经济已高速发展20多年。
Thanks to market-oriented reforms, the Chinese economy has been growing rapidly for more than two decades.

亿万富豪财富代际移交 inter-generational billionaire wealth transfer
2015年,中国的造富能力在亚洲处于领先地位,同时经历了首个亿万富豪财富代际移交。
China led Asia in creating billionaires in 2015 and underwent its first inter-generational billionaire wealth transfer.

义务兵役制 compulsory military service; conscription
以色列是世界上唯一对妇女普遍实行义务兵役制的国家。

Israel is the only country in the world that applies compulsory military service to women.

义务教育 compulsory education
有专家指出，中国在基础公共设施方面的投入是全球最低的，应该加强相关领域的改革，比如社会保障、义务教育、公共卫生及住房等。
Experts say that China's investment in its basic public services is among the lowest in the world. More efforts should be made in the reforms in related areas including social security, compulsory education, public health and housing.

义演 performance for charity; charity performance
为帮助希望工程筹款，他们举行了一场隆重的义演。
In order to raise funds for the Project Hope, they gave a grand performance for charity.

义演收入 proceeds from a charity performance
义演收入捐给了贫困山区的学校。
The proceeds from charity performances go to schools in poverty-stricken mountainous areas.

异地高考 children of migrant workers sit college entrance exams locally
中国有更多的省市已公布教育改革方案，允许外来务工人员的子女在当地就读高中并参加高考。
More Chinese provinces and municipalities have announced education reforms that would allow children of migrant workers to enter senior high schools and sit college entrance exams locally.

疫苗接种 vaccine jab
中国将为6～35月龄的儿童免费接种甲流疫苗。
Children aged from 6 to 35 months in China will get A/H1N1 flu vaccine jabs free of charge.

疫情防控 plague prevention
中国疾控中心已经往震区运了8万本用汉藏双语写的疾病防控手册和1万份疫情防控宣传单，之后还将发放更多。
China Centers for Disease Control and Prevention (CDC) already had delivered 80,000 bilingual disease prevention brochures in Chinese and Tibetan, and 10,000 plague prevention leaflets to the quake zone, with more to go.

疫情监测系统 epidemic surveillance system
国家疫情监测系统已经得到显著改善。
The national epidemic surveillance system has been significantly upgraded.

意向成员 prospective member
亚洲基础设施投资银行(亚投行)理事会通过决议,批准13个新的意向成员的加入,这使得该行获批的成员总数扩至70个。
The Board of Governors of the Asian Infrastructure Investment Bank (AIIB) adopted resolutions approving 13 new prospective members to join the bank, bringing its total approved membership to 70.

因材施教 student-specific approach; student-specific teaching method; teach students according to their aptitude
特殊人才群体应该特殊培养,也就是说要因材施教。
A specific group of students should receive a specific education, which is a student-specific approach.

因公殉职 perish in the line of duty; be killed in the line of duty
市政府新闻办通报,已经确认身份的66名遇难者中有5人为因公殉职。
Of the 66 identified victims, five perished in the line of duty, according to the Information Office of the municipal government.

阴阳合同 dual contract
阴阳合同指交易双方针对同一笔交易签订两份合同。
Dual contract refers to a contract between parties who have made two contracts for the same transaction.

银发族海啸 silver tsunami
"银发族海啸"就要来了。婴儿潮一代将开始进入退休年龄,公司必须做好准备应对大量员工离休的局面。
The "silver tsunami" is coming. The baby boomer generation is beginning to hit retirement age, and companies must prepare for what could be a major exodus.

银行挤兑 bank run
韩国金融委员会在一份声明中说,"最近由于另外两家银行被勒令停业整顿,他们都遭遇了挤兑"。
They have suffered a bank run after the recent suspension of two other banks, Republic of Korea's Financial Services Commission (FSC) said in a statement.

引力波 gravitational wave
由中山大学主导的我国本土引力波探测工程"天琴计划"已于2015年7月正式启动,目前正在立项中。
Tianqin, China's domestic gravitational wave research project initiated by the Sun Yat-sen University in July 2015, is awaiting governmental approval.

饮食疗法 food therapy; dietary treatment; diet therapy
城市人越来越接受饮食疗法。
People in cities are catching up with the idea of food therapy.

隐患 hidden danger
电暖气是办公室火灾隐患,经常有人下班回家时忘记关掉电暖气。
Electric heaters are a hidden danger for fire in the office. People often forget to turn them off when they leave the office for home.

隐瞒 cover up/conceal
国务院安全生产委员会周四就某国有企业下属公司试图瞒报华北地区铁路隧道工程爆炸致人死亡事故的行为提出批评,并要求对此行为从重处罚。
The state council's work safety committee on Thursday condemned a subsidiary of a State-owned enterprise which tried to cover up a deadly explosion at a railway tunnel project in North China and called for heavier punishment for such violations.

隐私面单 privacy waybill
国内多家快递公司开始使用只显示发件人和收件人部分信息的隐私面单,作为保护客户隐私的新举措。
Chinese express delivery companies have taken a new measure to protect the privacy of customers, by using privacy waybills that show partial information about the sender and the receiver.

隐私条款 privacy policy
该政策调整是网信办对网络服务和应用程序隐私条款评审结束后推出的。
The policy change came after the Cyberspace Administration of China's inspection of the privacy policy of online services and mobile apps.

隐形贫困人口 the invisible poverty-stricken population; the invisible poor
"隐形贫困人口"指那些花的比挣的多的人。他们生活讲究质量,在美食、衣服、健身房、水疗按摩以及其他日常支出方面开销很大,银行账户里基本没什么钱。
The invisible poverty-stricken population, or the invisible poor, refers to people

whose consumption exceeds their income. They usually live a quality life and spend a lot of money on food, clothing, gym, spas and other daily expenses, which leaves them little or no money in their bank accounts.

隐形战机 stealth jet fighter
中国很多博客和新闻网站都发布了歼20隐形战机在四川成都试飞成功的消息。
The test flight of the J-20 stealth jet fighter in Chengdu, Sichuan province, has been widely reported on Chinese internet blogs and online news sites.

隐性饥饿 hidden hunger
发展中国家1/3的人口正遭受"隐性饥饿",该疾病患者更易遭受感染、出生缺陷及发育性残疾。
One out of three people in developing countries suffers from hidden hunger, which increases their vulnerability to infection, birth defects, and impaired development.

隐性就业 unregistered employment
这些越来越多的隐性就业在就业率中根本反映不出来。
Increasingly unregistered employment cannot be reflected in the employment rate.

隐性失业 recessive unemployment
该计划扶助待业人员,或者说隐性失业人员。据说他们有几万之多。
The program helps those still in the plight of job-waiting or recessive unemployment, believed to be numbering tens of thousands.

隐性收入 invisible income; off-payroll income
部分隐性收入几乎无法征税。
There exists some invisible income that is almost impossible to levy taxes on.

印花税 stamp duty; stamp tax
专家建议国家应该逐步降低印花税率。
Experts suggest that the country should gradually lower the stamp duty.

英国脱欧 Brexit
英国脱欧对英国和欧洲都是个坏消息。这标志着欧盟理念需要变革了。
Brexit is bad news for Britain and Europe. It is a sign that the EU concept needs to change.

英国脱欧法案 Brexit bill
英国议会上议院通过了"脱欧"法案,扫清了触发《里斯本条约》第五十条的障碍,英国可以正式启动脱欧程序。

The House of Lords has passed the Brexit bill, paving the way for the government to trigger Article 50 of the *Lisbon Treaty*, so the UK can leave the EU.

英语水平 English proficiency
一份报告显示，中国人的英语水平已达到2011年以来的最高水平。
The English proficiency of people in China has reached its highest level since 2011, according to a report released.

婴童纺织品国标 national standards for infants and children's textile
我国首个针对婴幼儿及儿童纺织产品的强制性国家标准于2016年6月1日国际儿童节当天正式生效。
China's first mandatory national textile standards for children—both infants and older children—took effect on International Children's Day, 2016.

荧幕恋情 showmance; show romance
韩剧《太阳的后裔》在中国大热，男主宋仲基和女主宋慧乔的荧幕恋情也让许多观众心神荡漾。
Descendants of the Sun, a South Korean drama, gained great success in China and the showmance of actor Song Joong-ki and actress Song Hye-kyo touched the hearts of many.

盈利能力 profit ability
公司希望今年能够增强盈利能力，扭亏为盈。
The company hopes to increase its profit ability, turning around from loss to gain this year.

营改增 replace business tax with value-added tax (VAT)
2016年5月1日起，我国开始推行营业税改征增值税，这被视为一项重大的税制改革。
China's replacing business tax with value-added tax, or VAT, from May 1, 2016 is seen as a major taxation reform.

营销管理 marketing management
课程由4个模块组成，包括自我管理技能、会计、人力资源与营销管理。
The course is composed of four modules, including personal management skills, accounting, human resources, and marketing management.

营养补助 nutrition subsidy
国务院近日宣布，中央政府将为农村地区的2600万贫困学生提供营养补助。
The State Council announced that the central government will offer nutrition subsidies to 26 million poor students in rural areas.

营业额 turnover; volume of business
营业额少得可怜，只有几千元，厂子能熬到年底不关门就是奇迹。
With a turnover in the paltry range of a few thousand yuan, it'll be a miracle if the factory survives this year.

营业税 business tax
10月30日，国务院常务会议决定废止实施了60多年的营业税。
The State Council executive meeting on Oct 30 decided to abolish the business tax, which has been in force for over 60 years.

营业外收入 non-business income
版权及其他营业外收入在我们的总收入中占很大比重。
Income from copyrights as well as other non-business income makes a big proportion of our total income.

营业许可证 business permit
申请办理营业许可证过去要花几个月，现在几个礼拜就解决了。
Application for a business permit used to take months. Now it's done in a couple of weeks.

赢得市场 gain a share of the market; carve a niche in the market
由于实行了改革创新，这家企业的产品占据了更大的市场份额。
Because of the innovation, the product of the enterprise gained a larger share of the market.

影子贷款 shadow loan
国家发改委下属的国际合作中心主任说，珠江三角洲的许多企业都牵涉影子贷款或陷入房地产融资困境。
Director of the International Cooperation Center affiliated to the National Development and Reform Commission, said many of the enterprises on the Pearl River Delta are involved in shadow loans or real estate businesses that they had trouble financing.

影子内阁 shadow cabinet
昨晚在辞职正式公布之前，影子内阁内部的权力争夺就开始了。
Even before the formal resignation announcements, the jockeying for position within the shadow cabinet was well under way last night.

应酬 socialize; engage in social activities; have social intercourse
他所谓的应酬就是大吃大喝。

What he means by socializing is to wine and dine in grand style.

应急避难所 emergency shelter
上海市政府日前表示,计划于5年内在30个公园修建若干座应急避难所。
The Shanghai government said it will build emergency shelters in 30 parks within 5 years.

应急储备基金 Contingency Reserve Arrangement (CRA)
金砖国家同意建立一个应急储备基金,由各成员国的中央银行管理1000亿美元的基金。该基金将在避免短期资金流动压力和加强全球金融稳定方面起到预先防范作用。
The BRICS agreed to form a Contingency Reserve Arrangement, a 100 billion dollars fund to be managed by the central banks of the member countries. The facility will provide precautionary effect to forestall short term liquidity pressures and strengthen global financial stability.

应急措施 emergency measure
预计下午将有暴风雨,政府正在采取应急措施。
The government in anticipation of heavy rainstorms this afternoon is taking emergency measures.

应试教育 examination-oriented education
应试教育在中国根深蒂固。
Examination-oriented education is deeply rooted in China.

硬X射线调制望远镜 Hard X-ray Modulation Telescope
项目内部人士表示,硬X射线调制望远镜将帮助科学家更好地了解宇宙。
The Hard X-ray Modulation Telescope will help scientists better understand the universe, according to project insiders.

硬道理 overriding importance
发展才是硬道理。
Development is of overriding importance.

硬通货 hard currency
美元和英镑是典型的硬通货。
The US Dollar and the British Pound are good examples of a hard currency.

硬着陆 hard landing
政府承诺中国经济不会出现"硬着陆",这不是空话。

The government's pledge to prevent Chinese economy from a hard landing will not be empty talks.

拥堵费 congestion fee
北京或将跟随其他国际大都市的脚步对中心城区车辆征收拥堵费。
Beijing may follow other international metropolises by imposing a congestion fee for cars in the center of the city.

永久正常贸易关系 permanent normal trading relations (PNTR)
美国国会通过了对华永久正常贸易关系法案。
The US Congress passed the bill of permanent normal trading relations (PNTR) with China.

涌潮 tidal bore
许多游客都来到华东地区的浙江,希望能一睹钱塘江9年来最大的涌潮。
Tourists are flocking to East China's Zhejiang province in the hope of seeing the biggest tidal bore on the Qiantang River in nine years.

用工荒 labor shortage
这些年来,珠三角地区的公司极其依赖劳动密集型制造业。这次的用工荒可能有助于这些企业转向高科技的生产方式。
For many years, companies in the Pearl River Delta have relied heavily on intensive labor manufacturing. The labor shortage may help them become more high-tech.

优化资源配置 optimize the allocation of resources
金融机构的作用发挥得十分好,就能够优化资源配置。
If financial organizations bring their functions into full play, they may optimize the allocation of resources.

优化组合 optimum/preferred clustering; optimized grouping; optional regrouping
据中国农业银行广东省分行的调查,33%的居民对存款、股票、债券、基金、保险等金融资产的优化组合感兴趣。
The survey conducted by the Guangdong Branch of Agricultural Bank of China showed that 33 percent of citizens have an interest in the optimum clustering of financial assets, such as deposits, stocks, bonds, funds and insurance.

优惠关税 preferential tariff/duty
优惠关税待遇,又称特殊关税地位,通常是出于外交考虑为推动同某些国家的贸易而设计的。

The free and preferential tariff treatments, often called the special tariff status, are often designed to promote trade with countries for reasons of foreign policy.

优胜劣汰；适者生存 survival of the fittest
中国企业现在懂得市场经济中优胜劣汰、适者生存的意思了。
Chinese firms now know what survival of the fittest means in the marketplace.

优势互补 complement each other's advantages
通过平等协商、互谅互让，寻求利益契合点和平衡点，尤其是在国际多边规则下，应一视同仁，不能将单边规则强加于人，最终实现优势互补、双赢多赢。
Based on the principal of equal consultation, mutual understanding and accommodation, as well as equal treatment without discrimination, countries must seek convergent interests and complement each other's advantages to achieve win-win results.

优秀网络文化成果 online cultural works of excellence
浙江大学在其微信公众号发布了一项在校师生优秀网络文化成果的认定试行办法。
Zhejiang University issued a draft proposal recently via its WeChat official account to recognize online cultural works of excellence by its teachers and students.

邮递协议 Post Office Protocol（POP）
邮递协议让你可以从互联网服务提供者那里找回你的邮件。
The Post Office Protocol enables you to retrieve mail from your internet service provider（ISP）.

邮购新娘业务 mail-order bride trade
在全球化时代，国际婚介机构，也就是很多人所谓的"邮购新娘"业务，正迎来前所未有的繁荣发展。
In the age of globalization, the international matchmaking industry—still known in many circles as the mail-order bride trade—is thriving like never before.

邮政快件 express mail
我把它通过邮政快件给你寄过去。这样，你在3个工作日内就能收到。
I'll send it by express mail. You can get it in three working days.

游戏障碍 gaming disorder
世界卫生组织拟在更新版的国际疾病分类草案中，将"游戏障碍"列为精神疾病。
The World Health Organization is considering adding "gaming disorder" to the list of mental health conditions in its next update of the International Classification of Diseases (ICD), according to a beta draft of the document.

游行乐队 marching band
这次游行包括22辆彩车、2支舞龙队、3支舞狮队、30支游行队伍、8支游行乐队,参加游行的还有官员和其他重要人物。
The parade featured 22 floats, 2 dragon teams, 3 lion teams, 30 marching groups, 8 marching bands and officials and dignitaries.

游学 study tour
韩亚航空坠机事故发生后,浙江衢州市教育局已要求各学校及相关代理机构暂停所有夏令营和游学项目。
Quzhou Municipal Education Bureau in Zhejiang has told schools and related agent institutions to suspend all summer camps and study tours after the deadly Asiana Airlines crash.

友善之墙 wall of kindness
青岛一家慈善创意工厂发起了一项"友善之墙"活动,鼓励路人捐赠他们闲置的保暖衣物,也倡导有需要的人们将这些衣物带走。
A "wall of kindness", the creation of local charity Chuangyi Workshop in Qingdao, invites passers-by to leave their spare warm clothes and encourages those who are in need to take them.

有奔头 have something to look forward to; have something nice to expect
新政策的推行让农民觉得有奔头。
The new policy made farmers feel they have something to look forward to.

有偿贷款 onerous loan
许多人不愿意接受有偿贷款来修铁路和公路,会使这个本来就贫困不堪的县背上更沉重的债务负担。
Many did not want to accept onerous loans for building railways and roads, which would push the poverty-stricken county further into debt.

有偿新闻 paid news
我们目前需要和假新闻、有偿新闻以及新闻中的软广告做斗争,另外还存在一些不关注社会事务和公众利益的报道。
We are facing a battle against fake news, paid news, and soft advertising in news. It is also about reports that are unconcerned about social affairs and public interests.

有毒朋友 toxic friends
"有毒朋友"是指为了受到关注而在社交场合使你难堪的人。
"Toxic friends" refer to those who embarrass you in social situations in order to

gain attention.

有法可依，有法必依，执法必严，违法必究 There must be laws to resort to and abide by; the laws must be enforced strictly, and law-breakers must be prosecuted.

有腐必反，有贪必肃 fight every corrupt phenomenon, punish every corrupt official

我们要坚定决心，有腐必反、有贪必肃，不断铲除腐败现象滋生蔓延的土壤，以实际成效取信于民。

We must have the resolution to fight every corrupt phenomenon, punish every corrupt official and constantly eradicate the soil which breeds corruption, so as to earn people's trust with actual results.

有管理的浮动汇率制度 managed floating exchange rate regime

中国表示要加强市场在有管理的浮动汇率制度中的作用，使汇率更具弹性。

China affirmed its intention to enhance the flexibility and strengthen the role of market forces in its managed floating exchange rate regime.

有机污染物 organic pollutant

有些有机污染物对人体健康是有害的。

Some of the organic pollutants can be hazardous to human health.

有理想、有道德、有文化、有纪律 with lofty ideals, moral integrity, intellectual abilities and a strong sense of discipline

发展社会主义文化的根本任务，是培养一代又一代有理想、有道德、有文化、有纪律的公民。

The fundamental task of developing a socialist culture is to cultivate generations of citizens with lofty ideals, moral integrity, intellectual abilities and a strong sense of discipline.

有识之士 people of vision

我们热忱欢迎金融家、企业家和有识之士参与新区的开发建设。

We warmly welcome bankers, entrepreneurs and people of vision to participate in the development of the new district.

有效降水 effective precipitation

气象台预报称，长江中下游沿岸省市近两天仍无有效降水，尽管有零星小雨，但仍将持续干旱。

The observatory said there will be still no effective precipitation in the coming two days in provinces and municipalities along the lower and middle reaches of the Yangtze River and dry weather will continue to develop in spite of scattered drizzle.

逾期贷款 overdue loan
逾期贷款是未来不良贷款的一个指标。
Overdue loans is an indicator of future nonperforming loan, or NPLs.

舆论 public opinion
当今信息时代,舆论的威力很大。
Public opinion is a powerful weapon today in the age of information.

舆论导向 direct public opinion; direction of public opinion
正如世界各国的新闻一样,这里的新闻也要有舆论导向的义务,只是各国形式不同。
The media here are also expected to direct public opinion, as are media anywhere in the world, each in its own way.

与国际惯例接轨 be compatible with internationally accepted practices
为吸引人才,数学与系统科学研究院应加快科研体制改革,建立与国际惯例接轨的各项机制。
In order to attract talents, research institutes of mathematics and systematic sciences should speed up the reform of the scientific research system and set up various mechanisms compatible with internationally accepted practices.

与邻为善,以邻为伴 build friendship and partnership with neighboring countries
中国将继续执行"与邻为善、以邻为伴"的基本方针。
China will stick to the policy of "building friendship and partnership with neighboring countries".

语感 sense of language
老师经常强调语感对于学习外语的重要性。
Teachers often stress that a sense of language is very important in learning foreign languages.

语音识别 speech recognition
作者在书中讨论了语音识别、语音合成、语音信号等问题的基本原理。
The author discusses fundamentals of speech recognition, speech synthesis and speech signal, etc. in this book.

育婴假 parental leave
国内首个性别平等条例草案在去年10月的初稿中,建议给家有3岁以内宝宝的爸爸妈妈每年5天的育婴假,在去年12月份的二稿中,育婴假被延长到10天。
The draft, as the nation's first gender equality regulation, granted five days of parental leave every year for both parents of a child younger than age 3 in its first version last October and extended the leave to 10 days in its second version last December.

预购 pre-order
在线零售商亚马逊周四表示,轰动英国歌坛的苏珊·波伊尔即将发行的首张专辑已成为亚马逊有史以来全球预购数量最大的专辑。
The upcoming debut album by British singing sensation Susan Boyle has become the largest global CD pre-order in the history of Amazon.com, the online retailer said on Thursday.

预留车位 reserve parking spaces
浙江杭州一个大型居民区开始为看望老人的子女预留车位,方便子女定期看望父母。
A large residential community in Hangzhou, Zhejiang province, has begun to reserve parking spaces for people visiting their elderly parents, making it easier for children to drop by on a regular basis.

预算外收入 extra-budgetary revenue
据统计,目前财政预算外收入相当于财政总收入的50%。
According to statistics, the current fiscal, extra-budgetary revenue accounts for 50 percent of the total fiscal revenue.

预算外支出 off-budget expenditure
一般性的预算外支出由财政部门核定支出计划,按月拨付,年终结余由政府调控使用。
For routine off-budget expenditure, the fiscal department will check and ratify the expenditure plan and allocate it monthly. The government will control the surplus at the end of year.

预选赛 qualifying game
虽然美国和墨西哥队总是入围世界杯的热门球队,但是预选赛阶段从来都不是轻松的。
Though the US and Mexico are always heavy favorites to advance to the World

Cup, qualifying games are never easy, especially on the road.

欲速则不达 More haste, less speed.

御准 (give) royal assent

英国女王伊丽莎白二世御准一项法案，允许该国首相特蕾莎•梅触发《里斯本条约》第五十条，启动英国脱离欧盟的程序。

Britain's Queen Elizabeth II gave royal assent to a bill allowing British Prime Minister Theresa May to trigger Article 50 of the *Lisbon Treaty*, beginning the process through which the UK will leave the European Union.

誉满全球 be famed around the world; be famed all over the world

美国迪士尼公司推出的卡通明星米老鼠誉满全球。

The brand image of Mickey Mouse, a cartoon star produced by the US Disney Company, is famed around the world.

冤家宜解不宜结 Better to make friends than (to make) enemies.

冤家宜解不宜结。可是我不知道两家的世仇什么时候能结束。希望我这一代能看到那一天。

I know it's better to make friends than enemies. But I don't have an idea when the feud between the two families will end. I hope it does in my generation.

冤假错案 wrongful conviction

我们要充分认识到，律师是法律职业共同体的重要一员，是人民法院的同盟军，是有效防范冤假错案的无可替代的重要力量。

We should fully understand that lawyers are an integral part of the legal community, an ally of the courts and an irreplaceable force in preventing wrongful convictions.

元首外交 head-of-state diplomacy

国家主席习近平与来访的美国总统特朗普同意继续发挥元首外交对两国关系的战略引领作用。

President Xi Jinping and visiting US President Donald Trump agreed on maintaining the strategic leading role of head-of-state diplomacy in developing bilateral relations.

员工考核 employee evaluation

员工考核可作为决定员工工资的基础。

An employee evaluation can be used as a basis for determining pay.

原版 original edition
以下原版唱片均从港台购入,价格已包含运费。
The following original editions of discs are bought from Hong Kong and Taiwan, whose prices include the transportation costs.

原产地 place of origin
今后,爱茶人士可以通过特殊的原产地防伪标识来鉴别著名的龙井茶。
From now on, tea lovers will be able to identify the well-known Longjing Tea by a special logo authenticating its place of origin.

圆桌会议 round-table conference
圆桌会议没有取得任何进展,双方决定下周一继续会谈。
The two sides, failing to make any progress at the round-table conference, agreed to meet again next Monday.

远程视频庭审 remote video links for judicial hearings; remote video hearings
北京市将从9月1日起在部分法院实行"远程视频庭审"。
Several courts in Beijing will begin using remote video links for judicial hearings on Sept 1.

远光灯 full-beam headlight
近日,深圳交警对使用远光灯的驾驶员采取让他们看远光灯一分钟的处罚方式。
Traffic police in Shenzhen are punishing drivers who use full-beam headlights by making them stare into the lights for a minute.

远景规划 long-term plan; perspective long-term plan
根据水利部的消息,中国政府正在起草一项控制黄河洪水、截流、污染和沉积物积淀问题的远景规划。
The Chinese government is drafting a long-term plan for controlling floods, building dams, preventing pollution and tackling the build-up of sediment on the Yellow River, according to the Ministry of Water Resources.

月球背面 far side of the moon
我国一名探月科学家表示,中国计划成为首个实现月球探测器在月球背面着陆的国家。
China is planning to be the first country to land a lunar probe on the far side of the moon, a Chinese lunar probe scientist said.

阅兵式 military review
这次彩排从周六凌晨开始,包括将近20万市民参加并动用了60辆模拟彩车的群众欢庆游行、大约1.2万人参与演出的联欢活动以及阅兵式。
Starting early Saturday morning, the rehearsal featured a mass pageant involving nearly 200,000 citizens and 60 simulated floats, a gala by around 12,000 performers and a military review.

粤港澳大湾区 Guangdong-Hong Kong-Macao Greater Bay Area
粤港澳大湾区将作为一座桥梁，为香港带着创新技术进入规模可观的大陆市场提供更加便捷的途径。
The Guangdong-Hong Kong-Macao Greater Bay Area will serve as a bridge, offering Hong Kong easier access to the sizeable mainland market for its innovative technologies.

孕前健康检查 pre-pregnancy physical examination
中国于周四开始启动第二轮免费孕前健康检查项目，该项目涵盖了31个省、市、自治区的120个试点县（市、区）。
China started the second wave of free pre-pregnancy physical examinations in 120 pilot counties (cities or regions) in 31 provinces, municipalities and autonomous regions on Thursday.

载人飞船 manned spacecraft
据报道,中国第一艘载人飞船神舟五号于北京时间周三下午15时57分完成轨道运行一周。
China's first manned spacecraft Shenzhou-V completed an orbit shift at 15:57 Wednesday (Beijing time), according to reports.

再生水/中水 reclaimed water
虽然北京市有明确的指导方针要求高尔夫球场利用再生水进行灌溉,但是按此要求做到的球场却不到7%。
Fewer than 7 percent of Beijing's golf courses use reclaimed water for irrigation, despite Beijing's guidelines that strongly suggest they should all do so.

再生资源 renewable resource
煤炭与石油都不是再生资源。
Coal and gasoline are not renewable resources.

在家教育 home schooling
随着经济不断紧缩,越来越多居住在中国的外籍人士用在家教育的方式来应对学费持续上涨。
With a crimped economy tightening belts, a growing number of expatriates in China are seeing home schooling as a solution to the soaring cost of tuition.

赞赏功能 tipping function, cash reward feature
根据苹果的应用内购买政策,腾讯日前关闭了iPhone手机上的微信内容生产者赞赏功能。
Tencent has disabled its popular tipping function for WeChat content providers on the iPhone to comply with Apple's policy on in-app purchases.

暂停偿债 debt standstill
迪拜世界已拒绝为偿抵债务而廉价出售资产,因此将被迫寻求暂停偿债。
Dubai World has refused to offload assets at fire-sale prices to repay obligations, forcing it to seek a debt standstill.

暂行条例 provisional regulation; interim regulation
按暂行条例规定，行人过马路只能走人行横道。
Under provisional regulations, pedestrians are not allowed to cross the street unless through the pedestrian's stripe.

赞助费 sponsorship fees
根据新政策，非京籍学生不再需要缴纳赞助费，之前赞助费的缴纳标准大约为每年10000元。这意味着非京籍学生今后也可以在京接受免费义务教育。
With the new policy, non-native students are exempted from sponsorship fees—set at around 10,000 yuan annually. This means they will also have access to compulsory education for free.

赃款 ill-gotten money
广东省将对举报贪官的人予以奖励，奖金具体数额将与案件涉及的赃款金额挂钩。
South China's Guangdong province may reward those who report corruption according to the amount of ill-gotten money involved in the case.

赃款赃物 proceeds of crime; spoils
他们3人涉嫌盗窃11起，涉案财物、现金总额150万元。但是，在被捕之前，他们已挥霍掉大部分赃款赃物。
The three culprits were suspected of perpetrating 11 robberies involving cash and goods with a total worth of 1.5 million yuan. But most of the spoils had been splurged when police captured them.

造假账 falsified accounts
我们必须减少税收拖欠，采取可行措施解决造假账问题并逐渐建立新的税收管理体制。
We must reduce taxes in arrears, take practical measures to solve the problem of falsified accounts and gradually establish a new system in tax collection and management.

责权利相结合 combination of responsibility, power and interest
要求他们承担责任，就必须给予他们相应的权利待遇，然后才能要求他们出业绩。汉语行话可叫作责权利相结合。
If you want them to take certain responsibilities, you must also give them appropriate power to carry out the responsibilities plus monetary incentives before you can demand for results. In Chinese, it is sometimes referred to as the combination of responsibility, power and interest.

责任督学 educational inspector
北京市教委表示，市内每所幼儿园都要配备一名责任督学，监督幼儿园的运营。
Every kindergarten in Beijing will be staffed with an educational inspector to oversee their operation, local authority said.

炸弹之母 the mother of all bombs
投放的GBU-43/B巨型空爆炸弹被称为"炸弹之母"，是美军在行动中投放过的最大的非核武炸弹。
The GBU-43/B Massive Ordnance Air Blast Bomb (MOAB), known as "the mother of all bombs", is the largest non-nuclear bomb ever used by the US in a conflict.

债券通 Bond Connect
该交易平台正式名称为"债券通"，将与已经开通的内地和香港之间的"沪港通"和"深港通"股票互联互通交易平台并行，彰显了我国将资本市场全球化的决心。
The trading platform, called Bond Connect, would operate alongside the two existing cross-border Stock Connect programs between the Chinese mainland and Hong Kong, in a sign of the nation's determination to make its capital market more global.

债台高筑 be/become debt-ridden
发言人指出一些现有公司债台高筑，扭亏几乎无望。
The spokesman pointed out that some existing firms are debt-ridden with little hope of ever making money.

债务减记 write-down
但分析人士怀疑究竟有多少银行会自愿对希腊债务减记50%，并质疑额外救助基金的来源。
But analysts wondered how many banks would adopt a voluntary 50 percent write-down on Greek bonds and questioned where the money for the enlarged bailout fund would come from.

债务上限 debt ceiling
众议院和参议院的共和党和民主党领导人已经达成协议，同意提高政府的债务上限以避免产生违约风险。
Republican and Democratic leaders in the House and Senate have reached an agreement to raise the government's debt ceiling and avoid a default.

债转股 debt-to-equity swap
债转股使这家公司当年扭亏为盈。
The debt-to-equity swap helped the company to turn out a profit that very year.

战略定力 strategic focus
改革是推动发展的制胜法宝，中国应该保持其"战略定力"。
Reform is the recipe for boosting development and China should maintain its "strategic focus".

战略伙伴关系 strategic partnership
为建立战略伙伴关系，该项声明呼吁APEC成员间加强对话。
To build up a strategic partnership, the statement calls on APEC members to engage in further dialogue.

战略性新兴产业 emerging sectors(industries) of strategic importance
政府将为战略性新兴产业提供管理提升方面的政策支持，加强知识产权的保护力度并提供财政支持。
The government will provide policy support for managerial improvements, strengthen intellectual property rights protection and offer financial assistance to emerging sectors of strategic importance.

站队 take sides
美国于周一表示，不会在中菲黄岩岛问题上站队，并重申希望通过外交途径解决领土争端。
The United States said on Monday that it would not take sides in the Huangyan Island standoff between China and the Philippines and reiterated support for a diplomatic resolution to the territorial dispute.

招聘意愿指数 hiring intentions index
在所有调查监控的行业中，地产和建筑行业的招聘意愿指数最高，在第三季度达到了77.1。
The hiring intentions index of the property and construction industry is the highest among all monitored industries, reaching 77.1 for the third quarter.

招商引资 attract/invite investment (from overseas)
研讨会期间，北京还将推出总投资超过150亿美元的80个左右的招商大项目，以吸引海外投资。
Also during the seminar, Beijing will present some 80 major projects, with a total worth of more than $15 billion, to attract overseas investments.

肇事逃逸 hit-and-run
今年上半年,北京市共发生了148起卡车驾驶事故,造成178人死亡,占北京交通事故伤亡人数的32%。醉驾司机、闯红灯者和肇事逃逸司机也引发了多起交通事故。

The city recorded 148 truck-related accidents involving 178 deaths, 32 percent of Beijing's road fatalities in the first half year. Drink-drivers, people who ran red lights, and hit-and-run drivers were also involved in many accidents.

折旧费 depreciation expenses
该项目的主要成本是土地费、基础设施费、设备折旧费等。

The main costs of the project are land, infrastructure and equipment depreciation expenses.

珍稀濒危动物 rare or endangered species
华南虎是世界上十大珍稀濒危动物之一。据估计,野生华南虎现最多有20只。

It is estimated that there are no more than 20 South China tigers known to be in the wild, which have been listed as one of the ten most endangered species in the world.

真人秀 reality show
很多面向年轻人的真人秀非常受欢迎。

Many youth-oriented reality shows are very popular.

枕边风 pillow talk
我老婆吹了太多的枕边风给我,我才慢慢开始收取贿赂。

My wife gave me too much pillow talk to persuade me into taking bribes.

振兴经济 revitalize the economy
他说政府将不遗余力努力振兴经济。

He said his government would make every effort to revitalize the economy.

振兴中华 the revitalization of China; revitalize the Chinese nation; make China powerful and strong
他在典礼上作了演讲,希望大家记住这一时刻,尽自己最大的努力振兴中华。

In a speech delivered at the ceremony, he voiced the hope that everyone will remember this moment and do their bit to contribute to the revitalization of China.

争抢生源 poaching of talented students
中国高校争抢生源的竞争愈演愈烈,上海两所著名高校近日卷入争抢生源的激烈纷争中。

Two of Shanghai's leading universities are involved in a fierce dispute over alleged poaching of talented students, as competition among Chinese universities continues to intensify.

征兵 draft someone into the army
据全国征兵电话会议消息，中国将吸收更多高学历的年轻人入伍。
China will draft more well-educated young people into the army, according to a national conscription tele-conference.

征集意见 solicit opinion
一般来讲，召开公开听证会对征集各界意见很有必要。
Normally, a public hearing is necessary to solicit opinions from various circles.

征信 credit investigation
这个新条例将是中国第一个针对征信制度的全国性法规。
The new rule would be China's first nationwide regulation regarding the credit investigation system.

正式成员资格 full membership
联合国教科文组织周一接受巴勒斯坦成为该组织正式成员国，这是巴勒斯坦作为一个独立国家在寻求世界认可的长期努力中向前迈进的一步。
The United Nations Educational, Scientific and Cultural Organization granted the Palestinians full membership on Monday, a step forward in their long-running efforts to achieve recognition before the world as an independent state.

正式照会 formal note
他在记者招待会上说古巴拒绝阿根廷外交部的正式抗议照会。
He told the press conference that Cuba had rejected a formal note of protest presented by the Argentine Foreign Ministry.

证据审查 evidence review
有关死刑案中的证据审查和刑事案件中非法证据排除的这两项规定要求，只有在通过合法途径获得充分证据的情况下才能宣判死刑。
A death sentence should be pronounced only with sufficient evidence acquired through legal means, stipulate the two regulations: One on evidence review in death sentence cases, and the other on excluding illegal evidence in criminal cases.

政策性贷款 policy-based lending; government-directed loan
近来政策性贷款和商业贷款有分离趋势，这是迈向逐步取消对某些群体的优惠贷款与鼓励性贷款的一个受欢迎的步骤。

The recent trend to separate policy-based lending from commercial loans is a welcome step towards the phrasing out of preferential and subsidized lending to some groups.

政策组合 policy mix
渣打银行对中国和日本进行了比较后说,到目前为止中国的改革增长政策组合要优于日本等其他亚洲国家采取的政策。

In comparing both China and Japan, Standard Chartered said that China had so far pursued a better reform-growth policy mix than Japan and many other Asian countries.

政府特殊津贴 special government allowance
他是仅有的两位享受政府特殊津贴的教授之一。政府特殊津贴用于表彰特殊贡献者。

He was only one of two professors receiving special government allowances honoring people of outstanding contributions.

政企分开 separate the administrative functions from business/enterprise management
国家也将加快行政改革,转变政府职能,使政企分开,减少政府对经济的干预。

The country will also enhance reforms in administrative departments, transform the functions of the government, separate the administrative functions from business management and reduce its intervention in economic affairs.

政治规矩 political discipline and rules
领导干部应以政治规矩自觉维护党中央权威。领导干部必须遵守政治规矩,在任何时候任何情况下,言行思想都应与党中央一致。

Political discipline and rules exist to enable CPC cadres to defend the authority of the CPC Central Committee. Cadres must follow these rules, aligning themselves with the committee in deed and thought, at all times and in any situation.

政治生态 political ecology
政治生态和自然生态一样,稍不注意,就很容易受到污染,一旦出现问题,再想恢复就要付出很大代价。

Political ecology is like natural ecology; it is easily vulnerable to pollution in an unguarded moment. Once problems arise, a great price must be paid for recovery.

政治体制改革 reform of the political structure; political structure reform
我们必须继续积极稳妥推进政治体制改革,发展更加广泛、更加充分、更加健全的人民民主。
We must continue to make both active and prudent efforts to carry out the reform of the political structure, and make people's democracy more extensive, fuller in scope and sounder in practice.

支付产业 payment industry
我国将以均衡有序的方式对外开放其支付产业。
China will open up its payment industry in a balanced and orderly way.

支付能力 payment capacity
企业的现金流被认为是分析企业支付能力的重要手段。
A company's cash flow is considered to be the key tool for the analysis of its payment capacity.

支付体系 payment/clearing system
中国的支付体系主要包括基于票据的异地支付、银行同业电子支付、地方结算、跨行网银支付、国内银行卡支付（自动取款机和借记卡）以及邮局支付等形式。
China's payment systems mainly include paper-based, non-local fund transfer systems, electronic interbank systems, local clearing houses, electronic intra-bank clearing systems, internal card-based payment systems（ATM and debit cards）and post office clearing.

知识产权 intellectual property right
该论坛使您有很好的机会了解中国有关知识产权保护的政策法规。
The forum gives you a great opportunity to learn about laws and policy of China's intellectual property right protection.

知识密集型 knowledge-intensive
综合能力和学习能力是知识密集型产业的关键部分。
Integrated ability and learning capacity are the key elements in the knowledge-intensive industry.

脂肪税 fat tax
印度喀拉拉邦政府对品牌外卖店供应的比萨、汉堡、三明治、炸玉米饼和其他垃圾食品征收14.5%的"脂肪税"。
The government of Kerala in India collects a 14.5% fat tax on pizzas, burgers, sandwiches, tacos and other junk food served in branded outlets.

直播答题 live streaming quiz
几天之内参与人数创纪录，直播答题应用在中国爆红，成为直播行业下一个增长前沿。

Live streaming quiz applications are witnessing an explosive surge in China by drawing in a record number of participants in just a few days, making it the next growth frontier of the live streaming sector in China.

直销银行 direct bank

中国搜索巨头百度公司与中信银行建立直销银行，在线提供投资产品与贷款服务。

Chinese search giant Baidu Inc and China Citic Bank Corp set up a direct bank, which offers investment products and loans online.

职场冷暴力 emotional office abuse

智联招聘网开展的一项调查显示，超过70%的办公室职员遭遇"职场冷暴力"，其中3/4的人是80后。

More than 70 percent of office workers encounter "emotional office abuse", three-quarters of which are from the post-80s people, a survey conducted by zhaopin.com says.

职务犯罪 work-related crime

全国大检察官研讨班会议表示，2017年上半年，全国立案侦查职务犯罪人数达30538人。

A total of 30,538 Chinese officials were investigated for work-related crimes in the first half of 2017, according to a seminar for chief procurators.

职务消费 position-related consumption

该文件在薪资结构和支付、职务消费以及监督和管理等方面制定了指导方针，目的是为了建立健全规范国有企业高管薪酬的激励和约束机制。

The document set guidelines in salary structure and payment, position-related consumption, and supervision and management, in a bid to establish and perfect incentive and restraint mechanisms regulating SOE executives' salaries.

职业病 occupational disease

新发布的规划要求当地政府和企业加强职业病防护措施，职业病患者将得到更多的福利补偿。

Those suffering from occupational diseases will receive more welfare benefits following a newly issued plan urging local governments and companies to strengthen preventive measures.

职业高中（职高） vocational school

这所职业高中主要为制造业和建筑业输送人才。

This vocational school mostly trains people for manufacturing and construction businesses.

职业倦怠 job burnout
数据显示，相当高比例的职员患有"职业倦怠"，这个术语出自20世纪60年代格雷厄姆·格林所著的《一个自行发完病毒的病例》，目前被定义为"情感耗尽、自我成就感降低的心理状态"。
Statistics find a shockingly high proportion of employees suffering "job burnout", a term coined in the 1960s from the Graham Greene novel *A Burnt-out Case*. It is now defined as "a psychological condition of emotional exhaustion and reduced sense of personal accomplishment".

职业年金 occupational pension
我国发布了政府雇员职业年金详细标准，这是建立一个多层级、可持续的养老金体系的举措之一。
China announced detailed standards of occupational pension for government employees as a move to build a multi-level and sustainable pension mechanism.

职业瓶颈 career bottleneck
在职业发展中，女性职业有瓶颈。在企事业高管层面，女性的数量还是远远不够。
Women have come to a career bottleneck, and the number of women decision-makers in companies is far from enough.

职业议价员 professional bargainer
在贵阳有不少这样的职业议价员，有些人甚至组建了议价网站和议价组织。他们提供的服务覆盖范围很广，包括购买汽车、家具、房产和婚庆服务等。
In Guiyang, there are quite a few such professional bargainers. Some of them even set up bargaining networks and groups. They provide a wide range of services, including buying cars, furniture, property and wedding services.

植入式广告 product placement
"植入式广告"首次获准在英国的电视节目中出现。
Product placement is to be allowed on British television programs for the first time.

纸包不住火 Truth will come to light sooner or later./wrap up a flame of fire with paper
他知道犯这么大的事儿不可能永远隐瞒下去。用他自己的话说，纸包不住火。两周后，他投案自首了。

He knew he could not hide a crime like that forever. It's like trying to wrap up a flame of fire with paper, he said. Two weeks later, he handed himself in.

纸上谈兵 be an armchair strategist
他绝不是纸上谈兵，他的确想出了利用清洁能源短期内改善我国环境质量的计划。
Far from being an armchair strategist, he worked out a plan of utilizing clean energy to improve the environment in our country in a short time.

指纹比对 fingerprint comparison
嫌疑犯石某在北京已经居住了4年。他称自己是以游客身份进入故宫的，作案动机就是缺钱。他是通过指纹比对被警方发现的。
Shi has lived in Beijing for four years. He allegedly entered the Palace Museum as a tourist and conducted the theft for money. He was identified by police through fingerprint comparison.

质量管理 quality control
政府与成员企业促进产业信息交流和质量管理，协调制定产业标准并组织国际交流。
The government and member enterprises promote information exchange and quality control in the industry, coordinate the formulation of industrial standards and organize international exchanges.

质量认证 quality certification
国务院表示，要加强质量认证，营造公平的市场环境，提高中国制造品质。
The State Council said that it will strengthen quality certification to help create a fair market environment and raise the quality of Chinese-made products.

治则兴，乱则衰 order leads to prosperity and chaos to decline

致命弱点 Achilles' heel
过去，没有铁路运输是西藏经济发展的致命弱点，但青藏铁路通车以后情况就不同了。
The lack of rail transport used to be Tibet's Achilles' heel for its economic development. Now it is different with the operation of Qinghai-Tibet railway.

智慧健康养老业 smart health and elderly care industry
工业和信息化部表示，我国计划在未来4年发展智慧健康养老产业，以基本普及健康管理服务和居家养老。
China plans to develop the smart health and elderly care industry in the next four years to grant universal access to health management services and home-based elderly care, the Ministry of Industry and Information Technology said.

智力投资 intellectual investment
在西部开发过程中智力投资胜于经济扶贫，这已经成为共识。
It is widely agreed that intellectual investment has advantages over economic support in the development of the western regions.

智力引进 recruit talents; attract (foreign) talents
西部发展战略的实施促使西部许多地方政府争相从外部引进智力和人才。
With the implementation of the western development strategy, many local governments in western regions have been vying to recruit talents from other places.

智囊团；思想库 brain trust; think tank
几乎每个政府都有自己的智囊团。
Almost every government has its own think tank.

智能轨道快运系统 Autonomous Rail Rapid Transit(ART)
"智能轨道快运系统"车身长约30米，并安装了传感器，可以检测道路状况。
The Autonomous Rail Rapid Transit is around 30 metres long and is fitted with sensors that detect the dimensions of the road.

智能识别系统 intelligent identification system (IIS)
广东省深圳市的一处交叉路口设立起一个智能识别系统，用于曝光闯红灯的行人。
An intelligent identification system (IIS) has been set up on an intersection in Shenzhen, Guangdong province tasked with exposing pedestrians who jaywalk on red lights.

智能制造 intelligent manufacturing
智能制造是基于新一代信息通信技术与先进制造技术深度融合的新型生产方式。
Intelligent manufacturing is a new mode of manufacturing based on the deep integration of new generation information and communications technology and advanced manufacturing technology.

滞后影响 lagged effect
一些美国分析家说失业报告反映了今年春天经济几乎是零增长的状况对就业市场的滞后影响。
Some US analysts said the unemployment report reflects a lagged effect on job markets from the economy's near-zero growth this spring.

中等收入陷阱 middle-income trap
汇丰银行发布的一份报告称，中国正成为创新驱动的发展中经济体。如果创新持续下去，将帮助中国避开"中等收入陷阱"。

China is becoming an innovation-driven developing economy, and innovation, if continued, will help the country ward off the "middle-income trap", according to a HSBC report.

中国梦 the Chinese Dream
实现中华民族伟大复兴,是近代以来中国人民最伟大的梦想,我们称之为"中国梦",基本内涵是实现国家富强、民族振兴、人民幸福。

The rejuvenation of the Chinese nation has been the greatest dream of the Chinese people since the beginning of modern times; we call this "the Chinese Dream". The idea in essence is to make the country prosperous and strong, rejuvenate the nation, and see that the people are happy.

中国模式 China model
直到今日,中国的政治和经济体制仍需要进一步完善,"中国模式"正在世界和本国的经验基础上不断发展。

Up until today, China's political and economic system has yet to be perfected, and the "China model" is evolving based on world and Chinese experiences.

中国品牌日 Chinese Brands Day
国务院同意自2017年起,将每年5月10日设立为"中国品牌日"。

China's State Council has approved a "Chinese Brands Day" to be held on May 10 each year starting in 2017.

中国式过马路(乱穿马路的行人)jaywalker; cross the road in the Chinese style; the Chinese-style road crossing
北京市交管部门负责人宣誓要严厉打击乱穿马路的行人。从本周起,过马路时不等绿灯信号就穿行的行人将被现场罚款10元。

Beijing traffic chiefs have vowed to crack down on jaywalkers. From this week, people who do not wait for the "green man" signal to cross at intersections will receive on-the-spot fines of 10 yuan.

中国特色大国外交 major-country diplomacy with Chinese characteristics
中国特色大国外交要推动构建新型国际关系,推动构建人类命运共同体。

Major-country diplomacy with Chinese characteristics aims to foster a new type of international relations and build a community with a shared future for mankind.

中国特色自由贸易港 free trade port with Chinese characteristics
我国发布支持海南全面深化改革开放的指导意见,列出将海南建设成为自由贸易试验区和中国特色自由贸易港的详细举措。

China unveiled guidelines on supporting the southern island province of Hainan to deepen reform and opening up, with details on turning it into a pilot free trade zone and creating a "free trade port with Chinese characteristics".

中期借贷便利 medium-term lending facility (MLF)
我国央行对14家金融机构新增中期借贷便利操作。
China's central bank has offered new medium-term lending facility (MLF) loans to 14 financial institutions.

中日友好四项原则：和平友好，平等互利，互相信赖，长期稳定 The four principles of Sino-Japanese friendship: peace and friendship, equality and mutual benefit, mutual trust, and long-term stability

中医 traditional Chinese medicine (TCM)
我国药理学家屠呦呦荣获2015年诺贝尔奖生理学或医学奖，凸显了传统中医研究及其潜力正得到更多关注。
China's pharmacologist Tu Youyou received the 2015 Nobel Prize in physiology or medicine, highlighting more attentions are paid to traditional Chinese medicine researches and its potentials.

终身禁令 lifetime ban
经过3年的调查，中国足协向33人开出终身禁止从事足球活动的处罚，其中包括之前因操纵比赛而入狱的相关人员。
After a three-year investigation, the Chinese Football Association issued lifetime bans on 33 people in football-related activities, including some previously jailed for involvement in match-fixing.

终身责任制 lifelong accountability system
为遏制土壤污染进一步恶化，我国将对污染者实行终身责任制。
China will carry out a lifelong accountability system for polluters to arrest worsening soil pollution.

钟摆族 pendulum clan
有很多像张某这样的白领每周往返于两座城市之间，这样的人群被形象地称为"钟摆族"。
Many white-collar workers like Zhang commute every week between the two cities, earning themselves the moniker, "pendulum clan".

众创、众包、众扶、众筹 crowd innovation, crowdsourcing, crowd support and crowdfunding
打造众创、众包、众扶、众筹平台。

Platforms will be created for crowd innovation, crowdsourcing, crowd support and crowdfunding.

众口难调 It is difficult to cater to all tastes.
由于众口难调，这位聪明的老板在她的饭店制作了各式家常菜来招揽顾客。
Since it is difficult to cater to all tastes, the smart owner has created many kinds of home-style dishes in her restaurant to attract customers.

重大疾病保险 serious illness insurance
官方数据显示，目前大病保险制度已覆盖10亿多城乡居民。
According to official statistics, more than 1 billion urban and rural residents are now covered by the serious illness insurance system.

重型运载火箭 heavy-lift carrier rocket
我国发射了首个重型运载火箭长征五号，这是我国航天工业的又一个里程碑。
China launched its first heavy-lift carrier rocket, the Long March 5, marking a new milestone in the country's space industry.

重症病例 case of serious conditions
到目前为止，近75%的甲流患者已康复。285例重症病例中，54例已治愈。
So far, nearly 75 percent of the A/H1N1 patients have recovered. Among the 285 cases of serious conditions, 54 have been cured.

逐步淘汰 phase out
我国宣布将逐步淘汰白炽灯泡，从而减少碳排放量。
China has announced a plan to phase out incandescent bulbs and subsequently reduce emissions.

逐梦者 Dreamers
美国总统特朗普终止了一项对童年时期非法进入美国的年轻移民的特赦令，在华盛顿和全国各地均引发抗议。这一无证移民群体约80万人，他们常被形容为"逐梦者"。
US President Donald Trump ended an amnesty for young immigrants brought illegally to the US as minors, triggering protests in Washington and across the nation. This group of some 800,000 undocumented immigrants are often described as "Dreamers".

主场优势 home advantage
他表示，不希望自己的主场优势变成主场劣势，于是向裁判申请重跳。
He said he did not expect the home advantage turned to be home disadvantage, and

he spoke to referees to apply for repeating a dive.

主观能动性 personal initiative
我们鼓励员工积极进取，开拓创造性思维并互相交换想法。发挥个人主观能动性是我们创业精神的核心。

Our people are encouraged to be proactive, think creatively and share their ideas with each other. This personal initiative is at the core of our entrepreneurial spirit.

主力军 major driving force
一家出版社近日发布的一份蓝皮书指出，农民将成为中国网民增长的"主力军"。

Farmers will become a "major driving force" in the growth of China's internet population, according to a blue paper recently released by a publishing house.

主权债务评级 sovereign debt rating
穆迪下调中国主权信用评级没有影响人民币的价值，也没有影响中国全球市场大国的地位。

Moody's downgrading China's sovereign debt rating did little to affect the value of the renminbi or China's status as a global market powerhouse.

住房补贴 housing allowance; rental allowance
为鼓励员工到中国工作，公司每月还给他们一笔丰厚的住房补贴，数额达到他们月薪的一半以上。

To encourage people to work in China, the company also gives them a hefty monthly housing allowance that represents more than half of their salary.

住房空置率 housing vacancy rate
据国内媒体报道，某些大城市的住房空置率高达50%。虽然官方没有公布正式数据，但这却点燃了一些网民实地调查的热情。

The absence of authoritative figures on the nation's housing vacancy rate, reported as high as 50 percent in major cities by domestic media, has led some netizens to carry out a field investigation themselves.

住房信息系统 housing information system
随着全国住房信息系统的建立，会逐步取消限购政策。

The restrictions on house purchasing will be phased out upon the establishment of a national housing information system.

注册资本 registered capital
海外归来的学子已在上海注册了1300多家公司，注册资本达2.1亿美元。

Returning students have registered to run more than 1,300 companies in Shanghai with a registered capital of $210 million.

驻港部队 PLA Garrison in HKSAR
国家主席习近平视察了中国人民解放军驻香港部队石岗营区。
President Xi Jinping inspected the Chinese People's Liberation Army (PLA) Garrison in the Hong Kong Special Administrative Region (HKSAR) at Shek Kong barracks.

驻京办 liaison offices in Beijing
一些专家表示撤销驻京办的决定是合理的,因为它常常滋生腐败。
Some experts said it is reasonable to dismiss liaison offices in Beijing because they breed corruption.

转基因作物 genetically modified agricultural products
我国农业主管部门已批准安全证书的转基因作物包括棉花、水稻、玉米和番木瓜;其中只有棉花、番木瓜批准商业化种植。
Chinese agricultural authorities have granted certificates of safety to 4 types of genetically modified agricultural products—cotton, rice, corn and papaya, of which only cotton and papaya have been allowed for commercial production.

转授权 sublicense
达成合作后,腾讯音乐娱乐集团将代理的环球、索尼、华纳等大型唱片公司的版权转授权给阿里巴巴旗下的阿里音乐,以此换取阿里音乐代理的滚石、华研国际、寰亚等音乐版权的使用权。
The deal sees Tencent Music Entertainment Group sublicense its rights with major labels like Universal, Sony and Warner to Alibaba's Ali Music, in exchange for access to some of Asia's biggest labels like Rock Records, HIM International and Media Asia Entertainment Group.

转租房屋 sublet houses
根据国家税务总局11月中旬公布的最新法规,今后房东以及任何通过转租房屋获利的个人均需纳税。
According to a regulation from the State Administration of Taxation in mid-November, landlords and anyone who profits from subletting houses have to pay tax.

壮士断腕 cut one's own wrist
李克强总理将政府削权比喻成"壮士断腕",以展示他转变政府角色的决心。
Premier Li Keqiang compared reducing government power to "cutting one's own wrist" to demonstrate his resolve to transform government roles.

追平 score an equalizer
在与法国队的世界杯决赛中,意大利队的马特拉齐在上半场将比分追平。
Materazzi scored an equalizer in the first half of the World Cup Finals between Italy and France.

追索流散文物 retrieve lost cultural relics
北京故宫博物院计划追索流散文物。
The Palace Museum, also known as the Forbidden City in Beijing plans to retrieve its lost cultural relics.

追尾 rear-end
我的车被一辆卡车追尾。
My car was rear-ended by a truck.

准备金 capital reserve; reserve fund
今年由于外资引进态势平稳,世界经济增长缓慢对中国贸易平衡的影响相对减小,中国准备金进一步增加了。
China's capital reserves have climbed even higher this year as foreign capital flows remain healthy and the impact of the global slowdown on China's trade balance has been relatively reduced.

准生证明 birth permission certificate
我国夫妇在进行体外受精前不再需要获得准生证明。
Chinese couples no longer have to get birth permission certificates before they opt for in vitro fertilization(IVF).

桌游 role-playing board games
越来越多的青少年不再成天泡在网上,转而玩起了纸牌游戏和桌游。
A growing section of teenagers are cutting back on cyberspace to spend more time playing cards and role-playing board games.

资本外逃 capital flight
资本外逃是存在于国际金融体系中的重大问题。我们必须面对并解决这个问题。
Capital flight is a major problem in the international financial architecture. It must be fronted and solved.

资产剥离 peel off the (bad) assets of a company
准备明年上市的很多公司都会尽快对其不良资产进行资产剥离,以符合上市要求。
Planning to get listed in the stock markets next year, many companies will peel off the bad assets as soon as possible to be in accord with the requirement of the listing.

资产重组 reorganized assets; assets reorganization
这一措施是中国汽车工业资产重组的重要环节,双方都将从中受益。
This measure, as an important step of assets reorganization in China's automobile industry, will benefit both sides.

资产负债表 balance sheet
由于年储蓄增长率一直保持在8.2%,所以从资产负债表上看,香港银行拥有大量流动资产。
On the balance sheet, Hong Kong banks have plentiful liquid assets due to a continuous annual growth rate of 8.2 percent in deposits.

资产泡沫 asset bubble
专家称资产泡沫和债务风险已成为最可能导致流动性危机和经济动荡的因素。
Experts say the asset bubble and debt risks have become the most likely factors to trigger a liquidity crisis and economic turbulence.

资金池 capital pool
今年的重点是防止银行在同一资金池中经营不同风险水平的理财产品,并确保固定收益和浮动收益理财产品分账经营。
The focus this year should be to prevent banks from operating products with different risk levels in the same capital pool, and make sure they use separate accounts for products with fixed and non-fixed income.

资金划拨 funds allocation
他们部门负责资金划拨。
Their department is in charge of funds allocation.

资金密集型 capital-intensive
近年来,有更多的资金密集型和技术密集型私营企业纷纷涌现,活跃在各种行业中。
More capital-intensive and technology-intensive private businesses have emerged and been active in various industries in recent years.

资源合理配置 rational allocation of resources; better allocate resources
政府鼓励关闭规模小、效率低的矿或国营大矿将其兼并,实现资源合理配置。
Small, low-efficiency mines were encouraged to close or be merged with major State-owned mines to better allocate the resources.

资源环境承载能力 environmental and resource capacity
我国政府宣布建立资源环境承载能力监测预警机制,对环境造成损害的责任主体进行处罚。

The Chinese government announced that it had built an alert system to monitor regional environmental and resource capacity conditions, and punish those responsible for environmental damage.

资源税 resource tax
按数量征收资源税是没有道理的。
It is unreasonable to levy resource tax by quantity.

资源型城市转型 transform resource-dependent cities; transformation of resource-dependent cities
全面振兴东北地区等老工业基地,继续推进资源型城市转型。
We will fully revitalize old industrial bases such as northeast China and continue to transform resource-dependent cities.

自动对接 automatic docking
我国的神舟十一号载人飞船与天宫二号空间试验室成功实现自动对接,使我国距离建造空间站的梦想又近了一步。
The successful automatic docking of China's Shenzhou-11 manned spacecraft with Tiangong-2 space lab takes China one step closer to its dream of building a space station.

自动驾驶车辆 autonomous vehicle
北京市相关部门发布了国内首份自动驾驶车辆道路测试细则,表明了我国加速发展这项技术的决心。
China's first guideline on road tests of autonomous vehicles was released by local authorities in Beijing, signaling the country's determination to accelerate the development of the technology.

自动收票款装置 automatic fare collection (AFC)
自动收票款装置系统的引入标志着纸制公交车票时代的结束。
An automatic fare collection (AFC) system was introduced, marking the end of paper ticket in public transportation.

自律公约 self-discipline pact
来自140家门户网站和其他网站的代表周一在北京签署了行业自律公约,宣誓要抵制非法网络公关行为。
Representatives from 140 portals and websites signed a self-discipline pact Monday in Beijing, which vows to protest against illegal public relations on the internet.

自媒体 We Media
在自媒体时代,民众可以在网上发布、传播信息和观点,建立自己的用户概要,成为独立的"媒体"。
In the era of We Media, citizens can publish and circulate information and opinions online, develop their own user profiles, and become independent "media entities".

自拍 selfie
她还摆姿势和他自拍合影,似乎他们还交换了手机号码。
She posed with him for a selfie, and they appeared to exchange numbers.

自然保护区 nature reserve
西藏已将拉鲁列为地区自然保护区,以保护这片湿地。
To protect the wetland, Tibet has turned Lhalu into a regional nature reserve.

自然指数 Nature Index
10月19日发布的"2017自然指数—科研城市"中,北京高居榜首,上海位列第五。
Beijing tops the list of cities for research output while Shanghai ranks the fifth, according to Nature Index 2017 Science Cities supplement released on October 19.

自由港 free port; free-trade port
说到繁荣的自由港,就想到新加坡是个好例子。
Speaking of a flourishing free port, Singapore is a good example that comes to mind.

自由竞争 free competition
为了促进自由竞争,培育市场经济,制定反垄断法势在必行。
In order to promote free competition and cultivate a market economy, it is imperative to introduce an anti-monopoly law.

自愿申请倒闭 voluntary bankruptcy
它一面寻求资本重组和债务重组计划,一面考虑其他选择方案,包括宣布自然破产或转变为自愿申请倒闭。
It will evaluate its options, which may include seeking a dismissal of the involuntary filing or converting it to a voluntary bankruptcy case while it continues to pursue a recapitalization and a debt-restructuring plan.

自证其罪 self-incrimination
现行的刑事诉讼法已将非法取证和自证其罪列入禁止范围。
The prohibition of illegal evidence extraction and self-incrimination has already

been included in the current Criminal Procedure Law.

自主创新 self-dependent innovation
通过自主创新和国际合作，中国大型客机将在国际上崛起。
Self-dependent innovation and international cooperation will help Chinese large passenger aircraft soar around the world.

自主经营，自负盈亏 make one's own management decisions and take full responsibility for one's own profits and losses
市场经济条件下，企业应该自主经营，自负盈亏，来提高竞争力。
In the market economy, enterprises should make their own management decisions and take full responsibility for their own profits and losses to enhance competition.

自主招生 independent recruitment
推荐制的原则在于学生整体的综合素质。只有整体素质优秀的学生才能被提名参加北京大学的自主招生考试。
The principle of our recommendation lies in the comprehensive overall quality of students. Only the overall-excellent student will be nominated to attend the independent recruitment of students test of Peking University.

自助银行 self-service bank
随着自助银行、电话银行、网上银行、手机银行的相继问世，一种新型的虚拟银行——信息银行在上海出现。
Following the heels of the self-service bank, the telephone bank, the online bank and the mobile bank, a new type of virtual bank—the information bank—has made its debut in Shanghai.

自作自受 stew in one's own juices
他们的失败完全是他们自作自受的结果。
Their failure was considered the result of stewing in their own juices.

综合整治 comprehensive improvement
我们的工作重点应该是西部地区的科技教育发展、基础设施建设、生态环境改善和综合整治。
Priority should be given to the development of science and technology, education and infrastructure facilities, and the improvement of the ecological environment and comprehensive improvement in the western regions.

纵向横向经济轴带 north-south and east-west intersecting economic belts
要形成沿海沿江沿线经济带为主的纵向横向经济轴带，培育一批辐射带动力强的城市群和增长极。
We should form north-south and east-west intersecting economic belts along the coastlines, the Yangtze River and major transportation routes, and foster new growth poles and city clusters that facilitate the development of surrounding areas.

"走出去"战略 "go global" strategy
一些大型民企周末在广东珠海就"走出去"战略交换了意见。
Some top non-State companies exchanged views on their "go global" strategies in Zhuhai, Guangdong province, over the weekend.

走过场；走形式 go through the motions; formality
他走过场般地欢迎了一下她的朋友，转眼就离开了房间。
He went through the motions of welcoming her friends but quickly left the room.

租房市场 home rental market
我国正在推进大中城市租房市场的发展，以解决城市新市民日益高涨的租房需求。
China is pushing development of the home rental market in large and medium cities to address rising rental demand from urban newcomers.

租购并举 encourage both housing purchase and renting
坚持房子是用来住的、不是用来炒的定位，加快建立多主体供给、多渠道保障、租购并举的住房制度，让全体人民住有所居。
We must not forget that housing is for living in, not for speculation. With this in mind, we will move faster to put in place a housing system that ensures supply through multiple sources, provides housing support through multiple channels, and encourages both housing purchase and renting. This will make us better placed to meet the housing needs of all of our people.

足改方案 soccer reform plan
足改方案的一个重要特点是将简化其广受诟病、适得其反的管理体系。
One important feature of the soccer reform plan is to streamline the sport's widely criticized counterproductive management system.

足球腐败 soccer corruption
第一轮中国足球腐败案审理进入第二天，一位前足球俱乐部的管理者于周二早上出庭受审。
A former soccer club manager was put on trial Tuesday morning as the first round of Chinese soccer corruption trials went into the second day.

足球投资 soccer investment
一份报告显示,中国的足球投资位列世界第一。中国投资者对足球俱乐部的投资额达21.5亿欧元,成为全球最大的球队收购者。
China tops the world in soccer investment, according to a report. Chinese investors have spent EUR2.15 billion on soccer clubs, making them the world's biggest buyer of teams.

足球一流强国 top-class soccer nation
根据国家发改委、国家体育总局等部门联合发布的一项规划,我国计划在2050年前实现成为足球一流强国的目标。
China aims to realize the goal of becoming a top-class soccer nation by 2050, according to a plan jointly released by several government agencies, including the National Development and Reform Commission and the General Administration of Sport.

阻碍司法 obstruction of justice
此人因阻碍司法被判入狱6年。
The man was sentenced to six years in prison for obstruction of justice.

钻空子 exploit loopholes
我们不断修改和完善法规,以防有人钻空子。
We constantly amend and improve the regulations in case some people exploit loopholes.

最不发达国家 least-developed countries (LDCs)
世界上50个最不发达国家中的大多数在非洲。
Most of the 50 least-developed countries in the world are located in Africa.

最低工资保障制度 minimum-wage guarantee system; subsistence wage
白皮书提出政府应该制定最低工资保障制度以确保工人能拿到报酬。
The white book says that the government should work out the minimum-wage guarantee system to ensure payment for workers.

最低生活保证制度 system for ensuring a minimum standard of living; system for ensuring a subsistence level of living
在城市建立居民最低生活保证制度,在农村积极推进社会保障体系。
The system for ensuring a minimum standard of living for residents has been set up in cities, and the building of a social security system is being vigorously promoted in rural areas.

最后关头达成的协议 last-ditch agreement

经过数天磋商,欧洲各国领导人终于在最后关头达成协议。按照计划,希腊债务将减记50%,同时将欧元区救助基金EFSF(欧洲金融稳定基金)的救助基金规模从4400亿欧元放大到1万亿欧元。

European leaders sealed a last-ditch agreement after days of negotiation. Their plan is to reduce Greece's debt by 50 percent and expand the European Financial Stability Facility (EFSF), the Eurozone's bailout fund, to 1 trillion euros from 440 billion euros.

最惠国待遇 Most Favored-Nation status

正常贸易关系就是以前所谓的最惠国待遇。

Normal Trade Relations (NTR) was formerly known as Most Favored-Nation status.

最佳时机 sweet spot

我们正在步入经济发展的最佳时机。

We are moving into a sweet spot for the economy.

座卧转换动车 bullet train that can convert sleeping berths to seats

我国已研制出一种具有"座卧转换"功能的动车,以满足全天候运营的需求。

China has developed a bullet train that can convert its sleeping berths to seats to meet demand for around-the-clock operations.

附录 Appendices

社交媒体常用语

关注 follow
取消关注 unfollow
粉丝 follower
分享 share
回复 reply
转发 repost; forward
评论 comment
赞 / 点赞 like
加好友 friend
删除 / 解除好友 unfriend
私信 private message; direct message
（微信的）朋友圈 Moments（official name）; Friend Circle
@（音 at）
#（音 hashtag）
简介，个人资料 profile

常用军事词汇

xx 军区 xx Military Area Command (MAC)
xx 省军区 xx Provincial Military Command
xx 军分区 xx Military Sub-Command
预备役部队 the PLA's reserve force
驻港 / 澳部队 the PLA Hong Kong/ Macao Garrison
武警部队 the Armed Police Force
火箭军 the PLA Rocket Force
总参谋部 the General Staff Headquarters of the PLA

总政治部 the General Political Department of the PLA
总后勤部 the General Logistics Department of the PLA
总装备部 The General Armaments Department of the PLA
中国人民解放军陆军领导机构 the PLA Army general command
中国人民解放军战略支援部队 the PLA Strategic Support Force
集团军 army
军 corps
师 division
旅 brigade
团 regiment
营 battalion
连 / 排 / 班 company/platoon/squad
民兵 militia（总称）/militiaman（个体）
空降兵 airborne force
陆战师 marine division
装甲旅 armored brigade
军衔 military titles of the People's Liberation Army
陆军、空军（Army and Air Force） 上将（General），中将（Lieutenant General），少将（Major General），大校（Senior Colonel），上校（Colonel），中校（Lieutenant Colonel），少校（Major），上尉（Captain），中尉（Lieutenant），少尉（Second Lieutenant）
海军（Navy） 上将（Admiral），中将（Vice-Admiral），少将（Rear Admiral），大校（Senior Captain），上校（Captain），中校（Commander），少校（Lieutenant Commander），上尉（Lieutenant），中尉（Lieutenant Junior Grade），少尉（Ensign）

报纸行业相关词汇

【版面】
头版 the front page
头版头条 above the fold
注：报纸头版露在外面的上半页，如果是网页就相当于首屏。
广告 advertisement
分类广告 classified ads
国内版 nation
国际版 world
财经版 business

体育版 sports
生活版 life
专版 special
社论 editorials
评论版 op-ed
注：这是"opposite the editorial page"的缩写形式，一般都在社论版的对面，主要刊登非本报员工撰写的评论文章。
花絮报道 sidebar
书评 book review
副刊 supplement
连载小说 serial story
讣闻 obituary notice
公告 public notice
增刊 extra
文艺评论 literary criticism
周日特刊 Sunday features

【稿件】

标题 headline
（新闻标题下的）记者署名 byline
电头 dateline
注：
新闻报道事件发生的时间和地点，有时还包括通讯社的名称，比如：OSLO。May 10 (Xinhua) —The Norwegian government said on Tuesday it would extend its internal Schengen border controls for an additional 30 days in order to ensure its "public order and internal security".
现在很多电头都省去时间，直接写地点和通讯社的名称，比如：BEIRUT (AP). The outlook was uncertain today as ...
图片说明 caption
导语 lead
注：一般是报道的第一段，简要交代这篇报道的核心内容。
新闻报道 news article
通栏标题 banner headline
插图 cut
头条新闻 big news
最新新闻 hot news

独家新闻 exclusive news
抢先报道的独家新闻 scoop
交稿期限 deadline
特稿 feature article
读者来信 letters to the editor (letters from readers)

【从业人员】

采访对象 interviewee
采访人员 interviewer
新闻报道者 reporter
新闻记者 journalist
Journalist 与 reporter 的区别：
  Journalist 指实地采访收集新闻事件的相关信息，进行深入分析并写出相关新闻报道的工作人员；reporter 则指收集某个新闻事件的相关信息并将其通过音频或视频的形式展示出来的工作人员。不过，现在很多场合都能见到这两个词混用。

版面编辑 copy editor
主编 editor
总编辑 editor-in-chief
特约通讯员（在特殊事件发生时为报纸撰稿的记者）special correspondent
投稿者 contributor
新闻来源 news source
自由撰稿人 free-lancer

【其他相关词汇】

记者席 press box
新闻口 newsbeat(beat)
注：每个记者专门跟的领域，比如经济口，教育口，政法口，等等。
记者招待会 news conference, press conference
发行 distribution
发行量 circulation
报摊 newsstand; kiosk
订报费 subscription (rate)
新闻用纸 newsprint

房屋词汇

房子 House
并联别墅 semi-detached house
独立式房子 detached house
连栋房屋 terraced houses; row houses
篱笆 fence
房子前门 front door
车库 garage
车库通向道路的小路 driveway

公寓 Flat/Apartment
公寓楼 block of flats
第一层 first floor（美）/ground floor（英）
第二层 second floor（美）/first floor（英）
电梯 lift; elevator
楼梯 stair
楼外的台阶 step
阳台 balcony

租房 Renting
房东 landlord/landlady
房租 rent
房屋租赁合同 house leasing contract
定金 deposit
有家具的房子 / 公寓 furnished house/apartment
无家具的房子 / 公寓 unfurnished house/apartment
空房 vacant room; spare room
单人间 single room
双人间 double room
水、电、煤气和垃圾处理等费用 utilities
合租者 flatmate
房屋中介 letting agency
中介费 agent commission
寄宿家庭 home stay
学校宿舍 university accommodation

私人住房 private accommodation
起居室；客厅 living room; lounge
卧室 bedroom
主卧 main bedroom
地毯 carpet
（置于沙发前的）茶几 coffee table
单人沙发 armchair
沙发 sofa
遥控器 remote control
暖气片 radiator
中央供暖 central heating
冰箱 fridge; freezer
电烧水壶 kettle
厨房高脚椅 stool
烤箱 oven
洗碗机 dishwasher
水龙头 tap
洗碗池 sink
橱柜 cupboard
淋浴 shower
浴缸 bath
卫生间 bathroom
主卫 main bathroom
马桶 toilet

买房 Buy a flat/an apartment
房地产 real estate
按揭 mortgage
首付 down payment
现房 completed apartment
期房 forward-delivery housing
二手房 second-hand house
经济适用房 affordable housing
房价 housing price

交通词汇

交通规则 traffic regulation
超车道 passing bay
路标 guide post
上下高速公路的环形匝道 loop
安全岛 safety island
红绿灯 traffic light
自动红绿灯 automatic traffic signal light
红灯 red light
绿灯 green light
黄灯 amber light
交通岗 traffic post
岗亭 police box
交通警 traffic police
单行线 single line
双向行驶 two-way traffic
前面窄桥 narrow bridge ahead
拱桥 hump bridge
双向车道 dual carriageway
平交道口 level crossing
斑马线 zebra crossing
交通干线 artery traffic
车行道 carriage way
单行道 one way only
辅助车道 auxiliary lane
自行车道 cyclists only
不平整路 rough road
弯路 curve road; bend road
连续弯路 winding road
之字路 double bend road
道路交叉点 road junction
十字路 cross road
交通管制 traffic control
交通拥挤 traffic jam/congestion

划路线机 traffic line marker
修路 road works
潮湿路滑 slippery when wet
陡坡 steep hill
下坡危险 dangerous down grade
此路不通 road closed
安全第一 safety first
无证驾驶 drive without a license
危险驾驶 dangerous driving
左转 turn left
右转 turn right
靠左 keep left
靠右 keep right
让路 give way
速度限制 speed limit
恢复速度 resume speed
超速 excessive speed; speeding
禁止驶入 no entry
禁止超车 no passing; no overtaking
禁止转弯 no turn
禁止掉头 no U-turn
禁止通行 no thoroughfare
禁止停车 no parking
只停公用车 public car only
小心行人 caution pedestrian crossing
小心牲畜 caution animals
酒后驾车 drunk driving/DUI（driving under the influence）
交通肇事 commit traffic offences
轻微碰撞 slight impact
相撞 collide
连环撞 chain collision
撞车 car crash
肇事逃逸司机 hit-and-run driver

美容词汇

护肤 Skin care
洗面奶 facial cleanser
爽肤水 toner; astringent
紧肤水 firming lotion
柔肤水 smoothing toner
保湿霜 moisturizer
美白霜 whitening cream
活肤霜 revitalizer
面膜 face mask
剥撕式面膜 pack
敷面剥落式面膜 peeling
眼霜 eye gel
眼膜 eye mask
日霜 day cream
晚霜 night cream
磨砂膏 facial scrub
去黑头 deep pore cleanser
护手霜 hand lotion
润肤霜 body lotion
沐浴露 body wash

化妆品 Cosmetics
遮瑕霜 concealer
粉底霜 foundation cream
粉饼 pressed powder; pancake
散粉 loose powder
闪粉 shimmering powder
眼影 eye shadow
睫毛膏 mascara
眉笔 brow pencil
唇线笔 lip liner
唇膏 lipstick
唇彩 lip gloss/color
腮红 blusher

卸妆乳 make-up remover
指甲油 nail polish
洗甲水 nail polish remover

化妆工具 Cosmetic applicator
粉扑 powder puff
眉刷 brow brush
睫毛刷 lash curler
吸油纸 oil-absorbing sheet
化妆棉 cotton pad

护发用品 Hair-care products
洗发水 shampoo
护发素 hair conditioner
焗油膏 hairdressing gel
发型啫哩 styling gel
染发 hair dye

夏日防晒 Summer care
防晒霜 sunscreen
涂防晒霜 wear sunscreen
防晒霜的防晒系数 SPF (Sun Protection Factor)
晒后啫哩 after-sun lotion
被晒黑的 suntanned

手机词汇

蓝牙技术（无线耳机接听）bluetooth
全球定位系统 Global Positioning System (GPS)
客户身份识别卡；SIM 卡 Subscriber Identity Module（SIM）
手机用户 mobile phone user/subscriber
手机入网费 initiation charges for mobile phones; mobile access fee
手机充电 cellular phone replenishing/recharging
关机 power off
漫游（服务）roaming service
手机费 mobile phone fee
储值卡 pre-paid phone card

语音提示 voice prompt
按键 keypad
按键音 keypad tone
提示音 warning tone
手机铃音 mobile phone ringtone
彩铃 polyphonic ring tone
振动 vibrate
壁纸 wallpaper
短信 short message; text message
图片短信 picture message
待机模式 standby mode
快捷图标 short-cut icon
应用程序 application(app)
智能手机 smart phone
自动重拨 automatic redial
快速拨号 speed dial
语音拨号 voice dial
限制呼叫 fixed dial
呼出通话 outgoing call
被叫通话 incoming call
近来的呼叫 recent call
呼叫转移 call diverter
未接电话 missed call
已接电话 received call
不在服务区 out of reach

旅游词汇

旅行 journey; trip
旅行日程 itinerary
旅行路线 route
旅游者 tourist
游览 pleasure trip
商务旅行 business trip
出境游 outbound tourism; outbound travel

出境游客 outbound tourist
背包旅行者 backpacker
自由行 free walker
往返旅行 return journey; round trip
单程旅行 outward journey
套餐游；包办游 package tour; inclusive tour
远足 excursion; outing
探险 expedition
旅行支票 traveler's checks
旅游散客 independent traveler
旅游团 tour group
度假区 holiday resort

票 Ticket
票价 fare
单程票 single ticket
往返票 round-trip ticket; return ticket
半票 half-fare ticket; half-price ticket
全价票 full-fare ticket; full-price ticket

乘火车 Traveling by train
铁路 railroad（美）/railway（英）
轨道 track
火车 train
铁路系统 railway system; railway network
特快车 express train
快车 fast train
直达快车 through train
高铁 high-speed train
动车 bullet train
慢车 stopping train; slow train
游览列车 excursion train
市郊列车 commuter train; suburban train
车厢 coach; carriage
卧铺 sleeper
餐车 dining car; restaurant car; luncheon car

双层卧铺车 sleeper with couchettes
铺位 berth; bunk
上行车 up train
下行车 down train
行李车厢 luggage van; baggage car
车站大厅 station hall
收票员 ticket-collector; gateman
月台；站台 platform
站台票 platform ticket
小卖部 buffet
候车室 waiting room
行李暂存处 left-luggage office
列车员 car attendant; train attendant
列车长 guard; conductor
行李架 rack; baggage rack
在（某地）换车 change trains at...
（火车）在（某时）到达（The train）is due at...

乘飞机 Traveling by air
护照 passport
签证 visa
安全通行证 safe-conduct; pass
起飞 take off
落地 touch down
登机牌 boarding pass
办理登机手续 check in
候机室 departure lounge
航班号 flight number
国际抵达处 international arrival
国内抵达处 domestic arrival

行李 Luggage
推行李车 luggage barrow
私人用品 personal effects
团体行李 group baggage
行李票 claim tag

行李牌 handbag tag
行李标签 baggage tag; luggage label
行李房 luggage office
行李搬运车 baggage train
航运收据 airway bill
手提行李 hand luggage

住宿 Accommodation
旅馆 hotel
汽车旅馆 motel
提供住宿和早餐的旅馆 bed and breakfast (B&B)
青年招待所 youth hostel
豪华饭店 luxury hotel
公寓旅馆 residential hotel
寄宿公寓 boarding house
单人房间 single room
双人房间 double room
套房 suite
空房 vacant room
旅馆大厅 lobby
旅馆登记薄 hotel register
在一家旅馆住宿 put up at a hotel
订房间 book a room
登记 check-in
结账 check-out
预订房间 reservation
行李托管证 baggage check
接待 reception
登记表 registration form
门房 porter
侍者 bellboy
清理房间的女服务员 chambermaid
餐厅领班 headwaiter
半膳 half board
全膳 full board

工作及薪酬词汇

人事制度 personnel system
人事管理 personnel management
办公时间 office hour
工作时间 work hour; office hour
八小时工作制 eight-hour shift
轮班 shift
上午班 morning session
小／大夜班 evening/night shift
日班 day shift
签到本 attendance book
迟到本 late book
休息日 day off
上班中的休息时间 coffee break
工作日 workday
工作环境 working condition
工作证 work permit
加班 work overtime
节假日轮流值班 holiday rotation
差旅费 traveling allowance
工资册 payroll
薪水（指付给一个人的固定劳动补偿）salary
工资（为劳动或服务所付的报酬，尤指按小时、天数、周或按工作量所付的薪酬）wage
加薪 salary raise
外快 windfall
年薪 annual pension
年终奖 year-end bonus
奖金 bonus; premium
加班费 overtime pay
打卡 punch the clock
打卡机 time recorder
开溜 sneak out
实习 internship
试用 on probation

试用人员 probation staff
雇佣协议 employment agreement
员工考核 employee evaluation
考核表 employee evaluation form
绩效工资 merit pay
扣薪 dock pay
无薪假 unpaid leave
税前薪水 before tax salary
所得税 income tax
税后净薪 take-home pay; after-tax salary
遣散费 release pay
解雇费 severance pay
罚薪 deduction of salary
事假 casual leave
病假 sick leave

"五险一金" Insurance and Housing Fund
养老保险 endowment insurance
医疗保险 medical insurance
失业保险 unemployment insurance
工伤保险 employment injury insurance
生育保险 maternity insurance
住房公积金 housing fund

环保词汇

联合国环境与发展大会（环发大会）United Nations Conference on Environment and Development (UNCED)
环发大会首脑会议 Summit Session of UNCED
联合国环境规划署 United Nations Environment Programs（UNEP）
国际生物多样性日 International Biodiversity Day (29 December)
世界水日 World Water Day (22 March)
世界气象日 World Meteorological Day(23 March)
世界海洋日 World Oceans Day (8 June)
人与生物圈方案 Man and Biosphere (MAB) Program
中国生物多样性保护行动计划 China Biological Diversity Protection Action Plan

中国跨世纪绿色工程规划 China Trans-Century Green Project Plan
生物多样性公约 Convention on Biological Diversity
防治荒漠化国际公约 Convention to Combat Desertification
联合国气候变化框架公约 United Nations Framework Convention on Climate Change
国家环境保护总局 State Environmental Protection Administration (SEPA)
坚持环境保护基本国策 adhere to the basic state policy of environmental protection
污染者负担的政策 the Polluter Pays Principle
强化环境管理的政策 policy of tightening up environmental management
环保执法检查 environmental protection law enforcement inspection
限期治理 undertake treatment within a prescribed limit of time
生态示范区 eco-demonstration region; environment-friendly region
国家级园林城市 Nationally Designated Garden City
工业固体废物 industrial solid wastes
白色污染 white pollution (by using and littering of non-degradable white plastics)
可降解塑料袋 bio-degradable plastic bag
放射性废料积存 accumulation of radioactive waste
有机污染物 organic pollutants
三废综合利用 multipurpose use of three types of wastes (waste water, waste gas, solid waste)
城市垃圾无害化处理率 decontamination rate of urban refuse
垃圾填埋场 refuse landfill
垃圾焚化厂 refuse incinerator
防止过度利用森林 protect forests from overexploitation
森林砍伐率 deforestation rate
水土流失 water and soil erosion
土壤盐碱化 soil alkalization
生态农业 environment-friendly agriculture; eco-agriculture
水资源保护区 water resource conservation zone
海水淡化 sea water desalinization
造林工程 afforestation project
绿化面积 afforested areas; greening space
森林覆盖率 forest coverage
防风林 wind breaks
防沙林 sand breaks
速生林 fast-growing trees

降低资源消耗率 slow down the rate of resource degradation
开发可再生资源 develop renewable resources
环保产品 environment-friendly product
自然保护区 nature reserve
野生动植物 wild fauna and flora
保护生存环境 conserve natural habitats
濒危野生动物 endangered wildlife
珍稀濒危物种繁育基地 rare and endangered species breeding center
美化环境 landscaping design for environmental purposes
环境恶化 environmental degradation
温饱型农业 subsistence agriculture
空气污染浓度 air pollution concentration
酸雨、越境空气污染 acid rain and transfrontier air pollution
工业粉尘排放 industrial dust discharge
烟尘排放 soot emission
矿物燃料（煤、石油、天然气）fossil fuels (coal, oil and natural gas)
清洁能源 clean energy
汽车尾气排放 motor vehicle exhaust
尾气净化器 exhaust purifier
无铅汽油 lead-free gasoline
天然气汽车 gas-fueled vehicle
电动汽车 electric car
小排量汽车 small-displacement vehicle
温室效应 greenhouse effect
工业废水处理率 treatment rate of industrial effluent
城市污水处理率 treatment rate of domestic sewage
集中处理厂 centralized treatment plant

选举词汇

选举 election
投票 cast a ballot
计票 count of votes
投票日 polling day
投票箱 ballot box

选举程序 electoral procedures
选举大会 election meeting; electoral meeting
选举规则 election regulation
选民 voter
初选 primary election
普选 general election
决定性竞选 runoff
当选 be elected
个人投票 individual vote
公开投票 open vote
合格选民 eligible voter
候补者 alternate candidate
候选人 candidate
候选人名单 slate
被选举权 right to be elected
补缺选举 supplementary election（美）/ by-election（英）
不记名投票 secret vote; anonymous ballot
差额选举 competitive election
差额投票 differential voting
等额选举 single-candidate election
弃权不投票 abstention from voting
发表政见 express one's political views
法定程序 due course of law
法定人数 quorum
废票 invalid vote; void ballot
否决权 veto power
改选 re-election
记名投票 disclosed ballot
决定性票 decisive vote
抗议票 protest vote
监票员 ballot examiner
拉票 soliciting votes
冷门当选者；黑马 unknown elected nominee; dark horse
落选 lose an election; be voted out
民意测验 public opinion poll

投票后民调 exit poll
导向性民意调查 push polling
提名 nominate
提名者 nominator
领先者 front runner
压倒性胜利 landslide victory
险胜 narrow victory
在选举期间一连串的演讲、集会、旨在吸引选票的活动 campaigning
浮动选民（即还未决定给谁投票的选民）floating voter
竞选纲领 manifesto

夏季奥运会词汇

水上运动 Aquatics
游泳 swimming
自由泳 freestyle
仰泳 backstroke
蛙泳 breaststroke
蝶泳 butterfly
个人混合泳 individual medley
自由泳接力 freestyle relay
混合泳接力 medley relay
水球 water polo
跳水 diving
十米跳台 10m platform
三米跳板 3m springboard event
双人十米跳台 synchronized diving from 10m platform
双人三米跳板 synchronized diving from 3m springboard
赛艇 rowing
帆船 sailing
皮划艇运动 canoeing

田径 Track and field
径赛 track
跨栏跑 hurdles

障碍赛 steeplechase
接力 relay
跳跃 Jumping
跳高 high jump
撑杆跳高 pole vault
跳远 long jump
三级跳远 triple jump
投掷 throwing
推铅球 shot put
掷铁饼 discus
掷链球 hammer
标枪 javelin
男子十项全能 decathlon
女子七项全能 heptathlon

公路赛 Road events
马拉松 marathon
竞走 walk

球类运动 Ball games
羽毛球 badminton
男子单打 men's singles
女子单打 women's singles
男子双打 men's doubles
女子双打 women's doubles
混合双打 mixed doubles
棒球 baseball
篮球 basketball
足球 football
手球 handball
曲棍球 hockey; field hockey
垒球 softball
乒乓球 table tennis
网球 tennis
排球 volleyball
沙滩排球 beach volleyball

自行车 Cycling
公路自行车赛 road cycling
场地自行车赛 track cycling
山地自行车赛 mountain bike
追逐赛 sprint
计时赛 time trial
计分赛 points race
争先赛 pursuit

马术 Equestrian
障碍赛 steeplechase
盛装舞步 dressage
综合全能马术赛；三日赛 three-day event
击剑 fencing
花剑 foil
重剑 epee
佩剑 saber

体操 Gymnastics
竞技体操 artistic gymnastics
自由体操 floor exercises
鞍马 pommel horse
吊环 rings
跳马 vault
双杠 parallel bars
单杠 horizontal bar
高低杠 uneven bars
平衡木 balance beam
艺术体操 rhythmic gymnastics
蹦床 gymnastics trampoline

现代五项 Modern pentathlon
射击 shooting
击剑 fencing
游泳 swimming
骑马 riding
越野跑 cross-country running

射击 Shooting

10 米气步枪 10m air rifle

10 米气手枪 10m air pistol

男子 10 米移动靶 men's 10m running target

男子 50 米步枪卧射 men's 50m rifle prone position

50 米步枪 3 种姿势 50m rifle three positions

男子 50 米手枪 men's 50m pistol

女子 25 米手枪 women's 25m pistol

男子 25 米手枪速射 men's 25m rapid fire pistol

多向飞碟 trap

双多向飞碟 double trap

双向飞碟 skeet

铁人三项 Triathlon

游泳 swimming

自行车 cycling

跑步 running

举重 Weightlifting

抓举 snatch

挺举 clean and jerk

格斗 Combat sports

摔跤 wrestling

古典式摔跤 Greco-Roman

自由式摔跤 free style

拳击 boxing

柔道 judo

跆拳道 tae kwon do

射箭 Archery

冬季奥运会词汇

有舵雪车 bobsleigh

无舵雪车 skeleton

无舵雪车男子单人座 men single

雪橇男子双人座 men doubles

自由式滑雪 freestyle skiing
自由式滑雪男子雪上技巧 men moguls
自由式滑雪女子空中技巧 women aerials
跳台滑雪 ski jumping
跳台滑雪普通台男子单人 men NH individual
跳台滑雪大台男子团体 men LH team
高山滑雪 alpine skiing
男子高山回转 men slalom
男子高山滑降 men downhill
高山男子全能 men combined
女子高山大回转 women giant slalom
越野滑雪男子短距离 men sprint
越野滑雪男子4×10公里接力 men 4×10km relay
越野滑雪女子7.5+7.5公里追逐 women 7.5km+7.5km pursuit
越野滑雪女子30公里集体出发 women 30km mass start
单板滑雪 snowboard
男子单板平行大回转 men parallel giant slalom
男子单板障碍争先 men snowboard cross
北欧两项（越野滑雪和跳台滑雪）Nordic combined
冬季两项（越野滑雪和步枪射击的混合项目）biathlon
冰球 hockey
滑冰 skating
花样滑冰 figure skating
花样滑冰男子单人滑 individual men
花样滑冰双人滑 pairs figure skating
花样滑冰冰舞 ice dancing
速度滑冰 speed skating
速度滑冰男子团体追逐 men team pursuit
速度滑冰女子500米 women 500m speed skating
短道速滑 short track speed skating
短道速滑女子3000米接力 women 3000m relay
冰壶 curling

体育比赛结果词汇

优胜者 winner

纪录保持者 record holder
打破纪录 break the record
打破纪录者 record breaker
创造新纪录 set a new record
世界纪录 world record
冠军 champion
亚军 runner-up; the second place
季军 the third place
奖牌获得者 medalist
金牌获得者 gold medalist
银牌获得者 silver medalist
铜牌获得者 bronze medalist
决赛成绩 final result
总分 total points
名次；排名 placement; ranking
决赛名次 final placing
奖牌榜 medal tally
败给 lose to
击败 defeat
晋级 advance to
淘汰 be eliminated
完全击败；完胜 whitewash
夺魁 win the title
夺取金牌 go for gold
卫冕 defend the title
颁奖仪式 awarding ceremony
公布成绩 announce results
升国旗，奏国歌 raise the national flag and play the national anthem
风格奖 sportsmanship trophy
公平竞赛奖 fair play trophy
奖杯 cup; trophy
奖金 prize money
奖品 prize; trophy; award
颁发奖品 present award
绕场一周向观众致意 do a lap of honor